ICT Influences on Human Development, Interaction, and Collaboration

Susheel Chhabra
Lal Bahadur Shastri Institute of Management, India

Managing Director:	Lindsay Johnston
Senior Editorial Director:	Heather A. Probst
Book Production Manager:	Sean Woznicki
Development Manager:	Joel Gamon
Assistant Acquisitions Editor:	Kayla Wolfe
Typesetter:	Alyson Zerbe
Cover Design:	Nick Newcomer

Published in the United States of America by
Information Science Reference (an imprint of IGI Global)
701 E. Chocolate Avenue
Hershey PA 17033
Tel: 717-533-8845
Fax: 717-533-8661
E-mail: cust@igi-global.com
Web site: http://www.igi-global.com

Library of Congress Cataloging-in-Publication Data

ICT influences on human development, interaction, and collaboration / Susheel Chhabra, editor.
     p. cm.
  Includes bibliographical references and index.
  Summary: "This book creates awareness on how ICTs contribute to human development in multiple areas, including the link between ICTs and economic, social, and political aspects of human development"--Provided by publisher.
  ISBN 978-1-4666-1957-9 (hardcover) -- ISBN 978-1-4666-1958-6 (ebook) -- ISBN 978-1-4666-1959-3 (print & perpetual access) 1. Information technology--Social aspects. 2. Rural development--Effect of technological innovations on. I. Chhabra, Susheel.
  HM851.I28 2013
  303.48'33--dc23
                              2012009687

British Cataloguing in Publication Data
A Cataloguing in Publication record for this book is available from the British Library.

The views expressed in this book are those of the authors, but not necessarily of the publisher.

Table of Contents

Detailed Table of Contents

Chapter 1

Ricardo Gomez, University of Washington, USA
Kemly Camacho, University of Washington and Sula Batsú Research Cooperative in Costa Rica, USA

Libraries, telecenters, and cybercafés offer opportunities for wider public access to information and communication technologies (ICT). This paper presents findings of a global exploratory study on the landscape public access venues in 25 countries around the world. The goal of the project was to better understand the users of public access venues and their needs, this being one of several papers that result from the global study. This paper identifies profiles of the users of the different types of venues with respect to age, income, education and gender. While findings are not new, their value lies in the compelling evidence drawn from 25 countries and across different types of public access venues, which has never been done before. Results highlight the importance of strengthening public access venues in non-urban settings and to strengthen programs that reach out to underserved populations. The authors also point to special challenges faced by libraries and telecenters given the immense growth of cybercafés as public access venues in most of the countries studied.

Chapter 2

Muneesh Kumar, University of Delhi, India and Groupe ESC-Pau, France
Mamta Sareen, University of Delhi, India

The virtual environment of B2B e-commerce interactions has been considered to be a barrier in building trust of trading partners. There is adequate empirical evidence that supports the relationship between various trust related technology issues such as security, privacy, authentication, etc. However, there is dearth of evidence confirming the causal relationship between environment related trust issues such as social-cultural characteristics, technology standards, and regulatory framework. Based on a survey of 106 Indian companies using inter-organizational systems, this paper makes an attempt to identify specific attributes of these three environment-related issues that have the potential to influence trust in B2B e-commerce.

Chapter 3

Ahmed I. Saleh, Mansoura University, Egypt

As PCS networks aim to provide "anytime-anywhere" cellular services, they enable Mobile Terminals (MTs) to communicate regardless of their locations. However, in order to guarantee a successful service delivery, MTs' real time location should be continuously managed by the network. Location management plays the central role in providing ubiquitous network communications services, which includes two fundamental processes, i.e., registration and paging. Registration is concerned with the reporting of the current locations of the MTs, while paging is used to locate the MT. Both processes incur signaling cost, and due to the scarcity of PCS wireless bandwidth and for more scalable mobile services, it is important to reduce that signaling cost. As The blanket paging in current PCS networks wastes a lot of wireless bandwidth, the author focuses on the subject of paging in attempt to reduce the paging signaling cost under delay bounds. This paper challenges the signaling cost problem and successfully establishes a family of probability based paging strategies. The author will introduce a novel topology for the network registration area, which is called the hot spot topology (HST) and based on HST, a novel location management strategy, which is called "Flower Based Strategy" (FBS) is also introduced.

Chapter 4

Alemayehu Molla, RMIT University, Australia
Konrad Peszynski, RMIT University, Australia

This paper explores the e-readiness of firms in the Australian horticulture supply chain. The paper draws from the perceived e-readiness model (PERM) and relies on data collected from a survey of firms in the horticulture sector in Australia. The results indicate that while horticulture firms demonstrate relative organizational preparation for the conduct of e-business, the value network within which they operate does not appear to encourage and support their endeavour. In particular, government and industry associations do not appear to play supportive roles in encouraging the use of e-business among members of the horticulture supply chain. This paper highlights factors that are likely to facilitate or inhibit e-business in agribusiness, an area lacking in research globally. Practitioners such as governments, horticulture associations, growers and growers' associations, and digital marketplace operators, through understanding the e-readiness factors affecting e-business, can make effective decisions to develop their support, capabilities and offerings respectively.

Chapter 5

An exploratory, qualitative study in 25 countries around the world identifies success factors for centers that offer public access to Information and Communication Technologies (ICT). The study considered public libraries, telecenters, and cybercafés, and grouped the findings into four types of success factors: (1) understand and take care of local needs first, (2) train info mediaries and users, (3) build alliances with other venues and collaborate with other community services, and (4) strengthen sustainability. Results corroborate the findings of previous studies of libraries and of telecenters which identify success factors that include the four themes presented. However, this is the first systematic comparison across multiple countries to identify success factors in different types of public access venues. The findings highlight critical variables to be considered in policy decisions, funding allocations, and program implementation to reach underserved populations in developing countries with equitable access and meaningful use of ICT. They also provide valuable direction for future research to better understand the interactions between libraries, telecenters, and cybercafés as venues that can contribute to community development through public access to ICT.

Chapter 6

ICT plays a vital role in human development through information extraction and includes computer networks and telecommunication networks. One of the important modules of ICT is computer networks, which are the backbone of the World Wide Web (WWW). Search engines are computer programs that browse and extract information from the WWW in a systematic and automatic manner. This paper examines the three main components of search engines: Extractor, a web crawler which starts with a URL; Analyzer, an indexer that processes words on the web page and stores the resulting index in a database; and Interface Generator, a query handler that understands the need and preferences of the user. This paper concentrates on the information available on the surface web through general web pages and the hidden information behind the query interface, called deep web. This paper emphasizes the Extraction of relevant information to generate the preferred content for the user as the first result of his or her search query. This paper discusses the aspect of deep web with analysis of a few existing deep web search engines.

The term Information Communication Technology (ICT) includes any communication device or application. In malaria control, ICTs can ease communication, improve doctors' training, and increase access to information by individuals and groups that are historically unaware of malaria. Successful malaria vector control depends on understanding causes, prevention, and treatment. This paper examines the possibilities of using ICTs to eradicate malaria in Tanzania. It also explores the coverage of the malaria subject related to Tanzania on various electronic databases and e-journals. This paper concludes that Tanzania's Ministry of Health must put forth more effort on ICT management and be more active in their approach of disseminating malaria information.

Ghazi Al-Weshah, Al-Balqa Applied University, Jordan
Khalil Al-Hyari, Al-Balqa Applied University, Jordan
Amjad Abu-Elsamen, University of Jordan, Jordan
Marwan Al-Nsour, Al-Balqa Applied University, Jordan

This study provides a deep understanding of the current status of electronic networks in the Jordanian handicrafts sector from managers' perspectives. More specifically, this study enhances utilisation of the e-environment to gain market share in local, regional, and international markets. Four cases of handicraft projects are selected to conduct face to face interviews. The results show that handicraft projects have initial attempts to use E-electronic in their activities, but these attempts are still in embryonic stages, and they do not use E-networks effectively to gain market share. However, project managers believe that there is a direct link between the use of electronic networks and increases in the business's market share. Furthermore, it is intended that these initiatives be treated as innovative and at the end utilised to enhance the business development of similar enterprises belonging to the small and medium enterprises sector. The study recommends that such projects consider adoption of e-networks in their future plans, enhance their staff skills in terms of improving their IT and English language skills, and develop their own internet website to create new marketing channels.

Aarti Kawlra, Indian Institute of Technology Madras, India

Inspired by the potential of Information and Communication Technologies, henceforth ICTs, for socio-economic development, and supported by a university based technology and business incubator, Rural Production Company, henceforth RPC, was set up in 2007 employing an ICT-mediated distributed production model. This paper reveals how RPC, initially an exploratory project whose key innovation was its Internet kiosk-facilitated model of crafts production and local empowerment, morphed into a social enterprise catering to global demands. The context of innovation provided by the Incubator led to a transformation of an ICT4D (ICT for Development) project into a business venture through the practice of formal and informal questioning at every stage of its implementation. This paper focuses on the iterative method adopted while highlighting the role of the incubator in the overall design and development process of the enterprise. This paper is a reflexive mapping of the organization's evolution from the original research agenda of outsourcing production cum rural employment, to one that privileges local networks both as a conscious business strategy and as an arena for collaborative change for human development.

Chapter 10

Ali Acilar, Bilecik University, Turkey
Çaglar Karamasa, Bilecik University, Turkey

Internet use has grown and spread rapidly around the world during the last decade. Today, computers and the Internet have become an integral part of modern societies. The Internet has created a new medium for communication and commerce for businesses. It is hard to imagine a business working without using a computer. These technological advances have also largely affected small and medium-sized enterprises (SMEs). While large companies have been quick to adopt the information and communication technologies (ICTs), SMEs have been slow to adopt these technologies in general for various reasons, especially in developing countries. This study explores the factors affecting the adoption of e-commerce by small businesses in a developing country. To attain this purpose a case study was conducted in a small hotel, which is using its website to keep up with customer expectations and competition in a small Turkish city. Conclusions and suggestions derived from this study provide a meaningful contribution to the understanding of e-commerce adoption among small businesses in developing countries.

Chapter 11

Hakikur Rahman, University of Minho, Portugal
Isabel Ramos, University of Minho, Portugal

Adoption of innovation strategies in entrepreneurship is an age old phenomenon, but inclusion of open innovation or collaborative innovation strategies in the business processes is a newly evolved concept. By far, most research reveals that the majority of successful global ventures are adopting open innovation strategies in their business proceedings. However, despite their contribution to entrepreneurship and national economy, the small and medium scale enterprises (SMEs) are well below the expectation level in terms of acquiring this newly emerged trend of doing business. Moreover, not much research is being conducted to investigate SMEs potencies, expectations, delivery channels and intricacies around the adoption, nourishment and dissemination of open innovation strategies. This research proposes a contextual framework leading to an operational framework to explore the lifecycle of open innovation strategy management activities focusing technology transfer (inbounds or outwards). It discusses a few issues on future research in empowering SMEs through utilization of open innovation strategies.

Chapter 12

Isabel Ramos, Centre Algoritmi, University of Minho, Portugal
José Fernandes, Centre Algoritmi, University of Minho, Portugal

In the past year, knowledge and innovation management have acquired increasing relevance in organizations. In the last decade, open innovation strategy, and in particular, crowdsourcing innovation model has also gained increasing importance. This model is seen as a new innovation model, capable of accelerating the innovation process. Therefore, it is important to understand how organizations can best take advantage of this innovation model. This paper approaches in two ways for commercializing intellectual property: crowdsourcing innovation, and intellectual property marketplaces. Thus, with the intention of understanding the concepts and practices, the study started by collecting scientific articles through bibliographic data bases. The paper provides knowledge about concepts and practices underlying the ways for commercializing intellectual property. It also contributes with a proposal of architecture for an intellectual property marketplace, based on the analysis of practices about crowdsourcing innovation and intellectual property marketplaces. This architecture is still in a draft stage, but already includes helpful insights for organizations interested in applying the open innovation strategy.

Chapter 13

N. D. Oye, Universiti Teknologi Malaysia, Malaysia
N. A. Iahad, Universiti Teknologi Malaysia, Malaysia
Nor Zairah Ab Rahim, Universiti Teknologi Malaysia, Malaysia

This study examines the acceptance and use of ICT by Nigerian university academicians. The model validated is the Unified Theory of Acceptance and Use of Technology (UTAUT). Using a pilot study, one hundred questionnaires were administered and collected at the University of Jos Plateau State, Nigeria. The construct was significantly correlated with behavioral intention (BI). This implies that the university ICT system makes tasks easier to accomplish, thereby making academicians more productive. The survey shows that 86.5% agree. Effort expectancy (EE) was significantly correlated with BI. The result shows that 84.3% agreed that they could use ICT. Among the four UTAUT constructs, performance expectancy exerted the strongest effect. The UTAUT model shows age effects for older workers and a stronger willingness for the younger workers to adopt new IT products. According to this study age and gender do not have significant effect on acceptance and use of ICT. Performance expectancy (PE) and Effort expectancy (EE) are found to be the most significant predictors of academic staffs' acceptance of ICT and use.

Chapter 14

Kavitha Ranganathan, Indian Institute of Management, Ahmedabad, India

The leapfrogging theory claims that instead of following the conventional digital trajectory set by the west, emerging regions can straightaway use cutting-edge technology to "leapfrog" the digital-divide. To explore the possibility of digital leapfrogging by an emerging region, this study looks at the three domains of hardware, software and connectivity. In each domain the default technology and its potential is evaluated as a digital inclusion tool while being juxtaposed with the latest "cutting-edge" alternative that could be used instead for "leapfrogging". Three specific scenarios are developed in telephony, banking and the World Wide Web, which illustrate how a combination of these different technologies help emerging regions 'leapfrog the digital divide.' Finally, the paper suggests certain leapfrogging trajectories that ICT4D projects should explore.

Chapter 15

Muneesh Kumar, University of Delhi, India and Groupe ESC-Pau, France
Mamta Sareen, University of Delhi, India
Susheel Chhabra, Lal Bahadur Shastri Institute of Management, India

There is increasing evidence that e-commerce adoption among SMEs is expanding rapidly. In spite of that, SMEs, particularly in developing countries, have not been able to adequately benefit from the new opportunities offered by e-commerce technologies. Previous studies have identified lack of trust as one of the major hurdles in achieving the potential benefits by the SMEs. This paper identifies technology-related trust issues that need to be addressed while building e-commerce infrastructure for SMEs. The evidence offered in the paper is based on a survey of the relevant practices regarding deployment and effective implementation of relevant technology tools to address these issues and enhance the levels of trust in e-commerce infrastructure. The paper also examines the relationship between the perceived level of trust and the level of assurance in respect of various technology-related trust issues. The paper suggests an approach of collaboration among the SMEs while building the e-commerce infrastructure and focusing their attention on the technology-related trust issues.

Chapter 16

Chia-Wen Tsai, Ming Chuan University, Taiwan
Pei-Di Shen, Ming Chuan University, Taiwan
Yen-Ting Lin, Ming Chuan University, Taiwan

India is the third most HIV (Human Immunodeficiency Virus) /AIDS (Acquired Immune Deficiency Syndrome) -infected country in the world. The behavior of adolescents puts them at an increased risk for HIV and other STIs (Sexually Transmitted Infections). Additionally, their knowledge about HIV/AIDS is often inadequate. A quasi experiment was designed to be conducted at four high schools with a random sampling of 451 students. Two high schools used computers and other multimedia methods to promote AIDS education while two other schools used traditional lectures. Each school had two class-hours of AIDS education. Findings determined a gap in knowledge, attitude and behavior about HIV/AIDS issues within these different groups. The implications for current teaching approaches are discussed in this study.

Preface

The expectation of individuals and groups for accelerated development in the shortest possible period has been increased in this virtual environment. Information Communication Technologies (ICTs) are playing a vital role in enhancing interaction, collaboration, and hence, human development.

The development paradigm of human beings is widespread and multiple fields are creating a positive impact for accelerated growth. ICT is one of the most powerful forces that have influenced human development in all walks of life. Bridging the gap between rich and poor and equitable distribution of resources is one of the greatest challenge our society is facing today.

ICT can help to bridge this gap by facilitating the creation of process-oriented architectures for the equitable distribution and sharing of resources. The increasing use and pervasive impact of ICT can substantially enhance the ability of developing countries to address the full range of development goals. ICT can be a powerful enabler of development initiatives targeting specific development goals contributing to the critical mass and the threshold levels needed to ignite a virtuous cycle of development. It can influence the level of development by adoption of multidimensional approach, achieving coordinated actions, interactions and local implementation, and facilitating national and international linkages.

ICT driven interaction and collaboration in this virtual environment has shortened the gap, and people have come together to share their energies for the overall benefit of society. Interaction and communication has proven to be central to the concept of human development, and it is the single-most important factor to the success or failure of our efforts. The enhanced attention has been given to this dimension since today's multi-dimensional structures are based on ICT mediated communication. It has been estimated that 65% of the population in advanced countries is engaged in creating and processing information.

The availability of ICT infrastructure is not adequate to facilitate interaction and collaboration. The awareness and creation of public access points plays important role in use of ICT resources. Numerous research studies have been taken on this dimension; the major facts discovered are the convenience and use of these access points by the users. The creation of trust in a virtual environment, as well as development of search engines and advanced networks, is an important aspect which is influencing the wide-spread use of ICT for human development. The community participation in sharing and use of natural resources as well as health-related information has also been found to be successful in this technology-based society.

WHERE THE BOOK STANDS

ICT Influences on Human Development, Interaction, and Collaboration creates awareness on how ICTs contribute to human development in multiple areas. It describes the link between ICTs and human development, which includes economic, social, and political development. It identifies potential applications for the development of human beings and provides insightful analysis about those factors (also contextual and institutional ones) that affect ICTs for human development initiatives. This book addresses future challenges by proposing strategies to both governments and international cooperation organizations for moving forward.

ORGANIZATION OF THE BOOK

The book has been divided into sixteen chapters. The brief coverage of each chapter is given below.

Public access to ICTs in less privileged areas has been important keeping in view their impact on daily lives. Libraries, telecenters, and cybercafés offer opportunities for wider public access to Information and Communication Technologies (ICT). Chapter 1 presents findings of a global exploratory study on the landscape public access venues in 25 countries around the world in a global study. The research uses profiles of the users of the different types of venues with respect to age, income, education, and gender. Results highlight the importance of strengthening public access venues in non-urban settings and to strengthen programs that reach out to underserved populations. The research also points to challenges faced by libraries and telecenters given the immense growth of cybercafés as public access venues.

Trust has become a central issue for enhancement of e-commerce interactions in this virtual environment. The virtual environment of B2B e-commerce interactions has been considered a barrier in building trust of trading partners. Chapter 2, through empirical evidence, supports the relationship between various trust-related technology issues, such as security, privacy, authentication, etc. However, there is a dearth of evidence confirming the causal relationship between environmentally related trust issues, such as social-cultural characteristics, technology standards, and regulatory framework. Based on a survey of 106 Indian companies using inter-organizational systems, this research makes an attempt to identify specific attributes of these three environmentally-related issues that have the potential to influence trust in B2B e-commerce.

Personal Communication Service (PCS) networks aim to provide "anytime-anywhere" cellular services which enable Mobile Terminals (MTs) to communicate regardless of their locations. However, in order to guarantee a successful service delivery, MTs' real-time location should be continuously managed by the network. Location management plays the central role in providing ubiquitous network communications services, which includes two fundamental processes, i.e., registration and paging. Registration is concerned with reporting of the current locations of the MTs, while paging is used to locate the MT. Both processes incur signaling cost, and due to the scarcity of PCS wireless bandwidth and for more scalable mobile services, it is important to reduce that signaling cost. The blanket paging in current PCS networks wastes a lot of wireless bandwidth. Chapter 3 focuses on the subject of paging in an attempt to reduce the paging signaling cost under delay bounds. The research challenges the signaling cost problem and successfully establishes a family of probability-based paging strategies. The chapter introduces a novel topology for the network registration area, which is called the Hot Spot Topology (HST) and based on HST, a novel location management strategy, which is called "Flower Based Strategy" (FBS) is also introduced.

There is a need to strengthen e-business interactions in agribusiness. Chapter 4 explores the e-readiness of firms in the Australian horticulture supply chain. It uses Perceived E-Readiness Model (PERM) and relies on data collected from a survey of firms in the horticulture sector in Australia. The results indicate that while horticulture firms demonstrate relative organizational preparation for the conduct of e-business, the value network within which they operate does not appear to encourage and support their endeavor. In particular, government and industry associations do not appear to play supportive roles in encouraging the use of e-business among members of the horticulture supply chain. This chapter highlights factors that are likely to facilitate or inhibit e-business in agribusiness, an area lacking in research globally. Practitioners such as governments, horticulture associations, growers and growers' associations, and digital marketplace operators, through understanding the e-readiness factors affecting e-business, can make effective decisions to develop their support, capabilities, and offerings, respectively.

Community development through public access to ICT is becoming popular in this virtual environment. Chapter 5, through a comprehensive research study, considered public libraries, telecenters, and cybercafés, and grouped the findings into four types of success factors: (1) understand and take care of local needs first, (2) train info mediaries and users, (3) build alliances with other venues and collaborate with other community services, and (4) strengthen sustainability. The findings highlight critical variables to be considered in policy decisions, funding allocations, and program implementation to reach underserved populations in developing countries with equitable access and meaningful use of ICT. They also provide valuable direction that can contribute to community development through public access to ICT.

Search engines have become part and parcel of communication and interaction. ICT plays a vital role in human development through information extraction and includes computer networks and telecommunication networks. One of the important modules of ICT is computer networks, which are the backbone of the World Wide Web (WWW). Search engines are computer programs that browse and extract information from the WWW in a systematic and automatic manner. Chapter 6 examines the three main components of search engines: Extractor, a Web crawler which starts with a URL; Analyzer, an indexer that processes words on the Web page and stores the resulting index in a database; and Interface Generator, a query handler that understands the need and preferences of the user. It concentrates on the information available on the surface Web through general Web pages and the hidden information behind the query interface, called deep Web. Emphasis has been placed on the extraction of relevant information to generate the preferred content for the user as the first result of his or her search query. It also discusses the aspect of deep Web with analysis of a few existing deep Web search engines.

Health information systems are facilitating medical practitioners to control diseases. In malaria control, ICTs can ease communication, improve doctors' training, and increase access to information by individuals and groups that are historically unaware of malaria. Successful malaria vector control depends on understanding causes, prevention, and treatment. Chapter 7 examines the possibilities of using ICTs to eradicate malaria in Tanzania. It also explores the coverage of the malaria subject related to Tanzania on various electronic databases and e-journals. It concludes that Tanzania's Ministry of Health must put forth more effort on ICT management and be more active in their approach of disseminating malaria information.

e-Environment has become major factor in gaining market share for businesses. Chapter 8 provides a deep understanding of the current status of electronic networks in the Jordanian handicrafts sector from managers' perspectives. More specifically, the study enhances utilization of the e-environment to gain market share in local, regional, and international markets. Four cases of handicraft projects are selected to conduct face-to-face interviews. The results show that handicraft projects have initial attempts to use e-electronic in their activities, but these attempts are still in embryonic stages, and they do not use e-networks effectively to gain market share. However, project managers believe that there is a direct link between the use of electronic networks and increases in the business's market share. Furthermore, it is intended that these initiatives be treated as innovative and at the end be utilized to enhance the business development of similar enterprises belonging to the small and medium enterprises sector. The study recommends that such projects consider adoption of e-networks in their future plans, enhance their staff skills in terms of improving their IT and English language skills, and develop their own internet website to create new marketing channels.

Rural Production Company, henceforth RPC, was set up in 2007 by a university-based technology and business incubator employing an ICT-mediated distributed production model. Chapter 9 reveals how RPC, initially an exploratory project whose key innovation was its Internet kiosk-facilitated model of crafts production and local empowerment, morphed into a social enterprise catering to global demands. The context of innovation provided by the Incubator led to a transformation of an ICT4D (ICT for Development) project into a business venture through the practice of formal and informal questioning at every stage of its implementation. It focuses on the iterative method adopted while highlighting the role of the incubator in the overall design and development process of the enterprise. It is a reflexive mapping of the organization's evolution from the original research agenda of outsourcing production cum rural employment, to one that privileges local networks both as a conscious business strategy and as an arena for collaborative change for human development.

Use of ICTs in Small and Medium Enterprises has become essential to bridge the digital divide. Internet use has grown and spread rapidly around the world during the last decade. Today, computers and the Internet have become an integral part of modern societies. The Internet has created a new medium for communication and commerce for businesses. It is hard to imagine a business working without using a computer. These technological advances have also largely affected Small and Medium-Sized Enterprises (SMEs). While large companies have been quick to adopt the Information and Communication Technologies (ICTs), SMEs have been slow to adopt these technologies for various reasons, especially in developing countries. Chapter 10 explores the factors affecting the adoption of e-commerce by small businesses in a developing country. To attain this purpose, a case study was conducted in a small hotel, which is using its website to keep up with customer expectations and competition in a small Turkish city. Conclusions and suggestions derived from this study provide a meaningful contribution to the understanding of e-commerce adoption among small businesses in developing countries.

Adoption of innovation strategies in entrepreneurship is an age-old phenomenon, but inclusion of open innovation or collaborative innovation strategies in the business processes is a newly evolved concept. By far, most research reveals that the majority of successful global ventures are adopting open innovation strategies in their business proceedings. However, despite their contribution to entrepreneurship and national economy, the Small and Medium-Scale Enterprises (SMEs) are well below the expectation level in terms of acquiring this newly emerged trend of doing business. Moreover, not much research is being conducted to investigate SMEs potencies, expectations, delivery channels, and intricacies around the adoption, nourishment, and dissemination of open innovation strategies. Chapter 11, through research, proposes a contextual framework leading to an operational framework to explore the lifecycle of open innovation strategy management activities focusing technology transfer (inbounds or outwards). It discusses a few issues on future research in empowering SMEs through utilization of open innovation strategies.

In the past year, knowledge and innovation management have acquired increasing relevance in organizations. In the last decade, open innovation strategy, and in particular, crowdsourcing innovation model, has also gained increasing importance. This model is seen as a new innovation model, capable of accelerating the innovation process. Therefore, it is important to understand how organizations can best take advantage of this innovation model. Chapter 12 approaches in two ways for commercializing intellectual property: crowdsourcing innovation and intellectual property marketplaces. Thus, with the intention of understanding the concepts and practices, the study started by collecting scientific articles through bibliographic databases. It provides knowledge about concepts and practices underlying the ways for commercializing intellectual property. It also contributes with a proposal of architecture for an intellectual property marketplace, based on the analysis of practices about crowdsourcing innovation and intellectual property marketplaces. This architecture is still in a draft stage, but already includes helpful insights for organizations interested in applying the open innovation strategy.

The acceptance and use of ICT plays an important role in the enhancement of value to individuals and groups. Chapter 13, through a research study, examines the acceptance and use of ICT by Nigerian university academicians. The model validated is the Unified Theory of Acceptance and Use of Technology (UTAUT). Using a pilot study, one hundred questionnaires were administered and collected at the University of Jos Plateau State, Nigeria. The construct was significantly correlated with Behavioral Intention (BI). This implies that the university ICT system makes tasks easier to accomplish, thereby making academicians more productive. The survey shows that 86.5% agree. Effort Expectancy (EE) was significantly correlated with BI. The result shows that 84.3% agreed that they could use ICT. Among the four UTAUT constructs, performance expectancy exerted the strongest effect. The UTAUT model shows age effects for older workers and a stronger willingness for the younger workers to adopt new IT products. According to this study, age and gender do not have significant effect on acceptance and use of ICT. Performance Expectancy (PE) and Effort Expectancy (EE) are found to be the most significant predictors of academic staffs' acceptance of ICT and use.

The leapfrogging theory claims that instead of following the conventional digital trajectory set by the West, emerging regions can straightaway use cutting-edge technology to "leapfrog" the digital-divide. To explore the possibility of digital leapfrogging by an emerging region, chapter 14 looks at the three domains of hardware, software, and connectivity. In each domain, the default technology and its potential is evaluated as a digital inclusion tool, while being juxtaposed with the latest "cutting-edge" alternative that could be used instead for "leapfrogging." Three specific scenarios are developed in telephony, banking, and the World Wide Web, which illustrate how a combination of these different technologies helps emerging regions "leapfrog the digital divide." Finally, the chapter suggests certain leapfrogging trajectories that ICT4D projects should explore.

There is increasing evidence that e-commerce adoption among SMEs is expanding rapidly. In spite of that, SMEs, particularly in developing countries, have not been able to adequately benefit from the new opportunities offered by e-commerce technologies. Previous studies have identified lack of trust as one of the major hurdles in achieving the potential benefits by the SMEs. Chapter 15 identifies technology-related trust issues that need to be addressed while building e-commerce infrastructure for SMEs. The evidence offered in the chapter is based on a survey of the relevant practices regarding deployment and effective implementation of relevant technology tools to address these issues and enhance the levels of trust in e-commerce infrastructure. It also examines the relationship between the perceived level of trust and the level of assurance in respect to various technology-related trust issues. Chapter 15 suggests an approach of collaboration among the SMEs while building the e-commerce infrastructure and focusing attention on the technology-related trust issues.

The behavior of adolescents in developing countries put them at an increased risk for HIV and other STIs (Sexually Transmitted Infections). Additionally, their knowledge about HIV/AIDS is often inadequate. An ICT-based quasi experiment was designed to be conducted at four high schools with a random sampling of 451 students. Two high schools used computers and other multimedia methods to promote AIDS education, while two other schools used traditional lectures. Each school had two class-hours of AIDS education. Findings determined a gap in knowledge, attitude, and behavior about HIV/AIDS issues within these different groups. Chapter 16 provides implications for current teaching approaches in this study.

CONCLUSION

Information and Communication Technologies (ICTs) are making a significant impact on human development, interaction, and collaboration among individuals, groups, and societies. The efforts of various research initiatives and outcomes highlighted in this book have suggested some of the useful and relevant strategies, which are expected to promote awareness in this domain. The important ICT dimensions that have made significant influence for human development, interaction, and collaboration are given.

ICT has made an important contribution in facilitating public access points for interaction among a less privileged section of society, which will help to bridge the level of development between various sections of society. The creation of trust in the virtual collaborative environment is essential for use of ICT resources for human development. The use of advanced security systems and Personal Computer Networks (PCN), along with search engines, has made a remarkable contribution in this area, which influences e-commerce in all facets of life. The impact of ICT interaction and collaboration in agribusiness and health information has made an important stride in human development. The users in these areas are making themselves e-ready to harness the opportunities of development.

e-Environment has become a major factor in gaining market share for small and medium businesses. SMEs should consider adoption of e-networks in their future plans, enhance their staff skills in terms of improving their IT and English language skills, and develop their own Internet website to create new marketing channels. This will help entrepreneurs to enhance their skills using innovative strategies for collaboration and achieve their goals.

The interaction and collaboration using ICT provides knowledge about concepts and practices underlying the ways for commercializing intellectual property. It also contributes with a proposal of architecture for an intellectual property marketplace, based on the analysis of practices about crowd-sourcing innovation and intellectual property marketplaces. The convenience and direct use of ICTs for human development has facilitated the development of leapfrogging theory, which claims that instead of following the conventional digital trajectory set by the West, emerging regions can straightaway use cutting-edge technology to "leapfrog" the digital-divide.

Susheel Chhabra
Lal Bahadur Shastri Institute of Management, India

Acknowledgment

This book reflects contributions of several individuals. First of all, I would like to express my gratitude to all the authors of chapters in this book. Second, I am grateful to the many research institutions, companies, and generous individuals who supported the research that formed the basis of these chapters' contributions.

I would like to thank everyone who helped with the review process. Without their timely efforts and constructive criticism, this book would not have been possible. I am grateful to Heather A. Probst for giving me the opportunity to bring this publication into reality. The support staff deserves special appreciation for providing guidance during the development of this book.

I would be remiss if I failed to thank Shree Anil Shastri, Chairman, Dr. Gautam Sinha, Director, and Dr. G. L. Sharma, Advisor, of the Lal Bahadur Shastri Institute of Management, Delhi, India, for all the encouragement and support they provided.

I would also like to place on record a word of appreciation for my parents, Mr. Ram Krishan Chhabra and Mrs. Kailash Rani, and also my family members, Mrs. Shilpa Chhabra, Bhavya, and Ram Vaibhav, who have helped bring this project into reality.

Susheel Chhabra
Lal Bahadur Shastri Institute of Management, India

Chapter 1
Users of ICT at Public Access Centers:
Age, Education, Gender, and Income Differences in Users

Ricardo Gomez
University of Washington, USA

Kemly Camacho
University of Washington and Sula Batsú Research Cooperative in Costa Rica, USA

ABSTRACT

Libraries, telecenters, and cybercafés offer opportunities for wider public access to information and communication technologies (ICT). This paper presents findings of a global exploratory study on the landscape public access venues in 25 countries around the world. The goal of the project was to better understand the users of public access venues and their needs, this being one of several papers that result from the global study. This paper identifies profiles of the users of the different types of venues with respect to age, income, education and gender. While findings are not new, their value lies in the compelling evidence drawn from 25 countries and across different types of public access venues, which has never been done before. Results highlight the importance of strengthening public access venues in non-urban settings and to strengthen programs that reach out to underserved populations. The authors also point to special challenges faced by libraries and telecenters given the immense growth of cybercafés as public access venues in most of the countries studied.

INTRODUCTION

Information and communication technologies (ICT) can play an important role in human development. Venues such as libraries, telecenters, and cybercafés, which offer public access to ICT, can help offer more access and use of ICT for development among underserved populations in developing countries. While there have been many previous studies about public libraries and ICT (Rutkauskiene, 2008; Walkinshaw, 2007), especially in the US (Becker et al., 2010; Bertot, McClure, Thomas, Barton, & McGilvray, 2007),

DOI: 10.4018/978-1-4666-1957-9.ch001

about telecenters for community development (Best & Kumar, 2008; Gomez & Ospina, 2001; Kuriyan & Toyama, 2007; Proenza, Bastidas-Buch, & Montero, 2002), and to a lesser degree, about cybercafés and their contribution to social and digital inclusion (Finquelievich & Prince, 2007; Gurol & Sevindik, 2007; Haseloff, 2005; Salvador, Sherry, & Urrutia, 2005; Wheeler, 2007), we found no previous studies that have done a systematic comparison of the different types of venues and across multiple countries.

Who are the users of public access to ICT in developing countries around the world? To answer this question and other questions related to the user needs and opportunities to strengthen public access venues for human development, in 2008-2009 we conducted an exploratory, mostly qualitative study of libraries, telecentres and cybercafés in 25 countries around the world. The study was designed to help understand who is using these public access venues, how different types of public access venues are meeting the needs of underserved communities in different countries, and how they can be strengthened to better contribute to human development. This paper is focused on presenting a profile of users of public access venues as part of the results of the study. Other papers that result from this study analyze user needs, user perceptions, venue differences and similarities, and contributions to development, among other topics (Gomez, 2011).

The study was done in partnership with local researchers in each country, and designed with multiple data-collection and analysis methods to provide broad insight into the nature of these public access venues and their users. Approximately 25,000 people were surveyed in 25 countries, providing a thorough picture of the types of users who visit libraries, telecenters and cybercafés. This study does not include surveys of non-users, a sector of the population that deserves further research but requires a different data gathering strategy than what was used in this study.

We defined *Public Access Venue* as an institutional venue with a mission to offer public access to information tools and resources, with services that are available to all and not directed to one group in the community to the exclusion of others.[1] Based on this definition, we identified three main types of public access venue of importance in most countries, and grouped them under the generic headings "public library", "telecenter" and "cybercafé", with room for "other" venues of interest and importance in a particular country. Public libraries are often confused with school libraries, other specialized libraries, and community or popular libraries. Telecenters are often labeled community technology centers, communication community centers, or eCenters. We used the following definitions for each one of the three main types of venues included in this study, based on Wikipedia.org:

- **Public Library:** A library which is accessible by the public and is generally funded from public sources.
- **Cybercafé:** An internet café, or cybercafé, is a place that is open to the public, set up as a for-profit business where people can use a computer with Internet access, usually for a fee. It may also offer food and drinks, as well as other services.
- **Telecentre:** A place that is open to the public, set up as a non-profit service intended for community development, where people can use computers with or without Internet access, as well as services such as training courses and other development activities (usually related to health, education, agriculture, etc.). Sometimes there are fees for service, sometimes they are free.

We did not analyze use of ICT in non-public venues (home, school, or work), or the use of newer technologies, such as mobile phones or wireless plazas (hotspots), or the use of older technologies such as community radio, TV, and press. Important as these communication technologies are, they fall outside the boundary of this study. Further research can shed more light on the interactions between ICT in public and private venues, and between ICT and other communication technologies of importance for community development.

The study is exploratory in nature, and provides an initial perspective of broad patterns in the profiles of users, based on aggregated data across all countries, with special attention to commonalities across them. Local teams followed a shared research design that included document review, expert and operator interviews, qualitative user surveys, site visits and, in some cases, focus groups. Data was collected in each country in local languages, and researchers reported findings in English. The findings presented here are based on the reports produced by the local research teams, which we cite individually. All country reports for this study are available online[2].

The remainder of the paper is organized as follows: we present a description of the research methods used in this study, followed by findings and discussion around five issues: the urban prevalence of public access venues, the predominance of cybercafés, and an analysis of users of public access venues by gender, age, education, and income. The paper concludes with a discussion of the implications of the findings and questions for further research.

RESEARCH METHODS

In this section, we briefly describe the research methods to select the countries, collect and analyze the data. Note that this is a large and complex project and the complexity of the research methods cannot be fully described in detail here. For a detailed description see Gomez (2010). The general research question of this study was: what is the landscape of public access to ICT in developing countries? This broad question was followed by specific questions including: who are the users of public access venues? This specific research question is addressed in this paper. To better understand how it is placed in the broader research agenda, we will briefly describe the process followed to select the 25 countries included in the study, the data collection strategy and the data analysis.

Country Selection

A careful selection of countries was critical to this study, in order to focus on developing countries in the "middle of the pyramid" (Prahalad, 2006). Of 237 possible countries and territories in the world, the final 25 countries (Algeria, Argentina, Bangladesh, Brazil, Colombia, Costa Rica, Dominican Republic, Ecuador, Egypt, Georgia, Honduras, Indonesia, Kazakhstan, Kyrgyzstan, Malaysia, Moldova, Mongolia, Namibia, Nepal, Peru, the Philippines, South Africa, Sri Lanka, Turkey, Uganda) went through a selection process that used four successive sets of criteria to focus on a subset of developing countries with a mid-size geography and population, and with existing public library systems. The criteria for country selection were based on size, population, and other demographic data,[3] degree of freedom of expression[4] and political unrest,[5] a measure of "needs and readiness" criteria,[6] regional distribution, and availability of country research teams. The countries studied do not include very large and complex countries such as India and China, or countries with strong restrictions on freedom of expression, such as Bhutan or Cuba; the landscape of public access to ICT in those countries might vary greatly from what is presented here.

Research Rationale

The study of user profiles is part of a broader study of public access to ICT around the world. To address the broad goals of this research project we used as starting point the Real Access / Real Impact criteria developed in South Africa by Bridges.org (www.bridges.org). We adapted and refined Real Access to develop the Access, Capacity and Environment (ACE) Framework, in order to help understand the range of economic, political, educational, infrastructure, cultural, organizational, and other factors that affect the way people use ICT in public access venues. The three pillars of this framework are: equitable access: physical access, suitability, and affordability of the venue, as well as technology access; human capacity: human capacity and training (users and staff), meeting local needs, social appropriation; and enabling environment: socio-cultural factors, political will and legal and regulatory framework, as well as popular support. The ACE Framework is important to understand the broad scope of the research. The specific focus on users of public access venues was based on four key variables to be studied across all countries and all venue types: age, gender, education and income. Other variables were studied in specific contexts (for example, ethnicity, religion, caste, or language), but they do not offer a base for comparison across all countries.

Data Collection

Nineteen local research teams were chosen (with some researchers representing more than one country) following an international call for proposals. Lead researchers from each team were brought together twice – at the beginning and halfway through the research process – to discuss the purpose, methodology, and emerging findings of the study. Data was collected in all countries between December 2008 and August 2009. Each team conducted original research in local languages, using the following data collection methods:

- **Document Review:** Identify and review salient literature in the country, including existing statistical information about population, ICT penetration, public access

venues, government policies and previous studies relevant to the study. Sample: About 40 documents per country were reviewed.

- **Expert Interviews:** Identify at least ten specialists in the areas of interest of the project and conduct in-depth interviews with them. Interview guides were prepared in each country depending on the local needs and context. Sample: About 10 to 15 interviews with experts were conducted per country.

- **Site Visits:** Identify, visit and observe six or more venues of each type (library, telecentre, cybercafé, or other). Site visits were undertaken for a minimum of a half day, making sure to include both urban and non-urban sites (ideally three of each). In selecting sites, research teams identified typical case samples of each type of venue, including both urban and non-urban sites. Sample: there were about 20 visits per country, approximately 500 sites visited in total.

- **User Surveys:** User information was collected via a survey. A shared survey instrument was used to administer a questionnaire. Each country team was allowed to add questions that they felt were relevant to the local context to enrich the overall body of evidence. At each site every second or third user exiting the venue was surveyed. Teams surveyed between 40-50 users at each venue. Sample: Total users surveyed: around 1000 per country. Given limited time and resources, user surveys were not intended to provide statistically significant samples of the population or of the venues studied, but an exploratory indication of trends and patterns for comparison and further research.

- **Operator Interviews:** Identify at least one operator in each site visited and hold a structured interview to provide a more in-depth understanding of the venue, users and environment. Sample: around operators interviewed 20 per country.

Detailed country reports were prepared by each local research team using a data-collection template designed to help teams organize their local fieldwork in order to answer detailed questions about access, capacity and environment issues in each type of venue studied. The use of a shared research design and methodology across all countries helped make data more comparable, even though the specific ways in which data was collected varied from one country to another in order to make it more locally relevant.

The findings reported in this paper are mostly based on the results of the user surveys, with additional insight drawn from the other data collection methods, as reported by local researchers in each of their country reports. The structure of the report collected from each country team is as the following:

Structure of Each Country Report

1. Extended Executive Summary
2. Methodology
   2.1 Venue Selection
   2.2 Inequity Variables
   2.3 Data Gathering Techniques
   2.4 Research Trustworthiness & Credibility
3. Country Assessment
   3.1 Overall Country Assessment
   3.2 Research Framework
   3.3 Information Needs of Underserved Communities
   3.4 Charts: Information Needs, Users & Uses
   3.5 Economic, Policy & Regulatory Environment
   3.6 Probes for Emerging Insights from Phase 1

4. Venue-Specific Assessments
   4.1 Venue # 1: Public Libraries
   4.2 Venue # 2: Telecentres
   4.3 Venue # 3: Cybercafés
   4.4 Venue # 4: Other
5. Success Factors & Strategic Recommendations
6. Appendices

Data Analysis

The purpose of the data analysis particular to this paper was to identify and categorize trends in relation to users of public access venues. We conducted different types of analyses:

We cross checked the consistency of the data within and across different country reports and, when needed, verified the accuracy of data regarding counts of public libraries and other venues in different countries. We aggregated and analyzed the numerical data reported for the survey results in each country. In some cases, where information was missing from the country reports, we asked for additional input and clarification from our research partners. This numeric analysis is summarized and presented in the charts below, describing the distribution of the different types of public access venues, and the proportion of users by gender, age, education, and income.

We also did a detailed coding of all qualitative data using variables from the ACE Framework described above for each type of venue; this interpretive coding of the qualitative data was used to further understand the trends and patterns emerging in the analysis of the data. Therefore, qualitative data is used to explain or illustrate the findings of the analysis.

Finally, we undertook a detailed re-reading and discussion of the country reports to identify and group trends in the data and make sure we did not miss any significant insights from local research partners in relation to venue distribution, gender, education, age, and income of users. These are the main categories of findings we report in this paper.

Limitations of this Study

This study focused primarily on gathering qualitative data to assess the current state and future opportunities in public access to ICT across different types of venues in a sample of 25 countries. Even though there are numerous reports that compare statistical information of libraries (i.e., IFLA, 2007) and of ICT penetration and use across countries (i.e., ITU, 2009), his study is groundbreaking in its breadth and scope in that no other studies have systematically looked at different types of public access venues across multiple countries. Nonetheless, the breadth of the study also means that it does not provide an in-depth analysis of a particular venue, country, or experience, and findings cannot be easily generalized without a clear understanding of the specific context and the analytic framework used.

The tension between structure and flexibility in research design generally helped to strengthen the research results by providing a shared research methodology, while allowing flexibility to adapt to local priorities and context. A shared survey instrument was translated and adapted to meet the needs of each context, but users' profiles results were mostly shared as percentages, not absolute numbers, thus diminishing the ways in which we could analyze and use the survey results (i.e., percentage totals do not always add to 100). Other numerical data, such as counts of venues, percentages with ICT, and percentages in urban or non-urban settings, generally came from secondary sources consulted by local researchers.

Data about public libraries are generally more reliable than other venue data since most countries, and international bodies that work with libraries (i.e., IFLA, UNESCO), keep public records. When available, these official sources were used. Information about telecenters is more dispersed among international agencies and local non-profit organizations that sponsor the telecenters, making their records more difficult to access. Data about cybercafés is generally less comprehensive, or not available at all. Information, such as estimated number, characteristics, and locations of cybercafés and, to a lesser degree, telecenters, tends to be an informed estimate based on what they learned about those particular venues and the context in the country. Consequently, there is much variability in available estimates about the number of venues, especially cybercafés.

FINDINGS AND DISCUSSION

We will now discuss the main findings in relation to the **users** of public access venues, particularly in relation to gender, age, education, and income, as well as location (urban or non-urban[7]) of the venues.

Geographic Distribution of Public Access Venues

The next three figures describe the total distribution of public access venues included in this study, with proportions by type of venue and by geographic location (urban/non-urban) (Figure 1).

Cybercafés are by far the most common type of public access venue, representing 73% of the total number of venues included in this study. Libraries and telecenters account for only 11% and 12% (respectively) of the total count of public access venues. Four countries (Georgia, Honduras, Malaysia, and South Africa) did not report any numbers for cybercafés, and seven more countries reported numbers for cybercafés that are lower than other types of venues (Bangladesh, the Dominican Republic, Kazakhstan, Moldova, Mongolia, Namibia, and Sri Lanka). Based on the descriptions offered in the country reports, these low numbers can be attributed to strong public access initiatives leading to other types of public access venues (religious libraries, school libraries, health centers) as in the case of Sri Lanka (Wanasundera, 2008) and Namibia (James & Louw, 2008). See also Francisco Proenza's (2006) work

Figure 1. Distribution of public access ICT venues (based on aggregated data from 25 countries in the Landscape Study)

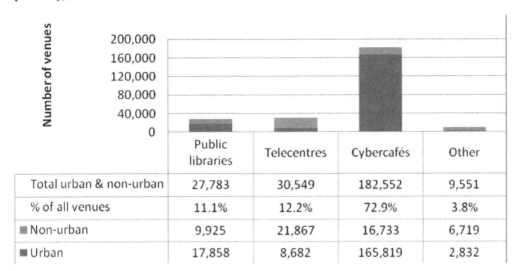

	Public libraries	Telecentres	Cybercafés	Other
Total urban & non-urban	27,783	30,549	182,552	9,551
% of all venues	11.1%	12.2%	72.9%	3.8%
■ Non-urban	9,925	21,867	16,733	6,719
■ Urban	17,858	8,682	165,819	2,832

for a detailed discussion of urban prevalence of public access initiatives. Furthermore, the Dominican Republic in particular mentions a lack of official data for their venue counts, which may lead to an underestimation of the number of cybercafés (Alfaro, Molina, & Camacho Jiménez, 2008). In any case, cybercafés are probably the most understudied, and these numbers are most likely to grow.

This analysis does not differentiate the numbers of computers, or computers with Internet connections, at the different types of venues in the countries studied. It is possible that fewer venues with more computers could serve the same number of people than more venues with fewer computers. More detailed research in this regard is currently underway as part of another global study at the University of Washington (www.globalimpactstudy.org) among others.

It appears a high concentration of public access venues is located in urban areas. While telecenters have a high proportion of non-urban locations, public libraries and cybercafés are primarily urban, with 64% and 91% of them respectively in urban locations. Furthermore, only 31% of the public libraries, on average, offer ICT as part of

their services. Given that cybercafés account for 73% of all public access venues studied (the great majority of them are urban), and given that over half the public libraries are urban, with only about 31% of the total libraries offering ICT services, it is clear that public access to ICT is mostly an urban phenomenon.

With a concentration on urban areas and populations, public access to ICT does not appear to serve the majority of the rural populations in the countries studied. The urban/non-urban divide is by far the most significant divide in public access to ICT. Further analysis is warranted to better understand the concentration of public access venues in relation to population, along the lines presented by Gomez (2009, pp. 14-19), but differentiating urban and non-urban population concentration and number of public access venues in each, in order to corroborate the degree to which public access venues serve both urban and non-urban populations.

In sum, cybercafés constitute the largest source of public access to ICT, and the majority of public access venues are located in urban areas. While data about number of public libraries and, to a lesser extent, telecenters is relatively easy to gather, the number of cybercafés is difficult to determine in any given country. Cybercafés are generally not grouped under any collective body or association, and they tend to appear and disappear with the local economy and market needs; their numbers are the result of "informed speculation," and may well be exaggerated for some countries while missing in others, as discussed earlier. In Georgia, Indonesia, and Malaysia, we have estimated the proportion of public libraries in urban locations, and in Brazil, Costa Rica, Ecuador, and Uganda, we estimated the proportion of cybercafés in urban locations based on information in the reports, since no actual numbers were provided by the research teams in those countries. These exceptions do not change the general trend of public access to ICT being mostly an urban and cybercafé-driven phenomenon.

This finding has two main implications:

1. There is an extreme urban predominance of public access initiatives. This imbalance has been reported before and is noted as a failure of telecenters to serve rural populations, (Kuriyan & Toyama, 2007; Proenza, 2006). If public access to ICT is to make a meaningful difference for underserved populations, non-urban populations need to be better served by public access ICT initiatives.
2. The importance of cybercafés in the field of ICT for community development has previously been reported by others (Haseloff, 2005), even if it is an "unintentional" social role (Finquelievich & Prince, 2007), an "instrumental" one (Robinson, 2006), or an expression of the "public sphere" (Salvador et al., 2005).

Even though there has been far more research about telecenters and public libraries than cybercafés, the sheer number of cybercafés makes it clear that their role in community development needs to be better understood in order to take full advantage of the increased access to ICT that they offer to the public. Furthermore, rather than competing with cybercafés by setting up new or alternative public access venues, government policy and public funds could be better directed to help make ICT services offered by cybercafés more equitable, accessible, and relevant to underserved populations (gender, age, education, income, as discussed below, as well as language, ethnicity, religion, caste, and other inequity variables of importance in each particular setting). Given the results of this study, more research on the role of cybercafés for community development, and the potential interactions between cybercafés, libraries and telecenters, is well warranted.

In this context of urban bias and strong predominance of cybercafés in the public access landscape, a closer look at the overall trends among the users of the different types of venues follows. Note that given the qualitative focus of this study and limitations in the data collection, results do not allow more complex statistical analysis such as t-test or ANOVA. More in-depth studies across different venue types, with representative samples and stronger statistical analysis of data, are warranted.

Gender Differences

Past experience and studies of public access venues (see detailed literature review by Sey & Fellows, 2009), especially studies of telecenters (Abbasi, 2007; APC WNSP, 2005, 2009; Gurumurthy, 2004; Kuriyan & Kitner, 2009; Obayelu & Ogunlade, 2006), indicate a significant gender gap in public access venues, which are, reportedly, visited and used primarily by men. However, as shown in the following figure, our study shows that overall trends in the proportions of users of the different types of public access venues tend to be quite similar among men and women around the world, with small differences that we will discuss in detail. These findings highlight the need to explore the issue of gender in public access venues in more depth (Figure 2).

Public libraries appear to have the smallest difference in gender distribution of users, with only a slightly higher proportion of women visiting libraries than men (Agosto, Paone, & Ipock, 2007; Applegate, 2008). Telecenters and cybercafés, on the other hand, tend to be visited more frequently by men than women. While the gender difference is smaller in the case of telecenters, in the case of cybercafés the difference may be more important. These data confirm the notion that access gaps still exist with regard to gender, but women were clearly using all of the public access venues we surveyed.

Francisco Proenza (personal communication) rightly notes that the apparent gender balance does not take into consideration the fact that 1) cybercafés are far more numerous than other venues (even if they are exaggerated), and 2) public access venues are more concentrated in urban settings. Our data does not allow a conclusive analysis of gender in relation to the urban/non-urban divide, but if we take into consideration the relative weight of the number of cybercafés vs. the number of libraries and telecenters, the gender

difference in use of public access venues becomes more significant. This difference/significance is displayed in Figure 3.

If we weigh the gender distribution of the users in relation to the number of venues in each type, the difference between men and women using cybercafés becomes clearer, given the fact that there are far more cybercafés than other types of venues Taking into account the numerical predominance of cybercafés, the gender difference in use of cybercafés appears to be more important. At the same time, this reading of the data also minimizes the gender disparity among users of libraries and telecenters, and over emphasizes the gender equity of the use of libraries and telecenters as public access venues.

Based on the above we suggest that public access initiatives that explicitly address and correct social inequities and gender differences, as is most frequently the case in public libraries and telecenters, are more successful at transforming the gender imbalance of women having more limited access and use of ICT in public access places. But this gender imbalance remains untouched or is further exacerbated by initiatives that only provide access to ICT, as is the case of cybercafés, without

Figure 2. Gender Differences in users by venue type (based on aggregated data from 25 countries in the landscape study; totals do not add to 100%)

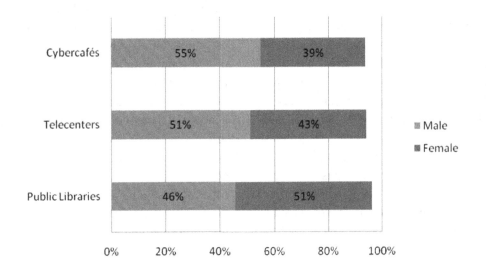

Figure 3. Gender differences in users by venue type (based on aggregated data from 25 countries in the landscape study)

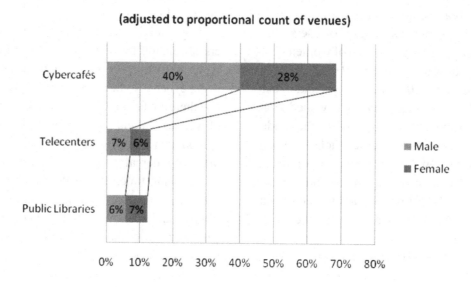

(adjusted to proportional count of venues)

proactive outreach to underserved populations such as women and minorities, as is frequently the case in libraries and telecentres. More in-depth research in each particular context is needed to assess a) whether the gender imbalance is larger or smaller than what our findings seem to imply, b) whether this difference is the result of numerical distortion in the count of venues, and c) whether it represents evidence that gender equity can be enhanced through purposeful social intervention (i.e., programs specifically designed to encourage participation of women) or undermined by public access driven by market forces that is limited to providing access to ICT alone, which ultimately reflects existing inequities in society.

Evidently, the number of users does not give the full picture of the full nature of public access venues: the frequency, intensity, purpose, and results of the use of ICT in public access venues is also important. For example, women face significant social restrictions in numerous countries, especially in some Muslim or Hindu countries where it is socially unacceptable for women to be alone or without a male in public places, or it is

not acceptable for women to interact with male operators of public access venues. An example from Egypt illustrates this reality for some women: "… local cultures also sometimes affect the people's access to public access venues. Among these is the factor of gender, which in some communities limits the access of women. Cyber cafés, as an example, witness a limited number of female users, more so in rural areas. While this is not as extreme in other venues, there is a limitation on the suitable hours for females to access these venues" (Wanas, 2008, p. 31).

These may be stronger barriers for women to use public access venues than just "no free time," or "no training in technology." Recent research in India and Chile by Kuriyan and Kitner (2009) offers additional valuable insight into issues of gender and shared computing. Gender interactions in public access ICT warrants further investigation, and tools, such as the Gender Evaluation Methodology (GEM) developed by the Association for Progressive Communications (APC WNSP, 2005, 2009; Goldfarb & Prince, 2008) would be useful in shedding additional light on this topic.

Significant Age Differences: Spaces Used Primarily by Youth

The most commonly reported result of all research teams around the world, and across all three types of public access venues surveyed – libraries, telecenters, and cybercafés – cited age as the most significant defining characteristic of the populations using these venues. Public access ICT venues are frequented mostly by youth. As the Argentina research team clearly stated, "Gender is not as relevant as age regarding the use of the information venues" (Rozengardt & Finquelievich, 2008, p. 22).

The following figure shows that the overwhelming majority of visitors to all three venues are between 15 and 35 years of age. While it would have been preferable to have a finer filter in the age brackets – for example, an age bracket between 15 and 24, and another between 25 and 35 – variations in the scales used in different countries make it impossible to more finely differentiate smaller age brackets between 15 and 35. The percentage of "senior" visitors aged 61 and older is the lowest of all age groups in all venues (Figure 4).

It has frequently been said that youth are "naturally close" to technologies, and that older populations are more removed: for example, in studies of populations over 60 years of age in developed countries (Raban & Brynin, 2006), older populations are shown to use ICTs very little. However, in this same study, the authors postulate that perhaps much of the relationship between age and technology use has to do with "secondary factors that are associated with age, such as reduced employment, diminished resources, and lower level of education" (Raban & Brynin, 2006, p. 49).

The concentration of users around youth, even largely defined as between 15-35 years of age, is clear across all types of venues and across all countries. There is little or no variation in the trend shown in the figure above when separating urban and non-urban venues, except for a slightly higher proportion of adult users in the small number of available, non-urban public libraries and telecenters. Furthermore, there are very few countries where there is a remarkable difference in the age distributions of the users from the averages shown above. More research in each country would be required to explain or correct the following extreme variations from the average:

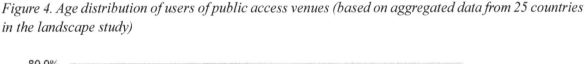

Figure 4. Age distribution of users of public access venues (based on aggregated data from 25 countries in the landscape study)

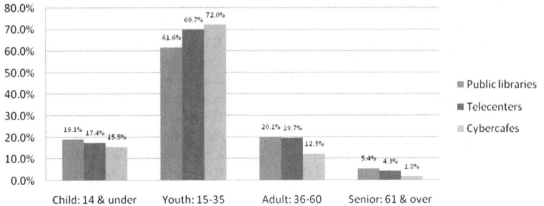

Significantly Higher Than Average

Honduras shows an unusually high proportion of children (ages 14 and under) using public libraries, and the Dominican Republic shows an unusually high proportion of children using telecenters. While anecdotal evidence would suggest a high concentration of school children using libraries and telecenters in these countries, it is more likely that the apparent extreme variations in these two countries are due to measurement error, since they both also report lower than average use of these venues for the youth age group, suggesting that the scale used to differentiate children from youth might have been different in these countries.

At the same time, Kazakhstan, Kyrgyzstan, and Namibia all show unusually higher proportions of youth using public libraries, and Honduras and Kazakhstan show unusually higher proportions of youth using telecenters than other types of venues. It is possible that these extreme variations are due to measurement errors in each country, since it is unlikely that all or almost all users of any age group would be exclusive users of any particular type of venue, as the data would seem to suggest. Finally, Peru and Mongolia both show a higher than average use of telecenters among adults, but we cannot find any apparent reason for this variation.

Significantly Lower Than Average

Few countries show a significantly lower proportion of youth using the public access venues: Costa Rica reports a low proportion of youth using telecenters, Dominican Republic reports much lower than average youth use of all venues, and Georgia and Honduras both report a relatively lower proportion of youth using public libraries. On the other hand, Peru reports an unusually low proportion of adult users of public libraries. As discussed above, the cases of Honduras and Dominican Republic may be attributed to errors in measurement; there is no obvious explanation for the variations in Costa Rica, Georgia, and Peru; further research is needed to assess whether they too are measurement errors, or if there are specific circumstances in those countries that explain this type of user distribution.

Finally, given the higher number of cybercafés over other types of venues, we created a projection of users by age that is proportional to the number of venues of each type. The result of this adjustment for age reconfirms the previously highlighted trend of youth as primary users of public access venues, emphasizing a stronger preference among youth for cybercafés over other types of venues, and eliminating a very slight preference among children, adults, and seniors for libraries over other venues, as is apparent in the analysis described above. Nonetheless, the differences are small enough not to warrant a solid conclusion. We have already indicated that the nature of the numerical data makes our analysis useful to identify higher-level trends, but not useful to explain small differences in each particular context.

The case of Ecuador appears to be a very typical illustration of the age distribution of users of the three types of public access venues, as described by the local research team:

- **Libraries:** "Library users are mainly young students (around 70% with education level up to high school), 79% between 15-35 in urban areas and 83% in the same range in non-urban areas. Most of the users are from medium [income bracket]" (Bossio & Sotomayor, 2008, p. 47).
- **Telecenters:** "Young people between 15-35 years old are most of the users of telecenters in urban areas; in non-urban areas users are mostly distributed by age (50% under 14, 17% 15-35 and 33% older than 35). People older than 61 are not telecenter users" (Bossio & Sotomayor, 2008, p. 60).
- **Cybercafés:** "Young people between 15-3 5 years old use cybercafés; this segment usually are incorporated to labor market,

so they can afford the cost of services... In non-urban areas a significant (36%) [number of] users are under 15 years old, and their use of cybercafés is mainly for education purposes because they usually don´t have other sources of information. In urban areas highly educated populations [are the] main users of cybercafés (70% with university degrees)" (Bossio, 2004; Bossio & Sotomayor, 2008, p. 75).

The fact that information needs can also be met at the workplace with a phone in the shop or a computer at work could indicate that adults do not use ICT less than youth, they just use public access venues less because they find other ways to access ICT at work or at home. As we will see, the same logic applies when discussing income differences.

Education Differences: Focus On Students and Users with Formal Educations

Results of our study show that, overall, most users of public access venues have high school or college educations, while a smaller proportion of them have elementary school educations, and only a small fraction have no formal education at all. Our study shows that the majority of ICT users in public access venues rea students, especially young students, across all types of public access venues.

Presented in a visual manner, the figure below emphasizes that when looking at education levels, a pattern emerges in which the smallest user group has no formal education at all, and the proportion of users grows as level of education goes up, reaching its maximum number of users at high school levels of education. The proportion of users with college level education then drops again, but it is still higher than for those with elementary education only. This pattern is consistent across all venue types (libraries, telecenters, cybercafés), and also across geographic locations (urban and non-urban

venues), except for a slightly higher proportion of elementary school level usage in non-urban locations than in urban ones. One limitation of the data presented here: for most countries, it is difficult to know whether the education level is the current level (students actively enrolled in education at that level) or the maximum level reached. Bearing in mind the predominantly young age of the majority of users described above, and on anecdotal evidence, we are inclined to think that the majority of users surveyed are youth currently enrolled in school at the level indicated here, and not that they are adults who record this level as the highest level of education reached (Figure 5).

Few countries have a large variation from the general trend expressed in the figure above, in which users are mostly educated to high school or college levels: Egypt reports 80% of users of public libraries are in elementary school, and Moldova reports almost half the users of telecenters and cybercafés have no formal education. Kazakhstan reports unusually high percentages of college level users in all venues. We have no particular explanation for these variations from the general trends further research in these countries would be needed to assess what lies behind the variations to the trends.

Most of the research teams around the world described education as being the primary factor of usage for public access information venues: these spaces are being visited mainly by young men and women doing their studies, primarily at the high school level. People with little or no formal education don't appear to be visiting these venues as frequently. This fact was expressed well by our Sri Lanka research team: "There are large numbers of people who are illiterate, who have no basic education, and are school drop outs. Very few of these people will use public access information venues" (Wanasundera, 2008, p. 19).

The figure above indicates a predominance of library use by elementary and high school level users. Nonetheless, this data does not necessarily indicate that these groups are making use of

Figure 5. Education levels of users of public access venues

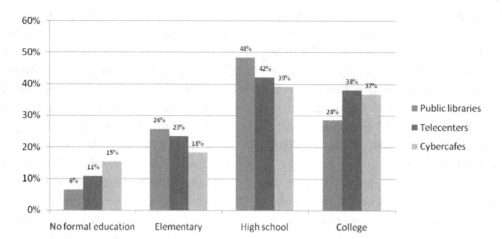

the public access venues to actually fulfill their school-related information needs or not. Information needs and uses are analyzed in a separate paper still in progress. Furthermore, while an important feature of public access venues is to fulfill the information needs of school-aged children and youth, most of whom are enrolled or have completed elementary, high school, or college level education, the apparent preference for libraries among elementary and high school students is erased when we factor in the relative weight of each type of venue: there are three times as many cybercafés as there are telecenters and public libraries combined. Based on the data on user age and education level alone, it's difficult to confirm whether libraries and telecenters are used more for education-related activities and cybercafés less, as the numerical data above would imply. But other qualitative data collected in the study does confirm the importance of education uses across all three venues. The following are typical examples of narrative descriptions local research teams made about the education-related information needs of users:

- **Libraries:** In Honduras, for example, "people access every day, the majority being kids and young people in school and university

students....Although the community has free access to the libraries, the adult population is the group who less visits them.... Students are the ones who consider it not only useful but necessary. But reading, information and knowledge as a way to improve the quality of lifestyle are still not as widespread amongst the rest of the community" (Arias & Camacho Jiménez, 2008, pp. 81, 82, 83).

- **Telecenters:** In the Philippines, for example, where telecenters are called Community E-Centers, "the users belong to the low- to medium-income range and possess intermediate education. They are below 25-years-old and live in rural areas... These students take the most advantage of accessing information through ICT while women, farm workers, the elderly and other underserved may have some difficulty finding time to access" (Ideacorp, 2008, p. 98).

- **Cybercafés:** In Kyrgyzstan, for example, where cybercafés are called Internet Clubs, "the majority of the users at Internet Clubs are students and school children. They usually look for thesis or dissertation references or subjects they are studying for their course work or thesis. In addition, students and school children come to Internet clubs to print out their presentations." (Ariunaa, 2008, p. 152)

While there is some evidence supporting an important education-related use of all types of public access venues, especially at the high school level, it is clear that people with no formal education are, for the most part, not using public access venues. This disparity points to an important social equity gap in the use of public access venues, especially challenging to the social role of public libraries and telecenters: how can they better include and serve the sectors of the population that are currently being excluded, i.e., those who do not have any formal education? More research into the education level and education uses of public access venues is needed to understand this issue in more depth.

Income Differences: Public Access Makes ICT Available to Lower Income Population

The last inequity variable for which we collected information in all countries is income level of the users of public access venues. Findings in relation to this variable appear to confirm that public access venues around the world are accessed primarily by low- and medium-income individuals

(low, medium, and high income brackets were determined relative to the specific context in each location, not to a set dollar value). There is less use of public access venues by people with higher incomes, especially of public libraries (Figure 6).

These results seem to support the idea that public access venues *do* make a difference in making ICT more accessible to lower- and middle-income populations, where private ownership and use do not support these needs.

Telecenters and cybercafés generally charge a fee for their services, so an interesting observation from the above figure is that there is not a large difference between low- and middle-income groups in their use of free public libraries versus fee-based cybercafés and telecenters (a small proportion of telecenters offer services for free; most charge some kind of fee for service, even if it is very low or subsidized and does not help to cover all the expenses of operating the telecenters). One might expect the differences in the patterns of use to be larger if cost was an important in determining choice of venues. Factors such as convenience, services offered, trust and preference of other friends, not cost, seem to more determinant in people's choice of which public access venue to visit. In other words, while defining the precise reason for income-related variations in public access to ICT is not possible with the data we

Figure 6. Income levels of users of public access ICT venues

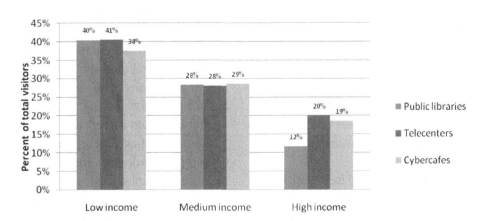

have, the observations provided by our research teams seem to indicate that charging a fee is not necessarily an important obstacle to accessing information in public access venues.

The situation described by the Brazilian team seems to be fairly typical, not exceptional: "poorer people were more likely to use cybercafés than their rich counterparts. Among internet users earning less than the minimum wage, 78% declared they access the web through paid public access centers. By contrast, only 30% of those who earned more than five times the minimum wage relied on cybercafés" (Voelcker, 2008, p. 16).

Populations also value other aspects of public access venues, such as the services they provide and the array of resources available. Our Nepal researchers, for instance, pointed out that low-income groups could not afford the services of telecenters and cybercafés, but they did view these venues as being important. At the same time, these researchers observed that high-income groups didn't need to go to cybercafés to get their work done, most likely because they have computers and Internet connection at home or at work (South Asia Partnership (SAP International), 2008, pp. 147-148).

This income-related usage is an important issue to explore further, especially in the face of increasing difficulties for financial sustainability of public access ICT services. Based on the preliminary information, public libraries (which generally offer ICT access for free) and telecenters (which are sometimes free but frequently charge low fees) could improve the financial sustainability of their ICT services by charging user fees without significantly altering the use of their ICT services: people of similar income brackets appear to make comparable use of different types of public access venues, regardless of fees, and use of public access venues seems to decrease as income bracket increases.

Finally, these findings confirm the notion that use of public access venues is not necessarily restricted to lower- or middle-income popula-

tions, although they do constitute the majority of users. In conversation with research partners, it was reported that public access venues are also used by people who have private access at home, at work, or at school: convenience, speed, or socializing with friends were strong drivers to use public access venues. The case of Peru is unique in that there is an unusually high proportion of Internet access in the country that happens through Cabinas Publicas, the local version of cybercafés, as opposed to through private access at home or work. The history of Internet penetration in the country, and the early spread of Cabinas Publicas, might explain this unusual trend, which is not replicated in any other country in the study. Additional research on whether higher income populations tend to use ICT less in public access venues because they use it at home, at work, or elsewhere is warranted.

CONCLUSION

This study shows that the typical profile of users of ICTs in a public access venue – a library, telecenter, or a cybercafé – in the countries we studied is very likely to be people in an urban location, very likely young (15-35), low- to middle-income, and those with a high school or college education. Overall, users are equally likely to be male or female (although a majority of users of cybercafés appears to be male; some differences do exist in particular countries and particular venues). This typical profile highlights the notion that public access venues are serving people who are already benefiting from other social services, especially formal education. In sum, public access venues are not primarily serving the poorest and most marginalized and excluded sectors of society.

The most salient divide revealed in our study is not based on gender, age, education, or income, but based on geographic location: public access venues are predominantly located in urban centers, while non-urban areas are dramatically underserved with very few exceptions. Reaching rural populations with public access to ICT is a far more difficult and costly task than reaching urban populations, but it is a task that governments, development agencies, and donors will have to address if they are to make further progress in overcoming further inequities in access to ICT.

If the driving force behind funding public access venues is the intent of contributing to human development by reaching underserved communities, as tends to be the case in public libraries and telecenters, this goal is partially being met: lower- and middle-income users are being served, women appear to be served as much as men, and children and youth appear to be the strongest users of these venues (adults and seniors far less so), and theses venues are also serving the information needs of students.

An important finding of this study: while public libraries and telecenters are serving human development needs, underserved communities, cybercafés appear to serve these needs just as well in urban areas of most countries we studied. In addition, cybercafés are much stronger players in the public access landscape, with more numerous facilities in operation in urban areas, and with similar patterns of users in regard to age, gender, education, and income (even though men appear to be more frequent users of cybercafés than women in most contexts). Cybercafés have frequently been excluded in research of public access venues, arguing that their user fees make them unaffordable to poorer sectors of the population or that to be truly equitable public access services have to be free. This study finds that even with user fees and their strong urban predominance; there is a strong potential role of cybercafés in social inclusion. This area has been studied very little, and opportunities for partnerships and collaboration between public libraries, telecenters, and cybercafés have rarely been explored.

Results of this study emphasize the need for creative solutions to harness the potential offered by cybercafés in urban areas, and to look for ways

(policies, partnerships, incentives) to make them more accessible and useful to adults and seniors, to women, to lower income users, and to those with no formal education, in sum, to those marginalized and excluded from goods and services in society. Other exclusion factors are likely to include language, literacy, ethnicity, religion, caste, etc., which should be also addressed in each particular context to make public access to ICT more truly equitable.

This paper does not analyze what people are actually doing in the public access venues, how this use differs by age, gender, education, or income, and how it differs by type of venue. Furthermore, we do not discuss private use of ICT (at home, work, or school), or the use of other communication technologies (mobile phones, community radio). More research is needed to better understand these spaces and their implications for public access ICT for human development.

We cannot make detailed country-level conclusions based on this initial exploration. Nonetheless, we can see broad patterns that suggest interesting questions for further research:

What can be done to improve access and broaden inclusion for truly underserved populations (such as low-education groups, very poor, and the elderly)? The predominance of young users with formal education suggests that just providing public access ICT does not necessarily result in further inclusion of marginalized sectors of the population. The sole provision of public access to ICT, without additional training and outreach to include people marginalized from social and economic goods and services, may not significantly transform inequitable relations and distribution of resources in the communities they serve. For example, the existing divide between urban and non-urban communities is magnified through the urban predominance of public access venues, and the prevalence of youth seems to be strengthening a new age divide, one that is permeating other sectors of life as well. Those already excluded from formal education are further excluded from public access venues, and it is likely that the poorest sectors of society are also being excluded. Providing access alone does not automatically result in stronger inclusion of marginalized and underserved populations. Other factors, such as ethnicity, religion, caste, or language are not included in this study for lack of comparable data, but should be explored further as well.

The high youth participation rates are intriguing. What are the social dynamics in these spaces? How are they configured as social spaces for interaction, both online and offline? Perhaps we should think in terms of how the technology enthusiasm of young users could be captured to benefit communities? How will the knowledge production processes of young people (influenced by new communication and information processes) affect how communities and countries operate?

More in-depth studies in each country, and in each type of public access venue, are needed to further understand the profiles of users, their uses of public access venues, and their implications for digital and social inclusion.

REFERENCES

Abbasi, S. (2007, August 30). *Role of Telecentres in Gender Empowerment: Do Telecentres Really Work for Women?* Paper presented at the Royal Holloway, University of London, London.

Agosto, D. E., Paone, K. L., & Ipock, G. S. (2007). The female-friendly public library: gender differences in adolescents' uses and perceptions of U.S. public libraries. *Library Trends*.

Alfaro, F., Molina, J. P., & Camacho Jiménez, K. (2008). *Public access to information & ICTs final report: Dominican Republic*. Seattle, WA: University of Washington Center for Information & Society (CIS).

APC WNSP. (2005). *Gender Evaluation Methodology for Internet and ICTs: A Learning Tool for Change and Empowerment*. APC WNSP.

APC WNSP. (2009). *Gender Evaluation Methodology*. APC WNSP.

Applegate, R. (2008). Gender Differences in the Use of a Public Library. *Public Library Quarterly*, *27*(1), 19–31. doi:10.1080/01616840802122468

Arias, M., & Camacho Jiménez, K. (2008). *Public access to information & ICTs final report: Honduras*. Seattle, WA: University of Washington Center for Information & Society (CIS).

Ariunaa, L. (2008). *Public access to information & ICTs final report: Kyrgyzstan*. Seattle, WA: University of Washington Center for Information & Society (CIS).

Becker, S., Crandall, M. D., Fisher, K. E., Kinney, B., Landry, C., & Rocha, A. (2010). *Opportunity for All: How the American Public Benefits from Internet Access at U.S. Libraries*. Washington, DC: Institute of Museum and Library Services.

Bertot, J. C., McClure, C. R., Thomas, S., Barton, K. M., & McGilvray, J. (2007). *Public Libraries and the Internet 2007: Report to the American Library Association*. Tallahassee, FL: College of Information, Florida State University.

Best, M., & Kumar, R. (2008). Sustainability Failures of Rural Telecentres: challenges from the sustainable access in rural India (SARI) project. *Information Technologies & International Development*, *4*(4), 14.

Bossio, J. F. (2004). *Social Sustainability of Telecentres from the Viewpoint of Telecentre Operators: A Case Study from Sao Paulo, Brazil*. London: London School of Economics.

Bossio, J. F., & Sotomayor, K. (2008). *Public access to information & ICTs final report: Ecuador*. Seattle, WA: University of Washington Center for Information & Society (CIS).

Finquelievich, S., & Prince, A. (2007). *El (involuntario) rol social de los cibercafés (Cibercafes' (involuntary) social role).* Buenos Aires, Argentina: Editorial Dunken.

Goldfarb, A., & Prince, J. (2008). Internet adoption and usage patterns are different: Implications for the digital divide. *Information Economics and Policy, 20,* 2–15. doi:10.1016/j.infoecopol.2007.05.001

Gomez, R. (2009). *Measuring Global Public Access to ICT: Landscape Summary Reports from 25 Countries Around the World (CIS Working Paper no. 7).* Retrieved from http://www.cis.washington.edu/depository/landscape/documents/CIS-WorkingPaperNo7.pdf

Gomez, R. (2010). Structure and Flexibility in Global Research Design: Methodological Choices in Landscape Study of Public Access in 25 Countries. *Performance Measurement and Metrics, 11.*

Gomez, R. (Ed.). (2011). *Libraries, Telecentres, Cybercafes and Public Access to ICT: International Comparisons.* Hershey, PA: IGI Global.

Gomez, R., & Ospina, A. (2001). The Lamp Without a Genie: using the Internet for development without expecting miracles. *The Journal of Development Communication, 12*(2).

Gurol, M., & Sevindik, T. (2007). Profile of Internet Cafe users in Turkey. *Telematics and Informatics, 24*(1), 59–68. doi:10.1016/j.tele.2005.12.004

Gurumurthy, A. (2004). *Gender and ICTs.* Brighton, UK: Institute of Development Studies.

Haseloff, A. M. (2005). Cybercafes and their Potential as Community Development Tools in India. *The Journal of Community Informatics, 1*(3), 13.

Ideacorp. (2008). *Public access to information & ICTs final report: Philippines.* Seattle, WA: University of Washington Center for Information & Society (CIS).

IFLA. (2007). *Access to libraries and information: Towards a fairer world (Vol. 7).* International Federation of Library Associations.

ITU. (2009). *Measuring the Information Society: The ICT Development Index.* Geneva, Switzerland: International Telecommunications Union.

James, T., & Louw, M. (2008). *Public access to information & ICTs final report: Namibia.* Seattle, WA: University of Washington Center for Information & Society (CIS).

Kuriyan, R., & Kitner, K. R. (2009). Constructing Class Boundaries: Gender, Aspirations and Shared Computing. *Information Technologies & International Development, 5*(1).

Kuriyan, R., & Toyama, K. (2007). *Review of Research on Rural PC Kiosks.* Retrieved from http://research.microsoft.com/research/tem/kiosks/

Obayelu, A. E., & Ogunlade, I. (2006). Analysis of the uses of information communication technology (ICT) for gender empowerment and sustainable poverty alleviation in Nigeria. *International Journal of Education and Development Using Information and Communication Technology, 2*(3).

Prahalad, C. K. (2006). *The Fortune at the Bottom of the Pyramid.* Upper Saddle River, NJ: Wharton School Publishing.

Proenza, F. (2006). The Road to Broadband Development in Developing Countries Is through Competition Driven by Wireless and Internet Telephony. *Information Technologies & International Development, 3*(2), 21–39. doi:10.1162/itid.2007.3.2.21

Proenza, F., Bastidas-Buch, R., & Montero, G. (2002). *Telecenters for Socioeconomic and Rural Development in Latin America and the Caribbean. Inter-American Development Bank 17.* Retrieved from http://www.iadb.org/sds/itdev/telecenters/exsum.pdf

Raban, Y., & Brynin, M. (2006). Older people and new technologies. In Kraut, M. B. R. E., & Kiesler, S. (Eds.), *Computers, phones, and the Internet: Domesticating information technology* (pp. 43–50). New York: Oxford University Press.

Robinson, S. (2006). The potential role of information technology in international remittance transfers. In Deen, J., Anderson, J., & Lovink, G. (Eds.), *Reformatting Politics: Information Technology and Global Civil Society* (pp. 121–128). New York: Routledge.

Rozengardt, A., & Finquelievich, S. (2008). *Public access to information & ICTs final report: Argentina.* Seattle, WA: University of Washington Center for Information & Society (CIS).

Rutkauskiene, U. (2008). *Impact measures for public access computing in public libraries.* Vilinius, Lithuania: Vilnius University.

Salvador, T., Sherry, J. W., & Urrutia, A. E. (2005). Less cyber, more café: Enhancing existing small businesses across the digital divide with ICTs. *Information Technology for Development, 11*(1), 77–95. doi:10.1002/itdj.20004

Sey, A. F. M. (2009). *Literature Review on the Impact of Public Access to Information and Communication Technologies* (Working Paper No. 6). Seattle, WA: Center for Infromation & Society, University of Washington.

South Asia Partnership (SAP International). (2008). *Public access to information & ICTs final report: Nepal.* Seattle, WA: University of Washington Center for Information & Society (CIS).

Voelcker, M. (2008). *Public access to information & ICTs final report: Brazil.* Seattle, WA: University of Washington Center for Information & Society (CIS).

Walkinshaw, B. P. (2007). *Why Do Riecken Libraries Matter for Rural Development? A Synthesis of Findings from Monitoring and Evaluation.* Washington, DC: Riecken Foundation.

Wanas, N. (2008). *Public access to information & ICTs final report: Egypt.* Seattle, WA: University of Washington Center for Information & Society (CIS).

Wanasundera, L. (2008). *Public access to information & ICTs final report: Sri Lanka.* Seattle, WA: University of Washington Center for Information & Society (CIS).

Wheeler, D. (2007). Empowerment Zones? Women, Internet Cafes, and Life Transformations in Egypt. *Information Technologies & International Development, 4*(2), 16.

ENDNOTES

[1] Adapted from: International Federation of Library Associations and Institutions (2001). The Public library service: IFLA/UNESCO guidelines for development. In P. Gill et. al. (Eds.), *The Section of Public Libraries*. The Hague: K. G. Saur Verlag GmbH München.

[2] All country reports in this study are available online at http://cis.washington.edu/landscape/library/working-documents.

[3] Size (exclude largest and smallest), population (exclude countries with population less than 1 million, and exclude highest population (India, China), per capita income (exclude countries with per capita income over $11,116), human development index (HDI below 0.5)

[4] Based on Freedom House index: http://www.freedomhouse.org.

[5] Based on U.S. Dept. of State travel advisories.

[6] **Needs criteria**: Income inequality based upon Gini index (2006) from United Nations Development Program; ICT usage: based upon CIA World Factbook (2007); ICT cost: based upon International Telecommunications Union's World Information Society

Report (2006). **Readiness criteria**: Politics: based upon World Economic Forum Global Information Technology Report (2006), Transparency International (2007), World Bank Worldwide Governance Indicators (2006); Skills: based upon International Telecommunication Union opportunity skills index (2007); ICT infrastructure: based upon International Telecommunication Union opportunity network index (2007).

[7] There was much discussion with our research partners on the use of urban vs. rural as each country has a different definition of what constitutes "rural," and there is always the issue of "peri-urban" locations… we have therefore simplified this distinction by focusing on the urban and non-urban geographic distribution.

Chapter 2
Impact of Technology–Related Environment Issues on Trust in B2B E–Commerce

Muneesh Kumar
University of Delhi, India and Groupe ESC-Pau, France

Mamta Sareen
University of Delhi, India

ABSTRACT

The virtual environment of B2B e-commerce interactions has been considered to be a barrier in building trust of trading partners. There is adequate empirical evidence that supports the relationship between various trust related technology issues such as security, privacy, authentication, etc. However, there is dearth of evidence confirming the causal relationship between environment related trust issues such as social-cultural characteristics, technology standards, and regulatory framework. Based on a survey of 106 Indian companies using inter-organizational systems, this paper makes an attempt to identify specific attributes of these three environment-related issues that have the potential to influence trust in B2B e-commerce.

INTRODUCTION

Research has shown that the virtual environment of B2B e-commerce interactions delays trust building and increases the risk perception of trading partners (Cheskin & Sapient, 1999; UNCTAD, 2002a; Olson & Olson, 2000). It is believed that technology has the potential to influence levels of trust in B2B e-commerce (Kumar & Sareen, 2009). There is an empirical evidence to support the relationship between various trust-related technology issues like security, privacy, non-repudiation, authentication, etc. and the levels of trust in B2B e-commerce. In addition to these company-specific technology issues, a number of

DOI: 10.4018/978-1-4666-1957-9.ch002

factors play an important role in creating a general environment of trust in e-commerce technologies among the members of user community and influence the general attitudes, perceptions, beliefs, etc. of users of e-commerce infrastructure, in general. This helps in appreciating the potential of the relevant technologies in building acceptable levels of assurance with regard to various technology-related trust issues. A number of such factors may be relevant in this context, however, the technology-related environment issues that have drawn the attention of researchers relate to social and cultural aspects, technology standards for e-commerce and the regulatory framework.

Though, the technology-related environment issues are influenced by initiatives from policy makers, professional associations and socio-culture background of the users, companies using B2B e-commerce can also take initiatives to influence the impact of these issues. In the absence of such initiatives, the levels of trust in B2B e-commerce may be lower. Though the impact of the social and regulatory issues on trust in B2B e-commerce has been suggested in the literature, there is dearth of evidence confirming the causal relationship between them. The present paper makes an attempt to identify some of specific attributes of these technology-related environment issues that have the potential to influence trust in B2B e-commerce.

Trust and E-Commerce: Theoretical Background

Trust has been posited as the one of the critical elements of successful e-commerce (Cheskin & Sapient, 1999; Corritore, Kracher, & Wiedenbeck, 2001). The importance of trust as a key facilitator of electronic commerce is increasingly being recognized by academic and practitioner communities (Bhattacherjee, 2002). The issue of trust is more relevant in e-commerce because of the higher degree of uncertainty of economic transactions in virtual environment as compared to the traditional settings (Grabner et al., 2003). Trust is considered as a valuable facilitator in e-commerce (Doney et al., 1998; Griffith et al., 2000; Marshall & Boush, 2001), especially in situations where control is lacking and future interactions are difficult to predict (Lane & Bachmann, 1996). Accordingly, trust is more relevant in e-commerce transactions because participants, at times, deal with greater ambiguity, uncertainty and risks outside their control. Previous research on trust and e-commerce has focused primarily on transaction specific investments and firm's performance (Doney & Cannon, 1997; Ganesan, 1994). Some scholars (Malone, 1994; lemons, 1993) have also focused on information technology as a means of reducing inter-organizational transaction costs (Kumar et al., 2009). The role of trust in economic perspective has been considered more profound due to interdependencies among trading partners (Ratnasingam, 2003). Rogio, A. (2010) predicted that at least 90 percent of e-commerce businesses would use some form of cloud computing in the next five years and at least nine in ten online retailers will be participating in a cloud by 2014. This move to cloud computing would imply that more and more e-commerce businesses would offload infrastructure, development, and software to the cloud. However, the issue of trust would be of great importance and as various issues like integrity, reliability, privacy, etc might create doubts in the mindset of the users.

Trust is often related with the user's disposition to trust. Disposition to trust is a measure of the extent to which an individual is willing to depend on others (Rotter, 1971) and is the result of general life experience and socialization (Mcknight et al., 2002). Developmental experiences, personality types, and cultural backgrounds of users have been believed to influence their inherent propensity to trust a vendor (Kim et al., 2000) It has been observed that trusting people are more likely to trust the virtual environment of Internet (Uslaner, 2000). Since trust makes people willing to take risks, trusting people are more willing to take risks online (Gefen, 2000). Individual users differ in their trusting personality traits and the rate at which they therefore acquire, from the website, the cues necessary to trust, and commence an online transaction with a vendor (Head et al., 2002). Similarly, regulatory environment and e-commerce technological standards may also define the risk perceptions of the user community and thus influence trust in e-commerce (Braga et al., 2005).

Literature Review

A number of studies have been conducted that attempt to relate socio-cultural characteristics, regulatory framework and technological standards to adoption of information technology including e-commerce. These studies can be classified into two broad categories namely: a) those that are relating to technology-related environment issues in adoption of IT and b) those that are relating to technology-related environment issues in adoption of e-commerce.

Studies Relating to Technology-Related Environment Issues in Adoption of IT

Schrammel et al. (2009) examined the relationship between personality traits, user patterns and information disclosure behaviors in different types of online communities. While the relationship between personality traits and usage pattern was found to be significant, no significant relationship could be observed between personality traits and information disclosure. They used the fife-factor model (McCrae, 1992) covering five dimensional traits namely neuroticism, extraversion, openness to experience, agreeableness and conscientiousness.

Butt and Phillips (2008) observed a negative correlation between conscientiousness and the use of internet. They found that extraversion play

a significant role in other online communication experiences. Neuroticism was found to play a key role in information control. They described how those who were high on the trait of neuroticism were likely to use the Internet.

Moghadam et al. (2008) studied the impact of differences in the national culture on IT implementation and adoption. The study used Hofstede theory as the primary theoretical framework and with an objective to identify the relationship between Iranian culture and implementation of IT. They observed that national culture could be a restraining or driving force in e-adoption. They, further, observed that IT adoption in individualistic societies is quicker than that in collectivistic societies.

Hwang (2005) examined the relationship between online trust and purchase intention. He also examined the role of uncertainty avoidance cultural orientation, social norms, and personal innovativeness in information technology as antecedents of online trust. He found that social norms influence all dimensions of online trust, while uncertainty avoidance cultural orientation affect only benevolence and ability dimensions of online trust.

Sanchez-Franco et al. (2004) evaluated the mediating role of personal factors affecting user web behavior. Focused attention, enjoyment, ultrarianism, and enjoyment were identified as the main personal factors. Further, they stated that higher the degree of experimental browsing more is the time spent on the virtual environment. In their later study in 2009, they examined the relationship between the national cultural and the acceptance and usage of ICT. They analyzed the cultural differences and their moderating effects on acceptance-based relationships between European universities. It was observed that cultural differences had a significant impact on attitudes and behaviors towards using web-based applications.

Studies Relating to Technology-Related Environment Issues in Adoption of E-Commerce

Mantymaki et al. (2010) found that trust and social presence are relevant determinants of loyalty-related behaviors in the Social virtual worlds (SVWs). Trust in the SVW staff was found to be relatively strong predictor of continuous use intention. Social presence was also found to not only as an important determinant of trust but also found to have significant direct positive effect on the customer loyalty.

Chin et al. (2009) found that trust in the Internet structure and social influence the willingness of consumers to purchase online. Their results were consistent with the study conducted by Limayem et al. (2000) where it was discovered that social influence of family and media was greatly associated with willingness to provide personal information online. Hwang (2005) supported that social dimensions like friends, family, media are significantly related to online trust.

Various scholars have studied the influence of national culture on trust beliefs (Gefen & Heart, 2006; Gefen et al., 2005; Doney et al., 1998; Fukuyama, 1995; Zucker, 1986). Gefen and Heart (2006) examined differences in three trust beliefs of vendor integrity, benevolence and ability between the US and Israel and were examined in terms of the influence of these beliefs on behavioural intentions. The study found significant differences in the paths from integrity to purchase intentions (with integrity showing a stronger effect in the American sample in relation to purchasing intentions). Their results indicated that conclusions based on US studies cannot and should not be automatically applied to other cultures and they accordingly emphasise the need for researchers to include national culture in e-commerce trust studies.

Lumsden and MacKay (2006) studied the influence of personality types onto a user's trust perception towards a website and stressed that a user's personality type influences his/her attitude towards trust in the virtual environment. The study focused whether a user's personality type influences their attitude towards trust assessment. However, their investigations did not lead to any statistically significant conclusions, indicating that a user's personality type does not affect his/her trust level towards a website. Nevertheless, they were able to discover some connections between trust and e-commerce.

Mutz et al. (2005) in their study of online buying behavior observed that higher levels of social trust could result in greater intent to shop via Internet. They also observed the positive trust condition was more effective in encouraging purchase intent in the case of first time online buyers. They suggested that levels of social trust in the user community can be modified by what they see, hear, and read.

Albrecht et al. (2005) identified need for marketplace and technology standards for successful e-commerce architectures. They found that there exist unfilled needs for systems that can reliably locate buyers and sellers in electronic marketplaces and also facilitate automated transactions. They developed an evaluation schema incorporating six fundamental standards that must be present in any e-commerce system if it is to successfully support widespread, efficient B2B transactions on a network. Using this schema, they found that no single technology provides a complete solution for all components of a standardized, loosely-coupled marketplace. B2B hubs have different data and transaction formats and limited market reach. The study found that although the technology toolbox of today is sufficient to support e-commerce, but there exist lack of standards on the seller side that leads to significant problems on the client side: namely, it is difficult to search and discover competing vendor services when different vendors offer heterogeneous interfaces.

In a comparative study of the bidding behavior of e-bay participants of Canada, France and Germany, Vishwanath (2004) observed that potential bidder's reliance on seller ratings was more in the low trust countries than that in the high trust countries. They concluded that buyers in countries in low trust levels look for information about trustworthiness of sellers from alternative sources while evaluating purchase options.

Sutherland and Tan (2004) introduced the concept of 'disposition of trust' in e-commerce and studied the influence of personality on user's intention to trust. The model emphasized that both institutional and interpersonal trust are reliant on dispositional trust. They found that extroversion and openness to experience had greater disposition to trust, whereas neuroticism and conscientiousness might lead to a lower disposition to trust.

Walczuch et al. (2004) identified antecedents of institution based trust in e-tailing. They observed that personality, perception, attitude, experience and knowledge had significant impact on institution based consumer trust. They observed that consumers trust is influenced more by perception based factors than knowledge-based and experience-based factors in e-retailing.

In order to examine the role of standardization in web interface design, Bernard (2002) carried out a study to determine where users expected to find "common e-commerce objects" on a page. The study involved a total of 302 participants (43% male, 57% female). Bernard stated that the expected locations correspond to the location of the objects on popular e-commerce sites such as Amazon.com, EddieBauer.com, BestBuy.com, and Target.com (2002). However, the study did not include a systematic analysis of e-commerce sites to determine to how closely actual practice aligns with users' expectations.

Adkisson (2002) examined 75 leading e-commerce sites (across 15 consumer product categories) to identify de-facto standards for e-commerce websites. He found relatively few design practices among those examined in this study met Nielsen's criteria for a de-facto standard (occurring in 90% or more of sites). The results indicated that relatively few defacto standards were

available and the lack of consistency among sites has implications for both designers and users. For designers, lack of meaningful de-facto standards means that design decisions can be difficult and time-consuming, increasing the costs of development. For users, the e-commerce user experience remains one in which they must adjust to how individual sites present hierarchical navigation and core e-commerce functions—reducing the overall usability of the e-commerce shopping experience.

McKnight et al. (1998) found that consumers' perceived control and confidence was positively influenced by three control mechanisms, i.e., regulations, guarantees, and legal recourse. If a consumer believes that he/she has control over the outcome of the online transactions, he/she is more likely to expect trustworthy behavior. In 2002, they further observed that disposition to trust was positively related to personal innovativeness, web experience relates positively to institution-based trust in the web.

Though most of the studies reviewed above have focused on various technology-related environment issues influencing adoption of IT and e-commerce, the emphasis has been primarily on the nature and role of social-cultural factors. Most of these studies did not focus specifically on B2B e-commerce. Moreover, there is a paucity of empirical evidence regarding other technology-related environment issues such as technological standards and regulatory environment and trust in B2B e-commerce. The present paper focuses on these issues and attempts to examine their relationship with the levels of trust in B2B e-commerce. The findings presented in this paper are based on the analysis of perceptions of the IT executives.

Sample Selection and Methodology

The findings presented in this paper are primarily based on a part of the data collected through a survey of the companies that are using inter-organizational systems for business relations. The survey was carried out in the year 2008. The instrument used to capture the perceptions of IT executives was a structured interview-guide which was administered with the respondents. In India, no formal list of various organizations focusing on inter-organizational activities is available. Hence, leading companies that are offering both the software and hardware solutions for inter-organizational systems were contacted to obtain the list of their customers. In this process, a list of 200 companies from all over India could be generated. These companies were contacted through post, e-mail, phone, etc. to seek their participation in the survey. However, only one hundred six (106) companies agreed to participate in the survey. The companies, located in different cities like Delhi, Mumbai, Pune, Chennai, Hyderabad, Bangalore, Chandigarh, etc. constituted the sample. The respondents were of the rank of the chief executive officer, chief information officer, or the IT head of the company.

Profile of the Sample

The two-third of the respondents belonged to large sized companies (having annual turnover of above Rs.250 crores and having more than 250 permanent employees). The focus of the B2B e-commerce operations of these companies varied from a) e-selling; b) e-procurement; c) e-services; and d) Hybrid focus, i.e., both e-selling and e-

procurement. Figure 1 shows the share of each category of the companies. As may be observed from the figure, one-third of the companies were focusing on e-procurement and almost one-fourth of the sample companies had their focus on e-selling and another one-fourth on e-services.

The respondents belonged to companies from different industries such as: a) Manufacturing-consumable goods b) Manufacturing-capital goods c) Banking sector and d) Information Technology and ITeS sector providing services to other companies like an intermediary. Figure 2 shows the share of each category of the companies.

64% of the companies belonged to the manufacturing sector, either capital goods or consumables. Thirty percent of the companies belonged to IT and e-services sector and the remaining (6%) from the banking sector.

In order to ascertain the relevance of the three environment related trust issues, the respondents of the survey were asked to give their opinions regarding various aspects of each of the issues on a 5 point Likert scale. The responses could range from strongly disagree (1) to strongly agree (5) to each of the questions related to different aspects of trust related environment issue. The following paragraphs present the brief description of the constructs used and the findings in this regard.

Figure 1. Size of the companies

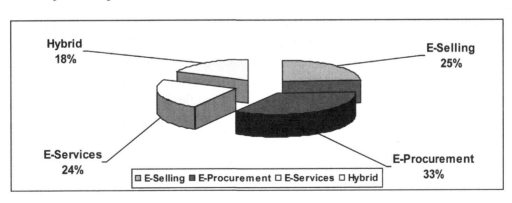

Figure 2. Industry verticals of the companies

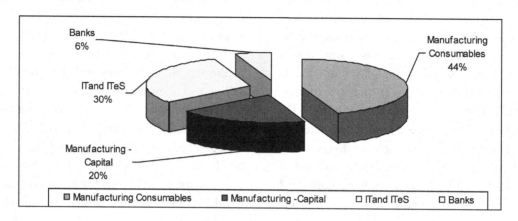

Social and Cultural Issues: Construct and Findings

The trust in B2B e-commerce may be a function of the social and cultural environment in which the user community is placed (Vatanasakdakul et al., 2004). There is adequate empirical evidence to suggest that differences in the national cultures can partly explain the behavioral patterns (Hofstede, 1991; Hani & Hsu, 2005; Money & Sharma, 2006). Various studies have emphasized the role of different cultural dimensions in the process of IT adoption (Rau & Liang, 2003; Karahanna et al., 2002). The rates of IT adoption may significantly differ in developing and developed countries due to the differences in their national cultures (Pare, 2001) and the level of trust in online trading environment may be influenced by the characteristics of the socio-cultural environment.

Based on the findings of Walczuch (2004) and other scholars, five psychological characteristics influencing trust in B2B e-commerce were hypothesized. These include: Personality-based characteristics; Perception-based characteristics; Organizational culture; IT Knowledge; and Attitude. These characteristics may vary between societies and cultures.

Personality-Based Characteristics

Trust has also been defined as: "a psychological state comprising the intention to accept vulnerability based upon positive expectations of the intentions or behavior of another" (Rousseau, 1998). Thus, trust is a personality characteristic and is a state of mind that encourages risk taking (Rotter, 1997). Trust is believed to be determined by a person's individual personality (Walczuch et. al. 2004). People who are more optimistic, cheerful and satisfied are more willing to build up trusting relationships than those who are pessimistic, neurotic and unsatisfied. The three personality based characteristics that may encourage risk taking are: extraversion, conscientiousness and openness to experience.

Extraversion is a characteristic of being focused on the outside world. This personality trait encourages quick adaptation to change (Gleitman, 1995; Carver & Scheier, 1992). In the context of e-commerce, extraversion could be useful characteristic in encouraging participation in the virtual trading environment and help in building trust.

Conscientious people are responsible, dutiful, and those who have positive beliefs towards others. These people tend to be more cautious in decisions making. On the other hand, people with low conscientiousness will be more trusting (Angenent, 1998; Olson & Suls, 1992).

Another personality based characteristic that influences the level of trust is the openness of an individual to experience (Walczuch et al., 2004). People who are more open to experience tend to more trusting. More openness to experience encourages people to adopt new concepts and perceive lesser risk in new situations and experiences (Olson & Suls, 1992).

Propensity to trust has also been called disposition to trust by other authors (Garbarino, 1999; Mcknight et al., 2002). Some people are more willing to trust and also have the capacity to take the risks in new situations and experiences (Walczuch et al., 2004). Such people are considered to have higher propensity to trust. Such people are likely to have greater trust in e-commerce (Ambrose & Johnson, 1992; Aubert & Kelsey, 2000; Cheung & Lee, 2000; Kim & Prabhakar, 2000).

These personality based characteristics of the user community may influence the level of trust in B2B e-commerce. In order to understand the significance of these personality based characteristics, the respondents were asked to give their opinion regarding the following statement on a 5-point Likert scale:

SC1: People who are extrovert, conscientious, 'open to experience' and have higher propensity to trust are more likely to adopt and trust B2B e-commerce system?

Perception Based Characteristics

Trust in e-commerce may be influenced also by the collective perception of the user community (Das et al., 1998; Friedman et al., 2000; Jarvenpaa, 2000). These perceptions may be based on the past experience, general reputation of the trading partner, and familiarity.

In the context of commerce, experience relates to first hand knowledge about the party and/or the trading environment (Walczuch et al., 2004). In an e-commerce environment, this first hand knowledge is acquired through multiple experiences in the online buying/selling process (Wordsmyth, 1999). In fact, various researchers investigating the customer perception have pointed out a positive correlation between trust and knowledge accumulated through experience in an e-commerce environment (Mcknight et al., 1998; Ganesan, 1994).

Reputation is built on the basis of the second hand information gathered about a potential trading party and the environment (Mcknight et al., 1998). Reputation reflects the collective opinion of the user community and thus helps in assuring the potential trading partners about the credibility of the party. According to McKnight et al. (1998), parties with a 'good reputation are seen as trustworthy, and those with a bad reputation as untrustworthy'. Reputation of the trading partner may be symbolized in brands. These brands communicate information that helps outsiders in evaluating the organization (Brown et al., 2006; Pitt & Papania, 2007). Familiarity relates to the frequency of exposure to a certain stimulus. Higher is the frequency of this exposure, lesser is the perceived risks as familiarity increases with each exposure A positive evaluation of this stimulus helps in enhancing the levels of trust (Brehm & Kassin, 1998).

These perception based characteristics of the user community may influence the level of trust in B2B e-commerce. In order to understand the significance of these perception-based characteristics, the respondents were asked to give their opinions regarding the following statements on a 5-point Likert scale:

SC2: Does the past experience have an influence on trust in B2B e-commerce?

SC3: Does the reputation and the brand of the trading partner influence trust in B2B e-commerce?

SC4: Do you, generally, place greater trust in familiar B2B e-commerce web sites?

Organizational Culture

Studies indicate that e-commerce adoption is influenced by the compatibility of the organizational and the national culture (Grandon & Pearson, 2004). Organizational culture can be an important barrier in the adoption of any technological change. The organizational culture in some Organizations discourage and resist adoption of new technologies, systems and processes Such barriers to change are fairly common in various cultures and have the potential to adversely influence trust in B2B e-commerce environment. Teo and Ranganathan (2004) identified organizational culture as an important barrier between firms collaborating in B2B e-commerce. Organizational cultures that discourage innovation change and use of new technologies may pull down the level of trust in B2B e-commerce adoption (Gibbs et al., 2003; Teo & Ranganathan, 2004).

The organizational culture of the trading partners may influence the level of trust in B2B e-commerce. In order to understand its significance, the respondents were asked to give their opinion on the following statement on a 5-point Likert scale:

SC5: Does the organizational culture influence trust in B2B e-commerce?

IT Knowledge

Trust in B2B e-commerce may be based on the knowledge about the information technology tools and practices. If the user community is knowledgeable about the effectiveness of the technology tools and practices, it helps in building trust in the B2B e-commerce trading environment. People with little knowledge about IT may perceive higher risks in B2B e-commerce and may be less trusting. Perceived knowledge about IT was also found to be an indicator of trust (Li et al., 1999).

The level of IT knowledge of the trading partners may influence the level of trust in B2B

e-commerce. In order to understand its significance, the respondents were asked to give their opinion regarding the following statement on a 5-point Likert scale:

SC6: Does prior knowledge of IT influences trust process in B2B e-commerce?

Attitude

According to the American Marketing Association (AMA), attitude can be defined as "a person's overall evaluation of a concept; an affective response involving general feelings of liking or favorability; a cognitive process involving positive or negative valences, feelings, or emotions… It is an interrelated system of cognition, feelings, and action tendencies". Attitude can be considered one of the most important concepts in the study of consumer behavior as, according to the literature, it is the direct determinant of this behavior. This functional view of attitude suggests that people hold attitudes to determine how to respond to their environment (Shavitt, 1989).The attitude of the user community towards the computers, information technology, Internet etc. could be an important factor in influencing levels of trust in B2B e-commerce (Milne, 1999; Jarvenppa, 2000; Cheung & Lee, 2000). A positive attitude towards IT, computers etc. could help in building positive evaluation of the B2B e-commerce trading environment and thus encourage online transactions.

The attitude of the user community towards IT, and/or e-commerce may influence the level of trust in B2B e-commerce. In order to understand its significance, the respondents were asked to give their opinion regarding the following statement on a 5-point Likert scale:

SC7: Does the attitude towards computers, IT and Internet influence trust in B2B e-commerce?

Table 1 presents the descriptive and other statistics with regard to the responses to the each

Table 1. Socio-culture environmental issues and trust

Socio-Culture Issues	Strongly Agree	Agree	Indifferent/ Disagree	Total Co.s	Mean Rating	Std Deviation	Kolmogorov Smirnov Z	Chi Square
SC1	59	25	21	106	4.37	0.797	3.627 [a]	26.057[a]
SC2	54	39	13	106	4.39	0.798	3.291 [a]	24.358 [a]
SC3	64	42	-	106	4.60	0.491	4.054 [a]	4.566 [b]
SC4	63	43	-	106	4.59	0.493	4.004 [a]	3.774 [a]
SC5	59	37	10	106	4.46	0.664	3.577 [a]	34.094 [c]
SC6	52	37	17	106	4.33	0.740	3.171 [a]	17.453 [a]
SC7	58	48	-	106	4.55	0.500	3.753 [a]	0.943 [d]

a. At 0.000 Asymptotic level of Significance and 2 degrees of freedom

b. At 0.033 Asymptotic level of Significance and 2 degrees of freedom

c. At 0.052 Asymptotic level of Significance and 2 degrees of freedom

d. At 0.331 Asymptotic level of Significance and 2 degrees of freedom

of the seven questions relating to social-cultural environment issues that have the potential to influence trust in B2B e-commerce.

As can be observed from the above table, all the seven socio-cultural environmental issues were considered significant in determining the levels of trust in B2B e-commerce. It may be noted that the mean rating was more than 4.3 out of 5 in all characteristics indicating fairly high credence given to these characteristics. Thus, it may be concluded that the social cultural characteristics of the user community play a significant role in determining the levels of trust in B2B e-commerce.

Specifically, the personality-based, perception-based, organizational cultural, IT knowledge and attitude towards IT are factors that have significant relationship with levels of trust in B2B e-commerce. Some of these characteristics can be influenced by deliberate attempts on the part of the companies who are desirous of enhancing the levels of trust of the trading partners in B2B e-commerce infrastructure. This could be done by suitable communication and, if necessary, by appropriate training programs for the user community. Such training programs can make user community more receptive to e-commerce adoption.

In order to examine the significance of differences between the mean perceptions of respondents from different types of companies, one way ANOVA was used on the overall mean perceptions regarding the role of all the social cultural issues. The statistics in Table 2, Table 3, and Table 4 were obtained in this regard.

As may be observed from the above statistics, the respondents from large size companies perceived greater role of social cultural issues in building trust in B2B e-commerce. However, the difference in the mean perceptions of respondents from large sized companies and small size was not found to be statistically significant. Similarly, no significant differences were noticed among the perceptions of respondents from different industry verticals and companies with different focus of B2B operations.

Table 2.

Focus	Mean
e-procurement	4.48
e-selling	4.37
e-services	4.46
Hybrid	4.62
$F_{(2,105)}=1.483$, $p>0.05$	

Table 3.

Size	Mean
Large size	4.53
Small Size	4.0
Medium	4.42
F(2,105)= 0.978), p>0.05	

Table 4.

Ind. Verticals	Mean
Mfg-consumables	4.43
Mfg-Capital	4.48
Bank & e-Services	4.33
IT and ITeS	4.56
F(2,105)=0.741), p>0.05	

E-Commerce Technology Standards

Standards can be defined as 'collection of system specific or procedural specific requirements that must be met by everyone' (Kouns & Minoli, 2010). Standards and protocols employed in recording, storage and transmission of digital information are important in ensuring meaningful communication between trading parties in e-commerce. Due to the proliferation of various technologies, methods and related practices, a large number of varying alternative solutions have emerged globally. Attempts have been made by different groups of organizations to develop technology standards that could facilitate e-commerce. These organizations include W3C consortia, UN/EDIFACT, BizTalk, RosettaNet, OBI Consortia, etc. Though these e-commerce standards have helped to resolve the difficulties in communication between different e-commerce resources, a lot of conflicts and incompatibilities still remain (Niwe, 2006).

B2B e-commerce requires regular interaction between the information systems of the trading partners. These information systems may be built on heterogeneous platform (H/W and S/W) and may use different formats for business documents like purchase order, sales order, invoice, dispatch schedule, etc. in their applications. This heterogeneity may lead to problems of inter-operability. Adherence to e-commerce standards can help in reducing the problem of interoperability between B2B e-commerce systems (Pincus, 1999; Reimers, 2001). Standards play an important role in e-commerce as they permit heterogeneous information systems in the network to exchange information by adhering to uniform methods of storage and exchange (Dean et al., 1999). Useful e-commerce technology standards, adhered to by all participants, allow computers to better accomplish their supporting role of finding possible suppliers, gathering comparative product and company data, and executing transactions. There is general consensus regarding the value addition by the adoption of standards in electronic communications (Niwe, 2006). In the absence of these standards, it may become very difficult for firms using different information systems to transact online with reliability and speed.

Compatibility between two systems can be achieved by each participant using the same technology or data formats as prescribed in the standards. Alternatively, it can also be done with the help of conversion (Farrell et al., 1992; Katz et al., 1994). From the perspective of the firm, following the standards entails upfront costs both in terms of cost of technology using emergent standards and the sunk cost of investment in legacy technology that is not compatible with the new standards (Chircu et al., 2001). On the other hand, conversion involves high cost of creating and maintaining the converters for each pair of incompatible formats and systems. The past experiences of using EDI standards indicate a distinct advantage of standards over converters.

The two main categories of e-commerce standards identified by Dean and Albrecht (2005) are: foundation technology standards and marketplace standards. The foundation technology standards relate to Data standards, Schema expression languages and Common communication methods. While the data standards prescribe the possible data types, Schema expression languages define data representation rules. For example, HTTP, XML, XHTTP etc. fall under these two categories. The Common communication methods relate to rules regarding physically transfer of information across a network. Standards like FTP, SMTP, TELNET, etc. fall under this category.

Marketplace standards attempt to define classification for various products and services, transaction templates, and business categories. Availability and acceptance of these standards can significantly minimize the risk of parties in B2B e-commerce. Unfortunately most of the standards in this category are either controlled by powerful organizations or are not comprehensive to meet the diverse needs of participants. However, a number of standards have been widely accepted and are in use for e-commerce in most of the countries. For example Business categorization schemes suggested by North American Industry Classification System (NAICS) (NAICS 2002) and the United Nations Standard Products and Services Code (UNSPSC) (UNSPSC 2002) have been widely adopted. eCl@ss, eclassOWL are the standards in Product and service representation.

In addition to the technology standards for development and transmission of transaction information, there is a need for standards pertaining to maintenance of privacy of information. These standards are defined by the privacy assurance providers such as Truste, BBB Online, PriceWaterhouseCoopers, WebTrust, etc. These standards help in assuring a minimum acceptable level of privacy and help in building trust of the user.

These technological e-commerce standards provide general system architecture and message protocols for ensuring smooth conduct of B2B e-commerce transactions as they help in improving functionality and interoperability of the participating trading partners. Their absence would hinder the adoption of B2B e-commerce particularly where the trading partners are using diverse e-commerce technologies.

Adoption of these e-commerce technology standards can remove glitches in the e-commerce systems thereby improving the reliability of such systems. This can help in enhancing the levels of trust in B2B e-commerce. In order to understand the significance of implementation of the technological standards in the e-commerce infrastructure, the respondents were asked to give their opinion regarding the following statement on a 5-point Likert scale:

S1: Availability and acceptance of various e-commerce technology standards influences trust in B2B e-commerce?

Table 5 presents the descriptive and other statistics with regard to the responses to the question relating to role of technological standard in building trust in B2B e-commerce.

As may be observed from Table 5, the availability and acceptance of various e-commerce technology standards was perceived to be a significant factor influencing trust in B2B e-commerce. Taking clue from this finding, companies can adopt appropriate technology standards and communicate this fact to trading partners in order to enhance their levels of trust in B2B e-commerce. Trade associations in IT industry should try to set

Table 5. Technology standard environmental issues and trust

Technology Standard Issue	Strongly Agree	Agree	Total Co.s	Mean Rating	Std Deviation	Kolmogorov Smirnov Z	Chi Square
S1	58	48	106	4.55	0.500	3.753 [a]	0.943[a]

a. At 0.000 Asymptotic level of Significance and 1 degrees of freedom

up and popularize the use of suitable technology standards so as to provide the needed assurance to the user community.

In order to examine the significance of differences between the mean perceptions of respondents from different types of companies, one way ANOVA was used on the mean perceptions regarding the role of e-commerce technology standards. The following statistics were obtained in this regard:

Mean: Large size= 4.63, Small Size=4.0; Medium Size=4.36, (F(2,105)= 2.847), p>0.05)

Mean: e-procurement=4.64, e-selling=4.35, e-services=4.47, Hybrid=4.68, (F(2,105)=2.647), p>0.05

Mean: Mfg-consumables= 4.48, Mfg-Capital Goods=4.55, Banking and e-Services=4.33, IT and ITeS=4.63, (F(2,105)=0.762, p>0.05)

As may be observed from the above statistics, the respondents from large size companies perceived greater role of e-commerce technology standards in building trust in B2B e-commerce. However, the difference in the mean perceptions of respondents from large sized companies and small size was not found to be statistically significant. Similarly, no significant differences were noticed among the perceptions of respondents from different industry verticals and companies with different focus of B2B operations

Regulatory Framework

A strong regulatory framework is essential for any successful trading environment. With the rapid growth of electronic commerce, development of separate legislation and associated administrative structures governing e-commerce transactions and other interactions is essential. Creating an efficient regulatory environment for e-commerce goes a long way in building confidence for this virtual trading environment. Most countries have taken initiatives in this direction creating legal

and administrative framework that provide legal sanctity to electronic processes and enable creation of digital evidences that could be recognized in case of dispute. For example US Federal Trade Commission and European Union (EU) have taken legislative and policy initiatives for encouraging trust in e-commerce.[1] Efforts have also been made to discourage and combat cyber crimes. As e-commerce cuts across political boundaries of nations, the harmonization of the laws and the administrative processes across nations is a challenge that needs to be met before e-commerce is adopted for international business.

The traditional trading environment used paper based systems for communication between the trading parties. This system had the advantage that the recording of the communication was permanent, any modifications could be easily detected, physical controls were available for restricting access to the documents/records, easy read-ability of the records, and well defined processes were available for establishing validity, authenticity, and reliability of the documents/records. Similar features need to be built up in electronic communications in order to encourage adoption of e-commerce. This can be achieved with the support of effective legal and administrative structures. Such structures must aim not only at incorporating the above mentioned features but also should deter e-frauds or abuse and other cyber crimes.

The regulatory framework for e-commerce should focus on making online transactions legally tenable and easily enforceable. This would require necessary changes in the contract laws, negotiable instruments laws, evidence laws, criminal laws, and banking laws. Though efforts have been made in most of the countries to create legal environment by making changes in the above mentioned laws, the effectiveness of such legal framework has often been questioned (Samtani & Harry, 2003)[2]. A number of initiatives have been taken in this direction including UNCITRAL Model Law on Electronic Commerce 1996; the UNCITRAL Model Law on Electronic Signatures

2001; the United Nations Convention on the Use of Electronic Communications in International Contracts 2005; the Asia-Pacific Council for Trade Facilitation and Electronic Business (AFACT); the International Trade Centre (ITC); the E-Trade Development Unit, etc. Inspite of the efforts by various multilateral agencies, the differences in the legal frameworks of various nations still continue. Differences also exist between nations in so far as their administrative structures for enforcement of such laws. Thus, the degree of effectiveness of regulatory framework for e-commerce is different in different countries. The extent to which the regulatory issues in e-commerce are addressed is likely to influence the level of trust in e-commerce.

Primarily, two broad categories of the regulatory issues are the impediments in equal treatment of electronic messages as compared to the paper based legal documents. The first category relates to meeting the traditional requirements of "writing", "document" "original" and "signature" (Moreno, 2001). The second category relates to the presence of dispute resolution mechanism for e-commerce transactions.

In the first category, there are primarily two legal issues namely electronic signatures and electronic contracting. The notion of document cannot be separated from the concept of signature. Signatures serve three purposes namely data origin authentication, message integrity and non-repudiation. Electronic documents need to have electronic signatures in order to get legal sanctity. The prevailing laws of the land must contain provisions that ensure electronic signatures serve the three purposes served by paper based signature in order to provide same legal status to the elec-

tronic documents. Countries also need to have well established rules regarding place of origin and permanent establishment, free movement of information, transparency obligations for ISPs and commercial communications, and conclusion and validity of electronic contracts.

In the second category, issues relate to development of an effective dispute settlement mechanism for e-commerce. Parties to e-commerce transactions should be able to resolve the disputes arising from online transactions at a speed that matches with the speed at which transactions are executed in e-commerce. The traditional dispute resolution mechanisms may not be effective in this regard. Moreover, the present environment is fraught with legal barriers in seeking redressal from courts in case of international transactions.

The extent to which these regulatory issues are addressed may influence the level of trust in B2B e-commerce. In order to understand the relevance of these regulatory issues in building trust in e-commerce, the respondents were asked to give their opinions regarding the following statements on a 5-point Likert scale:

L1: Does the similarity of legal treatment of online transactions with the off line transactions influence the level of trust in B2B e-commerce?

L2: Does the inadequacy of dispute resolution mechanism influence trust in B2B e-commerce?

Table 6 presents the descriptive and other statistics with regard to the responses to each of the two questions relating to regulatory framework.

Table 6. Regulatory framework environmental issues and trust

Regulatory Issues	Strongly Agree	Agree	Total Co.s	Mean Rating	Std Deviation	Kolmogorov Smirnov Z	Chi Square
L1	77	29	106	4.73	0.448	4.692 [a]	21.736 [a]
L2	84	22	106	4.79	0.407	5.016 [a]	36.264 [a]

a. At 0.000 asymptotic level of significance and 1 degrees of freedom.

As may be observed from the above table, similarity of legal treatment for online and offline transactions and the presence of adequate dispute resolution mechanisms were considered significant in determining trust in B2B e-commerce (as the mean rating in each case was more than 4.5 out of 5). This may imply that the perception regarding the efficacy of the regulatory framework in ensuring equal treatment to online and offline transactions and providing adequate dispute resolution mechanisms, enhances the levels of trust in B2B e-commerce. Companies must, therefore, communicate with their trading partners to influence their perception regarding the effectiveness of the regulatory framework so that their levels of trust could be enhanced. This could be achieved by offering additional legal evidences or documents that enhance the level of assurance to them in this regard.

In order to examine the significance of differences between the mean perceptions of respondents from different types of companies, one way ANOVA was used on the overall mean perceptions of role of all the regulatory issues. The following statistics was obtained in this regard:

Mean: Large size= 4.95, Small Size=4.3; Medium Size=4.59, (F(2,105)= 44.155), p>0.05)

Mean: e-procurement=5.00, e-selling=4.31, e-services=4.61, Hybrid=5.00, (F(2,105)=37.918), p<0.05

Mean: Mfg-consumables= 4.64, Mfg-Capital Goods=4.69, Banking and e-Services=5.00, IT and ITeS=4.89, (F(2,105)=2.936, p<0.05

As may be observed from the above statistics, the respondents from large size companies perceived greater role of regulatory issues in building trust in B2B e-commerce. However, the differences in the mean perceptions of respondents from large sized companies and small size was not found to be statistically significant. Interestingly, significant difference was noticed among the perceptions of respondents from different industry verticals and companies with different focus of B2B operations. The higher perceived role of regulatory issues in building trust in B2B e-commerce was observed in the case of respondents from companies with focus on e-procurement and companies with banking and e-services sector.

CONCLUSION

This study highlights the relationship between the environment related trust issues and the levels of trust in B2B e-commerce. The three basic technology related elements of this environment that need to be focused are social-cultural characteristics, technology standards and regulatory framework. The perceptions of respondents from companies with different profiles do not differ significantly except in the case of perceptions regarding role of regulatory issues. The focus of e-commerce operations and industry vertical to which the company belongs were found to be particularly significant differentiating factors in this regard.

Companies desirous of enhancing the levels of trust in their B2B e-commerce infrastructure should make deliberate attempts to influence the perceptions of the user community by appropriate training programs, adoption of technology standards and strengthening the legal position of the trading partner. Such attempts could reduce the risk perceptions of the trading partners while trading online. Of course, the role of the regulatory and the trade associations in strengthening the regulatory framework and the technology standards cannot be over-emphasized, in this regard. The new proposals of the European Union[3] for establishing a European trust mark to encourage cross border e-trading is a welcome initiative in this direction.

Contributions, Limitations and Scope for Future Research

An important contribution of this paper is in terms of identifying environment related issues that have the potential to enhance levels of trust in B2B e-commerce. This attempt is perhaps the first of its kind that focuses on various social and cultural or legal issues in addressing the trust related issues that arise in inter-organizational systems. The empirical evidence presented in the paper makes the paper unique in its scope and approach. This paper has attempted to measure the perceptions regarding the impact of environment factors on the levels of trust in B2B e-commerce.

Like any other study of this kind, this paper also suffers a number of limitations. The main limitation of this paper can be imputed to the research's coverage. The authors tried to include as many trust-shaping environment related factors as possible without trying to scope down the online trust problem to one particular aspect. This high-level aspect that resulted might therefore seem too general when viewed only from the perspective of a single discipline. The evaluation of various attributes of the environment factors has not been carried out, instead the perceptions about their implications on their trust in B2B e-commerce was measured and analyzed. Further, the environment related issues identified above have been considered to the matters for which initiatives are possible only at the macro level.

The present paper may provide motivations for conducting studies where the environment related factors are quantified and then related to levels of trust. A multi-country study comparing the differences in environment related factors can be useful in gaining better understanding of the issues that influence adoption of B2B e-commerce and offer specific suggestions for professional bodies and the policy makers in this regard. Triangulation of the results based on the perceptions of the respondents as presented in this study with data on the companies' actual usage of B2B

e-commerce would provide deeper understanding of the role of environment related trust issues in B2B e-commerce.

REFERENCES

W3C. (2002). *Web Services Architecture Working Group*.

Adkisson, H. (2002). *Identifying De-Facto Standards for E-Commerce Web Sites*. Retrieved from http://www.boxesandarrows.com/view

Ajzen, I., & Fishbein, M. (1980). *Understanding Attitude and Predicting Social Behavior*. Upper Saddle River, NJ: Prentice-Hall, Inc.

Albrecht, C. C., & Dean, D. L. (2005). Market Place and Technology Standards For B2B Ecommerce: Progress and Challenges. In *Proceedings of Standard Making: A Critical Research Frontier for Information Systems MISQ Special Issue Workshop* (p. 188).

Ambrose, P. J., & Johnson, G. J. (1998). A Trust Model of Buying Behavior in Electronic Retailing. In *Proceedings of the Americas Conference on Information Systems (AMCIS)*, Baltimore, MD.

Anderson, E., & Weitz, B. (1992). The Use of Pledges to Build and Sustain Commitment in Distribution Channels. *JMR, Journal of Marketing Research*, *24*, 18–24. doi:10.2307/3172490

Angenent, H. (1998). *Opvoeding en persoonlijkheidsontwikkeling*. Baarn, NL: Uitgeverij Intro.

Angenent, H. (2004). Psychological Antecedents of Institution-Based Consumer Trust in E-Retailing. *Information & Management*, *42*(1), 159–177.

Aubert, B. A., & Kelsey, B. L. (2000). *The Illusion of Trust and Performance*. CIRANO.

Bagozzi, R. P., & Fornell, C. (1982). Theoretical concepts, measurement, and meaning. In Fornell, C. (Ed.), *a Second Generation of Multivariate Analysis* (pp. 5–23). Praeger.

Bhattacherjee, A. (2002). Individual Trust in Online Firms: Scale Development and Initial Test. *Journal of Management Information Systems, 19*, 211–241.

Braga, C., & Primo, A. (2005). E-commerce Regulations: New game, new rules. *The Quarterly Review of Economics and Finance, 45*(2/3), 541–558.

Brehm & Kassin. (1998). *Social Psychology.* Boston: Houghton.

Brown, T. J., Dacin, P. A., Pratt, M. G., & Whetten, D. A. (2006). Identity, intended image, construed image, and reputation: An interdisciplinary framework and suggested terminology. *Journal of the Academy of Marketing Science, 34*(2), 99–106. doi:10.1177/0092070305284969

Burt, R. S., & Knez, M. (1995). Trust and Third Party Gossip. In Kramer, R. M., & Tyler, T. R. (Eds.), *Trust in Organizations: Frontiers of Theory and Research* (pp. 68–89). Thousand Oaks, CA: Sage.

Butt, S., & Phillips, J. G. (2008). Personality and self reported mobile phone use. *Computers in Human Behavior, 24*(2), 346–360. doi:10.1016/j.chb.2007.01.019

Carver, C. S., & Scheier, M. F. (1992). *Perspective on Personality.* Boston: Allyn and Bacon.

Cheskin. (2000). *Research, Trust in the Wired Americas.* Retrieved from http://www.cheskin.com/think/studies/trust2.html

Cheung, C., & Lee, M. K. O. (2000). Trust in Internet Shopping: A Proposed Model and Measurement Instrument. In *Proceedings of the Americas Conference on Information Systems (AMCIS),* Long Beach, CA.

Chircu, A. M., Kauffman, R. J., & Keskey, D. (2001). Maximizing the value of internet-based corporate travel reservation systems. *Communications of the ACM, 44*(11), 57–63. doi:10.1145/384150.384162

Connolly, R., & Bannister, B. (2007). E-commerce Trust beliefs: The influence of national culture. In *Proceedings of European and Mediterranean Conference on Information Systems (EMCIS2007),* Polytechnic University of Valencia, Spain.

Corritore, C. L., Kracher, B., & Wiedenbeck, S. (2003). On-line Trust: Concepts, Evolving Themes, A Model. *International Journal of Human-Computer Studies, 58,* 737–758. doi:10.1016/S1071-5819(03)00041-7

Das, T. K., & Teng, B. (1998). Between Trust and Control Developing Confidence in Partner Cooperation in Alliances. *Academy of Management Review, 23*(3), 491–512. doi:10.2307/259291

Davis, F. D. (1989). Perceived usefulness, perceived ease of use, and user acceptance of information technology. *Management Information Systems Quarterly, 13*(3), 319–340. doi:10.2307/249008

Dean, D. L., Lee, J. D., Pendergast, M. O., Hickey, A. M., & Nunamaker, J. F. Jr. (1998). Enabling the Effective Involvement of Multiple Users: Methods and Tools for Collaborative Software Engineering. *Journal of Management Information Systems, 14*(3), 179–222.

Dirks, K. T., & Ferrin, D. L. (2001). The role of trust in organizational settings. *Organization Science, 12*(4), 450–467. doi:10.1287/orsc.12.4.450.10640

Doney, P. M., Cannon, J. P., & Mullen, M. R. (1998). Understanding the Influence of National Culture on the Development of Trust. *Academy of Management Review, 23*(3), 601–620. doi:10.2307/259297 ebXML. (2001). *ebXML Technical Architecture Specification*.

Farrell, J., & Saloner, G. (1992). Converters, compatibility, and the control of interfaces. *The Journal of Industrial Economics*, *40*(1), 9–35. doi:10.2307/2950625

Fishbein, M., & Ajzen, I. (1975). *Belief, Attitude, Intention, and Behavior: an Introduction to Theory and Research*. Reading, MA: Addison-Wesley.

Friedman, B., Kahn, P. H., & Howe, D. C. (2000). Trust Online. *Communications of the ACM*, *43*(12), 34–40. doi:10.1145/355112.355120

Gambetta, D. G. (Ed.). (1988). *Trust: Making and Breaking Cooperative Relations*. New York: Basil Blackwell.

Ganesan, S. (1994). Determinants of long-term orientation in buyer-seller relationships. *Journal of Marketing*, *58*, 1–19. doi:10.2307/1252265

Garbarino, E., & Johnson, S. (1999). The Different Roles of Satisfaction, Trust, and Commitment in Customer Relationships. *Journal of Marketing*, *63*, 70–87. doi:10.2307/1251946

Gefen, D. (2000). E-Commerce: The Role of Familiarity and Trust. *Omega*, *28*, 725–737. doi:10.1016/S0305-0483(00)00021-9

Gefen, D., & Heart, T. (2006). On the Need to Include National Culture as a Central Issue in E- Commerce Trust Beliefs. *Journal of Global Information Management*, *14*(4), 1–30.

Gleitman, H. (1995). *Psychology*. New York: W. W. Norton & Company, Inc.

Grabner-Krauter, S., & Kaluscha, E. A. (2003). Empirical research in on-line trust: a review and critical assessment. *International Journal of Human-Computer Studies*, *58*, 783–812. doi:10.1016/S1071-5819(03)00043-0

Griffith, D. A., Hu, M. Y., & Ryans, J. K. Jr. (2000). Process standardization across intra- and inter-cultural relationships. *Journal of International Business Studies*, *31*(2), 303–323. doi:10.1057/palgrave.jibs.8490908

Hamburger, A. Y., Wainpel, G., & Fox, S. (2002). On the Internet no one knows I'm an introvert: Extroversion, introversion, and Internet interaction. *Cyberpsychology & Behavior*, *5*(2), 125–128. doi:10.1089/109493102753770507

Hani & Hsu. (2005). in Introducing Cultural Fit Factors to Investigate the Appropriateness of B2B Technology Adoption to Thailand by Savanid Vatanasakdakul. In *Proceedings of the 21st Bled eConference eCollaboration: Overcoming Boundaries through Multi-Channel Interaction*, Bled, Slovenia.

Head, M. M., & Hassanein, K. (2002). Trust in e-Commerce: Evaluating the Impact of Third-Party Seals. *Quarterly Journal of Electronic Commerce*, *3*(3), 307–325.

Hofstede, G. H. (1991). *Cultures and Organizations: Software of the Mind*. New York: McGraw-Hill.

Hofstede, G. H. (2001). *Culture's Consequences: Comparing Values, Behaviors, Institutions and Organizations across Nations*. Thousand Oaks, CA: Sage Publications.

Huang, H., Keser, C., Leland, J. W., & Shachat, J. (2003). Trust, the Internet and the Digital Divide. *IBM Systems Journal*, *42*(3), 507–518. doi:10.1147/sj.423.0507

Huang, Z., Brian, D., & Frolick, M. (2008). A comprehensive examination of Internet EDI adoption. *Information Systems Management*, *25*(3), 273–286. doi:10.1080/10580530802151228

Jarvenpaa, S. L., Tractinsky, N., & Vitale, M. (2000). Consumer Trust in an Internet Store. *Information Technology Management, 1*, 45–71. doi:10.1023/A:1019104520776

Karahanna, E., Evaristo, R., & Srite, M. (2002). Methodological issues in MIS cross-cultural research. *Journal of Global Information Management, 10*(1), 48–56.

Katz, M. L., & Shapiro, C. (1994). Systems competition and network effects. *The Journal of Economic Perspectives, 8*(2), 93–115.

Kim, K., & Prbhakar, B. (2000). Initial Trust, Perceived Risk and Adoption of Internet Banking. In *Proceedings of the International Conference on Information Systems (ICIS)*, Brisbane, Australia.

Konous, J., & Minoli, D. (2010). *Information Technology Risk Management in Enterprise Environments: A review of Industry practices and a pratical guide to risk management teams.* New York: John Wiley.

Kumar, N., & Benbasat, I. (2001). Shopping as Experience and Website as a Social Actor: Web Interface Design and Para-Social Presence. In *Proceedings of the International Conference on Information Systems (ICIS)*, New Orleans, LA.

Lewicki, R. J., & Bunker, B. B. (Eds.). (1995). *Trust in Relationships: A Model of Development and Decline.* San Francisco: Jossey-Bass.

Lumsden, J., & MacKay, L. (2006). How does personality affect trust in B2C e-commerce? In *Proceedings of the 8th international Conference on Electronic Commerce (ICEC '06)* (pp. 471-481).

Malone, T. W., Yates, J., & Benjamin, R. I. (1987). Electronic markets and electronic hierarchies. *Communications of the ACM, 30*(6), 484–497. doi:10.1145/214762.214766

Mäntymäki, M., & Salo, J. (2010). Trust, Social Presence and Customer Loyalty in Social Virtual Worlds. In *Proceedings of the 23rd Bled eConference eTrust: Implications for the Individual, Enterprises and Society*, Bled, Slovenia.

Marshall, R. S., & Boush, D. M. (2001). Dynamic decision-making: a cross-cultural comparison of U.S. and Peruvian export managers. *Journal of International Business Studies, 32*(4), 873–893. doi:10.1057/palgrave.jibs.8490998

McCrae, R. R. (1992). The five-factor model: Issues and applications. *Journal of Personality, 60*(2). doi:10.1111/j.1467-6494.1992.tb00970.x

McKnight, D. H., Choudhury, V., & Kacmar, C. (2002). Developing and Validating Trust Measures for ECommerce: An Integrative Typology. *Information Systems Research, 13*(3), 334–359. doi:10.1287/isre.13.3.334.81

McKnight, D. H., Cummings, L. L., & Chervany, N. L. (1998). Initial Trust Formation in New Organizational Relationships. *Academy of Management Review, 23*(3), 473–490. doi:10.2307/259290

Milne, G. R., & Boza, M. (1999). Trust and Concern in Consumers' Perceptions of Marketing Information Management Practices. *Journal of Interactive Marketing, 13*(1), 5–24. doi:10.1002/(SICI)1520-6653(199924)13:1<5::AID-DIR2>3.0.CO;2-9

Moghadam, A. H., & Assar, P. (2008). The Relationship Between National Culture and E-Adoption: A Case Study of Iran. *American Journal of Applied Sciences, 5*(4), 369–377. doi:10.3844/ajassp.2008.369.377

Money & Sharma. (2006). Referenced from Savanid Vatanasakdakul. 2008. Introducing Cultural Fit Factors to Investigate the Appropriateness of B2B Technology Adoption to Thailand. In *Proceedings of the 21st Bled eConference eCollaboration: Overcoming Boundaries through Multi-Channel Interaction*, Bled, Slovenia.

Moreno, C. (2001). Brief Overview of Selective Legal and Regulatory Issues in Electronic Commerce. In *Proceedings of the International Symposium on Government and Electronic Commerce Development*, Ningbo, China.

Mutz, D. C. (2005). Social Trust and E-commerce experimental evidence for the effects of social trust on individuals' economic behavior. *Public Opinion Quarterly, 69*(3), 393–416. doi:10.1093/poq/nfi029

Niwe Moses. (2006). Standards based B2B e-commerce Adoption. *Advances in Systems Modelling and ICT Applications*, 335-347.

Olson, B. D., & Suls, J. (1998). Self-, Other-, and Ideal-Judgements of Risk and Caution as a Function of the Five-Factor Model of Personality. *Personality and Individual Differences, 28*, 425–436. doi:10.1016/S0191-8869(99)00105-1

Olson, J. S., & Olson, G. M. (2000). i2i Trust in E-Commerce. *Communications of the ACM, 43*(12), 41–44. doi:10.1145/355112.355121

Pare, D. (2002). *B2B e-commerce services and developing countries: disentangling Myth from reality*. Retrieved from www.gapresearch.org/production/

Pare, D. (2003). Does this site deliver? B2B e-commerce services for developing countries. *The Information Society, 19*, 123–134. doi:10.1080/01972240309457

Pavlou, P. A., & Fygenson, M. (2006). Understanding and Predicting Electronic Commerce Adoption: An Extension of the Theory of Planned Behavior. *Management Information Systems Quarterly, 30*(1), 115–143.

Pincus, A. (1999). *Hearing on the Role of Standards in the Growth of Global Electronic Commerce*. Senate Committee on Commerce, Science, and Transportation Subcommittee on Science, Technology, and Space.

Pitt, L., & Papania, L. (2007). In the words: Managerial approaches to exploring corporate intended image through content analysis. *Journal of General Management, 32*(4), 1–16.

Ratnasingam, P., & Pavlou, P. A. (2003). Technology trust in internet based inter-organizational electronic commerce. *Journal of Electronic Commerce in Organizations, 1*, 17–41.

Ratnasingham, P. (1998). The importance of trust in electronic commerce. *Internet Research, 8*(4), 3–321. doi:10.1108/10662249810231050

Rau, P.-L. P., & Liang, S.-F. M. (2003). A study of the cultural effects of designing a user interface for a web-based service. *International Journal of Services Technology and Management, 4*(4-6), 480. doi:10.1504/IJSTM.2003.003627

Roggio, A. (2010). *Ecommerce Know-how: Cloud Computing in the Ecommerce Forecast. Ecommerce Notes*. Retrieved from http://www.practicalecommerce.com/articles

RosettaNet. (2001). *RosettaNet Background Information*.

Rotter, J. (1971). Generalised Expectancies for Interpersonal Trust. *The American Psychologist, 26*, 443–452. doi:10.1037/h0031464

Rousseau, D. M., Sitkin, S. B., Burt, R. S., & Camerer, C. (1998). Not So Different After All: A Cross-Discipline View of Trust. *Academy of Management Review, 23*(3), 393–404.

Sanchez-Franco, M., & Bodaba, J. P. (2004). Personal Factors affecting users' web session lengths. *Internet Research: Electronic Networking Applications and Policy, 14*(1), 62–80. doi:10.1108/10662240410516327

Sanchez-Franco, M., Francisco, J., Martínez-López, F., & Martín-Velicia, A. (2009). Exploring the impact of individualism and uncertainty avoidance in Web-based electronic learning: An empirical analysis in European higher education. *Computers & Education, 53*(3), 588–598. doi:10.1016/j.compedu.2008.11.006

Schrammel, J., Köffel, C., & Tscheligi, M. (2009). Personality Traits, Usage Patterns and Information Disclosure in Online Communities. In *Proceedings of the HCI – People and Computers XXIII – Celebrating people and technology*.

Shavitt, S. (1989). Operationalizing functional theories of attitude. In Pratkanis, A., Breckler, S., & Greenwald, A. (Eds.), *Attitude Structure and Function* (pp. 311–337). Hillsdale, NJ: Lawrence Erlbaum.

Sutherland, P., & Tan, F. B. (2004). The Nature of Consumer Trust in B2C Electronic Commerce: A Multi-Dimensional Conceptualization. In *Proceedings of the International Conference of the Information Resources Management Association: Innovations Through Information Technology*, New Orleans, LA (pp. 611-614).

UNSPSC. (2002). *United Nations Standard Products and Services Code.*

Uslaner, E. M. (2000). Social capital and the net. *Communications of the ACM, 43*(12), 60–64. doi:10.1145/355112.355125

Vatanasakdakul, S., Tibben, W., & Cooper, J. (2004). What prevents B2B e-commerce adoption in developing countries? In *Proceedings of a socio-cultural perspective, in the 17th Bled eCommerce Conference on eGlobal*, Bled, Slovenia.

Vishwanath, A. (2003). Comparing online information effects: A cross-cultural comparison of online information and uncertainty avoidance. *Communication Research, 30*(6), 579–598. doi:10.1177/0093650203257838

Walczuch, R., & Lundgren, H. (2004). Psychological Antecedents of Institution-Based Consumer Trust in E-Retailing. *Information & Management, 42*(1), 159–177.

Wolfradt, U., & Doll, J. (2001). Motives of adolescents to use the Internet as a function of personality traits, personal and social factors. *Journal of Educational Computing Research, 24*(1), 13–27. doi:10.2190/ANPM-LN97-AUT2-D2EJ

Wordsmyth. (1999). *Experience.* Retrieved from http://www.wordsmyth.net/cgibin

Zucker, L. G. (1986). Production of Trust: Institutional Sources of Economic Structure, 1840 – 1920. In Staw, B. M., & Cummings, L. L. (Eds.), *Research in Organizational Behavior* (*Vol. 8*, pp. 53–111). Greenwich, CT: JAI Press.

ENDNOTES

[1]   For details see ABA Task Force website at www.law.washington.edu/ABA-eADR

[2]   http://www.apdip.net/projects/2003/asian-forum/docs/papers/session7.pdf

[3]   For reference see www.europarl.europa.eu

This work was previously published in the International Journal of Information Communication Technologies and Human Development, Volume 3, Issue 1, edited by Susheel Chhabra and Hakikur Rahman, pp. 21-40, copyright 2011 by IGI Publishing (an imprint of IGI Global).

Chapter 3
A Novel Strategy for Managing User's Locations in PCS Networks Based on a Novel Hot Spots Topology

Ahmed I. Saleh
Mansoura University, Egypt

ABSTRACT

As PCS networks aim to provide "anytime-anywhere" cellular services, they enable Mobile Terminals (MTs) to communicate regardless of their locations. However, in order to guarantee a successful service delivery, MTs' real time location should be continuously managed by the network. Location management plays the central role in providing ubiquitous network communications services, which includes two fundamental processes, i.e., registration and paging. Registration is concerned with the reporting of the current locations of the MTs, while paging is used to locate the MT. Both processes incur signaling cost, and due to the scarcity of PCS wireless bandwidth and for more scalable mobile services, it is important to reduce that signaling cost. As The blanket paging in current PCS networks wastes a lot of wireless bandwidth, the author focuses on the subject of paging in attempt to reduce the paging signaling cost under delay bounds. This paper challenges the signaling cost problem and successfully establishes a family of probability based paging strategies. The author will introduce a novel topology for the network registration area, which is called the hot spot topology (HST) and based on HST, a novel location management strategy, which is called "Flower Based Strategy" (FBS) is also introduced.

INTRODUCTION

Recently, due to the exponential growth rate of Personal Communication Service (PCS) subscribers, the research in PCS networks has received a lot of attention (Singh & Karnan, 2010; Biswash & Kumar, 2009; Selvan, Shanmugalakshmi, & Nirmala, 2010). The most salient feature of such networks, as it is built upon an underlying cellular infrastructure, is the mobility support that enables network Mobile Terminals (MTs) to communicate with each others on the move (Singh & Karnan, 2010; Markande & Bodhe, 2009). Roughly speak-

DOI: 10.4018/978-1-4666-1957-9.ch003

ing, it is the main target of PCS network to deliver wireless calls among the network MTs on time at the minimal signaling cost. However, such target should be motivated by efficient techniques for managing the run time locations of the network MTs. In the existing PCS networks, a two-tire database structure is used to manage MTs' locations (Kumar & Tripathi, 2008).

The PCS network Service Area (SA), which is managed by a master database called Home Location Register HLR, is divided into a set of Registration Areas (RAs) (Kondepu & Kumar, 2009). HLR is a global database that maintains MTs' identity information including the mobile user information such as directory number, profile information, real-time location, authentication information, and billing information. Each RA is a collection of cells each serviced by a Base Station (BS). Several BSs are usually wired to a Base Station Controller (BSC). Furthermore, a number of BSCs are connected to one Mobile Switching Center (MSC). Usually one MSC is responsible of serving one RA. Another database type called Visitor Location Register (VLR) is attached to each MSC to store the profile information for the MTs currently visit its RA (Biswash & Kumar, 2009). For every MS, there is a permanent record in HLR (each MS is associated with a unique HLR). However, when a MS visits a new RA, a temporary record, for that MT, is created in the VLR serving such RA to reflect the current location of that MT (MT must register to the VLR before receiving any cellular service, and then HRL is also updated to reflect the real time location of that MT). When MT leaves such RA, the corresponding record in the VLR is deleted. When there is a call, PCS network always checks with the HLR to know the current VLR of the target MT, and then the call is delivered to the current VLR. Hence, HLR cooperates with a set of VLRs to track mobile users and find out the location of the target ones (Giner & Escalle, 2009; Zhao, Guo, & Liu, 2010; Bhadauria & Sachan, 2009).

In order to effectively deliver an incoming call to a MT, its precise location must be determined within a certain time limit. Location management is a key issue in PCS networks, which mainly involves two main operations; registration and paging (Zhang, Laurence, Jianhua, & Zheng, 2009; Kim & Choi, 2009). Registration is the process performed by each MT to report its up-to-date location to the network. Such location information is employed to find out the exact location of the MT whenever a new call is directed to it. On the other hand, paging is the process performed by the network to search the called MT (Bar, Feng, & Golin, 2007). It is carried out by sending polling signals to the cells with the highest probability of existence for the called MT. Hence, registration involves a MT initiated procedure, while paging involves a network initiated procedure (Kondepu & Kumar, 2009).

The problem of MT tracking can be considered using different strategies. The first is the "Always-Update" (AU), in which each MT registers itself whenever it crosses a new cell boundary (enters a new cell). According to the AU strategy, the signaling overhead due to transmissions of registration messages is so high. The impact of signaling overhead becomes troubleshooting with a small cell size and a large number of highly-mobile users. Moreover, the huge amount of location update events will significantly consume not only the limited network bandwidth, but also the electronic power of the MTs' battery. However, with the AU strategy, the exact MT location is always known, hence, the paging cost is always zero. The second strategy is the "Never-Update" (NU); in which MT never inform the network about its current location. Clearly, under the NU strategy, no overhead for registration, however, a network-wide search should be performed to find a particular MT. This certainly introduces a very high penalty. The third MTs' tracking strategy is the "Registration Area-Update" (RAU), which is the used by the current PCS networks. RAU is a combination of both AU and NU strategies. According to RAU, the network Service Area (SA) is portioned into a set of Registration Areas (RAs) (also known as location areas), in which each RA is sub-divided into a group of cells. Within the RA, NU strategy is used. When a MT moves into another RA, it must register itself (update his location information), and then the NU strategy is used within the new RA. Therefore, the network is always aware of the location information of each MT in the level of RA (Pratim, Anilesh, & Saradindu, 2009; Kim, Kim, Mani, Jun, & Agrawal, 2010).

An efficient location management system is the one that minimizes both the timing and signaling costs as much as possible (Prajapati, Agravat, & Hasan, 2010). However, both location update and paging costs can not be minimized at the same time. There is a trade-off between the both types of costs. Hence, the more the location information the system records about each MT (i.e., each MT updates its location more frequently), the less the paging cost as the network is continuously informed by the up-to-date location of each MT. Another trade-off exists between the paging signaling cost and the paging delay (Bar, Feng, & Golin, 2007). If all RA cells are paged simultaneously (blanket paging), the maximal signaling cost is reached while the paging delay, on the other hand, is the minimal. Many researches try to address the problem of minimizing the paging cost under the delay constraints by applying the selective paging approach (Baheshti, 2007). According to the selective paging, RA cells are paged sequentially by employing the callee MTs' existence probability in decreasing order, which in turn impacts well the paging costs. However, recent researches in selective paging are still theories and can not be applied successfully in the real world as they are either costly or difficult to be implemented. Hence, selective paging must continue to be researched and improved (Kondepu, Kumar, & Tripathi, 2008).

This paper focuses on the paging problem. We will try to minimize the paging costs under a time

delay pre-defined bounds. A set of paging schemes with the corresponding location update (registration) procedures by employing the time-varying location probability have been proposed through the paper. The aim is to accurately estimate the MTs' most probable locations within each network RA hopping to promote the paging hit rate with the minimal signaling and time costs. The main contributions of the paper can be summarized through the following points; (i) first, we have developed two novel probability based location management strategies for PCS networks, which are Probability Based Location Management (PBLM) and Modified Probability Based Location Management (MPBLM). (ii) Moreover, a novel Hot Spot Topology (HST) for the PCS registration area is introduced. (iii) Based on the proposed HST, another novel location management strategy called the Flower Based Location Management (FBLM) is then introduced. Excremental results have shown that the proposed location management strategies (PBLM, MPBLM, and FBLM) significantly reduce the paging cost under the time delay pre-defined constraints with a little increase in the registration cost.

BACKGROUND AND BASIC CONCEPTS

In this section, the basic architecture of a typical PCS network is illustrated. Then traditional registration and call delivery schemes for the current PCS networks are also introduced. Finally, the subject of selective paging is clarified in details.

PCS Network Architecture

As depicted in Figure 1, PCS Service Area (SA) is partitioned into a number of Registration Areas (RAs), which are sub-divided into several cells. A cell is the communication area covered by one Base Station (BS). Basically, a BC is used to communicate with mobile users visiting its cell

Figure 1. The structure of a typical PCS network

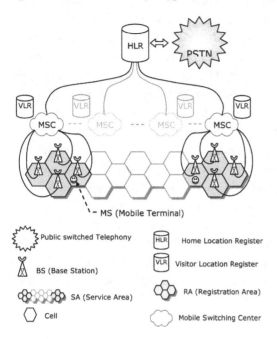

over pre-assigned radio frequencies. The location of a MT is thus the address of the cell where it currently resides. On the other hand, a group of neighboring cells constitutes a Registration Area (RA). BSs in the same RA are connected to one Mobile Switching Center (MSC), which is a dedicated telephone switch for PCS applications. It provides several switching functions and plays an active role in registration and call delivery. BSs are static and connected through land links to the MSC serving their RA. On the other hand, one or more MSCs are connected to one VLR to exchange location information through Signaling System Number 7 (SS7) network. An HLR is associated with a set of VLRs. A PCS network includes several SAs in which each one is managed by one HLR. Consequently, a PCS network may include several HLRs.

A PCS network uses distributed two-tire mobility database architecture to support roaming MTs. Location management is achieved by a continuous cooperation between HLR and VLR. For each MT, HLR stores the address of the cur-

rently visited VLR as well as the address of the MSC serving the BS of its current cell. On the other hand, VLR stores the address of the MSC (when the VLR manages several MSCs) as well as the ID of the cell where the MT currently resides.

Traditional Registration Scheme

There are two basic operations in the location management of PCS network, namely; registration and paging. Location registration is the process through which the network tracks the real time locations of its MTs. On the other hand, to deliver a call to a MT, it should be identified by the network. The process of searching for the callee MT within its current RA is referred to as paging. Location registration process is illustrated in Figure 2.

As depicted in Figure 2, when a MT enters a new RA, it registers itself at the VLR serving the new RA. This can be simply accomplished by sending a registration-request message to the new MSC through the BS of the current cell. Accordingly, the new VLR creates a temporary record for that MT, and then sends a message to inform the HLR of the MTs' new location. The location message is routed to a Signal Transfer Point (STP), which determines the HLR of the MT using its Mobile Identification Number (MIN). HLR iden-

Figure 2. Location registration scheme in PCS network

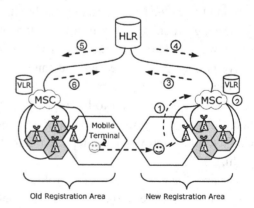

tification is achieved by a table lookup procedure called Global Title Translation (GTT). Finally, the message is forward to the MTs' HLR, which updates the MTs' record to reflect its real time location (current serving MSC). Finally, the MTs' HLR sends a registration acknowledgment to the new MSC as well as a registration-cancel message to the old VLR to delete the obsolete record of the moved MT.

Traditional Call Delivery Scheme

Basically, when a MT needs to call another one, the location of the callee MT must be identified. Identifying the location of the callee MT includes specifying its serving VLR as well as its currently visited cell. To deliver a call, the steps illustrated in Figure 3 should be followed.

The caller MT initializes the call by a cellular contact to the BS serving its current cell. Then, BS forwards the call initialization signal to the MSC serving the current RA. MSC then sends a message to the HLR of the callee MT (through STP where GTT is performed) asking for the location of the callee MT. The location request is forward to the callees' HLR. Then, the HLR of the callee MT sends a location request message to the MSC serving the RA of the called MS. MSC then determines the callees' current cell by paging the whole RA. This type of paging is called the

"blanket paging" as the whole RA is paged for identifying the cell where the callee MT resides. In spite of its simplicity and time saving, the blanket paging suffers from the high signaling cost.

Then, MSC assigns the callee MT a Temporary Location Directory Number (TLDN), then finally sends that TLDN to the callees' HLR. Afterward, HLR of the callee forwards the TLDN to the calling MSC. When the calling MSC receives the pre-assigned TLDN, it sets up a connection to the called MSC through which the call is routed.

Selective Paging

Usually, a MT has its own movement patterns in each RA. Within each RA, the movement patterns for each MT can be converted into a histogram that reflects the MTs' existence probability within each cell inside the considered RA. Hence, when a MT enters a specific RA, there will exist a set of cells that are probably host the MT with a high level of confidence. Hence, when paging for that MT, it will be better to page those highly probable cells first. Selecting a set of cells to be paged first is called the "selective paging" (Akyildiz, Ho, & Lin, 1996). The philosophy of selective paging is that; "if no long time has elapsed, the highest probability to find a MT would be the area closed to its last known location". Accordingly,

Figure 3. Call delivery scheme in PCS network

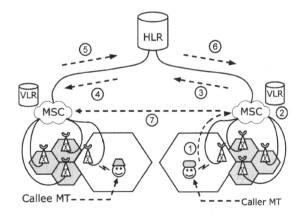

it will be desirable to search for that MT within such area as its existence probability is extremely high. However, if the MT does not found within such candidate area, the rest of the current MTs' registration area should be pages simultaneously.

Selective paging depends on two main aspects, which are; (i) in each RA, MT usually possesses regular moving behaviors. Hence, it often follows the same set of movement patterns. (ii) Within each RA, there exists a set of common cells where the existence probabilities of most MT are extremely high. Those cells are the ones that are located in the common paths. According to those two main aspects, for each MT in each RA, there are two types of cells; (i) cells which are regularly visited by that MT, and (ii) cells which are seldom visited. Based on this idea, the moving behavior of MT can be used to perfectly predict its location. As the most probable cells can be paged first, this can successfully promote the paging hit rate. Consider Figure 4 for more illustration. It is observed that an MT may spend a much longer period in a certain cells than in the rest within an LA. For example, an MT might remain in the cell covering his home or working place.

Selective paging hopping to reduce the signaling cost by minimizing the paging area (Akyildiz, Ho, & Lin, 1996). Hence, it divides the current MTs' RA into several smaller paging areas (PAs), then page all cells within each PA simultaneously in a separate paging round (PR). Noting

Figure 4. The highly probable cells for MT

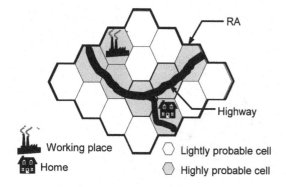

that; the PA with the maximal existence probability of the callee MT should be paged first. Then the rest PAs should be paged sequentially in a descending order with subject to the existence probability of the callee MT. However, estimating the size of each PA (number of cells) in each PR as well as the number of PRs are critical issues that should be calculated carefully hoping to not exceed the maximum allowable call delay (Akyildiz, McNair, Ho, Uzunalioglu, & Wang, 1999).

Generally, the main difference between selective paging and the fixed area (blanket) paging is the query directed to the Location Management Database (LMD) as well as the corresponding query results. In blanket paging, LMD returns the ID of the current RA for the callee MT. On the other hand, in the selective paging, LMD is first queried for the paging rounds for the callee MT, then, the corresponding paging area for each round can be identified. Figure 5 (A and B) shows LMD query procedures for both strategies.

Sequential steps for the selective paging are illustrated in Figure 6. Selective paging starts by identifying the paging area, which is simply the last registration area of the callee MT. Then, to avoid unnecessary paging, the current status of the callee MT is first checked (when a MT is voluntary switched off, it registers itself as "OFF" within its current RA. This informs the system to block any incoming call to that MT until it becomes "ON" again within the current RA or even at another RA).

As illustrated in Figure 6, if the callee MT is "ON", the cells within its last RA are organized in descending order based on the MTs' existence probability. The cells are paged then sequentially starting from the highly probable cell. This procedure continues until the callee MT is identified or the maximum delay bound is reached. In the latter case, all remaining RA cells are paged simultaneously. After the callee MT has been identified, the connection between the called and callee MTs is then established, and the call can then immediately start.

Figure 5. LMD query procedures (A) For blanket paging (B) For selective paging

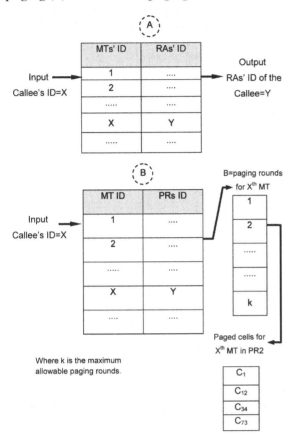

RELATED WORK

The research in PCS networks, especially under the subject of location management, has received a lot of interest in recent years. Location management involves two main operations, which are; (i) location update (registration), and (ii) paging. Selective paging, also called the multi-step paging was suggested in order to reduce the paging cost while maintaining the delay bound requirements (Abutaleb & Li, 1997; Akyildiz, Ho, & Lin, 1996). In each step, a subset of RA called paging area (PA) was searched in one polling cycle. Many schemes using ring-paging strategies had been proposed (Abutaleb & Li, 1997). However, sequentially paging the rings surrounding the MTs' last updated location may cause large paging cost

(Bar, Feng, & Golin, 2007). In Rose and Yates (1995) a highest-probability-first (HPF) scheme, in which the delay constraint was considered as a weighted factor in determining the minimum paging cost was introduced.

In Hwang, Chang, and Tseng (2000), a Direction-Based Location Update (DBLU) scheme had been introduced to minimize the paging cost using a line-paging strategy. A moving direction identification mechanism detects the change of moving direction and updates the MTs' location. Furthermore, a predictive paging scheme based on the movement direction of the MT can be found in Lee and Hwang (1999). An intra location area (Intra-LA) location update (LU) scheme was proposed to increase paging accuracy for PCS networks, which had been introduced in Xiao (2003).

All the previously mentioned mobility management techniques are static ones as they assume static borders of the network RAs (Hwang, Chang, & Tseng, 2000; Xiao, 2003). Hence, as soon as the MT crosses a new RA border, it has to register itself at the new RA. On the other hand, dynamic mobility management schemes (Bar, Kessler, & Sidi, 1995; Brown & Mohan, 1997) discard the notion of RA borders. A MT in these schemes updates its location based on either elapsed time, number of crossed cell borders, or traveled distance. All these parameters can be dynamically adapted to each mobile's traffic and mobility patterns. In Xie, Tabbane, and Goodman (1993) a novel scheme in which RAs are no longer static but, rather, determined dynamically per each MT had been proposed. Through such scheme, the fluid flow model was applied to represent the user mobility. Further, a signaling cost function for each user has been developed by the user's call arrival rate, as well as parameters which were determined by its mobility pattern. Then, an optimal RA size is determined for the user in terms of the pre-defined cost function (Xie, Tabbane, & Goodman, 1993). However, dynamic mobility management schemes are still uneconomical.

Figure 6. The sequential steps for selective paging

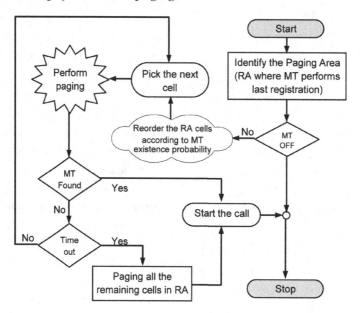

Several selective paging techniques rely on the concept of mobile terminal location prediction (Aljadhai & Znati, 2001; Rajagopal, Srinivasan, Narayan, & Petit, 2002; Bejerano, Smith, Naor, & Immorlica, 2006). Nevertheless, they assume the knowledge of the probability distribution not only for the MTs' velocity, but also its movement direction. This conditions the existence of sophisticated and costly equipments such as the Global Positioning System (GPS).

PROPOSED LOCATION MANAGEMENT STRATEGIES

In this section, a set of novel location management strategies will be introduced. Initially, a location management scheme based on the MTs' existence probability is introduced that will be considered as the base for the comparison. Then, a modification is introduced by considering the time in existence probability calculations. Afterward, a novel strategy for mining the users movement patterns have been introduced by considering a new Registration area (RA) topology. Such a new architecture allows

a novel registration methodology and accordingly a novel selective paging strategy.

Lazy and Active Moving Logs Collection Approaches

According to our proposed mobility management strategies, moving logs could be collected using two different approaches, which are; (i) lazy approach, and (ii) active approach. In the former, MTs' location is identified when it receives or performs a call. This is a lazy recording for the MT location. On the other hand, in the active approach, MTs' moving logs are collected by the MT itself. To accomplish such aim, each MT has a built-in internal cache. Whenever, the MT enters a new cell (receives a different base station ID), it records the new cell ID as well as the entrance time into its local cache. MT moving logs are sent to the VLR serving the current RA whenever its internal cache becomes full or the MT performs a de-registration process. Then, the internal cache is cleared to start recording a new moving log. Consider the two cases illustrated in Figure 7, the number of moving logs registered locations

Figure 7. Moving logs collection; (X) Low CMR (Y) High CMR

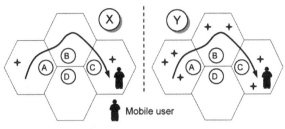

Approach	Cache contents (Registered locations)
Lazy	<A,C>
Active	<A,B,C>

Approach	Cache contents (Registered locations)
Lazy	<A,B,C>
Active	<A,B,C>

(entries) in the case of using lazy approach will never exceeds the registered locations when using the active approach even with high Call to Mobility Ratio (CMR). Although the lazy approach provides a little amount of location information, moreover, it can not provide an accurate MT tracking, it is simpler to be implemented as it needs no additional cost. Also, it minimizes the signaling cost since the lazy approach does not restrict each MT to send his moving logs to the corresponding VLR.

Probability Based Location Management (PBLM) Strategy

In the next subsections, the proposed Probability Based Location Management (PBLM) strategy using the active and lazy moving logs collection approaches will be illustrated in more details.

PBLM Using Lazy Moving Logs Collection Approach

Generally, the underlying computing system for PCS network generates a database record whenever a MT delivers or receives a call. Such call record stores detailed information about the call such as; the date, time, cell location where the call begins, etc. Table 1 gives an illustration. Hence, a daily large amount of data is recorded into the system database. This data contains huge hidden valuable information that can be used to improve the efficiency of the network location management schemes.

PBLM utilizes the accumulated data recorded in the systems database that summarizes the calls delivered to/from each MT, to enhance the efficiency of the system pager. Simply, PBLM uses the recorded data to predict the location (exact cell where MT resides) for the callee MT, and accordingly minimizing the paging cost. For each MT, its probability of existence, also called the existence support, in each cell of his current reg-

Table 1. A sample call logs for a specific MT

User ID	Call Date	Call Time	Cell where call initiated
5	1/2/2010	05:11:22	C_x
5	2/2/2010	08:09:12	C_y
5	2/2/2010	17:08:34	C_z
5	3/2/2010	12:13:21	C_m

istration area is continuously updated as a new call directed to or from it. The recorded existence probability, clarified in definition 1, is used to predict a candidate set of cells where the called MT is highly predicted to exist.

Definition 1: "Existence support of a Mobile Terminal"

The existence support of the mobile terminal MT_i to be located in the cell $c_j \in RA$ denoted as; $Support(MT_i,C_j)$ is the probability of existence of the mobile terminal MT_i in cell $C_j \in RA$, which is denoted as; $P(MT_i,C_j)$.

Under the lazy moving logs collection approach, $Support_L(MT_i,C_j)=P_L(MT_i,C_j)$, is the number of calls delivered to or from MT_i during which it resides at C_j divided by the total number of calls derived to or from MT_i during which it resides inside RA. Then, $P_L(MT_i,c_j)$ can be calculated as:

$$Support_L(MT_i,C_j) = P_L(MT_i,C_j) = \frac{Calls(MT_i,C_j)}{Calls(MT_i,RA)}$$

Hence, based on definition 1, as the number of calls delivered to or from MT_i during while it remains inside cell C_j increases, this increases its probability of occurrence at C_j, and also supports its existence in that cell. Assuming the maximum allowable call delay (MACD) to be; MACD=MAPD+T_c, where MAPD is the maximum allowable page delay, and T_c is the network latency time needed to set up the connection to the callee MT. Assuming the network delay for each paging round (PR) to be μ.. Hence, MAPD can be expressed as; MAPD=N_{MPR}*μ, where N_{MPR} is the maximum allowable paging rounds to find the callee MT inside its last RA.

Definition 2: "The Maximum Allowable Call Delay"

The maximum allowable call delay (MACD) is the maximum allowable delay time to setup and start a call between two MTs, it can be expressed as $MACD = N_{MPR} * \mu + T_c$, where μ is the delay time needed for one paging round, N_{MPR} is the maximum allowable paging rounds, and T_c is the network latency to actually setup the connection between the two mobile terminals.

Hence, the network has N_{MPR} paging chances to find the callee MT within its last RA. Initially, the maximum number of allowable paging rounds should be calculated based on the maximum allowable call delay and the paging delay for each paging round. Then, according to the probability of existence of the callee mobile terminal, all cells within its last RA are organized into N_{MPR} categories in descending order. The cells in each category are paged simultaneously aiming to identify the callee MT. If the callee mobile terminal still not identified even after paging all RA cells, this indicates that the mobile terminal either left the coverage area of the network or turned off without de-registration (i.e., sudden death of the power supply). The paging algorithm for PBLM is illustrated in more details in Figure 8, while the used parameters are listed in Table 2. Furthermore, identifying the paged cells in each paging round of the PBLM strategy is illustrated in Figure 9.

For illustration, consider the registration area RA shown in Figure 10, which consists of 16 cells. When a call is delivered to the mobile terminal MT_i that lies inside RA, the probability of existence for MT_i to be located inside each cell $C_j \in RA \ \forall \ 1 \leq j \leq 16$ is first calculated.

As illustrated in figure 10, the number of calls delivered to/from MT_i during while it remains inside RA equal to 34 calls. Hence, the probability of existence for MT_i to be inside each cell $C_j \in RA \ \forall \ 1 \leq j \leq 16$ is reported as follows;

$P(MT_i,C_j)_{\forall j \in \{2,4,5,8\}}=1/34=0.029411765$

$P(MT_i,C_j)_{\forall j \in \{9,12\}}=2/34= 0.0588235290$

Figure 8. Paging algorithm for PBLM

- **Input:**
  - A Registeration area *RA* of *n* cells, $RA=\{C_1, C_2, C_3, ..., C_n\}$
  - Probability of existence matrix for MT_i inside *RA*, expressed in a set of *n* pairs as; $PEM(MTi, RA)=\{<C_1,P(MT_i, C_1)>, <C_2,P(MT_i, C_2)>, ..., <C_n,P(MT_i, C_n)> \}$
  - Paging Delay (*time delay for one paging round*) μ.
  - Maximum Allowable Call Delay (MACD).
- **Output:**
  - *Cell_id* (the address of the cell where the called MT_i resides.

- **Steps:**

$MAPD=MACD-T_c$
If $(MAPD \bmod \mu)=0$ Then $N_{MPR}=MAPD/\mu$ Else $N_{MPR}=abs(MAPD/\mu)+1$
$N_{pc}=abs(n/ N_{MPR})$
For k=1 to N_{MPR}
    Construct the set $X=\{C_j| C_j \in RA$ and $C_j \in$ the set of N_{pc} cells with the maximum $P(MT_i, C_j)\}$
    If $k= N_{MPR}$ and $RA \neq \varnothing$ Then $X=X \cup RA$
    Simultanously_Page(C_j) $\forall C_j \in X$
    If Cell_Host(MT_i) $\in X$ then
        Identify the hosting cell ID, then start the call to MT_i
        Exit For
    End if
RA=RA-X
Next

$P(MT_i,C_j)_{\forall j\in\{11,14\}}=3/34= 0.088235294$

$P(MT_i,C_j)_{\forall j\in\{6\}}=4/34= 0.11764705900$

$P(MT_i,C_j)_{\forall j\in\{7,10\}}=5/34= 0.1470588240$

$P(MT_i,C_j)_{\forall j\in\{13\}}=6/34= 0.17647058800$

A graphical representation is also shown in Figure 11. Moreover, the paged cells in each page round are listed in Table 3.

Note that this method pages an equal number of cells in each paging round. However, in order to minimize the number of paged cells until the callee MT is identified, and accordingly minimizing the paging cost, the number of paged cells in each paging round should be increased gradually. To accomplish such aim, one suggested scheme is to use the logarithmic scale to subdivide the range of existence probability of the callee MT into a number of distinct clusters. Then, the cells in each cluster are paged simultaneously (cluster

Table 2. The used parameters for the PBLM algorithm

Item	Description
$PEM(MT_i,RA)$	Probability of existence matrix of MT_i inside RA.
MACD	Maximum Allowable Call Delay.
MAPD	Maximum Allowable Paging Delay.
N_{MPR}	The maximum number of paging rounds
T_c	The network latency to set up the connection to the callee MT.
n	The number of cells in RA.
N_{pc}	The number of cells in each paging round.

Figure 9. Identifying the paged cells in each paging round of the PBLM strategy

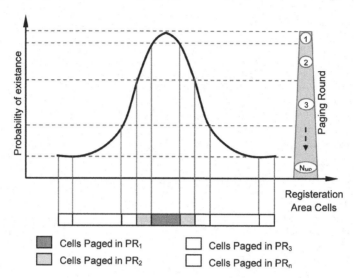

by cluster). The range of existence probability can be calculated using (1) as;

$$Avg\_Log\_Cost_F\big|_{RA} = \frac{\sum_{i=1}^{m}\left[abs\left(\dfrac{M_i}{y}\right)*\chi\right]}{m}$$

(1)

The next step is to divide the range defined in (1) using logarithmic scale into N_{MPR} clusters. Projection is then used, by employing the same scenario used in Figure 11, to identify the set of

Figure 10. The RA for the illustrative example

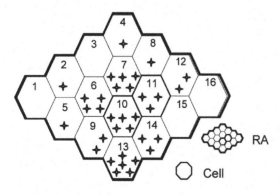

paged cells in each paging round. This mechanism allows starting paging a small set of highly probable cells hopping to find the callee MT with the minimal paging cost. If the called MT still not identified, the number of paged cells is then increased gradually in the next page round. This scenario continues until either the callee MT is identified or all cells (with in the current RA) are paged.

Using Active Moving Logs Collection Approach

Again, the same procedure followed in the previous section will be used here. However, existence support of a Mobile Terminal under active moving logs collection approach is clarified in definition 3.

Definition 3: *$Support_A(MT_i, c_j)$*

Under the active moving logs collection approach, $Support_A(MT_i,C_j)=P_A(MT_i,C_j)$, is the number of occurrences of MT_i in $C_j \in RA$ divided by the total number of occurrences of MT_i in all cells$\in$RA. Then, $P_A(MT_i,C_j)$ can be calculated as

Figure 11. Existence probability of MTi at all cells RA

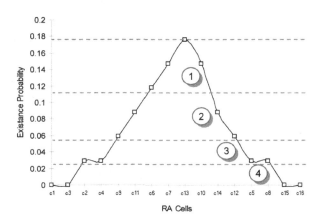

$$Support_A(MT_i, C_j) = P_A(MT_i, C_j) = \frac{Occurrances(MT_i, C_j)}{Occurrances(MT_i, RA)}$$

Hence, based on definition 3, as the number of occurrences of MT_i in cell C_j increases, this increases its probability of occurrence at C_j, and also supports its existence within that cell.

Modified Probability Based Location Management (MPBLM) Strategy

MPBLM is the same as PBLM but it considers the time when calculating the probability of existence for each MT. An existence probability spectrum (EPS) is constructed for each MT, which considers the time as a third dimension. Hence, the day time (24 hours) is divided into a set of smaller and equal time intervals (say each interval=1 hour), then the probability of existence of each MT in each cell∈RA is reported, then projected into the EPS(MT). Hence, the probability of existence of each MT can be estimated at any interval of the day time.

Assuming the active moving logs collection technique is used, when a MT enters a new cell C_j at the ith interval of the day time, the cell ID with the corresponding entrance time are stored in the MT local cache. Furthermore, if the ith interval has

finished and MT is still in C_j, MT has to record its existence in C_j at the $(i+1)^{th}$ interval of the day time within its internal cache. This procedure continues until MT leaves C_j. When MTs' cache becomes full, it sends the contents of its cache to the VLR serving its current RA, then clears the cache. The sequential steps needed by MPBLM for actively collecting the MT moving logs are illustrated in Figure 12.

Considering Figure 12, it can be concluded that, a MT stops collecting its moving logs only when it is turned OFF. Furthermore, a MT may be turned OFF either voluntary (in the case the user turned the power OFF) or involuntary (in the case the battery sudden death). During the former, before MT is turned OFF, it has to send the contents of its internal cache to the VLR serving its current RA. However, during the non-voluntary case, the pre-stored moving logs will be lost.

Table 3. The paged cells in each paging round for the illustrative example

Round	Paged Cells
PR_1	c_6, c_7, c_{13}, c_{10}
PR_2	$c_9, c_{11}, c_{12}, c_{14}$
PR_3	c_2, c_4, c_5, c_8
PR_4	c_1, c_3, c_{15}, c_{16}

Figure 12. Steps needed by MPBLM for active moving logs collection

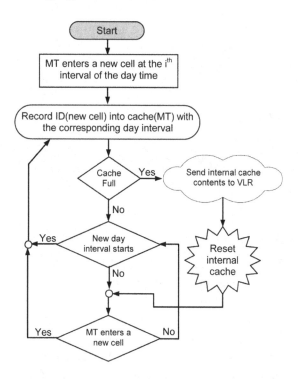

the time based existence probability table can be constructed, shown in the bottom part of Figure 14, which reflects the probability of existence for every MT in all RA cells at any day interval (the day interval was assumed to be one hour).

Figure 15, Table 4, Table 5, and Table 6 illustrate the existence probability of MT_i assuming the active moving logs collection during one month. The maximum existence probability of MT_i was found at the cells C_8 and C_{12}, which were found to be the cells hosting the home and work place of the user owning MT_i.

Hence, when a new call is delivered to MT_i, the current day interval is first identified, then the corresponding existence probability curve is extracted (for MT_i at the current day interval). For illustration, the existence probability curve for MT_i at 23th day interval is shown in Figure 16, which indicates that the maximum probable locations to find MT_i are the cells C_6, C_7, C_8, C_9, C_{10}, C_{11} (i.e., the most probable location to find the user owning MT_i is at the area surrounding his home).

Finally, after identifying the existence probability of MT_i at the current day interval, the same procedure followed before in PBLM strategy to page for the callee MT_i can be simply followed here in MPBLM strategy.

On the other hand, the operation will be simpler and straightforward when employing the lazy moving logs collection with MPBLM approach. MT in this case has no role in the call logs collection as it has no internal cache, however, logs collection is done totally by the VLR. When a new call arrives to a MT while it resides at cell C_j, the VLR serving the MTs' current RA reports the occurrence of that MT at C_j (after the paging process has been done) with the corresponding current day interval. Hence, no additional cost is required to send the collected call logs from MT to VLR as in the case of the active moving logs collection.

For illustration, consider RA_j, which is consists of 16 cells shown in Figure 13. The simplified data structure used to store all MTs movement information is shown in the top of Figure 14. Based on the information stored in that structure,

Figure 13. The registration area RA_j used for the illustrative example

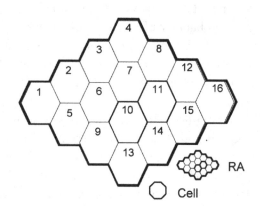

Figure 14. The structure used to store the existence probability of each MT in all RAs at every day interval

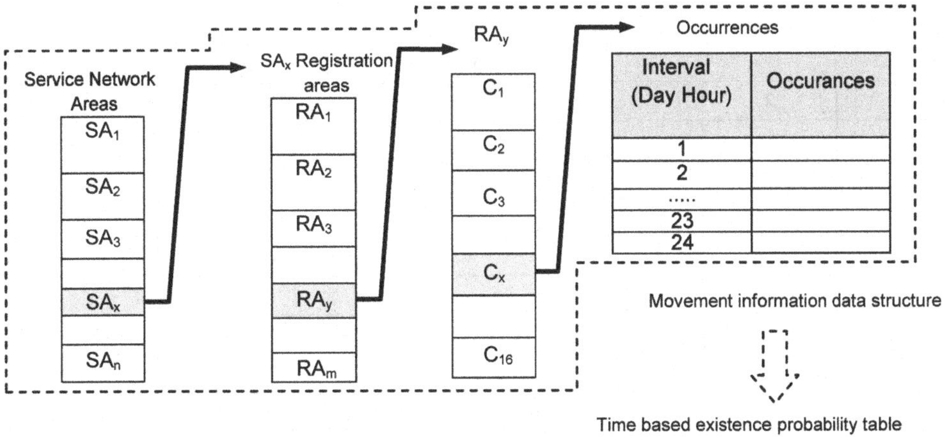

Service Network Areas	SA$_x$ Registration areas	RA$_y$	Occurrences	
			Interval (Day Hour)	Occurances
SA$_1$	RA$_1$	C$_1$	1	
SA$_2$	RA$_2$	C$_2$	2	
SA$_3$	RA$_3$	C$_3$	.....	
SA$_x$	RA$_y$	C$_x$	23	
SA$_n$	RA$_m$	C$_{16}$	24	

Movement information data structure

Time based existence probability table

Interval (Day Hour)	PE(C$_1$)	PE(C$_2$)	PE(C$_3$)	PE(C$_4$)	PE(C$_5$)	PE(C$_6$)	PE(C$_7$)	PE(C$_8$)	PE(C$_9$)	PE(C$_{10}$)	PE(C$_{11}$)	PE(C$_{12}$)	PE(C$_{13}$)	PE(C$_{14}$)	PE(C$_{15}$)	PE(C$_{16}$)
1	...	...	...	...	...	...	...	...	...	...	...	...	...	...	...	...
2	...	...	...	...	...	...	...	...	...	...	...	...	...	...	...	...
.....	...	...	...	...	...	...	...	...	...	...	...	...	...	...	...	...
23	...	...	...	...	...	...	...	...	...	...	...	...	...	...	...	...
24	...	...	...	...	...	...	...	...	...	...	...	...	...	...	...	...

Figure 15. Existence probability of MT$_i$ at all RA cells during all day intervals

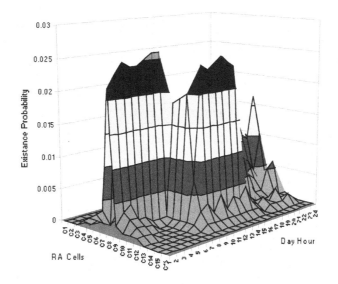

Table 4. Existence probability of MT_i assuming the active moving logs collection during one month (Day Intervals 1-8)

	Day Interval							
	1	2	3	4	5	6	7	8
C1	0	0	0	0	0	0	0	0
C2	0	0	0	0	0	0	0	0
C3	0	0	0	0	0	0	0	0
C4	0.00087	0	0	0	0	0	0	0
C5	0.001739	0.00087	0.00087	0	0.00087	0	0	0
C6	0.002609	0.00087	0.001739	0.00087	0.001739	0.00087	0.00087	0.00087
C7	0.003478	0.00087	0.002609	0.001739	0.00087	0.00087	0.001739	0.002609
C8	0.021739	0.023478	0.025217	0.024348	0.024348	0.025217	0.026087	0.026087
C9	0.001739	0.003478	0.004348	0.001739	0.001739	0.00087	0.00087	0.00087
C10	0.00087	0.002609	0.002609	0.00087	0.00087	0	0	0.00087
C11	0.00087	0.001739	0.001739	0	0	0	0	0.00087
C12	0.00087	0.00087	0.00087	0	0	0	0	0.00087
C13	0	0	0	0	0	0	0	0.00087
C14	0	0	0	0	0	0	0	0
C15	0	0	0	0	0	0	0	0
C16	0	0	0	0	0	0	0	0

Table 5. Existence probability of MT_i assuming the active moving logs collection during one month(Day Intervals 9-16)

	Day Interval							
	9	10	11	12	13	14	15	16
C1	0	0	0	0	0	0	0	0
C2	0	0	0	0	0	0	0	0
C3	0	0	0	0	0	0	0	0
C4	0	0	0	0	0	0	0.00087	0.00087
C5	0	0	0	0	0	0.00087	0.001739	0.004348
C6	0	0	0	0	0.00087	0.002609	0.002609	0.002609
C7	0.00087	0.00087	0.00087	0.00087	0.006087	0.005217	0.004348	0.003478
C8	0.001739	0.001739	0.001739	0.00087	0.02	0.02087	0.013913	0.013913
C9	0.018261	0.004348	0.00087	0	0.010435	0.013043	0.014783	0.006957
C10	0.01913	0.002609	0.00087	0	0.007826	0.004348	0.001739	0.004348
C11	0.02	0.001739	0.001739	0.002609	0.008696	0.007826	0.003478	0.001739
C12	0.006957	0.024348	0.023478	0.024348	0.002609	0.001739	0.00087	0.00087
C13	0.002609	0.003478	0.001739	0.004348	0.001739	0.00087	0.001739	0.00087
C14	0.00087	0.00087	0.00087	0.00087	0.00087	0	0.00087	0.00087
C15	0	0	0	0	0	0	0	0
C16	0	0	0	0	0	0	0	0

Table 6. Existence probability of MT$_i$ assuming the active moving logs collection during one month(Day Intervals 17-24)

	Day Interval							
	17	**18**	**19**	**20**	**21**	**22**	**23**	**24**
C1	0	0	0	0	0	0	0	0
C2	0	0	0	0	0	0	0	0
C3	0	0	0	0	0	0	0.00087	0.00087
C4	0	0	0.00087	0.00087	0.00087	0.00087	0.001739	0.00087
C5	0	0.00087	0.001739	0.004348	0.003478	0.002609	0.003478	0.004348
C6	0.00087	0.002609	0.002609	0.002609	0.002609	0.002609	0.004348	0.001739
C7	0.006087	0.005217	0.004348	0.003478	0.003478	0.006087	0.003478	0.002609
C8	0.02	0.02087	0.013913	0.013913	0.010435	0.009565	0.016522	0.011304
C9	0.010435	0.013043	0.014783	0.006957	0.006087	0.004348	0.010435	0.004348
C10	0.007826	0.004348	0.001739	0.004348	0.003478	0.002609	0.002609	0.00087
C11	0.008696	0.007826	0.003478	0.001739	0.001739	0.005217	0.006087	0.001739
C12	0.002609	0.001739	0.00087	0.00087	0.00087	0.001739	0.00087	0.00087
C13	0.001739	0.00087	0.001739	0.00087	0.002609	0.00087	0.00087	0
C14	0.00087	0	0.00087	0.00087	0.00087	0.001739	0.00087	0
C15	0	0	0	0	0	0	0	0
C16	0	0	0	0	0	0	0	0

Hot Spot Based (HSB) Topology for PCS Networks

To minimize registration cost, a PCS network forces each MT to register itself if it enters a new RA. Hence, no additional registrations are allowed

Figure 16. Existence probability of MT$_i$ during the 23th day intervals

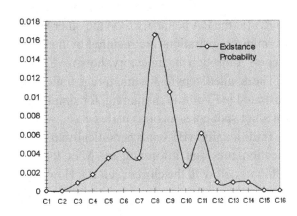

inside the entire RA. Although this behavior may have a great impact in minimizing the registration cost, it also offers the maximum paging cost. Much of traffic is needed to determine the precise location of the callee MT as all RA cells are paged simultaneously (blanket paging). Hence, there is a tradeoff between paging and registration costs.

In this section, we will present a new topology for reconstructing the network RA called "Hot Spot Topology" (HST) aiming to present a more precise location description for the network MTs. Then, an instance of HST called "Flower Based Topology" will be presented in more details.

Hot Spot Topology (HST)

HST attempts to minimize the paging overhead by allowing a precise prediction for the callees' MT location (hosting cell). To accomplish such aim, HST allows the MT to register (report) its current location at a predefined locations inside the RA called the "Hot Spots". The last reported location of MT at time t_i can be used to predict its current location at time t_{i+1}. HST is clarified in definition 4.

Definition 4: Hot Spots Topology. A Hot Spot based Topology arranges the cells of each RA to include a predefined locations (Hot Spots). Any MT is then forced to report its current location if it crosses any hot spot.

The concept of hot spots can be illustrated by considering Figure 17 in which the dark regions represent the considered hot spots. Any MT is forced to register itself if it enters any hot spot. Hence, two variants of registrations can be held in a network uses the HST as an underlying infrastructure (topology) for its RAs, namely; (i) macro-registration (Mac_Reg), and (ii) micro-registration (Mic_Reg).

Definition 5: Macro-Registration. A MT is forced to perform a macro-registration as soon as it enters a new registration area. Hence, the network can identify the current RA of that MT.

As depicted in definition 5, the macro-registration is needed so that the network can identify precisely the MTs' location. This is helpful in many circumstances such as directing a call to that MT or in deriving location based services. To accomplish such aim, whenever the MT enters a new RA, the address (ID) of the new RA should be recorded in the master HLR of that MT. The steps of the macro-registration process are the same as those steps of the traditional registration one introduced in section (2-2).

Definition 6: Micro-Registration. A MT is forced to perform a micro-registration as soon as it enters (pass through) a hot spot. Hence, the network can predict the current cell of that MT whenever a call is delivered to it.

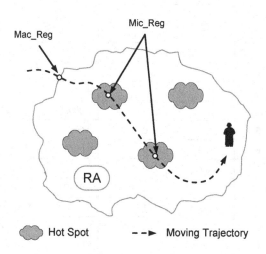

Figure 17. The hot spot based topology for PCS network RA

As depicted in definition 6, the micro-registration is needed by the network so that it can predict the location of every MT at any time. In this type of registration, every MT is forced to report its location as soon as it passes through any of the pre-defined hot spots. This can be helpful in predicting the current cell of the MT, which in turn has a great impact in minimizing the paging cost. Moreover, this type of registration is fully controlled by the VLR serving the current RA. Hence, no need to interrupt the master HLR of the MT that is performing a micro-registration. Figure 17 depicts the difference between the micro and macro registration types.

As illustrated in Figure 17, a MT is forced to perform a macro-registration whenever it enters the RA (at the RA boundary). On the other hand, two micro registrations are required by that MT if it passes through the trajectory shown in Figure 17. The detailed steps for the micro-registration are illustrated in Figure 18, assuming, for simplicity, that a hot spot consists of a single cell.

Traditionally, a BS sends periodically an identification message informing all MTs located within its cell with the current cell ID. However, when applying the Hot Spot topology, the identification message consists of double fields; (i) the current cell ID, and (ii) registration flag (Reg_Flag). This flag equals "1" if the cell is a hot spot; otherwise, it equals "0". Hence, when the MT receives an identification message with a new cell ID, it checks the Reg_Flag field to detect whether the micro-registration is needed or not. Whenever the MT receives an identification message with Reg_Flag=1, it sends a micro-registration message containing its ID to the BS serving the current cell (the hot spot it has entered). The BS of the current cell will forwards the MTs' ID as well as the hot spots' ID to the VLR serving the current RA. Hence, each VLR maintains a table (micro-registration table) to store IDs of all MTs currently located with the entire RA as well as the last registered hot spot (LRHS) as illustrated in Figure 18.

Figure 18. Detailed steps for the micro-registration process

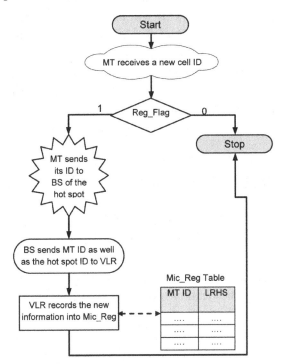

Flower Based Topology (FBT)

In this section, an instance of HST, which is called; "Flower Based Topology (FBT)" will be introduced. FBT is the basic infrastructure that will be used to implement a novel Flower Based Location Management (FBLM) Strategy for the PCS network, which will be introduced in the next section.

According to FBT, every RA is organized as a set of neighboring flowers as illustrated in Figure 19. A flower consists of an innermost cell, called the flower center or the master cell, which is surrounded with sex other leaves. Any MT is asked to register itself whenever it passes through any flower center. On the other hand, no registration is needed when the MT is moving across the flower leaves. For illustration, consider RA shown in Figure 19, which consists of seven adjacent flowers. According to the shown trajectory, MT has to perform one macro-registration at "point x", while four micro-registration are needed at "points y,z,m,n".

Flower Based Location Management (FBLM) Strategy

In this section, a new Flower Based Location Management (FBLM) strategy is introduced, which is based on the flower based topology for the network RA. As discussed before, the moving logs for network MTs in each RA can be collected either by lazy or active approaches. For illustration, consider the RA of seven flowers shown in Figure 20. Using the active approach with MT internal cache size able to store five cells IDs. Assuming that MT_i was "OFF" and is turned "ON" at "cell a". Hence, MT_i is assumed to be registered at the center of the flower in which "cell a" belongs to (i.e., F_2).

Assuming that MT_i is a new terminal that is the first to register at "*cell a*". Hence, at "*cell a*", the occurrence of MT_i in any cell $C \in RA$ equals 0 except at "*cell a*" itself where the occurrence

Figure 19. The flower based topology for constructing PCS registration areas

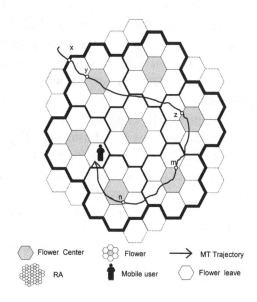

Figure 20. The RA of seven flowers for the illustrative example

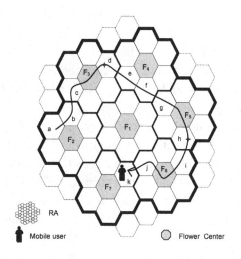

of MT_i equals one. According to the trajectory shown in Figure 20, MT_i sends his cache contents to the VLR serving its current RA, specifically when it enters "*cell d*" and "*cell h*". Hence, a part of the contents of the location database for MT_i at "*cell d*" and "*cell h*" are illustrated in Table 7 and Table 8 respectively.

Figure 21 shows the state diagram that reflects the conditional probabilities $P(C_j|Fi) \forall 1 \leq i \leq 7$ and $1 \leq j \leq 42$ for MT_i, which is the probability that MT_i is registered at flower center F_i but located at cell C_j. Considering the path shown in Figure 20 as the first path followed by MT_i in RA, the conditional probabilities for MT_i at cells $\{a,b,c,d,e,f,g,h,i,j,k\}$ are illustrated in Figure 21.

One problem that may affect the performance of the flower based location management strategy especially when using the lazy mobile logs collection approach is the "moving around problem", which is illustrated in Figure 22. This problem arises when the MT moves most of its time through the leaves of the flowers constituting its current RA without crossing the flower centers. However, the population of mobile users increases, which forces the PCS networks to use the cell splitting. This will minimize the impact of the moving around problem as the probability that MT crosses the flower centers increases. Moreover, even if the MT enters the RA at the cell C_x (flower leaf), it is forced to perform a micro-registration at the flower center F in which C_x belongs to. Consider Figure 22 for illustration.

ANALYTICAL MODEL

In the PCS network with HLR/VLR architecture, there are costs for location update and paging. Furthermore, there are two types of location updates, which are; (i) HLR location update that updates the location information at HLR database,

Table 7. A part of the contents of the location database for MT$_i$ at "cell d"

Flower Number	Occurrences at the trajectory cells												
	Center	a	b	c	d	e	f	g	h	i	j	k	l
1	0	0	0	0	0	0	0	0	0	0	0	0	0
2	0	1	1	1	0	0	0	0	0	0	0	0	0
3	1	0	0	0	1	0	0	0	0	0	0	0	0
4	0	0	0	0	0	0	0	0	0	0	0	0	0
5	0	0	0	0	0	0	0	0	0	0	0	0	0
6	0	0	0	0	0	0	0	0	0	0	0	0	0
7	0	0	0	0	0	0	0	0	0	0	0	0	0

Table 8. A part of the contents of the location database for MT$_i$ at "cell h"

Flower Number	Occurrences at the trajectory cells												
	Center	a	b	c	d	e	f	g	h	i	j	k	l
1	0	0	0	0	0	0	0	0	0	0	0	0	0
2	0	1	1	1	0	0	0	0	0	0	0	0	0
3	1	0	0	0	1	1	1	1	0	0	0	0	0
4	0	0	0	0	0	0	0	0	0	0	0	0	0
5	1	0	0	0	0	0	0	0	1	0	0	0	0
6	0	0	0	0	0	0	0	0	0	0	0	0	0
7	0	0	0	0	0	0	0	0	0	0	0	0	0

Figure 21. the conditional probabilities for MT$_i$ at all RA cells considering the pass of figure 20

Figure 22. The moving around problem

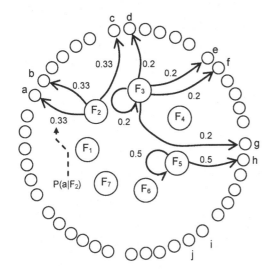

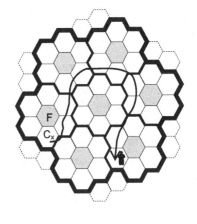

and (ii) VLR location update that updates the location information at VLR database. However, as we derive a new topology for construction the RA, the discussion here will concentrate on the paging costs and VLR database updates since the HLR database updates will be the same for both the traditional and the proposed location management strategies.

In this section, an analytical cost calculation procedure for paging and registration activities for the proposed location management strategies as well as the traditional one will be introduced. Although the probabilistic model was successfully applied to model the movement behavior as well as the call arrival rates (Bejerano, Smith, Naor, & Immorlica, 2006), we choose to follow a deterministic model to simplify the calculations. Here, we will try to estimate the additional and saved costs in both paging and registration activates introduced by the proposed location management strategies (probabilistic and flower based) compared with the traditional one.

Cost Analysis for the Proposed Probabilistic Approaches

In this subsection, we will consider the added and saved costs of paging and registration activities for PBLM and MPBLM strategies.

Paging Costs

Two different types of costs are considered here, which are; (i) signaling cost, and (ii) time cost. The former is the cost due to paging the RA cells until finding the target MT. On the other hand, the latter is the time delay (network latency) until the call starts. It is clear that the proposed probabilistic paging approaches try to decrease the signaling cost but it may increase the network latency (within the time limits constraints). The Additional Time Cost in paging for Probabilistic approaches denoted as; ATC_p(paging).

Assuming the delay time for each paging round to be μ. Hence, for traditional paging scheme (blanket paging), the paging delay=μ as the system pages the whole RA in one paging round. On the other hand, for our selective paging approaches (i.e., probabilistic and flower based), the paging delay for one call directed to MT_i can be calculated as; $paging\_Delay(MT_i) = \mu * n_i$, where n_i is the minimum number of paging rounds needed to find MT_i inside the RA under scope. The average paging delay for N calls directed to MT_i can be calculated using (2) as

$$Avg\_Pg\_Delay(MT_i) = \frac{\sum_{k=1}^{N} \mu * n_{ik}}{N} \qquad (2)$$

Where n_{ik} is the number of paging rounds needed to find MT_i inside RA during the kth call. Assuming that RA have m users, the average paging delay for one call directed to a MT resides in the RA under scope can be calculated using (3) as

$$Avg\_Pg\_Delay\Big|_{One\_Call} = \frac{\sum_{R=1}^{m}\left(\sum_{k=1}^{N_R} \mu * n_{Rk} \Big/ N_R\right)}{m} \qquad (3)$$

Where, N_R is the number of calls directed to the MT_R during the test period T, m is the number of users currently inside the RA under scope, and n_{Rk} is the number of paging rounds of the kth call for MT_R.

Hence:

$$Average\_ATC_p(Paging)\Big|_{One\_Call} =$$
$$Avg\_Pg\_Delay(Sel)\Big|_{One\_Call} - Avg\_Pg\_Delay(Blanket)\Big|_{One\_Call}$$

$$Average\_ATC_p(Paging)\Big|_{One\_Call} = \frac{\sum_{R=1}^{m}\left(\sum_{k=1}^{N_R} \mu * n_{Rk} \Big/ N_R\right)}{m} - \mu \qquad (4)$$

$$Average\_ATC_p(Paging)\big|_{One\_Call} = \frac{\sum_{R=1}^{m}\left(\sum_{k=1}^{N_R}\mu * n_{Rk}\Big/N_R\right) - \mu * m}{m}$$

(5)

On the other hand, the additional time cost of paging for probabilistic approaches for the *m* users during a test period *T* can be calculated using (6) as

$$ATC_p(Paging) = \sum_{R=1}^{m}\left[\left(\sum_{k=1}^{N_R}\mu * n_{Rk}\right) - \mu * N_R\right]$$

(6)

On the other hand, the saved signaling cost in the paging process compared with the traditional paging approach (blanket paging) denoted as; *SSC_p(paging)*, and can be calculated as; *SSC_p(paging)=SC_blanket-SC_p*, where *SC_blanket* is the signaling cost of blanket paging, and *SC_p* is the signaling cost of the proposed probabilistic approaches. Assuming that; *RA* has *X* cells, the signaling cost to page one cell is assumed to be *ξ*. Hence, the signaling cost for blanket paging to page for one MT can be calculated as; *X*ξ* as all RA cells are paged simultaneously to find the callee MT. For *m* MTs, *SC_blanket=X*ξ*m*. On the other hand, for the proposed probabilistic selective paging techniques, the signaling cost needed to page the entire RA MT$_i$ for one call can be calculated as; *Sig_Pg_Cost(MT_i)=n_i*C*ξ*, where n_i is the minimum number of paging rounds needed to find MT$_i$ inside RA, *C* is the number of cells paged in each paging round. The average signaling cost due to paging for *N* calls directed to MT$_i$ can be calculated using (7) as

$$Avg\_Pg\_Cost(MT_i) = \frac{\sum_{k=1}^{N}n_{ik} * C * \xi}{N}$$

(7)

Where n_{ik} is the number of paging rounds needed to find MT$_i$ inside RA during the kth call.

Assuming that RA have *m* users, the average signaling cost for one incoming call due to paging the RA under scope can be calculated using (8) as

$$Avg\_Pg\_Cost\big|_{One\_Call} = \frac{\sum_{R=1}^{m}\left(\sum_{k=1}^{N_R}n_{Rk} * C * \xi\Big/N_R\right)}{m}$$

(8)

On the other hand, the total Signaling Cost (*SC*) to page for the *m* users using probabilistic approaches can be calculated using (9) as

$$SC_p = \sum_{R=1}^{m}\left(\sum_{k=1}^{N_R}n_{Rk} * C * \xi\right)$$

(9)

Hence; the saved signaling cost of the paging process for the probabilistic approaches compared with the blanket paging approach considering *m* users can be calculated as

$$SSC_p(Paging) = SC_{blanket} - SC_p$$

$$SSC_p(Paging) = X * \xi * m - \sum_{R=1}^{m}\left(\sum_{k=1}^{N_R}n_{Rk} * C * \xi\right)$$

(10)

Moving Logs Update Cost

Due to the used moving logs collection scheme, another signaling cost should be considered. In the active moving logs scheme, whenever MT receives a new cell ID, it stores the new ID in its internal cache. When the cache becomes full or after a predefined cell crossing, MT sends the IDs of the previously visited cells to the VLR serving its current RA. The collected trajectories for each MT in the RA under scope are then used to update the MTs' existence probabilities. For simplicity, we assume that the cost for VLR database querying is negligible. This assumption is reasonable since the cost for querying VLR database is much smaller than the signaling (communication) cost.

Assuming each MT has to send its stored trajectory after crossing y cells. Let χ to be the signaling cost for sending the MTs' collected trajectory from MT to the BS serving its current cell, then from BS to the VLR serving the entire RA. The number of cell crossing for MT during the test period T is assumed to be M. Hence, the additional signaling cost due to the MT_i active moving logs update during T for the probabilistic location management strategies can be calculated using (11) as

$$Mov\_Log\_Cost_p(MT_i) = Integer\left(\frac{M_i}{y}\right) * \chi$$

(11)

With m MTs in the entire RA, the moving logs update cost can be calculated using (12) as

$$Mov\_Log\_Cost_p\Big|_{RA} = \sum_{i=1}^{m}\left[Integer\left(\frac{M_i}{y}\right) * \chi\right]$$

(12)

The average moving logs update cost for one user can be calculated using (13) as

$$Avg\_Log\_Cost_p\Big|_{One\_User} = \frac{\sum_{i=1}^{m}\left[Integer\left(\frac{M_i}{y}\right) * \chi\right]}{m}$$

(13)

Two important issues should be considered, which are; (i) for the lazy moving logs collection approach, no additional signaling cost for the moving logs update. This is simply because the system identifies MTs' moving trajectory by monitoring its incoming and outcoming calls. (ii) Within the proposed probabilistic location management strategies, no additional registration cost since MT has to perform macro-registrations only and no need to perform micro-registrations.

Total Costs for the Proposed Probabilistic Approaches

As illustrated in the previous subsections, two main types of costs can be considered, which are; signaling and time costs. In this section, the total costs from each type (signaling and time) are joined together to formulate the total signaling cost as well as the total timing cost. The total additional timing cost ATC_p for the proposed probabilistic location management strategies can be calculated using (14) as

$$ATC_p = ATC_p(Paging) = \sum_{R=1}^{m}\left[\left(\sum_{k=1}^{N_R}\mu * n_{Rk}\right) - \mu * N_R\right]$$

(14)

On the other hand, for the proposed probabilistic location management strategies, the total saved signaling cost SSC_p over the traditional scheme (using the active moving logs collection approach) can be calculated using (15) as;

$$SSC_p = SSC_p(Paging) - Mov\_Log\_Cost_p\Big|_{RA}$$

(15)

Substitute from (14) and (15), SSC_p can be calculated using (16) as

$$SSC_p = X * \xi * m - \sum_{R=1}^{m}\left(\sum_{k=1}^{N_R}n_{Rk} * C * \xi\right) - \sum_{i=1}^{m}\left[Integer\left(\frac{M_i}{y}\right) * \chi\right]$$

(16)

However, the third term of (16) should be eliminated for calculating the total saved signaling cost for probabilistic strategies in the case of using the lazy moving logs collection approach.

Cost Analysis for the Proposed Flower Based Strategy

In this subsection, we will consider the added and saved costs of paging and registration activities for the flower based location management strategy.

Paging Costs

The additional time cost of paging for the flower based strategy denoted as; $ATC_F(paging)$, which can be calculated in the same manner as $ATC_p(paging)$. Hence, $ATC_F(paging)$ can be calculated using (17) as;

$$ATC_F(Paging) = \sum_{R=1}^{m}\left[\left(\sum_{k=1}^{N_R}\mu * n_{Rk}\right) - \mu * N_R\right]$$

(17)

Where, μ is the network latency (delay time) for each paging round, N_R is the number of calls directed to the Rth MT during the test period T, m is the number of users currently inside the RA under scope, n_{Rk} is the number of paging rounds of the kth call for MT_R.

Also, the saved signaling cost of the paging process for the flower based strategy against the traditional paging approach $SSC_F(paging)$ can be calculated using the same procedure followed before to calculate $SSC_F(paging)$. Hence, $SSC_F(paging)$ can be calculated using (18) as

$$SSC_F(Paging) = X * \xi * m - \sum_{R=1}^{m}\left(\sum_{k=1}^{N_R} n_{Rk} * C * \xi\right)$$

(18)

Where, Where n_{Rk} is the number of paging rounds needed to find MT_R inside RA during the kth call, m is the number of users inside the RA under scope during the test period T, X is the number of cells in RA, ξ the signaling cost to page one cell, C is the number of cells paged in each paging round, and N_R is the number of calls directed to MT_R during the test period T.

Moving Logs Update Cost

Again, the same procedure followed in section 5.1.2 to calculate the moving logs update cost for the active moving logs collection approach

will also be followed here. Hence, the additional signaling cost for the active moving logs collection of MT_i during the test period T (for the flower based strategy) can be calculated using (19) as

$$Mov\_Log\_Cost_F(MT_i) = Integer\left(\frac{M_i}{y}\right) * \chi$$

(19)

With m MTs in the entire RA, the moving logs update signaling cost can be calculated using (20) as

$$Mov\_Log\_Cost_F\big|_{RA} = \sum_{i=1}^{m}\left[Integer\left(\frac{M_i}{y}\right) * \chi\right]$$

(20)

The average moving logs update signaling cost for one user can be calculated using (21) as

$$Avg\_Log\_Cost_F\big|_{One\_User} = \frac{\sum_{i=1}^{m}\left[Integer\left(\frac{M_i}{y}\right) * \chi\right]}{m}$$

(21)

Where, y is the number of cells crossing after which MT has to send its stored trajectory, χ is the signaling cost for sending MT trajectory from MT to the BS serving the current cell, then from BS to the VLR serving the entire RA, and M_i is the number of cell crossing for MT_i during the test period T.

Additional Registration Cost

In spite of its simplicity, the proposed hot spot topology, such as the flower based one, poses a new signaling cost for the micro-registration process. A MT is forced to register itself by sending its ID as well as the current cell ID to the VLR serving its current RA whenever it passes through a new hot spot (flower center in the case of the flower based topology). For simplicity, we assume that micro-registration cost is the same as the signaling cost for sending the MTs' trajectory to VLR (in the case of active moving logs collection), which was set to χ.

Assuming the MT_i passes through H hot spots (flower centers) during the test period T, the micro-registration cost for MT_i during T can be calculated as; $micro\_Reg\_Cost(MT_i)= \chi*H$. For m MTs, the total cost for the micro-registration process during T can be calculated using (22) as

$$mic\_Re g\_Cost\Big|_{RA} = \sum_{i=1}^{m} \chi * H_i \qquad (22)$$

Total Costs for the Proposed Flower Based Strategy

In this section, the total costs from each type (signaling and time) are joined together to formulate the total signaling cost as well as the total timing cost. The total additional timing cost ATC_F for the proposed flower based location management strategy can be calculated using (23) as

$$ATC_F = ATC_F(Paging) = \sum_{R=1}^{m}\left[\left(\sum_{k=1}^{N_R}\mu * n_{Rk}\right) - \mu * N_R\right] \qquad (23)$$

On the other hand, the total saved signaling cost SSC_F over the traditional scheme (using the active moving logs collection approach) can be calculated as

$$SSC_F = SSC_F(Paging) - Mov\_Log\_Cost_F\Big|_{RA} - mic\_Re g\_Cost\Big|_{RA}$$

Substitute from (18), (20), and (22), the SSC_F will be

$$SSC_F = X*\xi*m - \sum_{i=1}^{m}\left(\sum_{k=1}^{N_R}n_{ik}*C*\xi\right) - \sum_{i=1}^{m}\left[Integer\left(\frac{M_i}{y}\right)*\chi\right] - \sum_{i=1}^{m}\chi*H_i$$

$$SSC_F = X*\xi*m - \sum_{i=1}^{m}\left\langle\left(\sum_{k=1}^{N_R}n_{ik}*C*\xi\right) - \left[Integer\left(\frac{M_i}{y}\right)*\chi\right] - \chi*H_i\right\rangle$$

$$SSC_F = X*\xi*m - \sum_{i=1}^{m}\left\langle\left(\sum_{k=1}^{N_R}n_{ik}*C*\xi\right) - \chi*\left[Integer\left(\frac{M_i}{y}\right) - H_i\right]\right\rangle \qquad (24)$$

Where y is the number of cells crossing after which MT has to send its stored trajectory, χ is the signaling cost for sending the MTs' trajectory to the BS serving the current cell, then from BS to the VLR serving the entire RA, M_i is the number of cell crossing for MT_i during the test period T, n_{ik} is the number of paging rounds needed to find MT_i inside RA during the kth call, m is the number of users inside the RA under scope during the test period T, X is the number of cells in RA, ξ the signaling cost to page one cell, C is the number of cells paged in each paging round, and N_R is the number of calls directed to MT_R during the test period T.

PERFORMANCE EVALUATION AND EXPERIMENTAL RESULTS

The analytical model presented in the previous section allows us to study the performance evaluation of the proposed mobility management strategies as well as some of the traditional ones. Hence, to demonstrate the effectiveness of the proposed location management strategies, we will present some typical performance results by using the analytical model introduced in section 5.

Preliminary

Simulation was used to buildup an environment for implementing the experiments introduced in the next subsections. Real moving logs are not easy to be obtained as the active and lazy approaches to collect the moving logs are not implemented in the current PCS networks. We assume that there are 40 users who are free to roam within the considered RA and owning MT_i $\forall$ $i \in [1,40]$. Those 40 users are sub-divided into four sets S_1, S_2, S_3, S_4, which are defined as

$$S_1 = \begin{Bmatrix} MT_i | \text{ Office}\left(user\left(MT_i\right)\right) \in C_i \text{ and } Home\left(user\left(MT_i\right)\right) \in C_j \\ where \ C_i, C_j \in RA \ and \ 1 \leq i \leq 10 \end{Bmatrix}$$

$$S_2 = \begin{Bmatrix} MT_i | \text{ Office}\left(user\left(MT_i\right)\right) \in C_i \text{ and } Home\left(user\left(MT_i\right)\right) \in C_j \\ where \ C_i \in RA, \ C_j \notin RA \ and \ 11 \leq i \leq 20 \end{Bmatrix}$$

$$S_3 = \begin{Bmatrix} MT_i | \text{ Office}\left(user\left(MT_i\right)\right) \in C_i \text{ and } Home\left(user\left(MT_i\right)\right) \in C_j \\ where \ C_i \notin RA, \ C_j \in RA \ and \ 21 \leq i \leq 30 \end{Bmatrix}$$

$$S_4 = \begin{Bmatrix} MT_i | \text{ Office}\left(user\left(MT_i\right)\right) \in C_i \text{ and } Home\left(user\left(MT_i\right)\right) \in C_j \\ where \ C_i \notin RA, \ C_j \notin RA \ and \ 31 \leq i \leq 40 \end{Bmatrix}$$

Hence, the set S_1 represents the users who live most of their times in RA since their homes and work places lie within the RA under scope. S_2, on the other hand, represents the users who live outside RA but enter RA daily to reach their work places; hence, they spend their work times inside RA. The set S_3 represents the users who live inside RA but leave RA daily to their work places. Finally, S_4 represents the set of users who enter RA to perform some activities such as marketing, learning …etc. A grid of paths are assumed in RA (these paths pass through a set of pre-defined cells), which insures the connection between *Office(user(MT_i))*, *Home(user(MT_i))*, and a set of pre-defined locations that are assumed to introduce services to mobile users such as; markets and schools $\forall$ $1 \leq i \leq 40$.

For each MT, a set of trajectories are collected (using active and lazy logs collection approaches), then randomly divided into two groups, which are training and testing. The former is used to estimate the existence probabilities, while the latter is used to measure the performance of the

proposed mobility management strategies as well as the traditional ones.

During the next experiments, the delay time for each paging round (i.e., μ) is assumed to be 100 ms. Furthermore, the signaling cost to page for MT_i within one cell (i.e., ξ) is assumed to be greater than the signaling cost for sending the MT trajectory to VLR (i.e., χ) (it was assumed that $\chi \approx$ the cost for performing a micro-registration). Numerically, $\xi \approx 10 * \chi$. The RA under consideration is assumed to have 100 flowers, which in turn has 700 cells. Furthermore, the maximum network delay before starting a call was assumed to be 7 seconds. Hence, the maximum paging rounds=7000/100=70 (the network latency to setup the connection between the caller and callee MTs was neglected, i.e., $T_c \approx 0$). This means that 10 cells are paged in each paging round. Finally, the test period (i.e., T) was set to 1 hour in all experiments.

Competitors

For the purpose of comparing the performance of the proposed mobility management strategies, a set of competitors are illustrated in Table 9.

Experimental Results

Initially, the paging delay (measure in ms) is measured against the Call to Mobility Ratio (CMR). CMR can be defined as the percentage between the average number of calls per unit time to the average number of movements per unit time for the network mobile users. However, our definition for CMR that will be used through the next experiments has been modified to be $CMR = \frac{n}{m}$, where n is the number of calls directed to all MTs during the test period T, and m is the total number of movements of all MTs during T.

Figure 23 and Figure 24 illustrate the paging delay time measured in milliseconds against the number of mobile terminals using CMR=0.1 and

Table 9. The considered techniques used for the comparison

Technique	Description
Blanket	The blanket paging tries to page the whole RA for the target MT when a new call is delivered to it.
RP	Random Paging divides the cells of the current RA into groups (batches), then randomly pages those batches. All cells in each batch are paged simultaneously. The number of cells in each batch can be calculated as $$Batch\_Cells = \frac{Number\ of\ cells\ in\ RA * \mu}{Maximum\ Paging\ Delay}$$
PBLM(L)	Probability based location management with lazy moving logs collection approach.
PBLM(A)	Probability based location management with active moving logs collection approach.
MPBLM(L)	Modified probability based location management with lazy moving logs collection approach.
MPBLM(A)	Modified probability based location management with active moving logs collection approach.
FBS(L)	Flowed Based Strategy with lazy moving logs collection approach.
FBS(A)	Flowed Based Strategy with active moving logs collection approach.

Figure 23. Paging delay time using CMR=0.1

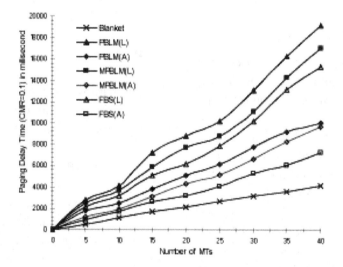

1 respectively. It was shown that the blanket paging introduces the minimal paging delay time as it pages the whole RA for the callee MT simultaneously in one round for each incoming call. On the other hand, strategies that employ the active moving logs collection approach outperform their peers which use the lazy moving logs collection one. FBS(A), MPBLM(A), then PBLM(A) respectively are most effective strategies that introduce the smaller paging delay time. On the other hand,

the RP strategy does not included in figures 23 and 24 as it introduces a very high delay time that can not be drawn using the scales of Figure 23 and Figure 24.

Figure 25 and Figure 26 illustrate the average paging delay time for each call measured in milliseconds against the number of MTs using CMR=0.1 and 1 respectively. It is approved that the blanket paging outperforms all other strategies. Furthermore, FBS(A) is the one that introduces

Figure 24. Paging delay time using CMR=1

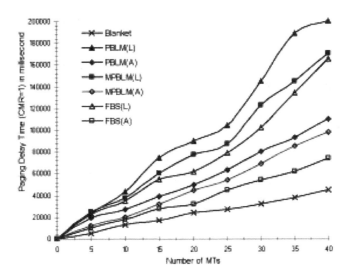

Figure 25. The Paging delay time using CMR=0.1

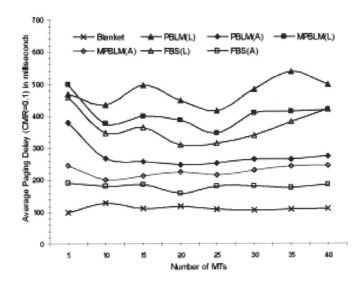

the smallest delay time for each incoming call over all other selective paging techniques.

The additional delay times measured in milliseconds introduced by the proposed selective paging techniques over the blanket paging using CMR=0.1 are illustrated in Figure 27. Moreover, the average additional delay time for one incom-ing call using CMR=0.1 is illustrated in Figure 28. By considering Figure 27 and Figure 28, it was shown that FBS(A) outperforms all other selective paging strategies as it introduces the smallest additional and average paging delay times. Furthermore, it can be concluded that; the strategies use the active moving logs collection

Figure 26. average Paging delay time using CMR=1

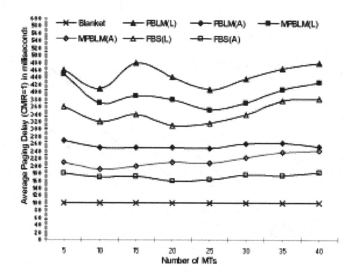

Figure 27. The additional paging delay for the proposed selective paging techniques over the blanket one using CMR=0.1

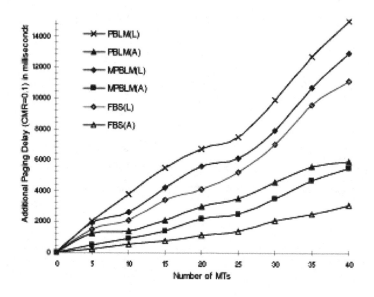

approach outperform their peers that use the lazy one.

Figure 29 and Figure 30 illustrate the total signaling cost introduced by the different location management strategies against the number of

mobile terminals using CMR =0.1 and 1 respectively. Each strategy has its own signaling cost. For illustration, the signaling cost for the blanket and RP is due to paging only. On the other hand, for the proposed selective paging strategies, some

Figure 28. The average additional paging delay for the proposed selective paging techniques over the blanket one using CMR=0.1

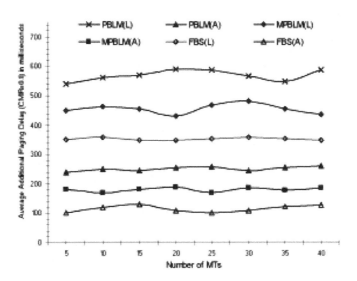

Figure 29. The total signaling cost for different location management strategies using CMR=0.1

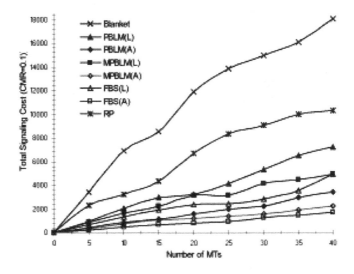

additional signaling costs are added such as; (i) the cost for the micro-registration (in the case of FBSs), and (ii) the signaling cost due to sending the moving logs when using the active moving logs collection approach. Considering figures 29 and 30, it can be shown that; (i) the blanket paging introduce the maximum signaling cost as it

pages the whole RA for each incoming call. (ii) Although there are additional signaling costs for micro-registration and sending the active moving logs, FBS(A) illustrates the minimal signaling cost as it finds the callee MT, in most cases, in the first paging rounds. (iii) The strategies use the active moving logs collection approach illustrate

Figure 30. The total signaling cost for different location management strategies using CMR=1

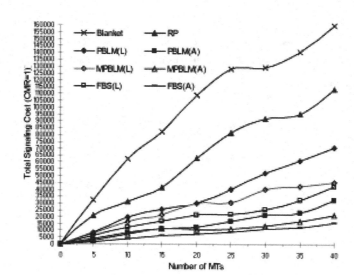

Figure 31. The total saved signaling cost for the proposed location management strategies against the traditional one using CMR=0.1

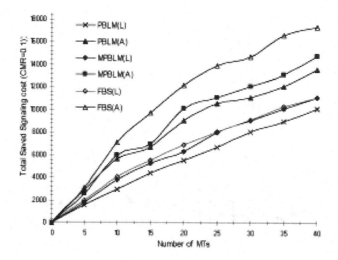

smaller signaling costs that their peers, which use the lazy moving logs one.

For the purpose of comparing the proposed location management strategies that use selective paging against the currently used one that uses the blanket paging, Figure 31 illustrates the total signaling costs saved by the proposed strategies against the traditional one. It can be concluded that; all the proposed location management strategies outperforms the traditional one as they successfully reduce the total signaling cost.

CONCLUSION

This paper focuses on the paging problem hoping to minimize the paging costs under the time delay pre-defined bounds. A set of paging schemes with the corresponding location update (registration) procedures by employing the time-varying location probability have been proposed through the paper. The aim is to accurately estimate the MTs' most probable locations within each network registration area hopping to promote the paging hit rate with the minimal signaling and delay time costs. The main contributions of the paper is to developed two novel probability based location management schemes for PCS networks, which are Probability Based Location Management (PBLM) and Modified Probability Based Location Management (MPBLM) schemes. Then, a novel Hot Spots Topology (HST) for the PCS registration area is introduced. Based on the proposed HST, a novel location management strategy called the Flower Based Location Management (FBLM) is then introduced. Although the proposed location management strategies may increase the delay time before starting a call, they all successfully reduce the signaling cost. From another point of view; the delay time is in the allowable range. Excremental results have shown that the proposed location management strategies significantly reduce the paging cost under the time delay pre-defined constraints with a little increase in the registration cost.

REFERENCES

Abutaleb, A., & Li, V. (1997). Location Update Optimization in Personal Communication Systems. *International Journal of Wireless Networks*, *3*, 205–216. doi:10.1023/A:1019157217684

Akyildiz, I., Ho, H., & Lin, Y. (1996). Movement-Based Location Update and Selective Paging for PCS Networks. *IEEWACM Transactions on Networking*, *4*(4), 629–638. doi:10.1109/90.532871

Akyildiz, I., Ho, H., & Lin, Y. (1996). Movement-Based Location Update and Selective Paging for PCS Networks. *IEEWACM Transactions on Networking*, *4*(4), 629–638. doi:10.1109/90.532871

Akyildiz, I., McNair, J., Ho, J., Uzunalioglu, H., & Wang, W. (1999). Mobility Management in Next-Generation Wireless Systems. *Proceedings of the IEEE*, *87*, 1347–1384. doi:10.1109/5.775420

Aljadhai, A., & Znati, T. (2001). Predictive mobility support for QoS provisioning in mobile wireless environments. *IEEE Journal on Selected Areas in Communications*, *19*(10), 1915–1930. doi:10.1109/49.957307

Baheshti, B. (2007). Review of Location Management in Cellular Networks. In *Proceedings of the IEEE Systems, Application and Technology Conference (LISAT 2007)* (pp. 1-6).

Bar, A., Feng, Y., & Golin, M. (2007). Paging mobile users efficiently and optimally. In *Proceedings of the IEEE Infocom 2007*.

Bar, A., Kessler, I., & Sidi, M. (1995). Mobile Users: To Update or Not to Update? *ACM/Baltzer. Wireless Networks*, *1*(2), 175–185. doi:10.1007/BF01202540

Bejerano, Y., Smith, M., Naor, J., & Immorlica, N. (2006). Efficient Location Area Planning for Personal Communication Systems. *IEEE/ACM Transactions on Networking*, *14*(2). doi:10.1109/TNET.2006.872555

Bhadauria, V., & Sachan, R. (2009). The Cost effective Location Management Scheme using Mobility Information and Received Signal Strength of Mobile Users in Wireless Mobile Networks. *IEEE International Conference in Advance Computing (IACC)*, 878-882.

Biswash, S., & Kumar, C. (2009). Distance-Direction-Probability Based Location Management Scheme for Wireless Cellular Network. In *Proceedings of the National Seminar on Recent Advances on Information Technology (RAIT – 2009)* (pp. 30-38).

Biswash, S., & Kumar, C. (2009). Dynamic VLR Based Location Management Scheme for PCS Networks. In *Proceedings of the International IEEE Conference on Methods and Models in Computer Science (ICM2CS 09)* (pp. 276-280).

Brown, T., & Mohan, S. (1997). Mobility Management for Personal Communication Systems. *IEEE Transactions on Vehicular Technology*, *46*(2), 269–278. doi:10.1109/25.580765

Giner, V., & Escalle, P. (2009). A Lookahead Strategy for Movement-Based Location Update in Wireless Cellular Networks. In *Proceedings of the Sixth International Conference on Information Technology* (pp. 1171-1177).

Hwang, H., Chang, M., & Tseng, C. (2000). A Direction-Based Location Update Scheme with a Line-Paging Strategy for PCS Networks. *IEEE Communications Letters*, *4*(5), 149–151. doi:10.1109/4234.846494

Kim, K., & Choi, H. (2009). A Mobility Model and Performance Analysis in Wireless Cellular Network with General Distribution and Multi-Cell Model. *International Journal of Wireless Personal Communications*, *53*(2), 179–198. doi:10.1007/s11277-009-9678-3

Kim, S., Kim, I., Mani, V., Jun, H., & Agrawal, D. (2010). Partitioning of Mobile Network Into Location Areas Using Ant Colony Optimization. *International Journal of Innovative Computing, Information, and Control*, *1*(1), 39–44.

Kondepu, K., & Kumar, C. (2009). An Effective Pointer-Based HLR Location Registration Scheme in Location Management for PCS Networks. In *Proceedings of the First IEEE International Conference on Communication Systems and Networks (COMSNETS-2009)* (pp. 570-571).

Kondepu, K., Kumar, C., & Tripathi, R. (2008). Partially Overlapping Super Location Area (POSLA): An Efficient Scheme for Location Management in PCS Networks. In *Proceedings of the IEEE 67th Vehicular Technology Conference (VTC-2008)* (pp. 2182-2187).

Kumar, C., & Tripathi, R. (2008). A Review of Mobility Management Schemes for the Wireless Networks. In *Proceedings of the National Seminar on Frontiers in Electronics, Communication, Instrumentation & Information Technology (FE-CIIT-2008)* (pp. 109-115).

Lee, B., & Hwang, C. (1999). A Predictive paging scheme based on the movement direction of a mobile host. In *Proceeding of IEEE Vehicular Technology Conference (VTC)* (Vol. 4, pp. 2158-2162).

Markande, S., & Bodhe, K. (2009). Cartesian Coordinate System based Dynamic Location Management Scheme. *International Journal of Electronics Engineering Research*, *1*(1), 63–69.

Prajapati, N., Agravat, R., & Hasan, M. (2010). Simulated Annealing for Location Area Planning in Cellular Networks. *International journal on applications of graph theory in wireless ad hoc networks and sensor networks (Graph-Hoc)*, *2*(1).

Pratim, B., Anilesh, D., & Saradindu, P. (2009). A New Fuzzy Logic Based Dynamic Location Update Scheme For Mobile Cellular Networks. *Advances in Wireless and Mobile Communications (AWMC) international journal*, *2*(1).

Rajagopal, S., Srinivasan, R., Narayan, R., & Petit, X. (2002). GPS-based Predictive Resource Allocation In Cellular Networks. In *Proceeding of the IEEE international conference on networks (IEEE ICON'02)* (pp. 229-234).

Rose, C., & Yates, R. (1995). Minimizing the Average Cost of Paging under Delay Constraints. *International Journal of Wireless Networks, 1,* 211–219. doi:10.1007/BF01202543

Selvan, C., Shanmugalakshmi, R., & Nirmala, V. (2010). Location Management Technique to Reduce Complexity in Cellular Networks. *IJCSI International Journal of Computer Science Issues, 7*(1).

Singh, J., & Karnan, M. (2010). Using a Novel Intelligent Location Management Strategy in Cellular Networks. In *Proceedings of the International Conference on Signal Acquisition and Processing* (pp. 238-242).

Singh, J., & Karnan, M. (2010). Intelligent Location Management Using Soft Computing Technique. In *Proceedings of the Second International Conference on Communication Software and Networks (ICCSN)* (pp. 343-346).

Xiao, Y. (2003). A Dynamic Anchor-Cell Assisted Paging with an Optimal Timer for PCS Networks. *IEEE Communications Letters, 7*(8), 358–360. doi:10.1109/LCOMM.2003.813812

Xie, H., Tabbane, S., & Goodman, D. (1993). Dynamic Location Area Management and Performance Analysis. In *Proceedings of the 43rd IEEE Vehicular Technology Conference* (pp. 536-539).

Zhang, Y., Laurence, T., Jianhua, Y., & Zheng, M. (2009). Quantitative Analysis of Location Management and QoS in Wireless Networks. *International Journal of Network and Computer Applications, 32*(2), 483–489. doi:10.1016/j.jnca.2008.02.012

Zhao, C., Guo, W., & Liu, F. (2010). An adaptive distance-based location management of LEO system using coordinates approach. *The International Journal for Computation and Mathematics in Electrical and Electronic Engineering, 29*(2), 468–476. doi:10.1108/03321641011014922

This work was previously published in the International Journal of Information Communication Technologies and Human Development, Volume 3, Issue 1, edited by Susheel Chhabra and Hakikur Rahman, pp. 41-76, copyright 2011 by IGI Publishing (an imprint of IGI Global).

Chapter 4

E-Business in Agribusiness:
Investigating the E-Readiness of Australian Horticulture Firms

Alemayehu Molla
RMIT University, Australia

Konrad Peszynski
RMIT University, Australia

ABSTRACT

This paper explores the e-readiness of firms in the Australian horticulture supply chain. The paper draws from the perceived e-readiness model (PERM) and relies on data collected from a survey of firms in the horticulture sector in Australia. The results indicate that while horticulture firms demonstrate relative organizational preparation for the conduct of e-business, the value network within which they operate does not appear to encourage and support their endeavour. In particular, government and industry associations do not appear to play supportive roles in encouraging the use of e-business among members of the horticulture supply chain. This paper highlights factors that are likely to facilitate or inhibit e-business in agribusiness, an area lacking in research globally. Practitioners such as governments, horticulture associations, growers and growers' associations, and digital marketplace operators, through understanding the e-readiness factors affecting e-business, can make effective decisions to develop their support, capabilities and offerings respectively.

INTRODUCTION

The volume and value of transactions on the Internet are still on the rise and are predicted to continue unabated for the foreseeable future. Likewise, national and international institutions are investing in policy and regulatory frameworks as well as infrastructure and services to facilitate the conduct of e-business (UNCTAD, 2010). The World Economic Forum monitors and reports the progress of nations in terms of their conducive environment for e-business, and citizens', governments' and businesses' preparation to and actual use of e-business (Dutta & Mia, 2010). However,

DOI: 10.4018/978-1-4666-1957-9.ch004

the adoption and infusion of e-business into the different sectors of an economy and among different countries remain uneven.

Particularly, the use of e-business by primary industries is an area that is largely under-researched (Bryceson, 2006; European Commission, 2008; Ng, 2005). One of these primary industries is Horticulture. Horticulture comprises fruits, vegetables, nuts, nursery, extractive crops, cut flowers and turf growing. In addition to growers, the horticulture supply chain includes production, harvesting, post-harvest, logistics and marketing service providers and industry associations. In Australia, horticulture is an AU$ 9 billion industry, with an export value of more than 800 million, comprising 30,000 enterprises and employing more than 80,000 people (Horticulture Associated Limited, 2009). Horticulture in Australia is the second-largest and fastest growing industry in Agriculture. In social terms, the industry forms the livelihood of many communities and economies in rural and regional Australia. Australia considers the application of digital technologies to enhance the competitiveness of agriculture as a key national priority.

Past innovations in transport communication technologies such as the telegraph and telephone have had significant impacts on the conduct of agribusiness. For example, the meteoric rise of the European trading houses and the Chicago commodity exchange has been partly attributed to the telegraph technology (Clasen & Muller, 2006). Agriculture is also one of the early adopters of electronic trading (such as the Egg Clearing House and the electronic cotton trading mechanism) long before the Internet (Montealegre et al., 2004). Applications of Internet and mobile based decision support systems in the production end of the agribusiness value chain are pervasive (Antonopoulou et al., 2009; Wang et al., 2006). Nevertheless, some reports consider agribusiness as an inefficient industry (Clasen & Muller, 2006). The industry is largely comprised of small farmers. Most have been characterized by investing more

on the production end and less on the marketing and distribution end of the agribusiness supply chain (Taragola, 2010; Xiaoping et al., 2009; Samuel et al., 1996). The majority tend to work *in* the business rather than *on* the business. Because of uneven adoption of technologies along the supply chain, transaction costs tend to be higher (Mueller, 2001).

Horticulture could benefit from the use of e-commerce practices (Taragola, 2010; Xiaoping et al., 2009; Clasen & Muller, 2006). During the "irrational exuberance" period of e-business, a number of dot-com companies established e-markets catering for the needs of agribusinesses. However most of these businesses were unable to attract a critical mass of agribusiness (Ng, 2005). Some of the business models were not reflective of the realities of agribusiness trading and technological sophistication (Stricker et al., 2003). This begs a question in regards to the e-readiness of horticulture agribusinesses. E-readiness, however defined, of countries and organizations has attracted a lot of research and practitioner interest (Molla & Licker, 2005b). The World Economic Forum's Global Information Technology Report provides valuable e-readiness benchmarking data at a national level (Dutta & Mia, 2010). There is, however, a need for second generation e-readiness studies (European Commission, 2008; Choucri et al., 2003) that go beyond national level assessments to look at specific sectors and e-business domains.

The objective of this paper is therefore to address the gaps identified above and investigate the e-readiness of horticulture agribusinesses. Specific questions addressed are (1) what framework can be used to assess e-readiness in agribusiness in Australia? (2) to what extent agribusinesses are prepared to exploit the potential of e-business in Australia? (3) to what extent do factors such as firm size, export orientation and supply chain positions influence the e-readiness of agribusiness? (4) how does e-readiness influence the adoption of e-business practices? To answer these questions, data are collected from the horticulture sector in Australia.

The remainder of this paper is structured as follows: the next section will provide a background review of agribusiness in general and horticulture specifically and the use of e-business in horticulture. The subsequent section will explore the concept of e-readiness and provide a research framework that will shape the remainder of the paper. The research design will be presented, before an analysis of the results. This will then be followed by a discussion of the findings and a conclusion.

E-BUSINESS IN HORTICULTURE

The horticulture industry is an open and highly complex sector. The supply chain includes growers, farm input and other service suppliers, logistics providers, processors and exporters and industry associations. The industry faces a number of challenges across the supply chain (Xu, 2009; Hewett, 2006). Some of these include lack of visibility of the supply chain; high cost of transaction fulfillment and logistics services; ever increasing customer demand for detailed and up-to-date information about the environmental and social characteristics of products, information asymmetry that affects trust among the members of the chain, trading practices that isolate growers from the rest of the supply chain; and emerging trend for more customization of agricultural products and need for developing track and trace capabilities.

The advent of e-business has enormous potential to address some of these challenges and improve horticulture agribusinesses abilities to communicate and trade with their partners efficiently (Taragola et al., 2010; Xiaoping et al., 2009). The Internet potentially opens new venues for organizations to create flexible supply chains by offering high-speed communication and tight connectivity. It allows supply chain members to digitize their business processes and to address

problems of information access, information asymmetry and uncertainty (Barua et al., 2004; Antonopoulou et al., 2009). Better information flow in supply chain facilitates effective coordination and collaboration with other members of the chain (Premkumar, 2000). Through effective supply chain collaboration and administration, firms can improve their planning and execution, reduce cost, minimize overall risk and improve customer satisfaction (Premkumar, 2000; Swaminathan & Tayur, 2003). In other words, from remote farm monitoring to soliciting traders online, to improving coordination and collaboration along the supply chain, the possibilities and potential benefits of e-business for horticulture are enormous.

In terms of international usage of e-business in agribusiness, Burke (2009) identified extensive use of computers and the Internet, especially for basic ICT functions such as email, online purchasing and online business-related research, regardless of firm size across SMEs. However, website ownership was less widespread where larger SMEs were more likely than micro-enterprises to have a website. Canavari et al. (2010) analyzed decision preferences regarding trust and control in transactions in food networks as a basis for the design of e-business environments for food-supply networks. They found that trust in food-network transactions, decision preferences for transactions in fresh produce, grain, milk–dairy, and meat chains were identified for the chain levels' primary production to manufacturing.

In regards to e-marketplace adoption, Xiaoping et al. (2009) analyzed the benefits and factors of B2B e-marketplace adoption in agriculture through a case study of Shandong Shouguang Vegetable Trading Market Online (SSVTMO), which is an information publishing system, visual digital transaction system and online auction system based on medium long-term spot trading. This B2B e-marketplace contributes to value creation in the Chinese agriculture industry by providing personalized information services, control of the fulfillment process, strategic partner networks and controlling complexity. However, Xiaoping et al. (2009) concluded that e-marketplace adoption in agriculture still faces technology and collaboration barriers. Cloete and Doens (2008) in their research, concluded that the majority of key decision makers in the South African agricultural industry are already participating in e-commerce of some form and that South African agricultural companies are keen to get more involved in e-markets as ICT improve in the immediate future.

In Australia, specifically, various State and Federal governments have been keen to promote greater use of e-business models, processes and technologies along the agribusiness supply chain and many regional and national organizations and associations have implemented policies and systems to support such use. Some examples include:

- Ex-Doc, a federal government e-business initiative that allows horticultural exporters to electronically file health and/or phytosanitary documentations with the Australian Quarantine Inspection Service (AQIS) in order to get an export certification (Molla & Peszynski, 2009);
- Excel-erate, an e-business system developed by the Australian Banana Growers' Council that provides growers with a framework to benchmark their business activities and performance against peers and targets (Molla & Peszynski, 2009);
- National Livestock Identification System (NLIS) (Tonsor & Schroeder, 2006), which enables rapid and accurate tracing of cattle, post-slaughter through RFID. This helps reduce potential losses by tracking cattle in the event of a disease breakout such as Creutzfeldt-Jakob disease; and
- Adoption and diffusion of RFID in the Australian livestock industry and the factors that influence a farmers decision (Hossain & Quaddus, 2010a, 2010b).

However, in order to ascertain the adoption or prospective adoption of e-business technologies, businesses should be assessed in terms of e-readiness. E-readiness is a critical capability that affects organizations' ability to convert e-business potential into a reality. The next section discusses the background concepts of e-readiness and develops the research framework.

RESEARCH FRAMEWORK

Although the proliferation of national level e-readiness frameworks has minimized with the emergence of the World Economic Forum's Network Readiness Index, the organizational e-readiness literature still seems fragmented. One of the ground breaking works in assessing e-readiness and its impact on e-business adoption at an organizational level is the Perceived E-readiness Model (PERM) (Molla & Licker, 2005a). The PERM posits e-readiness as a two dimensional construct representing both organizational and external factors that are likely to influence the decision of a business to engage in e-business: perceived organizational e-readiness and perceived environmental e-readiness. *Perceived Organizational E-readiness* (POER) describes the awareness, commitment and the stock of human, business and technological resources of a firm relevant to e-business. *Perceived External E-readiness* (PEER) is the degree to which managers believe that market forces, government, and other supporting industries are ready to aid in their e-business implementation. The PERM is comprehensive for identifying and unifying the e-business, managerial, organizational, and environmental factors that may affect the readiness of an organization for e-business. A number of studies have empirically examined and validated the PERM (Molla & Licker, 2005b; Lai et al., 2006, 2007; Tan et al., 2007; Ahmed et al., 2007) including the agri-food sector (Volpentesta & Ammirato, 2007). We drew from this model to develop the conceptual guideline for our research.

Given the development of e-business over the last few years and the improvement in national ICT infrastructures, we argue that the concept indicated in Molla and Licker's PEER construct should be separated into two distinct sub-constructs of Perceived Value Network Readiness (PVNR) and Perceived Institutional Readiness (PISR). PVNR refers to a firm's assessment of the readiness of its customers, competitors and suppliers. A firm can have partial control over the resources of its partner organizations and can use its power position to influence its business partners' adoption of e-business (Barua et al., 2004). In addition, businesses whose main rivals and customers are engaged in e-business can find themselves under market pressure to use e-business. However, the readiness of a firm to conduct business electronically depends not only on its own and partner efforts, but also on the readiness of the institutional environment. Institutions such as government and professional and industry associations can influence a firm's e-readiness either formally (through direct subsides, loans or incentives) or informally (through norms and rules that encourage use of e-business). Support giving industries

that develop e-business solutions applicable to a particular domain and their cost structure can also affect e-readiness. PISR therefore refers to a firm's assessment of support from such forces. Figure 1 captures the revised PERM framework used in this study. The dotted box and arrows represent areas that are not covered in this current paper.

The revised PERM relies on three constructs - POER, PVNR and PISR, to determine a firm's level of preparation to conduct business electronically. Applied to horticulture agribusiness, *Awareness* refers to horticulture agribusinesses perception and comprehension of the benefits and risks of e-business. For example, to use digital market spaces dedicated to agricultural machinery, input and products, traders should be aware of first, its existence and second, the value it can add to their business (Clasen & Mueller, 2006). E-business is normally suited for trading in digitised goods and services. Agribusinesses mostly deal with physical products and their knowledge of how to apply ICTs to trade with less effort influences their e-readiness (Cloete & Doens, 2008; Mueller, 2001). Awareness of e-business value can lead to managerial commitment, which in turn is essential for developing resources and assets.

Figure 1. The revised perceived e-readiness model

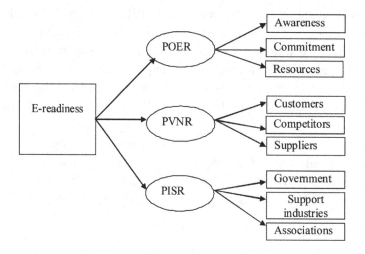

The physical nature of agricultural products, absence of uniform and widely accepted product standards and grades, the traditionally low information intensity of the agribusiness sector might dissuade managers from investing in e-business. The agribusiness value chain is archetypically dominated by family-owned small farmers. Small organizations have some distinct characteristics that either inhibit or facilitate e-business. Particularly, the commitment of the owner/manager is critical to any innovation decision and its implementation. That is, small size restricts access to relevant innovation/adoption resources such as human and technological. Stricker et al. (2003) opined that the ICT resources of most farmers are not very different to that of private households. Agribusinesses are also characterized by investing more on the production end and less on the marketing and distribution end of the agribusiness chain (Cameron, 1996). The level of automation is relatively limited (Montealegre et al., 2004). Lack of resources has been identified as one of the key determinants of organizational readiness, where resource has been defined as the stock of IT assets, finance and e-business know-how (Barua et al., 2004).

In terms of value network readiness, Montealegre et al.'s (2004) analysis of agricultural e-markets indicates that these markets have a limited life and low survival rate because of their inability to attract a critical mass of online traders. They further argue that despite predictions otherwise, agriculture might not be suitable for e-business. In Australia for example, studies indicate that agribusinesses generally lack supply chain management preparedness and make limited use of information technology (O'Keeffe & Mavondo, 2005). All these indicate that to assess the e-readiness of an agribusiness, it is important to assess the perception of the firm regarding the ability of its suppliers, competitors and customers to conduct business electronically.

In regard to supporting industries, and from an infrastructure point of view, rural areas generally fall on the negative side of the urban-rural digital divide with underdeveloped ICT infrastructure. E-business can only flourish in an environment where that ICT industry provides solutions that are both affordable and relevant to agribusiness (Pollard, 2003). Government's commitment to facilitate both the regulatory institutions and the development of rural ICT infrastructure can play a significant role in making e-business an attractive proposition for agribusinesses. Producer associations often wield a great deal of influential power in relation to the practice of commerce in agribusiness markets, which in turn, can have implications for the e-readiness of a firm. We will use the above nine variables to examine the e-readiness of firms in the Australian horticulture supply chain.

RESEARCH DESIGN

Operationalization of Constructs

The original perceived e-readiness instrument had 26 items for measuring the organizational e-readiness with a Cronbach alpha of 0.93; ten items for external e-readiness with a Cronbach alpha of 0.79 (Molla & Licker, 2005a). For the purpose of our study, we used a shorter version of this instrument by selecting only the items with higher factor loadings. We have also modified the wording of the items to make them more relevant to the horticulture sector. The final questionnaire consisted of six items related to organizational e-readiness, three items related to value network readiness, and four items related to institutional readiness. All items were based on a five point Likert scale ranging from 1=strongly disagree to 5=strongly agree. Table 1 summarizes the main constructs and the items used to operationalize them.

Table 1. Definition of constructs and items

Construct	Variables	Items
POER	Awareness	Our business has adequate awareness about the relevance of e-business to our practice
		We believe that e-business can provide benefits to our line of business
	Commitment	We are willing to provide the necessary resources for implementing e-business practices
	Resources	We have adequate resources to access and use the Internet
		Our business processes that can be automated have already been automated
		We have adequate managerial and technical capability for e-business implementations
PVNR	Customers	Our customers are ready to engage in e-business
	Suppliers	Our suppliers/partners are ready to engage in e-business
	Competitors	The nature of competition in horticulture encourages the use of e-business
PSIR	Support industries	E-business solutions and technologies relevant to the horticulture industry are widely available in Australia
	Associations	Industry association play active role in promoting the use of e-business
	Government	Government requires that we engage with them electronically
		Australian government provides incentives for e-business

Data Collection

The sample for data collection were 1335 micro, small, medium and large horticulture growers, horticulture associations, pre- and post-harvest service providers, horticulture marketing service providers, wholesalers and retailers. Of the 1335 mailed out questionnaires, 40 bounced back as undeliverable. Of the delivered questionnaires, 101 replied giving an 8% response rate. Nine were incomplete or have too many missing data points and are therefore excluded from the analysis. This resulted in 92 usable responses. Although less than 10% of the sample responded, our analysis of non-response bias indicates that, even if non-response bias cannot be completely ruled out, there was no significant difference between respondents and non-respondents. Therefore, cautioned generalization from this survey to others is possible. Summary information of the respondents is presented in Table 2 and further details of the sample including the non-response bias analysis are reported in Molla and Peszynski (2009, 2010).

DATA ANALYSIS

To analyse the data, first descriptive statistics were used to calculate the degree of agreement or disagreement on all the 13 items of e-readiness. The result is summarized in Table 3. As can be seen from Table 3, 70% appears to be committed to invest in resources to implement e-business practices; however, only 45% are willing to *provide* the resources. This is further reinforced by some 53% of the respondents who are convinced about the benefit of e-business to horticulture but a bit paradoxical when seen against the more than 50% who either do not believe or remain neutral as regards the adequacy of their awareness about the relevance of e-business. On the other hand, 64% (the highest disagreement percentage among the 13 items) perceive that the Australian government is not providing e-business incentives and 48% believe that industry associations has yet to play active role. 42% see that their suppliers and partners are not ready for e-business transaction. Indeed, of all the three dimensions of e-readiness,

Table 2. Summary of firms in the sample

Business age (years)	Percentage
<= 10	18%
11---25	36%
26-- 50	26%
51--100	8%
>101	2%
Missing	10%

Sector[1]	Percentage
Fruit Growers	50%
Vegetable growers	10%
Plant nurseries	13%
Cut flower and flower seeding	4%
Production and harvesting service	17%
Post-harvest and logistics services	13%
Marketing services	17%
Wholesale/retail	13%
Horticulture associations	11%

Business employee size (full time equivalent)	Percentage
Micro (<=4)	36%
Small (5-19)	37%
Medium (20-99)	3%
Large (>=100)	1%
Missing	23%

institutional readiness received the lowest percentage of agreement.

Only one-third of the respondents automated their business processes indicting limited potential for seamless business interaction and 25% believe that the government has set norms for e-business conduct. Overall, the perceived institutional e-readiness of the sample firms appears to be lower than both the organizational and perceived value network e-readiness. This perhaps shows that external push forces will not be that effective in developing the e-business capabilities of horticulture firms in Australia.

The descriptive statistics of the research variables based on Table 2's categorization is plotted in Figure 2.

Figure 2 reinforces the above observations that while the sample organizations showed a relatively better organizational e-readiness, the value network and institutional e-readiness is perceived as the least favorable. In particular, the government and industry associations have not been seen

as playing a supportive role in encouraging the use of e-business among members of the horticulture supply chain.

The data were further analyzed using the cluster analysis technique. Cluster analysis helps to organize data into meaningful structures, classify it into homogenous groups and develop taxonomies (Hair et al., 2005). Based on the K-means clustering algorithm, two clusters each containing 46 cases are produced. The between clusters variability (*Between SS 146*) is larger than the within cluster variability (*Within SS 26; F 169.88*) indicating a "good" and statistically significant classification. Figure 3 shows the e-readiness profile of the two groups.

The two groups differ in terms of their commitment, perceived competitive pressure and government support. In terms of organizational e-readiness, those firms that were relatively better prepared are more committed than those that are less prepared. In terms of value network e-readiness, better e-ready firms believe that the nature of competition in horticulture encourages the use of e-business whereas less e-ready firms are not influenced by competitive pressure. Better e-ready firms see government's support both in terms of providing incentives and in setting the norms for business-to-government or government-to-business as the least favorable of all the factors, whereas less e-ready firms see the competitive pressure (or the lack of it) as the least favorable.

Impact of Business Size and on E-Readiness

The Australian Bureau of Statistics classifies businesses with four or less full time employees (FTES) as micro; 5-19 as small; 20-99 as medium and the rest as large. On the basis of this classification, 1% of the respondents were large while the remaining 36, 37, and 3% were micro, small and medium, respectively. In order to assess if business size has any effect on e-readiness, the e-readiness profile of the businesses by size is plotted

Table 3. Response distribution

Items	Strongly Agree	Agree	Neutral	Disagree	Strongly Disagree	Mean	Std. Deviation
Our business has adequate awareness about the relevance of e-business to our practice	17%	28%	33%	11%	10%	3.3	1.2
We believe that e-business can provide benefits to our line of business	21%	32%	30%	8%	9%	3.5	1.2
We have adequate resources to access and use the internet	34%	36%	11%	8%	11%	3.7	1.3
Our business processes that can be automated have already been automated	11%	23%	38%	18%	11%	3	1.1
We have adequate managerial and technical capability for e-business implementations	15%	28%	26%	26%	5%	3.2	1.1
We are willing to provide the necessary resources for implementing e-business practices	12%	33%	35%	12%	9%	3.2	1.1
E-business solutions and technologies relevant to the horticulture industry are widely available in Australia	2%	18%	42%	26%	12%	2.7	1
Australian government provides incentives for e-business	1%	4%	32%	40%	24%	2.2	0.9
Industry association play active role in promoting the use of e-business	1%	19%	32%	29%	19%	2.5	1
Government requires that we engage with them electronically	6%	19%	38%	24%	14%	2.8	1.1
The nature of competition in horticulture encourages the use of e-business	9%	26%	31%	20%	14%	3	1.2
Our customers are ready to engage in e-business	6%	17%	40%	23%	14%	2.8	1.1
Our suppliers/partners are ready to engage in e-business	3%	20%	36%	28%	14%	2.7	1

Figure 2. E-readiness profile of sample firms

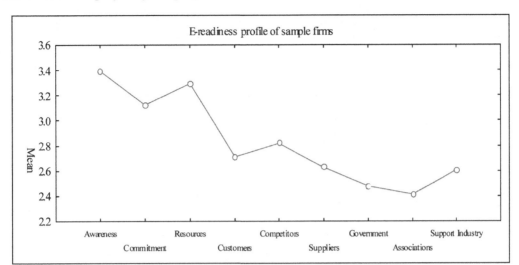

Examination of Figure 4 indicates that medium size organizations show a relatively better level of e-readiness on all the measures excepting awareness and competitive pressure than the rest of the groups. Micro organizations on the other hand show a relatively lower level of e-readiness. Further, a one way ANOVA (Table 4) with size as an independent predictor over e-readiness variables appears to indicate a statistically significant difference on perceived organizational e-readiness

(*Wilks Lambda= 0.678, F(12,143)=1.88, p=0.05*) due to size. The variables that cause the difference are awareness (*between SS 8.76, F= 3.28, p= 0.03*) and resources (*between SS 7.02, F= 2.97, p=0.04*). From Figure 4, it is clear that small organizations demonstrate a relatively better awareness of e-business compared to the rest of size categories where as large businesses appear to lack in e-resources.

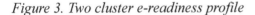

Figure 3. Two cluster e-readiness profile

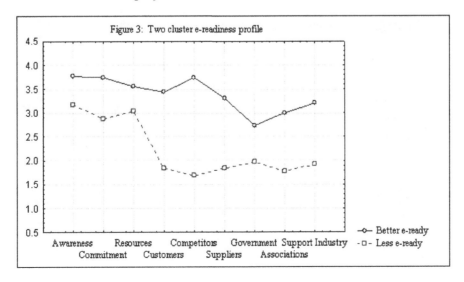

Figure 4. E-readiness profile by business size

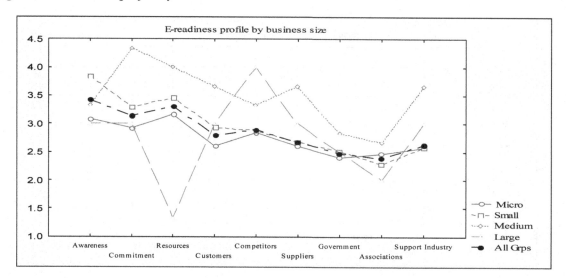

Impact of Sector on E-Readiness

The sample contained a mix of firms in the horticulture value chain including growers, pre-production, harvest and post-harvest service providers, retailers and wholesalers. In order to assess if the value chain position of the firms has any effect on e-readiness, the e-readiness profile of the businesses by supply chain position is plotted (Figure 5).

Based on Figure 5, horticulture associations demonstrate a relatively stronger profile of e-

readiness. Interesting to note in Figure 5 is how horticulture associations rate their commitment for e-business which according to Figure 2 is not something shared by other participants. The ANOVA test (*Wilks Lambda= 0.50, F(9, 36)=1.54, p=0.03*) with supply chain position as a predictor over e-readiness variables (Table 4) reveals that supply chain positions cause a statistically significant difference on e-readiness. The variables that are sensitive to supply chain position are commitment (*between SS 13.99, F= 2.81, p= 0.03*) and associations (*between SS 19.28, F=*

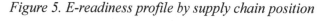

Figure 5. E-readiness profile by supply chain position

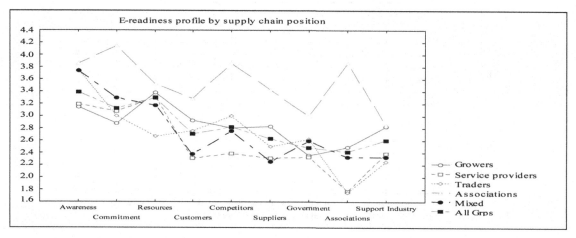

Table 4. Summary results of ANOVA tests

Predictor	Dependent variable	R²	SS	DF	F	P
Size	E-readiness	0.048	0.95	3	.965	0.42
	POER	*0.120*	*4.50*	*3*	*2.79*	*0.050.18*
	PVNR	0.080	4.72	3	1.71	0.36
	PISR	0.052	2.12	3	1.08	
Supply chain position	*E-readiness*	*0.349*	*13.9*	*4*	*2.81*	*0.03*
	POER	0.084	3.08	4	1.50	0.21
	PVNR	0.073	4.55	4	1.30	0.27
	PISR	0.123	5.06	4	2.33	0.06
Export Orientation	E-readiness	0.000	0.00	1	0.01	0.90
	POER	0.001	0.04	1	0.07	0.79
	PVNR	*0.121*	*2.65*	*1*	*2.20*	*0.02*
	PISR	0.012	0.51	1	0.87	0.35

4.99, p= 0.00). In the first case, growers appear to be least committed to e-business whereas in the second case, except the association themselves, none of the other members of the supply chain vote for the role the associations are playing in supporting e-business.

Impact of Export Orientation on E-Readiness

Of the respondents, 33% are involved in export activity. In order to assess if export orientation has any effect on e-readiness, the e-readiness profile is plotted (Figure 6). Inspection of Figure 6 indicates that no clear difference has emerged across the two groups. However, exporters appear to perceive the readiness of their value network, that is, customers, suppliers and competitors slightly better than that of non-exporters. On the other hand, non-exporters' perception of the institutional e-readiness is relatively better than that of exporters. A one way ANOVA (Table 5) with export orientation as an independent predictor produce a statistically significant difference in terms of perceived value network e-readiness (*Wilks Lambda=0.792, F(9, 760=2.2, p=0.02*).

Figure 6. E-readiness profile by export orientation

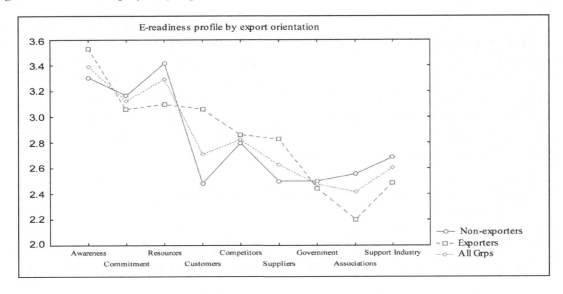

Table 5. Diffusion of e-business functions

Category	Item	Perform now	Plan to perform
Supply chain Information exchange	Exchanging information on growing, climatic conditions and harvest maturity electronically in real-time	18%	4%
	Use website to provide access to database relevant to horticulture	26%	2%
	Use website to provide information relevant to horticulture	33%	4%
Sense, monitor and track	Electronically monitor growth conditions of products on-farm and report the information back in real time	9%	4%
	Electronically monitor environmental conditions of containers in transit and report the information back in real time	2%	5%
	Use or provide on-line order/shipment tracking and tracing	11%	7%
Supply chain execution	Stock availability, prices or delivery times are shared with trading partners electronically in real-time	22%	8%
	Exchange trading information (orders, delivery notices, invoices, statements, remittance advice) online and in real-time	29%	8%
	Joining e-markets for on-line purchase or sale	6%	7%
Supply chain collaboration and co-ordination	Shipment and logistics management are facilitated with suppliers and distributors via the Internet	16%	3%
	On-line collaboration to schedule spraying and harvest programs	9%	7%
	Remote displaying/viewing of products during production	3%	3%
	Website supports online communities	7%	9%

The variable that are sensitive to export orientation difference is customers' pressure (*between SS 13.99, F= 2.81, p= 0.03*) and associations (*t= 2.38; DF= 68; p= 0.02*). It appears that those that are engaged in export business slightly tend perceive that their customers are ready to engage in e-business transactions.

The Effect of E-Readiness on E-Business

The effect of e-readiness can be seen through an inspection of the current level of diffusion of e- business functions performed electronically (Table 5) and through the correlation between e-readiness and e-business use. The use of the e-business and other Internet based technologies for performing 13 e-business functions were assessed. The justification for the selection of these 13 functions including the measurement's reliability is reported in Molla and Licker (2010).

The results indicate that, e-business practice in the Australian horticulture supply chain is at its infancy. Current e-business functions in horticulture tend to be informational (mostly via Websites) with limited sense, monitor and track, transactional and supply chain collaboration capabilities. Very few organizations e-enabled their supply chain execution activities with only 22% and 29% exchanging pre-transaction and post transaction trading information online respectively. In addition, use of e-markets for selling and/or buying is very limited. There is a statistically significant correlation between e-readiness and the maturity of the e-business functions (*r=0.533, p 0.001*).

DISCUSSION

In this paper we have investigated nine variables of e-readiness, classified into three constructs – organizational, value network and institutional e-readiness. Based on the analysis findings in the previous section, we discuss below five major empirical results and offer explanations and implications.

First, overall, the Australian horticulture supply chain lacks e-readiness. This seems to suggest that the agribusiness sector exhibit limited e-maturity and might require special attention to be integrated to Australia's digital economy. The finding is consistent with Australia's Business Readiness ranking which stands at 21, lower than for example Singapore (5), USA (8) and Korea (20) (Dutta & Mia, 2010). The empirical result demonstrates the differing level of internal, value network and institutional e-readiness. Furthermore, findings from this study generally indicate that the majority of organizations are small or micro players. As such, this impacts the amount of resources available to spend on implementing e-business solutions. This includes time and finances in implementing the necessary infrastructure and technologies.

Interestingly, when asked whether these companies are willing to allocate the necessary resources, the majority of respondents agreed. Therefore, it is argued that these organizations recognize the value of e-business for exporting both locally and internationally. The rationale behind this decision not to implement the necessary e-business technologies is that most organizations see their partners and suppliers as not ready to conduct business electronically. More support is required by industry associations in the agribusiness industry to promote and encourage the use of e-business. However, this support is not just limited to industry associations. Many organizations believe more encouragement is required by the government to support e-business.

Second, the effect of firm size on e-readiness is a mix of structural inertia and competitive pressure. The structural inertia associated with large firms appears to retard their internal e-business preparation. In economies where the e-business playing field for large and small firms is relatively more even, large firms usually face internal inertia

that negatively affects their e-business adoption (Xu et al., 2004). On the other hand, large firms appear to feel the competitive pressure and the need to develop e-business capabilities as more and more of their competitors engage in e-business.

Third, international operation shows some effect. Previous studies have mixed results about the relationship between e-business and export orientation. For instance, Raymond et al. (2005) argues that e-business might lead to expansion of export activities. Agribusinesses that might be facing sluggish demand for their produce might see e-business a vector of penetrating new export markets. Xu et al. (2004) argues state that global scope can be an incentive for e-business adoption due to potential transaction cost savings. On the other hand, the complexity of export operation and the higher costs to build e-business systems across country boundaries might dissuade exporting firms from adopting e-business. In our sample, it appears that these three effects seem to cancel one another out; hence we see the largely insignificant result of export orientation (excepting on customer readiness) as a predictor over e-readiness variables.

Fourth, there is an uneven profile of e-readiness along the horticulture supply chain with growers showing a lack of commitment for e-business. The horticulture industry is mainly spearheaded by growers. Most growers are small companies run by a family that hires help during peak seasons. The family would be on the farm daily for the majority of the day and would not have the time to explore or implement technology within their company. These growers seldom have the time to attend industry-relevant road-shows and demonstrations. Given the size of growers' organizations, it is not surprising that e-business is not seen as a priority. This implies that the nature of economic concentration and power imbalance among chain members is likely to affect the adoption, diffusion and assimilation of e-business and e-business-based alliances.

Fifth, the study has established that with existing implementation levels and further planned activities, the overall picture of e-business diffusion in the Australian horticulture supply chain is in its infancy. This finding can reflect Australian businesses' e-business usage ranking which stands at 30 below India (26) and far below United Kingdom (11) (Dutta and Mia, 2010). In fact, since 2002, Australia's e-business usage has fallen from third in 2003 to 24th in 2006/7 and 30th in 2009/10 (Figure 7). Capturing the implementation of electronically performed business functions provides a benchmark of the surveyed organizations' positioning.

CONCLUSION

This study was set out to address four basic questions and explore the e-readiness of firms in the horticulture supply chain in Australia. We draw from the Perceived E-readiness Model (PERM) and extend it into perceived organizational e-readiness, perceived value network readiness and perceived institutional readiness. The organizational e-readiness of a horticulture firm is captured through a manager's assessment of the firm's awareness, commitment, and resources. Likewise,

a manager's assessment of the e-readiness of suppliers and customers provides an insight into the firm's value network readiness while institutional readiness is captured in terms of government, associations and support industries.

Different members of the horticulture value chain demonstrate different combinations of e-readiness profiles. Overall though, survey respondents demonstrate a relatively stronger profile of organizational e-readiness and a weaker profile of value network e-readiness and weakest profile of institutional e-readiness. Of all the e-readiness variables, horticulture associations support for e-business in setting of norms (or rules of behavior) in business to association or association to business interactions received the lowest rating.

The study makes several contributions. First, it identifies the e-business strengths and weaknesses of a critical global economic sector that has received little e-business research attention, thus contributing towards a global understanding of the sector. Second, from an e-readiness point of view, we add to the empirical literature on sector and domain-specific e-readiness studies. Third from a theory perspective, we extend the Perceived E-readiness Model (PERM). Fourth, from a practitioner point of view, if agribusinesses are contemplating developing their e-business

Figure 7. Australia's e-business readiness and usage index Source: Based on Data from The World Economic Forum

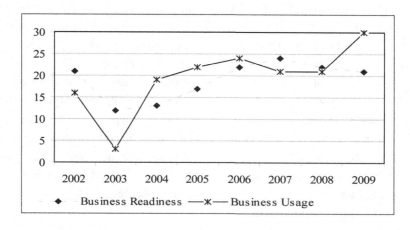

capabilities, our research indicates that it is instrumental that not only they consider their own resources and commitment but also the readiness of their supply chain and the wider institutions within which they operate in. Fifth, third party digital market makers can also benefit from the study as it reveals some of the potential inhibitors and enablers that might affect the participation of agribusinesses in e-markets.

A practical question that emerges from the discussion hitherto is how much of the desired attributes of e-readiness should businesses demonstrate? Or, putting it another way, how e-ready should organizations be? Our position is that e-readiness is a shifting goal post. The process requires continuous monitoring of organizational and environmental contexts and a capacity to routinely observe and understand organizations' e-business activity while simultaneously undertaking that activity. This is essential because the very organizational and environmental resources and conditions on which organizations draw to participate in e-business can at the same time be the basis for shaping and reproducing the internal and external environment under which they operate. As horticulture firms accumulate their capabilities, learn from their past experiences and interact with their environment (which in itself is in a state of change), their profile of e-readiness changes too

Finally, the study has some limitations in terms of its sample size and external validity. Ideally, a larger sample size is desirable for greater stability of the findings. Future research using a larger sample size is therefore needed to test if the results obtained here are replicable. Therefore, the extension of the findings documented here to other agribusiness industries in general and all horticulture firms in particular should be cautioned and requires further research. A replication of the study in other agribusiness industries will help shed light over interesting questions like: do the patterns identified in horticulture prevail in other sectors? What other relationships exist and how

are they different from the patterns that emerged in this study? The model described in this study constitutes a contribution to guide such further studies.

REFERENCES

Ahmed, M., Hussein, R., Minakhatun, R., & Islam, R. (2007). Building consumers' confidence in adopting e-commerce: A Malaysian case. *International Journal of Business and Systems Research*, *1*(2), 236–255. doi:10.1504/IJBSR.2007.015378

Antonopoulou, E., Karetsos, S. T., Maliappis, M., & Sideridis, A. B. (2009). Web and mobile technologies in a prototype DSS for major field crops. *Computers and Electronics in Agriculture*, *70*(2), 292–301. doi:10.1016/j.compag.2009.07.024

Barua, A., Konana, P., & Whinston, A. (2004). An empirical investigation of net-enabled business value. *Management Information Systems Quarterly*, *28*(4), 585–620.

Bryceson, K. P. (2006). *E issues in agribusiness, the what, why, how*. Oxford, UK: Cabi Publishers. doi:10.1079/9781845930714.0000

Burke, K. (2009). Internet ICT use in agriculture: Micro-enterprises and SMEs. *Journal of Developmental Entrepreneurship*, *14*, 233–254. doi:10.1142/S1084946709001260

Cameron, H. (1996). Investing in Australian agribusiness companies: A challenge to the industry. *Australasian Agribusiness Review, 4*(1).

Canavari, M., Fritz, M., Hofstede, G., Matopoulos, A., & Vlachopoulou, M. (2010). The role of trust in the transition from traditional to electronic B2B relationships in agri-food chains. *Computers and Electronics in Agriculture*, *70*, 321–327. doi:10.1016/j.compag.2009.08.014

Choucri, N., Maugis, V., Madnick, S., & Siegel, M. (2003). *Global e-readiness- for what?* Retrieved from http://ebusiness.mit.edu

Clasen, M., & Muller, R. (2006). Success factors of agribusiness digital marketplaces. *Electronic Markets, 16*(4), 349–360. doi:10.1080/10196780600999809

Cloete, E., & Doens, M. (2008). B2B e marketplace adoption in South African agriculture. *Information Technology for Development, 14*(3), 184–196. doi:10.1002/itdj.20105

Dutta, S., & Mia, I. (2010). *The global information technology report 2009/2010.* Geneva, Switzerland: World Economic Forum.

European Commission (EC). (2008). *The European e-business report 2008: The impact of ICT and e-business on firms, sectors and the economy.* Retrieved from www.ebusiness-watch. org/key_reports/synthesis_reports.htm

Hair, J. F., Black, W. C., & Babin, B. J. Anderson, R. E., & Tatham, R. L. (1995). *Multivariate data analysis* (6th ed.). Upper Saddle River, NJ: Prentice-Hall.

Hewett, E. W. (2006). Progressive challenges in horticultural supply chains: Some future challenges. *Acta Horticulturae, 712*(1), 39–50.

Horticulture Associated Limited (HAL). (2009). *Value of horticulture.* Retrieved from http://www. horticulture.com.au/areas_of_Investment/Environment/Climate/value_horticulture.asp

Hossain, M., & Quaddus, M. (2010a, March 30-April 1). An adoption diffusion model of RFID-based livestock management system in Australia. In *Proceedings of the IFIP WG 8.2/8.6 International Working Conference* on *Human Benefit through the Diffusion of Information Systems Design Science Research*, Perth, Australia (pp. 179-191).

Hossain, M., & Quaddus, M. (2010b). Impact of external environmental factors on RFID adoption in Australian livestock industry: An exploratory study. In *Proceedings of the Asia-Pacific Conference on Information Systems* (p. 171).

Lai, F., Dahui, L., Wang, J., & Hutchinson, J. (2006). An empirical investigation of the effects of e-readiness factors on e-business adoption in China's international trading industry. *International Journal of Electronic Business, 4*(3-4), 320–339. doi:10.1504/IJEB.2006.010869

Lai, F., Wang, J., Hsieh, C., & Chen, J. (2007). On network externalities, e-business adoption and information asymmetry. *Industrial Management & Data Systems, 107*(5), 728–746. doi:10.1108/02635570710750453

Molla, A., & Licker, P. (2005a). eCommerce adoption in developing countries: A model and instrument. *Information & Management, 42,* 877–899. doi:10.1016/j.im.2004.09.002

Molla, A., & Licker, P. (2005b). Perceived e-readiness factors in e-commerce adoption: An empirical investigation in a developing country. *International Journal of Electronic Commerce, 10*(1), 83–110.

Molla, A., & Peszynski, K. (2009). E-Business diffusion among Australian horticulture firms. *Australian Agribusiness Review, 17,* 78–93.

Molla, A., & Peszynski, K. (2010). The use of e-business in agribusiness: Investigating the influence of e-readiness and OTE factors. *Journal of Global Information Technology Management, 13*(1), 1–30.

Montealegre, F., Thompson, S., & Eales, J. (2004, June 12-15). An empirical analysis of the determinants of success of food and agribusiness e-commerce firms. In *Proceedings of the IAMA Forum Symposium*, Montreux, Switzerland.

Mueller, R. A. E. (2001). E-commerce and entrepreneurship in agricultural markets. *American Journal of Agricultural Economics, 83*(5), 1243–1249. doi:10.1111/0002-9092.00274

Ng, E. (2005). An empirical framework developed for selecting B2B e-business models: The case of Australian agribusiness firms. *Journal of Business and Industrial Marketing, 20*(4-5), 218–225. doi:10.1108/08858620510603891

O'Keeffe, M., & Mavondo, F. (2005). *Capabilities and competing: High performance in the food and beverage industry.* Retrieved from http://www.nfis.com.au/dmdocuments/final%20report.pdf

Pollard, C. (2003). E-service adoption and use in small farms in Australia: Lessons learned from a government-sponsored programme. *Journal of Global Information Technology Management, 6*(2), 45–66.

Premkumar, G. (2000). Interorganization systems and supply chain management: An information processing perspective. *Information Systems Management.*

Raymond, L., Bergeron, F., & Blili, S. (2005). The assimilation of e-business in Manufacturing SMEs: Determinants and effects on growth and internationalisation. *Electronic Markets, 15*(2), 106–118. doi:10.1080/10196780500083761

Stricker, S., Emmel, M., & Pape, J. (2003, July 5-9). Situation of agricultural ICT in Germany. In *Proceedings of the 4ᵗʰ Conference of the European Federation for Information Technology in Agriculture, Food and the Environment on Information Technology for a Better Agri-Food Sector, Environment and Rural Living,* Budapest, Hungary.

Swaminatha, J. M., & Tayur, S. R. (2003). Models for supply chains in e-business. *Management Science, 49*(10), 1387–1406. doi:10.1287/mnsc.49.10.1387.17309

Tan, J., Tyler, K., & Manica, A. (2007). Business-to-business adoption of eCommerce in China. *Information & Management, 44*(3), 332–351. doi:10.1016/j.im.2007.04.001

Tonsor, G. T., & Schroeder, T. C. (2006). Livestock identification: Lessons from the U.S. beef industry from the Australian system. *Journal of International Food & Agribusiness Marketing, 18*(4), 103–118. doi:10.1300/J047v18n03_07

UNCTAD. (2010). *Information economy report 2010: ICTs, enterprises and poverty alleviation.* New York, NY: United Nations.

Volpentesta, A. P., & Ammirato, S. (2007). Evaluating web interfaces of B2C e-commerce systems for typical agrifood products. *International Journal of Entrepreneurship and Innovation Management, 7*(1), 74–91. doi:10.1504/IJEIM.2007.012174

Wang, N., Zhang, N., & Wang, M. (2006). Wireless sensors in agriculture and food industry—recent development and future perspective. *Computers and Electronics in Agriculture, 50*(1), 1–14. doi:10.1016/j.compag.2005.09.003

Xiaoping, Z., Wu, C., Tian, D., & Zhang, X. (2009). B2B e-marketplace adoption in agriculture. *Journal of Software, 4*(3), 232–239.

Xu, S., Zhu, K., & Gibbs, J. (2004). Global technology, local adoption: A cross-country investigation of internet adoption by companies in the United States and China. *Electronic Markets, 14*(1), 13–24. doi:10.1080/1019678042000175261

Xu, X., Duan, Y., Fu, Z., & Liu, X. (2009). Internet usage in the fresh produce supply chain in China. *Computer and Computing Technologies in Agriculture II*, *3*, 2151–2160.

ENDNOTE

[1] Note that since some businesses operate in more than one category, the total is more than 92.

This work was previously published in the International Journal of Information Communication Technologies and Human Development, Volume 3, Issue 2, edited by Susheel Chhabra and Hakikur Rahman, pp. 1-18, copyright 2011 by IGI Publishing (an imprint of IGI Global).

Chapter 5
Success Factors in Public Access Computing for Development

Ricardo Gomez
University of Washington, USA

ABSTRACT

An exploratory, qualitative study in 25 countries around the world identifies success factors for centers that offer public access to Information and Communication Technologies (ICT). The study considered public libraries, telecenters, and cybercafés, and grouped the findings into four types of success factors: (1) understand and take care of local needs first, (2) train info mediaries and users, (3) build alliances with other venues and collaborate with other community services, and (4) strengthen sustainability. Results corroborate the findings of previous studies of libraries and of telecenters which identify success factors that include the four themes presented. However, this is the first systematic comparison across multiple countries to identify success factors in different types of public access venues. The findings highlight critical variables to be considered in policy decisions, funding allocations, and program implementation to reach underserved populations in developing countries with equitable access and meaningful use of ICT. They also provide valuable direction for future research to better understand the interactions between libraries, telecenters, and cybercafés as venues that can contribute to community development through public access to ICT.

INTRODUCTION

Public access to ICT can help marginalized communities gain access to new tools and sources of information that are critical to life in the 21st Century. What does public access to ICT look like in developing countries, and how can it be strengthened in order to make a better contribution to community development? This research identifies four key factors that contribute to the success of venues such as public libraries, cybercafés and telecenters. It is based on a qualitative study in 25 countries. The goal of the study was to better understand the landscape of public access to ICT across selected developing countries, inform policy and funding decisions, and contribute to

DOI: 10.4018/978-1-4666-1957-9.ch005

public knowledge about the importance of public access ICT for community development. By offering a better understanding of success factors, these findings can help strengthen venues that offer public access to ICT, and strengthen their contribution to improve the quality of life of marginalized communities around the world.

The last decade has seen an exponential growth of initiatives that offer public access to Information and Communication Technologies (ICT) in libraries, government and community centers, schools, cafés, and other small businesses. People visit libraries and other types of centers to use a computer, access the Internet, look for information, communicate with friends and family, play games, learn new things, or conduct business. Public access to ICT can play an important role in social and economic development, especially in underserved communities (Castells, 2007; Unwin, 2009; Warschauer, 2003). Although access to ICT alone does not automatically result in human development, it does enable new opportunities for human development beyond economic growth and western-style modernization.

Development is regarded as an activity to promote empowerment rather than economic modernization, as early development theories suggested(Servaes, 2008). "Empowerment is the mechanism by which individuals, organizations and communities gain control and mastery over social and economic conditions, over political processes, and over their own stories" (Melkote & Steeves, 2001, p. 366). This notion of development as empowerment is increasingly being adopted in the field of ICT for Development (ICT4D or ICTD). As noted by Unwin, "for many in the early 21st century, development is primarily seen as being concerned with economic growth, and identifying the ways in which the economic systems of poor countries can be made more effective...however, this is only one perspective, and others prefer to emphasize the importance of participation and empowerment in effective development...ICTs can have a key role to play in delivering both of

these contrasting interpretations of development" (Unwin, 2009, p. 1). Furthermore, "researchers have also argued that the impact of ICTs extends well beyond the economic domain, having positive spillover effects on numerous dimensions of social life. For example, these technologies have been harnessed to enhance learning [...], improve health [...], empower marginalized women [...], promote indigenous knowledge [...], and maintain good governance" (Ngwenyama & Morawczynski, 2009, p. 238).

This research project gathered detailed data regarding the current status, challenges, and lessons of public access computing across a broad spectrum of developing countries and emerging economies: Algeria, Argentina, Bangladesh, Brazil, Colombia, Costa Rica, Dominican Republic, Ecuador, Egypt, Georgia, Honduras, Indonesia, Kazakhstan, Kyrgyzstan, Malaysia, Moldova, Mongolia, Namibia, Nepal, Peru, Philippines, South Africa, Sri Lanka, Turkey, and Uganda (see country selection rationale below). Local research teams in each country conducted the study using a shared research design and rationale to examine how and why people use public access venues, with a particular emphasis on the information needs of underserved and marginalized populations. One of the salient results of the research project is a detailed analysis of the common factors that contribute to the success of public access ICT centers in 25 developing countries.

The next section will explore some of the most salient literature relevant to this topic, followed by a brief description of the research methods in this study. Research findings are then presented and discussed, ending with a final conclusion.

LITERATURE REVIEW

There have been many previous studies about ICT in public libraries, especially in the U.S.(Bertot, McClure, & Jaeger, 2008; Rutkauskiene, 2008; Walkinshaw, 2007), about telecenters for community development (Best & Kumar, 2008; Etta & Parvyn-Wamahiu, 2003; Gomez & Hunt, 1999; Parkinson, 2005; Proenza, Bastidas-Buch, & Montero, 2002)and, to a lesser degree, about cybercafés and their contribution to social and digital inclusion (Finquelievich & Prince, 2007; Gurol & Sevindik, 2007; Haseloff, 2005; Robinson, 2004). However, there are no previous studies that have done a systematic comparison of different types of venues across multiple countries, or studies that extract common factors that enable success in public access venues from a broad variety of settings, as undertaken in this study.

"Public access venue" is defined as one that offers public access to information and services that are available to all. It does not necessarily refer to information from public sources, or about services that are free. In recent years, two concepts have been used with regard to ICT public access: universality and usability (van Dijk, 2006; Vanderheiden, 2000). Universality means that all human beings are entitled to access information, and usability is the potential of a device or service to be utilized to meet users' needs. However, universal access is still an aspirational goal, not a reality in most parts of the world. For this reason, this research focused on libraries (open to the general population, funded by government sources, intended to meet local community information needs as a public service), telecenters (not-for profit centers open to the public, which offer ICT as part of their services or other activities that are intended to help community development, and may or may not charge a fee), and cybercafés (for-profit centers that are open to the public, offer ICT access and services, generally charge a fee, and do not necessarily have an intent to support community development).For the purpose of this study, the definition of public access venue includes cybercafés, which are open to the public even though they generally charge user fees. This study excludes schools and specialized libraries that are not open to the public because access is limited to students, faculty, and staff.

Threats to equitable ICT access also prevent equitable social and economic development. "The unequal access to technology between groups due to differences in demography, economic status, and locations has been suggested to affect worldwide globalization through Internet connectivity" (Kamssu, Siekpe, & Ellzy, 2004, p. 151). The findings of this study uncover distinct patterns underlying the global disparities that ICT access carries. These disparities increase in developing countries. As van Dijk observed:

Development is uneven as well, and increasingly so, because the overwhelming majority of the population does not participate at all. It is lagging behind compared with the diffusion of new media in the nodes of their own countries, and even more as compared with the developed countries. This majority has little access even to old media such as the telephone, radio, TV and the press and to essential services such as electricity[...] The few computers and network connections in developing countries are barely used for applications in agriculture, health, education, public works, water resources, public transportation, public information, population planning, rural and urban land development or public utilities. (van Dijk, 2006, p. 252)

For the discussion of success factors, it is important to clarify what constitutes success. Each community and each type of venue defines "success" its own way, and one person's failure may be another person's success. Furthermore, parameters for what constitutes success can change over time. Richard Heeks analyzes total failures, partial failures, and successes of information systems for developing countries, and defines "success" as instances where "most stakeholder groups attain their major goals and do not experience significant undesirable outcomes." He also notes that it is difficult to assess success or failure of ICT initiatives for development for lack of literature in general, lack of evaluation in particular, and excessive focus on case studies (Heeks, 2002, p. 102).

Gichoya analyzes factors for successful implementation of ICT projects in government, and points out that success factors are "occurrences whose presence or absence determines the success of an ICT project. They can be drivers or enablers [...] Their absence can cause failure and their presence can cause success" (Gichoya, 2005, p. 179). Based on these definitions, this research identifies and discusses the factors that contribute to equitable access and meaningful use of ICT by underserved sectors of the population through public access venues in the developing countries studied. "The evidence to date suggests that although ICTs can make a significant difference to the lives of poor and marginalized communities, many well-intentioned projects have failed" (Unwin, 2009, p. 26). By offering a better understanding of success factors across three types of public access centers in 25 countries, rather than just one type of center in one country or region, this research helps policy and decision-makers to focus their efforts on issues that make a difference and avoid the failures, partial or total, of past public access to ICT initiatives in developing countries.

RESEARCH METHODS

An iterative process of data collection and analysis (Barzilai-Nahon, Gomez, & Ambikar, 2009) was conducted in two phases: the first phase was exploratory, to test the initial framework and provide a preliminary analysis to help shape more in-depth data collection in each country. The research started using the Real Access/Real Impact framework, developed by Bridges.org in South Africa. After the preliminary analysis of the first phase, the team adapted and refined Real Access and called the resulting framework the Access, Capacity, and Environment (ACE) Framework, as a tool to understand the range of economic, political, educational, infrastructure, cultural,

organizational, and other factors that affect the way people use ICT in public access venues. The three pillars of the ACE Framework are: *Access* (physical access, suitability, and affordability of the venue; technology access; *Capacity*: (human capacity and training (users and staff); meeting local needs; social appropriation); and *Environment* (socio-cultural factors; political will and legal and regulatory framework; popular support). The ACE Framework offers a systematic way of understanding the different dimensions that affect the landscape of public access to ICT in its particular context.

Selection of Countries

Of 237 possible countries and territories in the world, the final 25 countries were selected based on four sets of criteria to allow us to focus on "middle of the pyramid" (Prahalad, 2006) countries. The criteria for country selection were based on:

1. **Demographic Data:** Size (exclude largest and smallest); population (exclude countries with population less than 1 million, and exclude India and China with the highest population); per capita income (exclude countries with per capita income over US$11,116); Human Development Index (HDI below 0.5) (Human Development Reports, 2007).
2. **Freedom of Expression** (based on Freedom House index) (Freedom House, 2007) and **Political Unrest** (based on US Department of State travel advisories) (http://travel. state.gov/travel/cis_pa_tw/cis_pa_tw_1168. html)
3. **Needs and Readiness Criteria:** (composite measures developed by research team using publicly available statistical data):
   a. **Needs Criteria**
      i. Income inequality (based on Gini index from United Nations Development Program (Human Development Reports, 2009).

ii. ICT usage per capita (based on United States Central Intelligence Agency World Factbook (2007).

iii. ICT cost (based on International Telecommunications Union (ITU) (2010) ICT Development Report.

b. **Readiness Criteria**

i. Composite measure of politics (based on World Economic Forum (2010) Global Information Technology Report, Transparency International's (2009) Corruption Perception Index, and World Bank's (2010) Worldwide Governance Indicators.

ii. Measure of ICT infrastructure

iii. ICTskills (based on ITU Opportunity Network Index and Opportunity Skills Index (International Telecommunications Union, 2007).

4. **Other Tipping Factors:** Existence of public library systems, regional distribution, and availability of qualified country research teams.

The country selection criteria are important to understand the scope of the success factors presented here. The study did not include the most populous countries (China and India) even though important changes in public access to ICT are taking place there, especially cybercafés in India. It does not include all the smallest or poorest countries (e.g., Haiti or The Gambia) even though they may need the most development assistance to provide broader public access to ICT, and it does not include the wealthiest countries (e.g., North America or the European Union) where the landscape of public access to ICT is significantly different than in developing countries. Finally, the study does not include countries where there are significant limitations to freedom of expression or political unrest (e.g., Iraq or Myanmar); conducting independent research in those countries is more difficult, and the landscape of public access to ICT might be significantly altered in those contexts as well.

Data Collection

Nineteen local research teams were chosen (with some researchers representing more than one country) following an international call for proposals. Lead researchers from each team were brought together twice, at the beginning and halfway through the research process, to discuss the purpose, methodology, and emerging findings of the study. Detailed country reports were prepared by each local research team using a report template. The template was designed to help each team organize their local fieldwork by answering detailed questions about Access, Capacity and Environment issues for each type of venue. In this way, the data collection in each country was based on and helped to further strengthen the ACE framework used in this study.

The teams conducted local research in local languages and reported their findings in English. All research teams used the following data collection methods:

- **Document Review:** Identify and review salient literature in the country, including existing statistical information about population, ICT penetration, public access venues, government policies, and previous research relevant to the study. About 40 documents per country were reviewed.

- **Expert Interviews:** Identify and conduct in-depth interviews with at least ten specialists in public access venues. Interview guides were prepared in each country depending on the local needs and context. About 10 to 15 interviews with experts were conducted per country.

- **Site Visits:** Identify, visit, and observe six or more venues of each type (library, telecenter, and cybercafé). Site visits were undertaken for a minimum of a half-day, making sure to include both urban and non-urban sites (ideally three of each). While selecting sites, research teams identified typical case samples of each type of venue, including both urban and non-urban sites. On average there were 20 visits per country with about 500 sites visited in total.

- **User Surveys:** User information was collected via a survey. A common survey instrument was used to administer a questionnaire. Each country team was allowed to add questions that they felt were relevant to the local context to enrich the overall body of evidence. At each site, every second or third user exiting the venue was surveyed. Teams surveyed between 40-50 users at each venue and conducted approximately 1000 surveys per country. Given limited time and resources, user surveys were not intended to provide statistically significant samples of the population or of the venues studied. The surveys were exploratory and the results indicated trends and patterns for comparison and further research.

- **Operator Interviews:** Identify at least one operator in each site visited and hold a structured interview to provide a more in-depth understanding of the venue, users, and environment. Around 20 operators were interviewed per country.

Data Analysis

After carefully reading each country report, the researchers did a detailed annotation of the success factors identified by each team. During a facilitated workshop and several group discussions, the different success factors across countries and venues were analyzed, grouped, and categorized,

all of which led to the formulation of the common themes described here. After finalizing the grouping and description of these factors, the authors went back to the detailed country reports to re-validate and document each one with examples from different countries. This process allowed combining multiple visions and readings of the rich data collected in the study, and resulted in higher-level, distilled lessons and success factors grounded in the data and the context of each country and venue.

Finally, the authors did a detailed re-reading and discussion of the country reports to identify and group trends in the data, selecting examples that best illustrated the key trends to make sure significant insights from local research partners were not missed.

Previous studies of particular countries and of libraries or telecenters have suggested success factors that included the four categories presented here. However, this is the first systematic comparison based on original research across multiple countries to identify success factors in different types of public access venues. The analysis devotes special attention to libraries and telecenters, since these venues generally intend to contribute to public wellbeing and development. Nonetheless, cybercafés are also included in the analysis.

This research is groundbreaking in its breadth and scope. There are no other studies that have systematically looked at the common success factors across different types of public access venues and multiple countries. However, the breadth of the study also means that it does not provide an in-depth analysis of a particular venue, country, or experience and the findings cannot be easily generalized without a clear understanding of the specific context and the analytic framework.

While the flexibility to translate and adapt the data collection tools to the needs and requirements of each country makes the study more locally appropriate, variations in the way data was collected or presented also makes the comparison of results across countries more problematic. The details discussed here may not be an in-depth reflection of any single country, but the combined results from 25 countries represent meaningful trends and patterns that clarify the common success factors for venues that offer public access to ICT.

Findings

The country reports prepared by local research teams were used as sources of evidence for the analysis. All original country reports are publicly available online (http://cis.washington.edu/land-scape/library/working-documents), and they are referred to by country to simplify the reading. Each local team of researchers identified around ten success factors for public access venues in their country, in addition to a detailed description and analysis of access, capacity and environment issues in each type of public access venue studied. These are some of the key themes found across all or most of the success factors identified in the study:

The critical importance of understanding and serving local needs first is clearly reflected in the findings and recommendations of the researchers in the majority of the countries studied. They show that for successful implementation of public access venues that serve local development, it is important to have accurate data about the user community, their information needs, and the information systems already in use, as described in the following examples. Nearly all 25 countries reported that while government efforts to expand ICT services are commendable, these efforts do not succeed if the ICT services fail to meet the needs of the local community.

Knowing the current distribution of information systems and practices in a community is an important consideration as well. The researchers in Honduras, for instance, stressed the need to avoid duplication of efforts. Malaysia's research team reported that the distribution of venues throughout the country was relatively successful, including rural areas where the venues are incorporated into post offices, libraries, or health clinics, i.e., "places where local communities can access them easily."

Training of users and, more importantly, of info mediaries (both formal and informal) is a strong common success factor across all 25 countries in this study. Honduras researchers described ICT training as "elemental" to success. They also suggested that the success of cybercafés ought to be passed along to society by taking responsibility for training the population in the use of ICT, thereby "boosting the capacities of the individuals and generat[ing] a major communal impact." Researchers in Indonesia took the call for increased digital literacy a step further, advocating universal free ICT training for all, especially for underserved populations, as critical to success. The Argentina team pointed out that information literacy training for users should encompass their real interests and needs in order "to make a real appropriation of ICTs." Similarly, the Ecuador team called for the development of ICT training programs that address the needs of special groups, such as "women, illiterates, non-Spanish speakers, and older people."

Researchers in Georgia extended the call for training to include venue operators, who should learn more about searching for health and education information. The Malaysia research team listed centralized training for venue operators as one of its main success factors. Along these lines, researchers in Kyrgyzstan noted the need to "renew training and education curriculum of the ICT specialists to meet requirements of fast growing industry." Local businesses could also benefit from training. Indonesia's team recommended that the government should support local e-commerce by training "small to medium businesses to enable them to upload their products to the Warmasif [telecenter] website." The Moldova team argued that librarians and venue operators should be trained in both fundraising and grant proposal development in order to acquire more financial support for ICT programs.

Most research teams in this study noted that collaboration takes many forms and leads to a variety of social impacts. Although this trend was noted across all countries, it was especially prevalent in Latin American countries. The Peruvian success factors for public access ICT centers included collaboration among similar venues: "the "rich practice of association and networking of special libraries… linked by a common theme: AIDS, agriculture, forestry… [They] may have different goals, but they share some common problems and may share learning."

In Costa Rica, some telecenters have partnered successfully with libraries. Telecenters organized within libraries benefit from an established infrastructure and the ability of librarians to teach ICT literacy. In turn, libraries that host telecenters can use the Internet to supplement out-of-date library resources and better serve their communities. Likewise, Brazilian researchers suggested some innovative solutions for creating new visions of public libraries – the creation of libraries in telecenters and vice versa. For example, a library in the state of Bahia bought computers with support from Identidade Digital, a program that supports telecenters.

From a different angle, Nepal's research team reported the use of a public/private partnership model where private, urban cybercafés serve "as capacity building and supporting partners for [public] telecenters in rural areas." The team in Nepal also calls for stronger "collaboration and networking among venues and relevant stakeholders to learn from each other and avoid duplication of effort." Moreover, the team in Honduras offers a slightly different perspective: "There should be joint efforts to know where the venues are located or where they try to settle, in order to avoid a double effort having several venues in the same place or, in other words, preventing a venue's sustainability to be affected due to the closeness of other venues that offer services at lower cost."

From a different angle, Nepal's research team reported the use of a public/private partnership

model where private, urban cybercafés serve "as capacity building and supporting partners for [public] telecenters in rural areas." This idea of public/private partnerships is now common in the development literature. Public access ICT venues offer a unique opportunity to develop a new partnership model that capitalizes on the strengths of both public (e.g., libraries, telecenters) and private (e.g., cybercafés) initiatives in a manner that will contribute to human development. Further research on the public/private partnership model is needed.

In this study, most research teams pointed out the importance of political sustainability, e.g., having government departments devoted to ICT development. Collaborating with other governmental units – a "Ministry of ICT," as it is called in Colombia – could oversee the provision of online content regarding citizens' rights and governmental services. Argentina's research team argued for the adoption of a transparent e-government concept: "Public information venues could become privileged places of training citizens to participate in E-Government and E-Democracy processes." Namibia's team advocated for more venues where citizens could access government information free of charge, such as information kiosks at Community Information Resource Centers.

Many countries highlighted the need for electricity and basic infrastructure to support ICT. Researchers in Bangladesh credited the relative success of urban (as opposed to rural) ICT venues to the availability of an uninterrupted power supply. The reports from Algeria, Ecuador, Georgia, Kyrgyzstan, and Peru all called for increased support of basic infrastructure in rural areas. Even where buildings, electricity, and computers were available, Internet access and bandwidth were problematic. The Bangladesh research team noted that "the performance of the venues with Internet connection is way better than the venues without Internet connection." In Brazil, researchers identified infrastructure in the form of "updated equipment (e.g., adequate computers, Internet bandwidth)" as a critical success factor for ICT.

The following section discusses the implications of these findings.

Discussion

In analyzing the findings, this research identified four themes as the most salient factors that enhance the success of public access venues, with a particular focus on meeting the needs of underserved communities. They are grouped under the headings of Access, Capacity and Environment, based on the ACE Framework that informed this research:

- **Access:** Understand and take care of local needs first
- **Capacity:** Train infomediaries and users
- **Environment:** Collaborate with other media and build alliances with other venues
- **Cross-Cutting:** Strengthen sustainability

Each one is discussed in more detail below, with examples from the study of libraries, telecenters, and cybercafés in all 25 countries.

Access: Understand and Take Care of Local Needs First

Successful implementation and maintenance of public access computing initiatives require a solid understanding of the information needs and resources of the communities they intend to serve. Most successful initiatives typically offer concrete solutions for specific issues of local contexts (e.g., their information needs) and the ability to build on existing practices in these communities. Community-needs assessment and social-development orientation are especially important if the public access initiatives are intended to reach underserved communities.

This finding is underscored by Schneiderman (2002, p. 2), many people cannot benefit from technology "because of high cost, unnecessary complexity, and lack of relevance to their needs." This assessment is also convergent with recent literature in the development field, where the concepts of participation, empowerment, and social capital are now fully integrated into development work (Cadiz, 2005; Servaes & Malikhao, 2005). Meeting local needs is also a cornerstone of community approaches in the field of library and information science (Aabo, 2005; Hillenbrand, 2005; Worcester & Westbrook, 2004), as well as Community Informatics (CI) or ICT for Development (Gurstein, 2000; Heeks, 2009; Raiti, 2007; Unwin, 2009).

There were several suggestions as to how public access centers could support local needs. For example, the creation of websites in local languages and with local content information (e.g., health, environment, and agriculture) and websites for youth (e.g., focusing on education and knowledge building) were frequently noted as critical for success. Bangladesh, Georgia, Sri Lanka, Peru, Namibia, South Africa, and Kazakhstan are all countries that deal with multiple languages spoken throughout the country. Georgia's research team, for instance, noted that information portals should disseminate information in both Armenian and Azerbaijani. For certain regions in Peru, the team recommended online information should be more readily available in Quechua, an indigenous language spoken by a large proportion of the population.

Local communities also need to take ownership of the development of ICT programs and content, engaging community members to create practical solutions that improve the lives of individuals in the community. This idea of "social appropriation of ICT" is expressed in different ways across the 25 countries. Social appropriation is a concept that is difficult to translate from its Spanish original, *apropiación social*. It refers to the local community's capacity to take ownership of ICT tools, incorporate the tools into their daily lives and routines, and turn the tools into practical solutions that help meet their needs. There was much interest in the concept of social appropriation by all researchers during the preliminary analysis of early research results, so it is not surprising most of them were able to document instances of social appropriation of ICT in the final country reports. For example, researchers in Sri Lanka recommended community involvement in order to "give ownership to the project and prevent it from being a purely top down exercise." In Argentina and the Dominican Republic, researchers reported that the population wanted to incorporate ICT use into their daily lives and to leverage building community. In Honduras, for example, community input has shown the potential to transform telecenters and libraries into spaces for knowledge exchange by creating meeting places not only for literacy training but also for "discussion, action, and struggles." In Bangladesh, telecenters were found to be successful, especially because they "are attracting users, as they could identify appropriate content and services."

Many of the research teams emphasized that for ICT to reach and effectively serve local communities, they need to promote a positive information culture that includes constructive attitudes to information sharing and public awareness of ICT services. Public libraries in particular are undermined by perceptions that they service students only, produce old and outdated information, or simply are not "cool" to visit. Mongolia's team described traditional libraries as places "where study happened, intellect was developed and newspapers were read." People traditionally consider public libraries as a place to go for reading and accessing print materials, and most research teams suggested that libraries need to create a new public image that embraces technology and offers ICT services. To address current perceptions of libraries as places strictly for students, other adult groups need to be made aware of the library's information services. Library outreach activities should also align with patrons' cultural and entertainment practices. The Dominican Republic's team, for instance, suggested that library

coordinators should develop "fun" activities, such as organizing chess tournaments to draw people into the library. An example of successful public libraries is found in Argentina: "In public and popular libraries, the success factors are their strong integration into communities, the gratuity and accessibility of their services, the varied activities they supply, the support they receive from the State, and the information and exchange networks they have established."

Creating a positive-awareness campaign and taking calculated risks might revive public libraries from the "current state of decay, lack of capacity, and tired mentality" observed by researchers in Mongolia and elsewhere. Moreover, public access venues need to address people's perceptions of information. The former Soviet republics have an extensive network of public libraries. Researchers in these countries noted that the extensive yet decrepit public library system in these countries no longer serves the community's actual needs. In Georgia, researchers found that many people believed they could not find high-quality information at the library because the building was poorly maintained (i.e., no heat, no funding). Perceptions affect the credibility of the venues more than the actual content or services they provide.

Utilizing positive awareness and public relations campaigns to improve images of public libraries can generate ideas to secure additional funding. For example, the Kazakhstan team recommended that the library system study the tactics used by banks in that country, which have been successful in raising public awareness of their mission and services. In the same way, Moldova's researchers suggested that local public authorities, such as the mayor or local councils, get involved in the publicity campaigns. The involvement of local authorities would also help local governments become aware of the needs of underserved populations.

Most cybercafés have no explicit strategy to assess community needs. They rely on growing demand for ICT services, even in marginalized communities, and the population's capacity to pay for these services. In this sense the mission of cybercafés is simpler, and their success does not require a sophisticated understanding of local needs or ways in which ICT can contribute to development. Libraries and telecenters do have a development goal, and they require a more in-depth understanding of local needs and how to serve the local population, not just with access to computers but with services that contribute to development.

Capacity: Train Infomediaries and Users

The second theme in the success factors that emerged from this study in 25 countries has to do with training users and operators of the public access venues. If communities are to benefit from public access to ICT, both users and operators need to have the basic training and know-how in order to use and operate the services. Building this capacity starts with basic literacy (reading and writing) training and includes basic digital literacy (use of computer, its basic applications and features). Strengthening the training and capacities of librarians and other operators of public access venues is also critical to the operator's success, especially if they are to provide guidance, training, and support services to users, directly or indirectly. Trained and motivated librarians and operators make better information brokers, or "infomediaries," who help make information resources more meaningful to the local communities, and help bring local knowledge and information resources to the public access venues. In the words of the research team from Bangladesh:

Either we have to make whole population literate over-night or we have to develop some mechanisms to make disadvantaged people immediately access benefit of ICTs. The research shows that one of such mechanisms is Infomediary deployed in non-urban telecenters. Infomediary is a human

interface between digital content and illiterate or print-disable people. The research shows, where there is an infomediary the user profiles are broader including illiterate people. Furthermore, the performance of the infomediary influences the performance of a telecenter, where such infomediary was found.

Formal infomediaries include librarians and operators of telecenters and cybercafés. As part of a broader literature review on ICT impact, Sey and Fellows (2009) point out that infomediaries "have been found to be important contributors to the viability and sustainability of a public access venue." Infomediaries are critical to the success of telecenters in particular (Best & Kumar, 2008; Gomez & Hunt, 1999).

Extending the notion beyond the formal role of librarians or telecenter operators, other informal infomediaries play a critical role as well. Abrahamson and Fisher (2007) describe this informal role as "lay information mediary behavior" (LIMB). For example, LIMB refers to the behavior of a person who finds information for another member of the family, for a friend, or a neighbor. This indirect usage was also analyzed by Schilderman (2002) who suggested that "social networks are the foremost source of information of the urban poor" and that the poor tend to believe people they trust rather than perhaps more informed contacts with which they do not have close ties. He then developed the concept of "key informants" (aka "infomediaries") defined as "people inside, or sometimes outside, a community who are knowledgeable in particular livelihoods aspects, and are willing to share that knowledge" (Schilderman, 2002, p. 5). In order to tap into this resource to help serve the information needs of this underserved population, he cited a number of success factors, including: involvement of the poor themselves as equal partners, building on local knowledge, the use of community-based communication methods, and building the capacity of community-based organizations and key individuals within them.

More research on LIMBs and the resulting indirect usage of ICT can help us better understand the role of Infomediaries and the diffuse effects of ICT use in public access locations, especially when dealing with underserved and marginalized communities.

In sum, training users and Infomediaries to become effective users of ICT is critical to the success of public access venues. While cybercafés tend to offer limited training to users, libraries and telecenters have a strong role to play in this domain. These venues offer basic digital literacy training and help users (and indirect beneficiaries who may be helped by these users) make effective use of ICT for community development. To do this well, libraries and telecenters need to start by making sure their staff (librarians and operators) are digitally literate and that they can, in turn, help train and support users, particularly those most marginalized and excluded by society. It can even be seen as a measure of success that libraries and telecenters train users who then go to cybercafés to make use of ICT services to advance their development goals. Public access to ICT is not a single or isolated event, but a system of practices and opportunities that enable underserved communities to take advantage of the ICT tools to promote empowerment and development. In this venture, there is a role for libraries, for telecenters and for cybercafés. And they will be all more successful if they work together.

Environment: Strengthen Alliances with Other Public Access Venues and Collaborate with Other Media

The most striking finding across all countries studied, indicated by most research teams in this study, is that collaboration among and between different public access venues is limited but can yield powerful results if it is promoted and strengthened. Networks of libraries, telecenter associations, and collaboration between cybercafés can be enhanced by partnerships between these venues within one community, which will make public access to ICT stronger and more effective at serving the needs of the local population. The collaborative model is convergent with current trends in understanding the power of networks as a distinctive characteristic of the information society. "Actors are no longer independent…They are dependent on each other. In networks, actors make agreements and more or less freely engage in associations. They cooperate on the basis of complementary strengths and they become interdependent" (van Dijk, 2006, p. 73). The research team in the Philippines recommends: "Internet cafe owners should organize themselves locally, regionally or nationally in order to have a proper forum where they can air their concerns regarding issues that may affect their businesses. They should engage their LGUs [local governments] in order to have a stake in ICT-related policies. They should also call for the creation of a local ICT council."

Public access venues were more successful when they extended partnerships and collaboration beyond public access venues to include other community services and media important to the community. Most notably, these collaborations include successful partnerships with community radio stations, health clinics, community organizations and government offices, as well as creative uses of mobile phones in combination with public access venues. This model is convergent with current research in other domains of public services. "Public services are now often provided by a complex network of partnerships, contracts, and alliances between government agencies, nonprofit organizations, and businesses, rather than by hierarchical government bureaucracy" (Huang & Provan, 2007).

Collaboration opportunities exist with other development organizations as well. For example, Namibia established information kiosks in Community Information Resource Centers for different community development activities. In South Africa, where HIV/AIDS centers operate as public access ICT venues, researchers noted the potential for leveraging further collaboration for program implementation: "The scoping of the HIV/AIDS centers strongly suggests that there is an opportunity to explore a programmatic intervention by ICT funders in partnership with one or more of the HIV/AIDS programs discussed."

Similarly, researchers from other countries offered innovative, concrete suggestions of the relation between public access to ICT and other media, most notably community radio and mobile phones. As Kazakhstan's team explained, "Combining various media types allows maximizing the impact and ensuring all groups involved are covered. Radio may not be appealing to young Internet users while rural elderly population will never choose [a different] option." Researchers in Algeria recommend the "mobilization of public mass media (Radio and TVs) to educate people (especially disabled and illiterate people) on best information practices." Uganda's researchers argued for "strategic establishment of a community radio at every Public Library facility per district." A strong linkage between public access venues and community radio is detected and requires further investigation.

Teams studying the Philippines and Argentina both observed that these countries have greater access to cell phones than computers and, therefore, recommended expansion of government services through cell phones. The Philippines' research team specifically advocated for the expansion of text messaging services with development-oriented information. Finally, Mongolia's team promoted "the range of information vectors (including radio, TV and mobile phone) that can be developed at community level." While this study did not explore the interaction of ICT in public access venues with other technologies such as community radio or mobile phones, additional research is warranted to get a better understanding of the opportunities presented by better collaboration with other media.

Cross-Cutting: Strengthen Sustainability

The ACE Framework, based on analyzing Access, Capacity and Environment for public access venues in 25 developing countries, was a useful tool to uncover key success factors for libraries, telecenters and cybercafés. Cross-cutting all dimensions, sustainability is a key challenge for all types of venues, in all countries studied, although it manifests itself in different ways in each case.

Sustainability of public access venues is a critical issue that touches on multiple dimensions: financial, political, technical, social, and cultural. Sustainability crosses all dimensions of access, capacity and environment of public access venues. Government funding and support for public libraries has been declining in many countries, and donors' interest in telecenters has declined as well, threatening the sustainability of these public access venues. Successful telecenters have found creative ways to generate revenues, and popular libraries have explored innovative ways to build strong community support. But local community involvement alone cannot ensure the sustainability of public access ICT. Governments must also work to create an environment that strengthens and sustains public access to information and ICT resources if they are to meet the needs of underserved communities.

Challenges to sustainability have been extensively reported in the literature about public access to ICT, especially for the telecenters (Bailey, 2009; Best & Kumar, 2008; Gurstein, 2005; Jensen & Esterhuysen, 2001; Proenza, 2001; Toyama et al., 2005). Many telecenter projects have simply failed after the original donors have left. Mayanja (2006) observed, "financial and social sustainability of telecenters remains one of the key challenges of the digital inclusion programming more than a decade after."

In an editorial of the *Journal of Community Informatics* dedicated to telecenter sustainability, Michael Gurstein suggests:

What is meant by "sustainability" in the ICT context is less a matter of a broad "configuration of civilization" and more to do with day to day slogging by community members in meeting the payroll and keeping the machines running amidst the wear and tear of daily life (both physical and electronic) while always keeping in mind how the technology could be used to respond to the needs (and opportunities) of their local communities. ... When we are speaking of "sustainability" in the context of ICTs we should perhaps be speaking of "sustainabilities" rather than "sustainability," for there are many dimensions of this issue which go much beyond the simple economic and the meeting of weekly payrolls. (Gurstein, 2005, p. 2)

As succinctly summed up by the team in Costa Rica, the "digital divide is only a small part of the economic divide." When governments plan and implement ICT services, they should be mindful of the needs of disenfranchised and marginalized communities. Kazakhstan's research team advocated "affirmative action" to serve the needs of marginalized groups in order to create a more inclusive information society. The country's Program on Reduction of Information Inequity has so far failed to identify vulnerable groups, such as the homeless or the disabled. These groups in particular need extra assistance to access information, including finding government services.

In addition to financial and political sustainability, technological sustainability needs to be ensured by making technology work in low-resource environments. Public access venues aimed at underserved communities frequently face technical limitations due to working in resource-constrained environments: poor electricity, connectivity, and outdated technology make it especially hard to operate effectively. Making ICT sustainable anywhere obviously requires basic infrastructure: electricity, equipment, and Internet connections. This infrastructure also includes support systems (e.g., technical support, trouble-shooting, and networks) to maintain information systems and ensure that they function efficiently, even in environments where resources are scarce.

Beyond basic infrastructure, further analysis of the success factors and recommendations revealed that many of the research teams addressed additional issues of sustainability. The Costa Rican team attributed the failure of many rural telecenters to the challenges beyond installation, including maintenance of the equipment and software updates. Because only government technicians are permitted to repair equipment or address software problems and viruses at these telecenters, many of them have only two out of six computers working at any given time while they await technical support. The Bangladesh team expressed this problem as a need to "strengthen the support system (e.g., technical, know-how, and operational) for the public access venues."

Maintenance is only part of the true cost of sustainable infrastructure. Ongoing costs must be considered in addition to initial investment. Researchers in Namibia found that "the cost of computers and their software is limiting their availability. Government should therefore have a policy to support the use of Free and Open Source software." In Bangladesh, where the availability of electricity in rural areas is "dismal" and unlikely to change soon, the recommendation is for an investment in "low power consuming device[s] with higher battery life" in order to bring ICT services to the public. These recommendations point to the need for forethought and planning in order to make technology sustainable in low-resource environments.

Issues of social and cultural sustainability were only tangentially reflected by the majority of the research teams, and yet they are critical to the success of any initiative that is to contribute to development (Melkote & Steeves, 2001). More research is needed to explore and better understand the implications of cultural and social sustainability of public access centers.

CONCLUSION

Understanding the factors that contribute to the success of ICT venues in the communities they serve makes it easier to fulfill the promise of ICT as a tool for empowerment and human development. Awareness of the success factors will also help avoid the partial or total failures of public access initiatives. Drawing on data from a study of public libraries, telecenters, and cybercafés in 25 developing countries, this research presents four common success factors for venues that offer public access to ICT:

- **Understand and Take Care of Local Needs First:** Failure to understand and respond to local needs may be the most frequent reason for failure of public access initiatives to ICT (and many other development projects). In public access ICT initiatives, meeting local needs is most clearly expressed in the production and availability of locally relevant content, available in local languages, and with appropriate support and help for users from marginalized groups to make effective use of such content (Gould, Gomez, & Camacho, 2010). Sound community needs assessment and continued interaction and reassessment to adapt to changing needs is a critical factor in the success of public access ICT initiatives, particularly to help realize the community development role of libraries and telecenters.

- **Train Infomediaries and Users:** Effective training includes training people to use the technologies and services, as well as training infomediaries (librarians, operators) to support and serve the needs of the disadvantaged communities who use their venues. Schilderman (2002) identified seven key characteristics of effective infomediaries: their capacity to provide information in an accessible format; their willingness to share information rather than hold onto it; their ability to get hold of information and adapt it to a local context; their experience, education, knowledge and reliability; their accessibility, proximity and helpfulness; their social sensitivity and capacity to involve residents; and their leadership qualities, influence and moral authority (Schilderman, 2002, p. 28). Combining all these with technical proficiency and digital literacy may be a tall order for any librarian, operator or staff of a library, telecenter or cybercafé. But effective attention to these skills and capacities may be, in turn, the solution to creating a new role for libraries and telecenters in the community.

- **Build Alliances with Other Venues:** In the literature, as in the practice of most of the local research teams that worked in this study, research on libraries, telecenters, or cybercafés tends to focus on one type of venue and excludes the other two types. With few exceptions, bridges for collaboration or comparison between different types of venues are rare. In fact, some of the research partners were surprised to discover similarities and opportunities for convergence with the other venue types. With telecenters and, especially, libraries in developing countries facing a crisis of credibility and trust (Gomez & Gould, 2010), partnerships between libraries, telecenters, and cybercafés might be the key to their survival and sustained relevance. More research on opportunities for collaboration and partnerships between libraries, telecenters, and cybercafés is needed to inform specific recommendations.

- **Collaborate with Other Media and Community Services:** Just as libraries, telecenters, and cybercafés need to work together and capitalize on their respective strengths, other media and community services complement and support the role of public access ICT initiatives and their contribution to development. Collaboration with community radio stations and partnership with community organizations that offer training, job placement, childcare, adult education, etc. are required for public access ICT to effectively contribute to human development. For example, more than ICT skills alone, soft skills and support services such as "training in general job-seeking skills (e.g., punctuality, interviewing, appropriate attire) and assistance with practical steps (e.g., job search, application process, transportation)" are essential to help low-income populations increase income and employment (Garrido, Rothschild, & Oumar, 2009). The interaction between public access venues and mobile phones also needs to be further investigated. While some believe mobile phones will replace computers and the proliferation of mobile phones in developing countries makes public access computers superfluous (Veeraraghavan, Yasodhar, & Toyama, 2009), it is more likely that mobile phones complement, not replace the information services and opportunities offered by computers and public access ICT.

- **Strengthen Sustainability:** Finally, this study underscores the importance of strengthening the sustainability of public access venues. Financial sustainability appears to be more easily accomplished in cybercafés, a phenomenon reported a decade ago by Proenza (2001). On the other hand, cybercafés experience a strong tension between their need for revenue generation and serving the needs of community development. All venues face difficulties related to technical sustainability (e.g., equipment maintenance and obsolescence), and all venues face different challenges related to political, social and cultural sustainability. More successful venues tend to have stronger political and community support, and serve local populations in a local and culturally appropriate manner. Nonetheless, financial

sustainability gets more attention than other types of sustainability for public access venues across all countries in this study. More research is needed on differences and similarities related to political, cultural, and social sustainability across public access venues. A larger question also warrants further study: if cybercafés are more successfully offering sustainable public access to ICT, what is the role for libraries and telecenters to ensure that public access effectively contributes to community development?

While deploying more infrastructure and technology is important, this research highlights the importance of attending to other issues that require attention for public access venues to be successful. Understanding local needs, providing effective training, supporting partnerships and strengthening sustainability are all critical aspects that require dedicated attention and resources, even though these activities do not necessarily give the quick illusion of success given by installing new computers in libraries or telecenters. The results of this study underscore the importance of a more comprehensive strategy to support public access to ICT, one that goes beyond setting up computers for public use.

This is the first systematic comparison across multiple countries to identify success factors in different types of public access venues. Previous studies identified similar success factors in one country or one type of venue. However, the broad-based validation in this study provides solid guidance to policymakers, donors, and practitioners to focus their efforts where they can make the most difference to the communities they serve: beyond offering public access alone, venues need to understand local needs, provide effective training, support partnerships and collaboration, and strengthen sustainability of the venues. Furthermore, the findings discussed here provide clear direction for future research in order to strengthen ways to offer public access to ICT for underserved communities around the world.

ACKNOWLEDGMENT

The author wants to acknowledge contributions by Melody Clark, Pamela Kilborn-Miller, Sylvain Cibangu, Elizabeth Mitchell, Khue Duong, Hepzibah Schenkelberg, Elizabeth Gould, and the Technology & Social Change group at the University of Washington, in addition to all the local research teams in 25 countries that made this study possible. This research was conducted during 2008-2009 with a grant from the Bill & Melinda Gates Foundation. An earlier version of this paper was presented at iConference 2010, Urbana-Champaign, Illinois, Feb 2010, and will be included as a book chapter in "Libraries, Telecenters and Cybercafes, International Comparisons", R. Gomez (Ed.), IGI Global, 2011.

REFERENCES

Aabo, S. (2005). The role and value of public libraries in the age of digital technologies. *Journal of Librarianship and Information Science, 37*(4), 205–211. doi:10.1177/0961000605057855

Abrahamson, J., & Fisher, K. E. (2007). What's past is prologue: Towards a general model of lay information mediary behaviour. *Information Research, 12*(4).

Bailey, A. (2009). Issues affecting the social sustainability of telecentres in developing contexts: A field study of sixteen telecentres in Jamaica. *The Electronic Journal on Information Systems in Developing Countries, 36*(4), 1–18.

Barzilai-Nahon, K., Gomez, R., & Ambikar, R. (2009). Conceptualizing a contextual measurement for digital divides: Using an integrated narrative. In Ferro, E., Dwivedi, Y. K., Gil-Garcia, J. R., & Williams, M. D. (Eds.), *Overcoming digital divides: Constructing an equitable and competitive information society* (pp. 630–644). Hershey, PA: IGI Global.

Bertot, J. C., McClure, C. R., & Jaeger, P. T. (2008). The impacts of free public Internet access on public library patrons and communities. *The Library Quarterly, 78*(3), 285–301. doi:10.1086/588445

Best, M., & Kumar, R. (2008). Sustainability failures of rural telecentres: Challenges from the sustainable access in rural India (SARI) project. *Information Technologies & International Development, 4*(4), 14.

Cadiz, C. M. (2005). Communication for empowerment: The practice of participatory communication in development. In Hemer, O., & Tufte, T. (Eds.), *Media and glocal change: Rethinking communication for development* (pp. 145–158). Göteborg, Sweden: NORDICOM.

Castells, M. (2007). Communication, power, and couter-power in the network society. *International Journal of Communication, 1*, 238–266.

Central Intelligence Agency. (2007). *The world factbook.* Retrieved from https://www.cia.gov/library/publications/the-world-factbook/rankorder/2153rank.html

Etta, F., & Parvyn-Wamahiu, S. (2003). Information and communication technologies for development in Africa: *Vol. 2. The experience with community telecentres. Ottawa.* On, Canada: IDRC.

Finquelievich, S., & Prince, A. (2007). *El (involuntario) rol social de los cibercafés* [Cybercafes' (involuntary) social role]. Buenos Aires: Editorial Dunken.

Freedom House. (2007). *Map of press freedom.* Retrieved from http://www.freedomhouse.org/template.cfm?page=251&year=2007

Garrido, M., Rothschild, C., & Oumar, T. (2009). *Technology for employability in Washington State: The role of ICT training on the employment, compensation and aspirations of low-skilled, older and unemployed workers.* Retrieved from https://digital.lib.washington.edu/dspace/handle/1773/16298

Gichoya, D. (2005). Factors affecting the successful implementation of ICT projects in government. *The Electronic Journal of E-Government, 3*(4), 175–184.

Gomez, R., & Gould, E. (2010). The "cool factor" of public access to ICT: Users' perceptions of trust in libraries, telecentres and cybercafés in developing countries. *Information Technology & People, 23*(3), 247–264. doi:10.1108/09593841011069158

Gomez, R., & Hunt, P. (Eds.). (1999). *Telecentre evaluation: A global perspective.* Ottawa, ON, Canada: IDRC.

Gould, E., Gomez, R., & Camacho, K. (2010). *Information needs in developing countries: How are they being served by public access venues?* Paper presented at the 16th Americas Conference on Information Systems AMCIS, Lima, Peru.

Gurol, M., & Sevindik, T. (2007). Profile of Internet cafe users in Turkey. *Telematics and Informatics, 24*(1), 59–68. doi:10.1016/j.tele.2005.12.004

Gurstein, M. (2000). Community informatics: Enabling communities with information and communications technologies. In Gurstein, M. (Ed.), *Community informatics: Enabling communities with information and communications technologies* (pp. 1–30). Hershey, PA: IGI Global.

Gurstein, M. (2005). Editorial: Sustainability of community ICTs and its future. *The Journal of Community Informatics, 1*(2), 2–3.

Haseloff, A. M. (2005). Cybercafes and their potential as community development tools in India. *The Journal of Community Informatics, 1*(3), 13.

Heeks, R. (2002). Information systems and developing countries: Failure, success, and local improvisations. *The Information Society, 18*(2), 101–112. doi:10.1080/01972240290075039

Heeks, R. (2009). *The ICT4D 2.0 manifesto: Where next for ICTs and international development?* Retrieved from http://www.sed.manchester.ac.uk/idpm/research/publications/wp/di/documents/di_wp42.pdf

Hillenbrand, C. (2005). Librarianship in the 21st century - crisis or transformation? *The Australian Library Journal, 54,* 164–181.

Huang, K., & Provan, G. K. (2007). Resource tangibility and patterns of interaction in a publicly funded health and human services networks. *Journal of Public Administration: Research and Theory, 17*(3), 435–454. doi:10.1093/jopart/mul011

Human Development Reports. (2007). *Fighting climate change: Human solidarity in a divided world.* Retrieved from http://hdr.undp.org/en/reports/global/hdr2007-2008/

Human Development Reports. (2009). *M economy and inequality.* Retrieved from http://hdrstats.undp.org/en/indicators/161.html

International Telecommunications Union. (2007). *Measuring the information society: ICT opportunity index and world telecommunications/ICT indicators.* Retrieved from http://www.itu.int/ITU-D/ict/publications/ict-oi/2007/

International Telecommunications Union. (2010). *Measuring the information society.* Retrieved from http://www.itu.int/ITU-D/ict/publications/idi/2010/Material/MIS_2010_without_annex_4-e.pdf

Jensen, M., & Esterhuysen, A. (2001). *The telecentre cookbook for Africa: Recipes for self-sustainability*. Paris, France: UNESCO.

Kamssu, J. A., Siekpe, S. J., & Ellzy, A. J. (2004). Shortcomings to globalization: Using Internet technology and electronic commerce in developing countries. *Journal of Developing Areas*, *38*(1), 151–169. doi:10.1353/jda.2005.0010

Mayanja, M. (2006). Rethinking telecentre sustainability approaches: How to implement a social enterprise approach: Lessons from India and Africa. *The Journal of Community Informatics*, *2*(3).

Melkote, S. R., & Steeves, H. L. (2001). *Communication for development in the third world. Theory and practice for empowerment* (2nd ed.). Thousand Oaks, CA: Sage.

Ngwenyama, O., & Morawczynski, O. (2009). Factors affecting ICT expansion in emerging economies: An analysis of ICT infrastructure expansion in five Latin American countries. *Information Technology for Development*, *15*(4), 237–258. doi:10.1002/itdj.20128

Parkinson, S. (2005). *Telecentres, access and development: Experience and lessons from Uganda and South Africa* (p. 176). Ottawa, ON, Canada: IDRC.

Prahalad, C. K. (2006). *The fortune at the bottom of the pyramid*. Upper Saddle River, NJ: Wharton School Publishing.

Proenza, F. (2001). Telecenter sustainability - myths and opportunities. *The Journal of Development Communication*, *12*(2), 15.

Proenza, F., Bastidas-Buch, R., & Montero, G. (2002). *Telecenters for socioeconomic and rural development in Latin America and the Caribbean*. Retrieved from http://www.iadb.org/sds/itdev/telecenters/exsum.pdf

Raiti, G. C. (2007). The lost sheep of ICT4D research. *Information Technologies and International Development*, *3*(4), 1–7. doi:10.1162/itid.2007.3.4.1

Robinson, S. (2004). Cybercafés and national elites: Constraints on community networking in Latin America. In Day, P., & Schuler, D. (Eds.), *Community practice in the network society* (p. 13). London, UK: Routledge.

Rutkauskiene, U. (2008). *Impact measures for public access computing in public libraries*. Lithuania: Vilnius University.

Schilderman, T. (2002). *Strengthening the knowledge and information systems of the urban poor*. Rugby, UK: Department for International Development (DFID).

Servaes, J. (Ed.). (2008). *Communication for development and social change*. Thousand Oaks, CA: Sage.

Servaes, J., & Malikhao, P. (2005). Participatory communication the new paradigm. In Hemer, O., & Tufte, T. (Eds.), *Media and glocal change: Rethinking communication for development* (pp. 91–103). Göteborg, Sweden: NORDICOM.

Sey, A., & Fellows, M. (2009). *Literature review on the impact of public access to information and communication technologies*. Seattle, WA: University of Washington.

Shneiderman, B. (2002). *Leonardo's laptop: Human needs and the new computing technologies*. Cambridge, MA: MIT Press.

Toyama, K., Kiri, K., Menon, D., Pal, J., Sethi, S., & Srinivasan, J. (2005). *PC kiosk trends in rural India*. Paper presented at the Freedom, Sharing and Sustainability in the Global Network Society Conference, Tampere, Finland.

Transparency International. (2009). *Corruption perceptions index.* Retrieved from http://www.transparency.org/policy_research/surveys_indices/cpi/2009/cpi_2009_table

Unwin, T. (Ed.). (2009). *ICT4D: Information and communication technology for development.* Cambridge, UK: Cambridge University Press.

van Dijk, A. G. M. J. (2006). *The network society* (2nd ed.). Thousand Oaks, CA: Sage.

Vanderheiden, G. (2000). Fundamental principles and priority setting for universal usability. In *Proceedings of the Conference on Universal Usability* (pp. 32-38).

Veeraraghavan, R., Yasodhar, N., & Toyama, K. (2009). Warana unwired: Replacing PCs with mobile phones in a rural sugarcane cooperative. *Information Technologies & International Development, 5*(1), 81–95.

Walkinshaw, B. P. (2007). *Why do Riecken libraries matter for rural development? A synthesis of findings from monitoring and evaluation.* Washington, DC: Riecken Foundation.

Warschauer, M. (2003). *Technology and social inclusion: Rethinking the digital divide.* Cambridge, MA: MIT Press.

Worcester, L., & Westbrook, L. (2004). Ways of knowing: Community information-needs analysis. *Texas Library Journal, 80*, 102–107.

World Bank. (2010). *Worldwide governance indicators.* Retrieved from http://info.worldbank.org/governance/wgi/sc_country.asp

World Economic Forum. (2010). *The global information technology report 2009-2010.* Retrieved from http://networkedreadiness.com/gitr/

This work was previously published in the International Journal of Information Communication Technologies and Human Development, Volume 3, Issue 2, edited by Susheel Chhabra and Hakikur Rahman, pp. 19-37, copyright 2011 by IGI Publishing (an imprint of IGI Global).

Chapter 6
Search Engine:
A Backbone for Information Extraction in ICT Scenario

Dilip Kumar Sharma
Shobhit University, India

A. K. Sharma
YMCA University of Science and Technology, India

ABSTRACT

ICT plays a vital role in human development through information extraction and includes computer networks and telecommunication networks. One of the important modules of ICT is computer networks, which are the backbone of the World Wide Web (WWW). Search engines are computer programs that browse and extract information from the WWW in a systematic and automatic manner. This paper examines the three main components of search engines: Extractor, a web crawler which starts with a URL; Analyzer, an indexer that processes words on the web page and stores the resulting index in a database; and Interface Generator, a query handler that understands the need and preferences of the user. This paper concentrates on the information available on the surface web through general web pages and the hidden information behind the query interface, called deep web. This paper emphasizes the Extraction of relevant information to generate the preferred content for the user as the first result of his or her search query. This paper discusses the aspect of deep web with analysis of a few existing deep web search engines.

INTRODUCTION

Information and communication technology have tremendous potential for social impact, human development and improving the lives of people they serve Through ICT peoples are able to communicate in better way and can access relevant information. It also helps in developing collaborative and research skills. People can gain confidence and avail opportunities on their potential. Information and communication technology provides appropriate hardware, software

DOI: 10.4018/978-1-4666-1957-9.ch006

and networking services to the search engine. To find out relevant pages instantaneously from billions of web pages available on the internet is a complex task. So, information extraction in web scenario is must to provide the relevant search to the user at the very first instant. An effective search engine is the necessity of today's information era. Search engine is a software program that searches for web sites that exist on the World Wide Web. Search engines search through its personal databases of information in order to provide the relevant information. A web crawler is an automated program that starts with a set of URLs called seeds and stores all the URL links associated with downloaded web page in a table called crawl frontier. The extractor sends all these information attached to the textual raw data to the analyzer. The analyzer then takes the entire HTML code of the downloaded web page and analyzes the code, keeping the relevant data and rejecting the rest. Some composing techniques are applied to link containing the similar types of information from the database to generate the relevant query results. Information and communication technology can be related to information extraction in web context or in search engine in a variety of ways (Anderson & Weert, 2002; Kundu & Sarangi, 2004). Traditional web crawling techniques

have been used to search the contents of the web that is reachable through the hyperlinks but they ignore the deep web contents which are hidden because there is no link is available for referring these deep web contents. The web contents which are accessible through hyperlinks are termed as surface web while the hidden contents hidden behind the html forms are termed as deep web. Deep web sources store their contents in searchable databases that produce results dynamically only in response to a direct request (Bergman, 2001) (Sharma & Sharma, 2011). Figure 1 shows the benefits of information extraction using ICT in human development in context of search engine.

ANALYSIS OF APPLICATION AREA OF ICT

Some of the area in which ICT plays a significant role in their development is analyzed below.

ICT in Education

In 1999 an analysis was done to find out the use of computer in schools. In that analysis it was found that a large number of students were sound enough to use the computers without taking help

Figure 1. Benefits of information extraction using ICT in human development in context of search engine

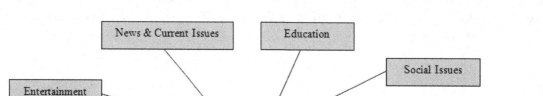

from school. The analysis also reveals that male and female students have different area of interest regarding the use of computer. A complete frame work can be divided into five modules.

Resource: It corresponds to a range of sources to access information.

Tutorial: It helps to acquire new knowledge along with feedback.

Exploration and Control: It investigates and provides the situations.

Support: It facilitates in communicating and providing the information to users.

Link: It facilities the interactive information exchange between individuals and groups.

Analysis of ICT evolution reveals that four specific approaches should be applied to adoption and use of ICT in educational organization. These four approaches are evolvement, application, hybridization and transformation (Hyper History, 2010; Anderson & Weert, 2002).

The deep web provides for a wide range of educational resources which varies from a student searching for an ideal school based on key personal requirements to an administrator looking for fund-raising resources. The key resources include directories and locators, general education resources, statistics resources etc.

ICT in Business

ICT is also useful in business environment. It underpins the achievement of current business and it offers government with a proficient communications. At the same time, ICT adds value to the processes of learning in the organization and management of learning institutions. The Internet is a driving force for large development and innovation in both developed and developing countries. The following competencies are gaining importance with reference to ICT:

- Decision-making
- Expert advice
- Control on dynamic situations
- Collaborative working
- Seamless communicating

Technological developments lead to changes in work and changes in the organization of work, and required competencies are therefore changing (Kundu & Sarangi, 2004).

ICT in Human Resource Development

ICT can be applied in rationalization and transformation of human resource development. ICT facilitates managers and employees to have direct accessibility to resources. Human resource development with ICT is termed as eHRDM. The public service commission (PSC) is an autonomous body for recruitment of human resource for government jobs. The Various steps in recruitment and selection process of PSC are to receive demands of human resource from government offices, verification of the given information, advertisement through media, receiving and sorting the applications, screening of applications, conduct pre-selection process, conduct interview process and final appointment.

Over the years, whole recruitment and selection process of PSC is in a typical paper based system. Recently, PSC has introduced the recruitment and selection database system which invites online job applications for the advertized jobs. The recruitment and selection (R&S) process developed by ICT personnel has objectives to find out the duplicity and redundancy in the R&S system, develop and maintain the system at par with the organization, which has successfully employed the ICT based R&S system, documentation of benchmark standard with recommendation, establishment of system implementation committee with technical personnel, implementation of the system, to conduct the workshops related to the system organization, formation of rollout process and establishment of monitoring and evaluation system.

Guidelines required for successful establishment of ICT based system for R&S are to establish LAN, MAN and WAN, procurement of leased line, increase the band width of system to facilitate the efficient data transmission. The requirements for system hardware and software for ICT based R&S system are to develop the system database server, backup server, windows based server and SQL based server, development of antivirus and firewall software, endorsement of physical access and control, connecting PCs website through World Wide Web, 24/7 browsing of advertisement by easy submission of online application and tracking of the job application (Wachira, 2010).

ICT in Social Issues

Planners, policy makers and researchers hold highly polarized and equivocal views on the diffusion of Information Communication and Technology (ICT). The role of search engine is significant in promoting objectives such as poverty alleviation, universal education, and reduction in mortality and health hazards, sustainable development and bridging the socio-economic divides in the world. It leads us with many online social work search that are providing number of free services to the social work and related professions.

ICT in Job Information

ICT can be used in job information extraction. It can therefore enhance human development. User can utilize a search engine for extracting job related data hidden behind the search forms and can identify the job according to their requirement. This makes the job searching easier and thereby

increasing the number of online job seeker and net users. Therefore, it is beneficial for both common people and Internet service providers. It helps us to provide the different and desired web pages related desired year of job and attaining the job according to their demand.

ICT in Shopping and Auctioning

ICT can also be useful in terms of web context in online shopping and online bidding. There are various shopping and auction sites such as amazon.com, ebay.com etc. that utilize the concept of ICT to support human development. User is required to enter the prerequisites on the website form and submit it online. The search engine then produces the list of items related to the user's query. It helps us in determining the current market trends by leading us to give the idea about the price raised and price fall for the smooth flow of business.

ICT in Database Related Information Extraction

Information from the database can also be extracted with the help of Web crawler that uses ICT. Tremendous amount of data remain hidden behind the database which can be explored using various programs which illustrates the use of ICT in database information extraction.

ICT in E Commerce/Banking

ICT plays a vital role in e commerce as well as e banking that has a better transparent system in which users can trade efficiently and can participate globally. Security is prime concern in this matter and requires further improvement. It helps to provide many E commerce development solutions to give the company many supports that are needed to run the day to day business (Kumar & Sareen, 2009).

ICT and Environment

The impact of ICT on environment has made tremendous changes like paperless offices and global society for environmental protection. ICT companies are working more upon green technologies and promoting biodiversity and preservation to reduce the impact of their own activities. It helps in optimizing many of the environmental health safety jobs and to use this employment by various workers.

In spite of the high-quality and authoritative information it provides, Deep web offers some excellent resources focusing on entertainment that are as useful as its serious counterparts. These entertainment resources such as movies, music, amusements, live performances, and other activities people do mostly for fun and pleasure.

ICT in Health

ICT has increased the access to information and has therefore increased the effectiveness of health care services by promoting the expansion of health and social services. It provides many links related to the health field showing numerous numbers of diseases and their related researches as well as their therapies concerned to it. The deep web avails a vast amount of authoritative information, offered by reputed health care organizations. Unlike the surface web resources that can even mislead the users, the deep web resources promises to provide the exceptionally high quality information on diseases, medical procedures, pharmaceutical drugs, nutrition, clinical trials, or other healthcare related issues.

ICT in E Government

The use of ICT in governance is increasing to deliver its services to the citizens at the location of their connivance in an efficient and transparent manner. Electronic governance is the application of ICT. Through the ICT, government can exchange information and services, communicate transactions between Government and citizen (G2C), Government and business (G2B). Therefore, being a service provider, Government should motivate their employees for delivering services through ICT (Sharma et al., 2007). Governments today are putting more and more information on the every day. Most of the portals to government information are covered by the surface web materials. The outstanding government Deep Web resources provide for sites that offer "general" type of information, directly from government entities themselves. These resources are useful for searcher who relies solely on the general purpose search engine.

ICT in Other fields

ICT can be used in online messaging and chatting. In general, web portals, classifieds, publications etc. use ICT. All of these areas use the concept of Information extraction based on form values. The Deep Web delivers many resources that meet all the important criteria required by the people who conduct legal research on the web by providing the correct, authoritative, and easy to access material in a timely manner. Real-time information is probably the "purest" type of Deep Web data, and it's not likely that general-purpose search engines will ever in their indices. Real-time information is almost always stored in databases that are constantly updated in real or near-real time. In some cases, such as stock quotes or airline flight arrival information, each update obliterates the previous data record. Even if a search engine could somehow crawl and index this information, it would be like isolating a single frame from a feature length movie. In other cases, real-time data is preserved, but the key point is that it is archived data in raw form, which a searcher cannot easily manipulate.

Figure 2 shows the distribution of websites based on content type. In order to utilize the full potential of web, there is a need to concentrate on web content so that it can prove to be a great

Figure 2. Distribution of web sites on content types (Bergman, 2001)

Content Types	Topic Databases	General Search	Messaging / Chatting	Jobs Search	Calculators	White / Yellow Pages	Library	Portals	Classified	Shopping	Publications	Internal Sites
Percentage	54%	1%	1%	1%	2%	2%	2%	3%	5%	5%	11%	13%

source of information i.e., information extraction should be done in the context of web which leads to utilization of Information Communication and Technology.

Deep web information are useful in education, business environment, human resources development, social issues, job information, shopping, in e-commerce/banking, database related information extraction, health, e-government, and other field such as messaging & chatting because the database can publish the result through direct query. Deep web sites post their result as dynamic web pages in real–time. These dynamic web pages have a distinct uniform resource locator address that permits them to be recovered again later. But in surface web pages, web pages are static and linked to other pages. Static pages do not have a unique URL address and therefore are not allowed to access information again later. Deep web sites also tend to improve the quality of search because it does not provides a long list of hits instead a right list.It means, it provides relevant information for each query. Through Deep web sites users can choose authoritative sites, but it is advisory to be careful about the selection of searchable sites. Users can make their own determination about the quality.

SEARCH ENGINE: A BACKBONE FOR INFORMATION VISUALIZATION

Search engine is a tool to gain information to the search of a specific collection; this may be a library, the internet, or have a personal collection. Search engine plays a vital role in extraction of information from World Wide Web. A search engine consists of web crawler whose function is to download web pages from the internet and store them into the database? The list of URLs is stored in the database queue, from where a scheduler selects URLs. These URLs are then downloaded by a multi-threaded downloader. Once downloaded, the text and meta data is stored in the database storage.

Need of Search Engine

The size of the World Wide Web is drastically increasing. Therefore, it is necessary to find out the required information in lesser time. Web crawlers are used to take all the links from the visited pages by the search engine and indexing is done in order to arrange them according to their preferences. Crawlers are used to carry out the maintenance by checking the links and HTML code. It is used to test web pages and links for valid syntax and structure. A Search engine should be able to search the information in World Wide Web in different formats from different sources. Search engine combines all the modules required for a particular application. Examples are online discovery, compliance of financial regulatory services, pharmaceutical research, counter measure for terrorisms sells prediction and customer support etc.

Working of the Search Engine

Figure 3 shows the working of a typical search engine. A crawler uses the HTTP network protocol in order to browse the internet which allows

Figure 3. Working of a typical search engine

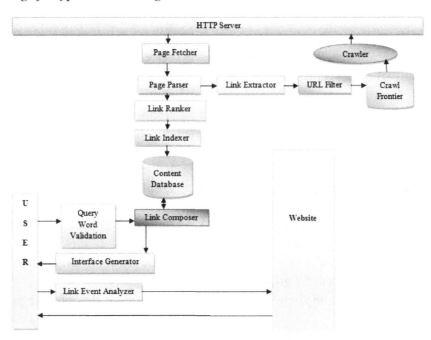

it to download or upload data from and to it. The crawler browses this URL and downloads the associated web page. It then looks for hyperlinks in the downloaded page. The URLs attached to these hyperlinks are then added to the queue. First of all, the crawler crawls over the http server through the search engine in which the crawl frontier, contains the links to be crawled. After the Links are extracted, they are parsed for further processing. After indexing, all the links are saved into the Content Database after applying ranking on them. Whenever the user enters the query in the search engine, it first checks the link from the Content Database and shows the corresponding results to the user. After that user does the event on the given link, the corresponding to which relevant pages are shown to the user from the web. A search engine consist of three major modules i.e. extractor, analyzer and indexer and interface generator (Brin & Page, 1998). Algorithm of these modules is given below.

Extractor

The Extractor is a Page Fetcher which fetches the web pages from the internet. A link extractor takes out a web address from a server reply to play it back as well as the dynamic parameters of the web address (Craven, 2003; Kaplan, Iida, & Tokunaga, 2009). The algorithm of the extractor is as follows:

- Extract the URL from the crawl frontier table which has not been parsed till now.
- Send HTTP GET request for that particular URL to the server.
- Download the URL's related page for further parsing procedure.
- Call the analyzer module to parse this URL.
- Repeat the steps from step1 until all the URL of crawl frontier are been parsed.

Analyzer and Indexer

Analyzer is an indexer that processes words of the web page and stores the resulting index in a database. The algorithm of the analyzer is as follows:

- Receive the downloaded URL's HTML code string.
- Check for internal links, and if present, convert them into external links.
- For each external hyperlink present in the HTML code, do:
  - Extract the URL attached to the hyperlink if not already present in the crawl frontier table else skip.
  - If this URL is unwanted (.gif, .jpg, .css, .xml, .doc, .pdf, .mp3 etc), then skip.
  - Else, insert this URL in the crawl frontier table.
  - Extract other information attached to the downloaded web page from its HTML string, like title, meta description etc.
  - If two of the strings are same then decide their precedence on the basis of HTTPs labelled.
  - Save all this information in the data table in the database.
- For each search word in the array, do:
  - Search the number of occurrences of the word in the database table data.
  - Arrange the search results in decreasing order of number of 'hits'.
- Stop

Interface Generator

Interface generator is a query handler that understands the need and preferences of the user.

The algorithm for the composer is as follows:

- The query that is to be searched is been entered.

- The query is been filtered by stemming process by removing white space, special characters, symbols etc from the user's search query.
- If search query is empty, then return, else continue.
- Break the search query into individual search words and store them into an array.
- Club together the search results of individual search words and again arrange them.
- Display the results on the output screen for the user.
- Stop.

Utility of Search Engine

These algorithms describe the procedure about how the URLs are been parsed and fetched from the web and how actually the crawler works by getting collected with all of the URLs from the web. They also describe the way the parsing should be done after fetching the HTML page related to that corresponding URL. Since the crawler is intended for getting the information depending upon the query fired, so these algorithms also describes that how query is processed and the related information to that of the query is displayed to the user. The main part of search engine is web crawler which is used for collecting and storing the information in database.

TYPES OF WEB CRAWLERS

The following are the general types of web crawlers.

Simple Crawler

Developed by Brian Pinkerton in 1994, is a, single-process information crawler which was initially made for his desktop. Later, it was extended on to the internet. It had a simple structure, and hence had limitations of being slow and having limited efficiency.

Parallel Crawler

Initially given by Junghoo Cho in 2002, this approach relied on parallelizing the crawling process, which was done by multi-threading. It had faster downloading and was less time consuming but required more bandwidth and computational power for parallel processing. It parallelizes the crawling process and uses the multithreading that reduces the downloading time. For example, Google Bot employs parallel, single-threaded processes (Yadav, Sharma, & Gupta, 2008).

Focused Web Crawler

This concept was given by Manczer in 1998, refined by Soumen et al. (1999). They focused on specific topics and get the relevant result. They are also called as topical crawler. They do not carry out the unnecessary task by downloading all the information from the web instead it download only the relevant one associated with those of the predefined topics and ignores the rest. This is advantageous for time saving factor. They are limited in its field. Examples: Healthline, Codase etc.(Chakrabarti, Berg, & Dom, 1999).

Distributed Web Crawler

Distributed web crawling is a distributed computing technique whereby Internet search engines employ many computers to index the Internet via web crawling. It uses distributed computing and reduces the overload on server. It also divides the works into different sub servers. Their main focus is on distributing the computational resources and the bandwidth to the different computers and the networks. Examples: YaCy: P2P web search engine with distributed crawling (Boldi, Codenott, Santini, & Vigna, 2004).

Deep Web Crawler

ICT provides various tools and one among them is deep web or web wrappers. But to have an access on these tools developer requires deep knowledge as web wrappers are site specific solutions that have dependencies with web structure and also, web a wrapper requires constant maintenance in order to support new changes on the web sites they are accessing. The deep web / hidden web refer to World Wide Web content that is not part of the surface Web, which is not indexed by surface web search engines. In Deep web, Pages are not indexed by search engine. It mainly requires registration and signing up. Example- Yahoo Subscriptions, LexiBot etc (Sharma & Sharma, 2010; Bergman, 2001). Table 1 shows a summary of the different types of web crawlers.

Issue of Network Interoperability in ICT

ICT is built upon numerous computers and telecom networks. For efficient communication on a global basis, all networks should be compatible to each other or some type of interface should be provided between networks. The main reasons to cope up with inter platform and architecture compatibility that enables the seamless information extraction. So research should be done in the direction of network cooperation and international standards should be made that can facilitate the cooperation among the diverse platforms (Acevedo, 2009).

Table 2 (Bergman, 2001) illustrates that Deep web searching would be useful for development work because it create dynamic content, response to a direct query and gave relevant information for market and all other domain. It more secure for professional contents, Government reports, strategy statements, research/sell reports, operational papers.

Table 1. Summary of different types of web crawlers

Name	Description	Advantage	Limitation
Simple crawler	Single process information, iteratively download the web pages and follow the breadth first traversal.	Simple structure, indexing process is straight forward.	Slow and limited efficiency.
Parallel crawler	Process is parallelized and indexing is done through identifying a keyword to make the search more relevant.	Faster downloading, less time consumption.	More bandwidth, more computational power.
Focused Web crawler	Downloaded web pages related to predefined topic or domain.	Relevant downloading, provide relevant results, reduces number of retrieving pages thereby regulating the visiting pages and analyses is more deep so as to define high quality pages.	Limited in field. Pre decided resource extraction.
Distributed Web crawler	Distributed computing technique and interact in peer to peer fashion.	Reduces overload on server, division of work in sub servers.	More computational power. Complex to manage.
Hidden/Deep crawler	Dynamic generation of web pages.	Access huge amount of online data.	More resource and processing needed

Table 2. Surface web versus deep web

Surface Web	Deep Web
1. Surface web page is static and linked to other pages. 2. They are not narrower with deeper content. 3. Total quality content of the Surface web is less. 4. Surface web is not relevant for every information need and for others domain. 5. The surface web does not publish the result through direct query. As search engines look through links, they are unable to access certain type of web pages These pages never enter the system and, therefore, are never indexed. 6. Surface web make static HTML pages that are less likely to be from professional content suppliers. 7. The Surface Web, crawled by popular search engines running today, contains only a fraction of the overall unstructured content available on-line today. 8. The surface web is the "general web" and is what one can find using general web search engines. It is also what one see in almost all subject directories.	1. Deep web page is dynamic content served up in real time from a database in response to a direct query. 2. Deep Web sites ought to be narrower with deeper content. 3. Total quality content of the Deep Web is thousand times much greater than Surface web. 4. Deep Web content is highly pertinent to every information need and other domain. 5. The Deep Web search is the content that resides in searchable databases, the results from which can only be discovered by a direct query. Without this direct query, one would not be able to reach the results. 6. Professional contents suppliers typically have the kind of database-based sites that are more secure in deep web. 7. The Deep Web contains all the "unknown or hidden", unstructured content that the surface web failed to provide to its users. 8. The Deep web is the "hidden web" and is what one cannot find using the normal search engine for this they need the Deep web crawlers to get the information fetched.

ANALYSIS OF SOME OF IMPORTANT DEEP WEB SEARCH ENGINES

Complete Planet (www.completeplanet.com)

Complete Planet is an invisible web portal with fast service, relevant results and an easy to use interface. Complete Planet searches over more than 7000 database and search engines. Complete planet's advanced search is pretty standard. It provides the option to search by title, keyword, description, date etc. Every database is extremely alert in character. While surfing the web, user can click on the links that are provided by the search engine, to reach the individual high value databases. It is easy to use, simple and broadens the search.

IncyWincy (www.incywincy.com)

IncyWincy is an invisible Web search engine and it behaves as a meta-search engine by tapping into other search engines and filtering the results by searching the web, directory, forms, and images. It discovers search engines when spidering the web. It features a unique search engine relevancy algorithm. It provides user listings, premium keyword purchase, and custom website spidering. Information may change quickly and become unavailable or may become the part of the visible web.

Scirus (www.scirus.com)

It contains the latest search engine technology and searches over 410 million- specific web pages that enable the user to quickly pinpoint the scientific, scholarly, technical and medical data on the web. It has a wide range of special features to help to get the scientific information which are needed. It can find specific conference, abstracts and patents. It helps to refine, customize and save the searches. Scirus is a search engine mainly made for science subjects. It concentrates simply on pages containing technical content.

DeepDyve (www.deepdyve.com)

DeepDyve is the largest online rental service for scientific, technical and medical research with over 30 million articles from thousands of authoritative journals. It makes research easy and affordable. It can copy entire sentences, paragraphs and even complete articles against the specific query. It also finds related information for every article by clicking the "More like this" button on search result page. Their search is not restricted to keywords or literals. It can search by simply pasting the whole of the article into the search bar. Some of the articles in the DeepDyve are "open access" and are marked as "free" for any user to read.

Biznar (www.biznar.com)

Biznar is a free, publicly available deep web search engine that uses advanced "federated search technology" to return high quality results against the search query in real time. It accelerates search by returning the most relevant results from over 60 authoritative business collections to one easily navigable page. It is very effective search engine created especially for those professional businesses that need to get access to specific information for their works. This system is a federated search which means that by using this tool one can look the information not from only one source but from many databases at the same time (Price & Sherman, 2001; Basu, 2010).

COMPARATIVE ANALYSIS OF DIFFERENT SEARCH ENGINES

After analyzing the different types of search engines, it is concluded that surface web search

Table 3. Query words versus Results counts for surface web search engines

Query words	Surface Web Search Engine			
	Google Search	**Yahoo Search**	**Bing Search**	**AOL Search**
Mobile computing	9,980,000	311,000,000	11,00,000	12,400,000
Electronic commerce	8,400,000	2,290,000	3,85,00,000	9,350,000
Digital signal processing	9,850,000	1,590,000	31,00,000	1,370,000
Compiler	15,200,000	965,000	1,68,00,000	4,820,000
Soft computing	3,110,000	1,510,000	1,39,00,000	2,690,000
Medical	465,000,000	57,100,000	38,60,00,000	136,000,000
Research	708,000,000	88,800,000	50,40,00,000	273,000,000
Numerology	38,20,000	7,190,000	31,70,000	1,380,000

Table 4. Query words versus results counts for deep web search engines

Query words	Deep Web Search Engine				
	Scirus	**deepdyve**	**biznar**	**IncyWincy**	**complete planet.com**
Mobile computing	1,794,169	4,232,459	2,781	114,154	177
Electronic commerce	1,096,216	3,446,266	2,969	1,18,746	238
Digital signal processing	18,88,306	7,953,655	1,446	46,248	73
Compiler	18,88,306	2,261,880	1,523	1,09,087	85
Soft computing	5,95,501	39,72,039	1,496	20,206	33
Medical	32,669	37,71,574	3,400	39,15,116	4,767
Research	9,55,84,523	44,19,671	3,495	53,21,514	5,000
Numerology	16,233	211,515,718	933	15,018	40

Figure 4. Variations of results counts versus query words for surface web search engines

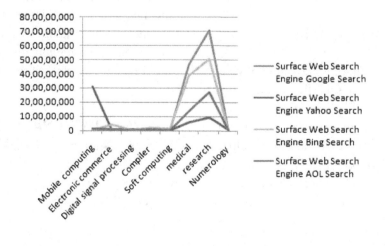

Figure 5. Variations of results counts versus query words for deep web search engines

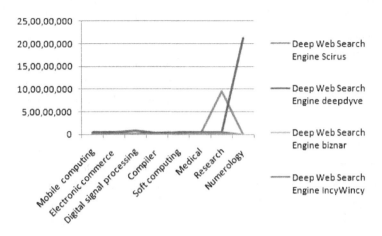

engine results in large number of surface web results, whereas deep web search engine extracts the hidden web data. Table 3 and Table 4 shows query words versus results counts for surface web search engines and deep web search engines respectively.

Figure 4 and Figure 5 reflects the graph between the results obtained against query words for the different search engines.

Deep web search engines shows small number of results as they are not so efficient as compared to surface web search engines due to less advancement in the field of deep web search.

CONCLUSION

This paper highlights the role of information extraction in human development. Information extraction is facilitated by ICT. Search engine plays a vital role in information extraction from World Wide Web. An important module of the search engine is a web crawler. Web crawler can result in desired information extraction from www. A lot of important information is hidden behind the deep web. Normal web crawlers are not capable of effective crawling of the deep web. For effective crawling of the deep web, a specialized web crawler is required, which is known as deep

web crawler. Finally, this paper also presents the analysis of some of the important deep web crawlers to find out their role in the information extraction from www. One of the two important areas of application of ICT i.e. education and human resource development are discussed in details. ICT can be applied in the education field very effectively. Educational organizations are the main contributors in the field ICT revolution. Use of ICT brings out the new teaching methods with the use of new gadgets. ICT becomes the common source of information in present knowledge age. ICT enables the commons users to access the relevant information at one click at their home. ICT improves the resource functioning of human resource development management practice by making the system cost effective by minimizing the cost by providing the resources to the people without a traditional paper work system. ICT makes information omnipresent without the limitations of time, place and availability. ICT minimizes the cost of the system by providing the information to various users from one source in less time. Using ICT human's resource development service can be improved by redefining the responsibilities of the employees through a improved strategic orientation of human resource development.

ACKNOWLEDGMENT

All the companies/products/services names are used for identification purposes.

REFERENCES

Acevedo, M. (2009). Network cooperation: Development cooperation in the network society. *International Journal of Information Communication Technologies and Human Development, 1*(1). doi:10.4018/jicthd.2009010101

Anderson, J., & Weert, T. V. (Eds.). (2002). *Information and communication technology in education.* Paris, France: UNESCO.

Basu, S. (2010). *Search engines to explore the invisible Web.* Retrieved from http://www.makeuseof.com/tag/10-search-engines-explore-deep-invisible-web/

Bergman, M. K. (2001). The deep web: Surfacing hidden value. *Journal of Electronic Publishing, 7*(1). doi:10.3998/3336451.0007.104

Boldi, P., Codenott, B., Santini, M., & Vigna, S. (2004). UbiCrawler: A scalable fully distributed web crawler. *Software, Practice & Experience, 34*(8), 721–726. doi:10.1002/spe.587

Brin, S., & Page, L. (1998, April 14-18). The anatomy of a large-scale hyper textual web search engine. In *Proceedings of the Seventh International World-Wide Web Conference*, Brisbane, Australia.

Chakrabarti, S., Berg, M., & Dom, B. (1999). Focused crawling: A new approach to topic-specific web resource discovery. In *Proceedings of the Eighth International Conference on World Wide Web* (pp. 1623-1640).

Craven, T. C. (2003). Html tags as extractor cues for web page. *Journal of Information Science, 6*, 1–12.

Hyper History. (2010). *History education and information communication technologies (ICT).* Retrieved from www.hyperhistory.org/images/assets/pdf/ict.pdf

Kaplan, D., Iida, R., & Tokunaga, T. (2009). Automatic extraction of citation contexts for research paper summarization: a co reference-chain based approach. In *Proceedings of the Workshop on Text and Citation Analysis for Scholarly Digital Libraries* (pp. 88-95).

Kumar, M., & Sareen, M. (2009). Building trust in e-commerce through web interface. *International Journal of Information Communication Technologies and Human Development, 1*(1). doi:10.4018/jicthd.2009092205

Kundu, A., & Sarangi, N. (2004). *ICT and human development: Towards building a composite index for Asia.* Amsterdam, The Netherlands: Elsevier.

Price, G., & Sherman, C. (2001). *The invisible web: Uncovering information sources search engines can't see.* Medford, NJ: CyberAge Books.

Sharma, D. K., & Sharma, A. K. (2010). Deep Web information retrieval process: A technical survey. *International Journal of Information Technology and Web Engineering, 5*(1), 1–21. doi:10.4018/jitwe.2010010101

Sharma, D. K., & Sharma, A. K. (2011). A Novel Architecture for Deep Web Crawler. *International Journal of Information Technology and Web Engineering, 6*(1), 25–48. doi:.doi:10.4018/jitwe.2011010103

Sharma, D. K., Varshneya, G., & Upadhyay, A. K. (2007). AJAX in development of web-based architecture for implementation of e-governance. *International Journal of Electronic Government Research, 3*(3), 40–53. doi:10.4018/jegr.2007070103

Wachira, F. N. (2010). *Improving the management of human resources in the public service through application of information and communication technologies (ICTs).* Paper presented at the AP-SHRMnet Workshop, Cotonou, Benin.

Yadav, D., Sharma, A. K., & Gupta, J. P. (2008). Parallel crawler architecture and web page change detection techniques. *WSEAS Transactions on Computers, 7*(7), 929–941.

This work was previously published in the International Journal of Information Communication Technologies and Human Development, Volume 3, Issue 2, edited by Susheel Chhabra and Hakikur Rahman, pp. 38-51, copyright 2011 by IGI Publishing (an imprint of IGI Global).

Chapter 7
Contribution of Information and Communication Technologies to Malaria Control in Tanzania

Restituta T. Mushi
University of KwaZulu-Natal, South Africa

Wanyenda Chilimo
Pwani University College, Kenya

ABSTRACT

The term Information Communication Technology (ICT) includes any communication device or application. In malaria control, ICTs can ease communication, improve doctors' training, and increase access to information by individuals and groups that are historically unaware of malaria. Successful malaria vector control depends on understanding causes, prevention, and treatment. This paper examines the possibilities of using ICTs to eradicate malaria in Tanzania. It also explores the coverage of the malaria subject related to Tanzania on various electronic databases and e-journals. This paper concludes that Tanzania's Ministry of Health must put forth more effort on ICT management and be more active in their approach of disseminating malaria information.

1. INTRODUCTION

Tanzania is in East Africa with the Indian Ocean to its southern part. It borders Uganda and Kenya to the north, Burundi, Rwanda, and Congo to the west and Mozambique, Zambia, and Malawi to the south. All these neighbouring countries are highly affected by malaria. Tanzania contains three of Africa's best-known lakes, Victoria in the north, Tanganyika in the west, and Nyasa in the south. Mount Kilimanjaro in the north, 19,340 ft (5,895 m), is the highest point on the continent. Because of its location being in the tropic region, Tanzania is highly infested with malaria parasite (Infoplease, 2009).

DOI: 10.4018/978-1-4666-1957-9.ch007

Malaria is a mosquito-borne disease caused by anopheles mosquito. Malaria parasite causes over 2.7 million deaths in Africa per year. Each year some, 500 million people are sick with malaria, and of those, over 2 million children (which is 90%) die of malaria cases (Goldring, 2009). A worrying trend which is emerging in the fight against malaria is that insecticides are becoming less effective against mosquitoes. Malaria parasite is becoming more resistant to anti-malarial drugs such as chloroquine and quinine (Goldring, 2009).

Ninety percent (90%) of the world's malaria cases occur in Africa of recent, malaria outbreaks are being reported in some locations of Africa such as the highlands of Kenya which were previously thought to be at elevations too high for malaria transmission(World Health Organization, 2008). There have been various opinions among scholars on account for this recent happening. Some scientists hypothesize that the emergence of malaria in areas which were previously free from the parasites is due to climatic change. For others, human migration is responsible for the spread of malaria to regions which were previously free from the parasites. Also, malaria has resurged in certain locations of Africa such as Madagascar, South Africa, and Zanzibar that previously had effective control programs. Throughout the world, malaria occurs in over 100 countries and territories. More than 40% of people in the world are at risk. Large areas of Central and South America, Hispaniola (Haiti and the Dominican Republic), Africa, the Indian subcontinent, Southeast Asia, the Middle East, and Oceania are considered malaria-risk areas (Uyaphi, 2008).

In June 2005, the United States Government selected the United Republic of Tanzania as one of the first of three countries to be included in the President's Malaria Initiative (PMI). During the launch, President George W. Bush urged African countries to fight malaria, the continent's leading killer disease, through the use of treated bed nets. The US government had set aside $1.2 billion under the initiative to fight malaria in 15

African countries, including Tanzania (Ubwani, 2008). The Tanzania Malaria Operational Plan for the 2009 fiscal year was divided into activities for mainland Tanzania and Zanzibar. This is because Mainland and Zanzibar have a separate and independent malaria control programs. The Mainland Malaria Control Programme (NMCP) serves the Mainland only (population 38.4 million) while the Zanzibar Malaria Control Programme (ZMCP) serves Zanzibar (population 1.1 million) (MOP Tanzania).

Out of the 15 PMI countries, Tanzania has the highest number of people at risk from malaria related illness. Approximately 40 million individuals of which 38.6 million are in the mainland (which puts 93% of the population in the mainland at risk) and 1.3 million in Zanzibar (where 100% of the population is at risk). Annual malaria deaths in Tanzania have been reduced to 60,000, of which an estimated 80% are children under five years of age. Approximately 14-18 million clinical malaria cases are reported annually by public health services. Over 40% of all outpatient attendances are attributed to malaria (Malaria Operational Plan (MOP) Tanzania: 2008). According to the Health Management Information System (HMIS), the disease is responsible for more than half of deaths among children under five years of age and up to one-fifth of deaths among pregnant women (MOP Tanzania, 2008). Information Communication Technologies (ICTs) is used properly may play a role in providing access to much needed information for malaria control

ICTs can be defined as an umbrella term which involve innovations in microelectronics, computing (hardware and software), telecommunications and opto-electronic. These innovations enable the processing, manipulation and storage of large amounts of information, along with rapid distribution of information electronically in digital form through communication networks (Human Development Reports, 2001). ICTs can be divided into the following categories: New ICTs; these include computers, satellites, wireless one-on-

one communications (including mobile phones), electronic mail (email) and internet. Old ICTs; these include radio, television, landline telephones and telegraph (SIDA, 2005).

To further define ICTs and differentiate them from other information-handling technologies Heeks (1999) divides information handling technologies as follows: ICTs which are based on digital information held as 1s and 0s and comprise computer hardware, software and networks. Other information-handling technologies include 'intermediate' technologies, which are based on analogue systems such radio, television and telephone; 'literal' technologies, which are based on information held as written word, such as books and newspapers; and 'organic' technologies such as the brain and sound waves. In establishing the Contribution of ICTs to Malaria Control in Tanzania this paper adopt a wider definition of ICTs which include not only computers and Internet but also mobile phones, radio and television

This paper examines the possibilities of using ICTs to eradicate malaria in Tanzania. In addition, the paper include the review of literature from websites of different organizations such as the ministry of health in Tanzania, hospitals, NGOs dealing with malaria and various electronic databases and e-journals, such as ScienceDirect, EbscoHost, and AJOL. In addition, information was sourced from the National Institute for Medical Research and from Ifakara Health Research. In addition, paper review the types of ICT's which can be used especially with disadvantaged families who unfortunately form the bulk of those affected by the disease. Furthermore the paper highlights how society can benefit from public health by using ICT. Finally, the paper discusses ways of dealing with malaria by using combinations of treatment and suggests some of the ICT's facilities which can be helpful.

2. MALARIA SITUATION IN TANZANIA

According to Malaria Operational Plan (MOP) Tanzania (2008), malaria is endemic across nearly all of mainland Tanzania. The operational plan states that 93% of the population lives in areas where Plasmodium falciparum is transmitted. Prevalence of malaria among children between 6 to 59 months of age ranges from 0.4% in the elevated region of Arusha to 41.1% in the northwestern region of Kagera. Unstable seasonal malaria transmission occurs in approximately 20% of the country, while stable malaria with seasonal variation occurs in another 20%. The remaining malaria endemic areas in Tanzania (60%) are characterized as stable perennial transmission Plasmodium falciparum accounts for 96% of malaria infection in Tanzania. The principal malaria vector in the mainland and Zanzibar is Anopheles gambiae. The population size of Tanzania (39.4 million) and level of malaria endemicity results in 35 million persons at risk for this disease-the largest number among all 15 Plan for Malaria Initiative (PMI) countries. Health facilities report malaria as the leading cause of outpatient and inpatient health care visits and the primary cause of deaths among children. Over 40% of all outpatient attendances are attributable to malaria approx. 16 million clinical malaria cases, NMCP estimates that 70,000 malaria deaths occur annually in Tanzania among all ages - extrapolated from under-5 mortality rate in 2004-05 TDHS, size of under-5 population, and the amount of deaths attributable to malaria MOP Tanzania. Malaria poses huge barriers to economic growth within endemic regions. Increasing resistance to affordable antimalarials has recently worsened these health and economic burdens.

In Tanzania there is need for the government to put more effort in the health sector to make people aware of the effects of malaria and how to deal with the problem. The importance of awareness in the fight against malaria can never be overemphasized.

Plasmodium falciparum is the most dangerous of the four species of human malaria (Plasmodium Falciparum, Plasmodium Vivax, Plasmodium Ovale, and Plasmodium Malaria) (MOP Tanzania, 2008). The use of effective ICTs is one of the ways to increase community awareness on the whole issue of malaria eruption and its prevention. This is why this study aim to encourage the government particularly department of health to use ICT's to inform society what can be done to eradicate or to reduce the spread of malaria.

3. MALARIA CONTROL IN TANZANIA

Efficient malaria control depends on embarking on measures which target groups at risk. These groups are defined by the level and pattern of malaria endemicity, since the intensity of Plasmodium falciparum transmission and the age pattern of clinical malaria are inversely related. In areas of high falciparum transmission, such as the Kilombero Valley in southern Tanzania, about half of all malaria hospital admissions and deaths are in children younger than 1 year. The clinical demonstration of falciparum infection can also be dependent on the age and intensity of spread, since younger children have a tendency to be affected with more severe malaria attack (Schellenberg, 2001).

Although international donor funding for malaria control in Africa has increased since 2002, funding remains inadequate and our understanding of how increased financial resources have influenced equitable and targeted coverage of key malaria control strategies across Africa is incomplete. This is perhaps an area that further research should be directed.

In Tanzania, various efforts have been made by government to fight malaria. The Act for health was officially made available in December 2006. The Minister of Health and Social Welfare, made the Act available in all government health facilities and faith-based organizations. According to

Tanzania's new Act treatment policy, combination malaria therapy translated in Kiswahili as *Dawa Mseto Ya Malaria* was officially launched on Africa Malaria Day April 25 2007 in the Kagera Region. The campaign aims to improve malaria treatment and awareness in Tanzania through multi-media such as television, radio, posters and music to promote and improve malaria treatment awareness. The communication campaign complements government's efforts to improve national access to malaria treatment (National Malaria Control Programme).

In Tanzania, malaria controls continue to bases on the diagnosis and prompt treatment of both suspected and long-established cases through the healthcare. The absence of microscopic examination in most of the health facilities continues to be a limiting factor in the fight against malaria. Such absence creates a scenario whereby health workers prescribe medication based on medical suspicion to identify the need of treatment for malaria without a proper knowledge of the nature of the parasite being treated. At times, doctors estimate and give treatment for malaria to patients which cause a lot of unnecessary and premature death. In addition, individuals assume the signs and symptoms of malaria without proper diagnosis. They sometimes take malaria drugs such as Quinn and chloroquine on the grounds that such a medication has worked for others (Brabin, Wort, & Warsame, 2006). A major challenge which faces the fight against the spread of malaria is the lack of adequate knowledge of the sickness.

4. GOVERNMENT EFFORTS TO CONTROL MALARIA

The government of Tanzania has implemented several interventions for malaria control. One of such interventions is the delivery of treated mosquito nets to families. In indoor spraying against mosquitoes and the use of insecticide-treated nets is one of the simplest and most cost-effective technologies in fighting malaria. If it is effectively utilized it can change the malaria situation in Africa (Erdman & Kain, 2007). The challenge facing weak health systems is how to deliver such communication. Experiences from places such as Morogoro rural area, Bagamoyo, Lindi and other remote areas with poor communication network shows that health workers are confronted with challenges in delivering information on malaria control, and maternal and child health. Improving communication network in these rural areas can create a situation whereby people become more aware of the benefits of availing themselves to use the healthcare facilities thus improving their quality of life (Ekman, Pathmanathan, & Liljestrand, 2008). In addition, Noor et al. (2009) adds that, insecticide-treated bed nets (ITNs) provide a means to improve child survival across Africa. It has also been pointed out that people should use DEET insect repellent on exposed skin and flying insect spray in the room where they sleep (Erdman & Kain, 2007). People need to wear long pants and long-sleeved shirts, especially from dusk to dawn since this is the time when mosquitoes that spread malaria bite. To sleep under a mosquito bed net implies having a treated net. This is where government can assist by either providing free treated mosquito nets or subsidizing the price of treated nets. Such a programme should cover the entire population instead of focusing on a particular section. Furthermore government can go into partnership with community in preparing malaria awareness workshops. Such workshops should be both informative and entertaining such that people will be more willing to attend. Whether you are living in a high-risk area or perhaps traveling to one, mosquito nets offer essential protection against mosquitoes, flies and other insects (Erdman & Kain, 2007).

Epidemiological supervision of malaria is also vital for malaria control and well-timed public health responses to outbreaks and plague. In endemic areas, monitoring malaria incident and resistance enables formulation of effective national prevention strategies and treatment protocols to reduce morbidity and mortality, and may even promote the return of drug-sensitive parasites. Observation efforts in endemic and non-endemic areas can be mutually beneficial: physicians in non-endemic areas often base malaria chemoprophylaxis and treatment decisions on trends in endemic regions, whereas unusual or drug-resistant imported malaria can serve as early warning signs for emerging trends in endemic areas. Tanzania government makes members of community and visitors aware of malaria pandemic through international and local media such as radio television and even the Internet. By providing this information, visitors and citizens are better placed to take the necessary safety measures before travelling to affected areas. Such measures include vaccinations and the use of prescribed anti-malaria drug.

5. ICTS AND MALARIA CONTROL IN TANZANIA

There has been much discussion on the role that recent advanced ICTs could play in improving health systems in different countries. Part of this is to help get rid of some of the myths that people hold with as regards to malaria. For in instance, some people in Tanzanian society have accepted malaria as a disease which children are born with. Such a distorted notion of the disease negatively impacts on the fight for the control and eradication of the disease. The use of ICTs can make a substantial contribution to improving health and healthcare through proper dissemination of information (Lucas, 2008).

The ICT to be introduced in public sector must be one that is user friendly and easily accessible. Dr James Ngwandu (Mvumi Hospital, Tanzania) argues that computers can be used in medical institutions to translate and adapt health information (Fahamu, 2002). Such facility will provide health workers with what they need to disseminate and store information about malaria. Tanzania has a predominantly rural population of subsistence farmers who mainly speak local languages and Swahili, while most of the information on malaria control from research and the academy is available in English language. Given this situation, there is a real need for reliable, up-to-date, locally relevant information in local languages and Swahili. Erdman and Kain (2007) argued that people tend to assume that ICT's is only Internet, it is much more. Information on malaria control can be communicated through various means such as posters, newspapers, community audio towers, drama, sustainable community radio, or even the links between radio and e-mail, dance, film and video. E-mail and fax could be used to transfer information taken from the Internet into communities. In a research with young people, Erdman and Kain (2007) used audiocassettes to record experiences and ideas relating to sexual health and these were then played through audio-towers in the communities. This proved to be effective way to communicate with the community. Erdman and Kain (2007) further played the tapes national radio to include those who did not benefit from the project locally (Fahamu, 2002). ICTs can be used in the control of malaria by facilitating health education and communication and in the training of the health professionals.

5.1. ICTs in Health and Education

Health education and communication is one of the key components in malaria control and prevention (Mboera, Makundi, & Kitua, 2007). Serious obstacles in most disease control strategies include lack of effective health information, education, and communication programs (Mboera, Makundi, & Kitua, 2007). Community and health providers need to understand the problem of malaria in all its relevant aspects. They must also be aware of all the options available in order to make improvement on those areas that are not so effective. Health providers and communities need to appreciate

the epidemiologic and technical dimensions of the malaria problem as well as the factors that affect whether particular control options will be feasible. For individuals and households, effective health communication can help raise awareness of health risks and solutions. Effective use of ICTs will provide motivation and skills needed to reduce these risks, help them find support from other people in similar situations, and affect or reinforce attitudes.

In Tanzania, available information indicates that health education and information communication provided to the community has had limited impact on behavioural change and hence disease prevention and control. In part, this is due to the ineffective communication strategies used in health education, communication programs between systems and providers. Although various studies in the country have indicated that healthcare facilities are the most reliable sources of health education, such facilities are often not accessed by many people particularly in rural areas because of their healthcare charges, long distances, inadequate and unaffordable transport systems, poor quality of care, equity, poor governance, and inadequate human resource (Mboera, Makundi, & Kitua, 2007). ICTs may play a significant role to improve the health education and communication within the health sector in general and in malaria control in particular.

ICT's facilities can be used to make people aware of malaria symptoms so that they can visit their healthcare as soon as possible. In some countries, ICT projects in public sectors such as health have become notorious for cost over-runs, delayed implementation and failure to meet intended objectives. This is true in the health sector in Tanzania where effective utilization of ICT's is hampered at times by the lack of personnel. In this situation, government has to put in place structures which will ensure that personnel are given adequate training and are properly monitored to make sufficient use of ICT's in the fight against malaria. An example of health education program on malaria control is the one provided by a nonprofit organization called Sesame which has established the Tanzanian series Kilimani Sesame program. The aim of this is to reach approximately five million Tanzanian children through television, radio, and outreach materials addressing basic educational needs on health and hygiene messages, and malaria prevention (Sesame, 2009). The focus on malaria is particularly significant because malaria is a major public health concern in Tanzania, particularly among children under the age of five. The organization has been advocating that the most cost-effective way to prevent malaria transmission is to sleep under a pesticide-treated mosquito net hung in the proper way. Unfortunately only 16% of Tanzanian children under the age of five sleep under a treated mosquito net (Sesame, 2009).

One of Kilimani Sesame's primary goals is to provide families with basic information about the malaria and methods to best prevent, recognize, and treat malaria. These messages are presented in a way that help children develop a sense of resilience and self-confidence by using age-appropriate and reassuring ways of communicating information and modeling behaviors. The Kilimani Sesame television episodes features adapted material from South Africa's Takalani Sesame with locally-produced live action films featuring the daily lives of children in Tanzania. These locally-produced documentary films portray the diversity of children in Tanzania and give viewers opportunities to engage with positive images of Tanzanians on-screen. The fact that 80% of the country's population lives in rural areas suggests the need to introduce ICT facilities through which people will be provided with proper education of Malaria campaign especially to the young girls and boys (Sesame, 2009).

From the national malaria control programmes in Kenya and Tanzania which was facilitated by Alasdair Unwin, a film titled 'A Mother's Story' was made by the Media Trust for the National Malaria Control. The film was created in Kenya in 2000 so that it could be shown at the annual Roll Back Malaria Global Partners Meeting held in Geneva. Although much has changed in the few years since the film was made, many of the underlying systemic problems continue to persist. The film highlights the underlying rationale behind the changes in anti-malarial drug policy and why attention should be paid to reducing the burden of malaria in Africa. The film can also be used as an effective training tool for health workers (Uyaphi, 2008).

5.2. Telemedicine and Malaria Control

The term telemedicine was used in the 1970s to describe situations in which physicians examined patients by means of telecommunications equipment (Lucas, 2008). However, of recent the term has become much more broadly applied, sometimes to cover almost any health-related use of communications technology. For the purpose of this paper a more limited approach of the term will be adopted such as in a situation where communication takes place between two medical providers or between a provider and a specific patient or where a telephone is used to seek health advice or assistance. At this level it seems obvious that health services in most developing countries would greatly benefit if every public health facility simply had access to a functional telephone. However, adoption of this strategy in Tanzania will only benefit a few since majority of the people in the rural areas lack access to the telephone as well electricity (Lucas, 2008). This situation is likely to change though, thanks to the availability of additional Internet and e-mail services through telecentres and multitude of private mobile phone kiosks which are mushrooming in even the poorest countries (Lucas, 2008).

5.3. The Use of ICT's in Effective Diagnosis of Malaria

The use of ICT's can help to provide information for effectively malaria diagnosis. In this case ICT are important for proving health care health professional with information. ICT's can provide the health professional with accurate information on proper diagnosis of malaria rather than generalizing signs of any other disease to be malaria. Malaria diagnostic tests must be rapid and accurate. Early recognition and treatment are critical to prevent progression to severe disease, and accurate species determination guides therapeutic decisions. Moreover, for effective implementation, tests must be practical in terms of cost, availability, and ease of use ICT application is very crucial (Erdman & Kain, 2007). In non-endemic areas, limited experience of physicians and laboratories with malaria leads to delays and inaccuracies in diagnosis, which can have fatal results. In endemic areas, rapid and accurate diagnostics are needed to identify infected individuals and avoid over-prescription of antimalarials based on unreliable clinical diagnosis. Misdiagnosis of malaria may distract from other potentially life-threatening illnesses, contributes to antimalarial resistance, and is increasingly unsustainable as expensive Artemisinin-based Combination Therapies (ACT) are instituted as first-line treatment (Erdman & Kain, 2007).

6. BENEFITS OF ICTS

- In malaria diagnosis images can be sent digitally using computers. In this way one department can work hand in hand with other departments to make sure patient results are retrieved as soon as they are requested.
- Use of consultants contacted phonically or by email. In this way programs can reach big number of people and patients. They will not need to go to the hospital before making arrangement with their doctors for their availability. This will save time and money for the patients.
- Making information relevant and interesting. Through ICT information always reach intended community which is affected by malaria while is still current. In addition information is provided in deferent format e.g. images, animations, music etc. whereby community do not get bored very easy.
- Through ICT's large amount of data such as patients admission records can be managed in different ways for instance using HTML format, DVDs, CDs, CD-ROM, Cassette etc.

7. LIMITATIONS OF ICT'S

- High cost in the purchase and maintenance ICT equipments limits their use to the majority.
- Although health information is readily available on the Internet and has changed the way people deal with their health in many ways, the retrieval of relevant information remains problematic, especially for elderly people. This is because most elderly people do not have ICT's skills and in addition, some of them cannot afford. (Marschollek et al., 2008)

8. CONCLUSION

ICT contributes to the increase in the efficiency and effectiveness of the delivery of information on malaria control and treatment. It provides attractive opportunities in terms of easiness of communication, improves doctors' training and access to patients by individuals and groups which are historically unaware of malaria. Careful consideration of advantages compared to the costs and finance of ICT's is required for proper assessment of ICT management.

9. RECOMMENDATIONS

- Use of solar energy instead of electricity especial in a rural areas, this will make ICTs more accessible. The use of biogas as a source of power for ICT's should be encouraged.
- More emphasis should be placed on ICTs which are readily available to the majority of people in the rural areas such as community radios.
- Training on the effective use of the ICTs is important so as to maximize their use in malaria control.

REFERENCES

Brabin, B., Wort, U. U., & Warsame, M. (2006). Birth outcomes in adolescent pregnancy in an area with intense malaria transmission in Tanzania. *Acta Obstetricia et Gynecologica Scandinavica, 85*(8), 949–954. doi:10.1080/00016340600756870

Demetre, L., Britta, O., & Debbie, M. (2008). *Information technology (IT) with a human face: A collaborative research project to improve higher nutrition training in Southern Africa.* Stellenbosch, South Africa: University of Stellenbosh.

Ekman, B., Pathmanathan, I., & Liljestrand, J. (2008). Integrating health interventions for women, newborn babies, and children: A framework for action. *Lancet, 372*(9642), 990–1000. doi:10.1016/S0140-6736(08)61408-7

Erdman, K. L., & Kain, K. C. (2007). Molecular diagnostic and surveillance tools for global malaria control. *Travel Medicine and Infectious Disease, 6*(1-2), 82–99. doi:10.1016/j.tmaid.2007.10.001

Fahamu. (2002). *Healthcare training and internet connectivity in Sub-Saharan Africa.* Retrieved from http://www.fahamu.org/downloads/Nuffieldwebreport.pdf

Goldring, J. P. D. (2009). *Malaria: Drugs, diagnostics and where is the vaccine? Royal society of South Africa lecture series.* Pietermaritzburg, South Africa: University of Kwazulu Natal.

Heeks, R. (1999). *Information and communication technologies, poverty and development, development informatics.* Retrieved from http://www.man.ac.uk/

Human Development Reports. (2001). *Human development report: Making new technologies work for human development.* Retrieved from http://hdr.undp.org/en/reports/global/hdr2001/

ICT4D. (2008). *The sustainable use of ICTs to enable poor people and marginalised communities to use the potential of ICT to transform their lives.* Retrieved from http://www.gg.rhul.ac.uk/ict4d/Malaria.html

Infoplease. (2009). *Tanzania.* Retrieved from http://www.infoplease.com/ipa/A0108028.html

Lucas, H. (2008). Information and communications technology for future health systems in developing countries. *Social Science & Medicine, 66*(10), 2122–2132. doi:10.1016/j.socscimed.2008.01.033

Marchant, T., Schellenberg, J. A., Edgar, T., Nathan, R., Abdulla, S., & Mukasa, O. (2002). Socially marketed insecticide-treated nets improve malaria and anemia in pregnancy in southern Tanzania. *Tropical Medicine & International Health, 7*(2), 149–158. doi:10.1046/j.1365-3156.2002.00840.x

Marschollek, M., Mix, S., Wolf, K. H., Effertz, B., Haux, R., & Steinhagen-Thiessen, E. (2007). ICT-based health information services for elderly people: Past experiences, current trends, and future strategies. *Informatics for Health & Social Care, 32*(4), 251–261. doi:10.1080/14639230701692736

Mboera, L. E. G., Makundi, E. A., & Kitua, A. Y. (2007). *Uncertainty in malaria control in Tanzania: Crossroads and challenges for future interventions*. Dar es Salaam, Tanzania: National Institute for Medical Research.

Menda, A. (2010). *ICT education project amid rural connectivity challenges*. Retrieved from http://www.businesstimes.co.tz/index.php?option=com_content&view=article&id=200:ict-education-project-amid-rural-connectivity-challenges&catid=45:ict-news&Itemid=73

Noor, A. M., Juliette, J., Mutheu, J. J., Andrew, J., Tatem, J. A., & Simon, I. (2009). Insecticide-treated net coverage in Africa: Mapping progress in 2000-07. *Lancet, 373*, 58–67. doi:10.1016/S0140-6736(08)61596-2

Rowland, M. (2007). Efficacy of pyrethroid-treated nets against malaria vectors and nuisance biting mosquitoes in Tanzania in areas with long-term insecticide-treated net use. *Tropical Medicine & International Health, 12*(9), 1061–1073. doi:10.1111/j.1365-3156.2007.01883.x

Schellenberg, D., Menendez, C., Kahigwa, E., Aponte, J., Vidal, J., & Tanner, M. (2001). Intermittent treatment for malaria and anemia control at time of routine vaccinations in Tanzanian infants: A randomised, placebo-controlled trial. *Lancet, 357*(9267), 1471–1477. doi:10.1016/S0140-6736(00)04643-2

SOUL BEAT. Edutainment. (2007). *National malaria control programme (NMCP)*. Retrieved from http://www.comminit.com/en/node/135350/304

Swedish International Development Cooperation Agency (SIDA). (2005). *ICTs for poverty alleviation: Basic tool and enabling sector*. Retrieved from http://www.eldis.org/fulltext/sidaictpoverty.pdf

TechTargent. (2007). *ICT*. Retrieved from http://searchciomidmarket.techtarget.com/

Ubwani, Z. (2008). *Tanzania: Bush calls for use of nets in malaria war*. Retrieved from http://allafrica.com/stories/200802190005.html

USAID. (2008). *President's malaria initiative: Malaria Operational Plan (MOP) Tanzania*. Retrieved from http://www.fightingmalaria.gov/countries/mops/fy09/tanzania_mop-fy09.pdf

Uyaphi. (2008). *Tanzania malaria*. Retrieved from http://www.uyaphi.com/tanzania/malaria.htm

World Health Organization. (2008). *World malaria report: The global fund: To fight AIDS, tuberculosis and malaria*. Retrieved from http://www.theglobalfund.org/en/malaria/background/

This work was previously published in the International Journal of Information Communication Technologies and Human Development, Volume 3, Issue 2, edited by Susheel Chhabra and Hakikur Rahman, pp. 52-60, copyright 2011 by IGI Publishing (an imprint of IGI Global).

Chapter 8
Electronic Networks and Gaining Market Share:
Opportunities and Challenges

Ghazi Al-Weshah
Al-Balqa Applied University, Jordan

Khalil Al-Hyari
Al-Balqa Applied University, Jordan

Amjad Abu-Elsamen
University of Jordan, Jordan

Marwan Al-Nsour
Al-Balqa Applied University, Jordan

ABSTRACT

This study provides a deep understanding of the current status of electronic networks in the Jordanian handicrafts sector from managers' perspectives. More specifically, this study enhances utilisation of the e-environment to gain market share in local, regional, and international markets. Four cases of handicraft projects are selected to conduct face to face interviews. The results show that handicraft projects have initial attempts to use E-electronic in their activities, but these attempts are still in embryonic stages, and they do not use E-networks effectively to gain market share. However, project managers believe that there is a direct link between the use of electronic networks and increases in the business's market share. Furthermore, it is intended that these initiatives be treated as innovative and at the end utilised to enhance the business development of similar enterprises belonging to the small and medium enterprises sector. The study recommends that such projects consider adoption of e-networks in their future plans, enhance their staff skills in terms of improving their IT and English language skills, and develop their

DOI: 10.4018/978-1-4666-1957-9.ch008

own internet website to create new marketing channels.

INTRODUCTION

Electronic networks can assist an organisation discover and share knowledge and learning within the organisation and from entities outside the organisation (O'Toole, 2003), as an innovative instrument for adding business value. The concept of electronic network is rarely mentioned in the networks literature, but used as e-business (Taylor & Murphy, 2004; Fillis *et al.,* 2004; O'Toole, 2003), e-relationships (O'Toole, 2003), or electronic market-place and e-business (Stockdale & Standing, 2004). Therefore, these terms are used interchangeably with e-networks.

Some studies used the terms e-commerce, internet commerce, and e-business in a compatible way (Stockdale & Standing, 2006; Poon & Swatman, 1998). Ramsey *et al.* (2003) stated that the term electronic business is used broadly and interchangeably with e-commerce and internet commerce to describe the internet activities and process in a business. Moreover, Fillis *et al.* (2004) confirmed that the terms e-business and e-commerce can be used interchangeably to describe firms' utilisation of E-technology in their activities and operations.

Most of the previous studies defined the term E-business to represent all electronic activities and process in a business (Liu & Arnett, 2000; Tang *et al.,* 2003; Fillis *et al.,* 2004). For example, Liu and Arnett (2000) considered e-business as a way of conducting business by companies and their customers performing electronic transactions through computer networks. Moreover, e-business is also defined as the enhancement and optimisation of a business's activities through the usage or creation of new, digital markets and value chains both for strategic and operational benefits (Tang *et al.,* 2003). Furthermore, Fillis *et al.* (2004) defined e-business as "any business carried out over an electronic network (exchanging data files, having a websites, using other companies' websites or buying and selling goods and services online" (p. 179).

The above-mentioned definitions used E-business as a broad term to describe all electronic activities that can be adopted in businesses operations in different ways to build relationships management with other parties. Specifically, small and medium size enterprises (SMEs) do not have the skills or time to implement all internet applications. Firm size affects the level of resources available for investment in information technologies and associated training which can support e-business adoption in SMEs (Serbanica & Militaru, 2008).

Currently, the Internet is most commonly used by SME firms in developing countries for communication and research; the Internet is least used for e-commerce. E-mail is considered an important means of communication. However, the extent of use is limited by the SMEs' recognition of the importance of face-to-face interaction with their buyers and suppliers (Andam, 2003).

In developing countries, there are many barriers and challenges for small business to adopt electronic networks as driver for electronic activities. The previous studies in developing countries have not defined electronic networks in a clear way. For example, Adekunle and Tella (2008) investigated the barriers of electronic networks adoption in Nigerian small businesses. Consequently, they concluded that E-commerce, E-business and e-networks could be used interchangeably.

Up to date, no any empirical study has investigated the use of E-networks in handicrafts sector in Jordan. This paper attempts to make contribution to the recognition of this knowledge gap. It also offers guidance for future research in a field of research.

The paper, first, presents a review of the literature pertaining to the concept of electronic networks, small businesses, E-networks environment, and the Handicraft industry scope. Thereafter, explained the methodology employed for this research. The study results are then analysed and interpreted in the light of theoretical evidence reported in extant literature. Finally, a number of conclusions drawn from this investigation were discussed, along with limitations of the study and avenues of future research.

The Concept of Electronic Networks

There is no single, uniformly acceptable definition of electronic networks term. The terms e-business, e-commerce, e-relationships, and e-network are used interchangeably in the literature. However, electronic network can be defined as all financial and informational electronically mediated exchanges between organisations and its external shareholders (Kulmala & Rauva, 2005). Therefore, the electronic networks can be considered as a tool of the e-commerce (Kulmala & Rauva, 2005; Stockdale & Standing, 2004).

The electronic networks in a study of e-marketplace defined as an inter-organisational information system that allows multiple buyers and sellers, and other shareholders to communicate and transact through a dynamic central market place that is supported by additional services (Stockdale & Standing, 2004).

Adekunle and Tella (2008) described the value and benefits of using e-networks. They mentioned that "using electronic information to boost performance and create value by forming new relationships between and among businesses and customers."

The level of confidence of using e-mail for communication with both suppliers and buyers increases only after an initial face-to-face interaction. E-mail, therefore, becomes a means for maintaining a business relationship (Andam, 2003). For the purpose of this study, the electronic network can be considered as all internet activities and process (such as e-mail and websites) that are adopted in businesses operations in different ways to communicate and build relationships with competitors, customers, marketing agencies, and other stakeholders. While gaining knowledge and capacity from internal and external sources for the value gain (Chesbrough, 2003), forms a dynamic knowledge acquisition system, belonging to the newly evolved open innovation paradigm.

Small Businesses and E-Networks Environment

Sparkes and Thomas (2001) investigated the use of internet as one of critical success factor for marketing in Welsh agri-foods small businesses. They concluded that there is need for appropriate support of SMEs to make them aware of the importance of the adoption of e-business as a critical success factor for their marketing because it provides a strong interaction with customers and international audience. O'Toole (2003) suggested that there are various implementation levels of the E-relationship using industry associations, consultants, government agencies, universities or network providers. The study recommended that institutions should play the key role in making the technology infrastructure cheaper and available.

Another benefit of adopting e-business in SMEs could be the higher efficiency obtained in business activities due to a fast and accurate processing of information. Web-enabled services increase the competitiveness of SMEs because they change the relationship with customers by creating a stronger link between firms and its clients (Lal, 2005). Collins *et al.* (2003) examined the causal relationship between enhancing the SMEs business performance and the utilization of e-networks in the tourism sector; Fink and Disterer (2006) examined to what extend is the information communication technologies (ICT) are infused into the operation of SMEs? They considered ICT a tool for SMEs to become international businesses; Fillis *et al.* (2004) argued that electronic network is an essential asset for small business development taking into consideration the macro trend of globalization which removes the geographic barriers and increase competitions among businesses. Therefore, they developed a conceptual model that increases the level of e-networks adoption.

Fillis *et al.* (2004) proposed some areas which confirm that "E-networks can create competitive advantage in small businesses such as: first, E-networks provide small firms the ability to access an information infrastructure. Second, adoption of E-networks provides small firms with internal and external communication among each others. Third, adoption of E-networks allows small businesses to communicate effectively with customers, suppliers, business partners and competitors. Fourth, small firm's competitive advantages can be provided by connecting to the internet. Fifth, the entrepreneurial owners' orientation of small businesses can create sustainable advantages.

SMEs use ICTs to develop new organizational models, compete in new markets or enhance their internal and external communication relationships (Sánchez *et al.*, 2007). Ramsey *et al.* (2003) emphasised that even in the well-developed countries, the adoption and effective use of e-business remains law among small and medium enterprises. However, e-networks can create a competitive advantage for small firms and the e-enabled small businesses are well placed to gain benefits of the electronic networks. Nevertheless, the studies of Stockdale and Standing (2006), Ramsey *et al.* (2003) have concluded that the successful adoption of e-business depends on the business owner's motivation, experience, focus on profitability, close relationship with customers, and the innovation and flexibility level of management.

Ramsey *et al.* (2003) identified that there are major difficulties for SMEs going online, these difficulties are mainly; the lack of strategic appreciation of the dynamics of the Web, and the development of capabilities for managing the information infrastructure for e-business. Therefore, the support of IT agencies, private sector, or national institutions is highly recommended to consider the decision of e-business adoption on the strategic plans. Serbanica and Militaru (2008) confirmed that the smaller businesses are often less aware of full benefits for e-business. In addition, SMEs have shown a greater uncertainty of the benefits of IT adoption than larger firms.

It is highly recommended by Chitura *et al.* (2008) that researchers seek to find new ways to help small businesses overcome e-business adoption barriers. Chitura *et al.* (2008) summarised some previous studies for barriers of e-commerce adoption by SMEs between 2001 and 2006. The study implications concluded that the future studies should stop searching for the barriers and instead focus on how SMEs can overcome these barriers to obtain the full benefits of the technology.

Lawrence (2008) investigated how SMEs use the internet in UK. More specifically, the benefits of using internet, issues countered in using the internet, and the impact of using internet on business activities. 400 questionnaires were distributed to SMEs in UK. The study concluded that SMEs are experiencing limited success with the use of internet in exposing their products or services to global audience and reaching new customers.

Allahawiah *et al.* (2010) investigated the level of Internet usage for business solutions by small and medium enterprises in Jordan. A random sample of 100 firms with less than 500 employees was selected from various sector in Jordan. They found that a majority of respondents use the Internet in business activities, the adoption of the Internet as a business tool is limited to a brochure, where Web site which primarily provides only one way and non-interactive information about the company and its products.

Hunaiti *et al.* (2009) investigated the main challenges facing the growth of e-commerce in SMEs in Libya. Questionnaire surveys have been distributed to forty business managers to concerning e-commerce situation in Libya. The study found many challenges facing Libyans' e-commerce like the expensiveness of internet pricing; the unsuitability of online shopping services and Libyan postal system; and the Libyans' culture and their limited trust in the online trading systems.

Other previous studies identified that there are many benefits for e-business adoption by small businesses such as cost of sales reduction, innovation, job creation, and low cost of transaction, in addition to many other indirect benefits (Adekunle & Tella, 2008; Sánchez *et al.,* 2007; Stockdale & Standing, 2004;). These studies concluded that the benefits gained by E-networks adoption are strongly linked to the flexibility and entrepreneurial orientation of small businesses.

Scope of Handicraft Industry

There are very limited studies in handicraft enterprises area. However, some studies attempt to define the scope of handicraft industries and investigate the characteristics of the Craft micro-enterprises (Fillis, 2002; McAuley & Fillis, 2004). Fillis (2002) identified the craft business characteristics; the study defined crafts as "a class of objects in which these objects must have a high-degree of hand made input, either by using the hand itself, hand-tools and hand-held power tools" (p. 915). Fillis (2002) also stated that a product can be called craft-product when traditional methods are using as part of the production process. Therefore, craft products are not necessarily to be produced using traditional materials. Consequently, craft products are produced by traditional production methods regardless of the used materials.

McAuley and Fillis (2004) defined *crafts* in the widest possible sense as involving of individuals to firms making or manufacturing a functional or decorative product which has a handmade element at some stage in its production. Moreover, Fillis (2002) distinguished between the production of hand crafts and the craft-based industries; craft production involves a single person who is completing the entire process from conceptualisation to fabrication. On the other hand, the crafts product itself must exhibit artistic appeal that been made of individual design and contain a large degree of manual skills in its production, either manufactured as one-off items or in small batches (Fillis, 2002).

McAuley and Fillis (2006) evaluated craft sector and what the practical options might be for the craft sector to survive after the credit crunch. Their findings stated that craft business sits at the micro end of the continuum of SMEs and the main component of this SME spectrum is being sole operator or having a few staff, or operating part-time, this is strongly supporting the craft business characteristics discussed by Fillis (2002). McAuley and Fillis (2006) concluded that during economic downturn, the craft businesses sales are expected to be decreased in compare with previous years because regular buyers and people who occasionally buy crafts will buy less.

Small craft businesses faces many barriers such as the high cost of hiring employees, the hardness of finding a craft expert, and the increase on the workload in case of businesses expanding. Thus, small businesses need to be supported by a technology provider in order to have sustained and cheap electronic services (McAuley & Fillis, 2006; Ramsey *et al.,* 2003).

In terms of market share, craft businesses are expected to maintain their loyal buyers. However, it is hard to get the attention of new customers to gain more market share. McAuley and Fillis (2006) proposed a survival strategy should consider many issues: first, develop training to improve craftsperson skills. They stated that "there is no better time than in a recession to get the training completed especially in improving the selling skills for the craftsperson" (McAuley & Fillis, 2006); Second, adopt cooperative with other business to share resources and especially promotional costs. Third, confirm the online business presence and shift to online sales.

Based on the above mentioned discussion, the study focuses on the contribution of electronic networks as a key success factor to gain market share in some selected handicraft small businesses in Jordan.

Market Share Strategies

Market share literature can be divided into economics literature and marketing literature (Falkenberg, 1984). Economics studies focus on the relationship between market share and profitability (Prescott *et al.,* 1986; Shanklin, 1992; Kuzma & Shanklin, 1992) and the relationship between market share and return on investment (Chussil, 1991). Marketing studies focus on how to develop market share using one or more of marketing mix tools (Falkenberg, 1984).

Therefore, there is no single definition for market share term. Many studies use market share term for "sales volume". In no growth markets, the two terms are synonymous. But in declining markets, growing share is the only way to maintain or grow sales (Chussil, 1991). However, most studies state that market share can be represented as the ratio between company's total sales and the total sales of its industry. Moreover, the nature of competition in market plays an important role in identifying the market share characteristics (Strouse, 2001). In this aspect, Falkenberg (1984) stated that from marketing view market share is determined by the relative attractiveness of a firm total offering.

Kuzma and Shanklin (1992) confirmed that market share reflects two types of forces that do cause high or low profits; first, relative scale and or experience based cost advantages and disadvantages. Second, relative success in designing, producing, and marketing products that meet the needs of customer in particular served market.

Broadly speaking, it is costly to gain market share against market leaders in a mature industry with flat or declining sales (Kuzma & Shanklin, 1992). In building market share a business should consider competitors reactions. Moreover, building the market share should be integrated in planning process particularly strategic plans (Chussil, 1991).

Strouse (2001) reported that market share can be increased by three different ways. The first is to take customers away from competitors. This increases one's own share and reduces the share of each competitor. However, the business should assume that competitors aren't taking as many customers from you as you are from them. More specifically, branding and service differentiation are the most effective method to attract customers from competitors. Second, strategic groups, regulatory initiatives, competitive entry into local markets, technology, and critical analysis of their customers' service experiences are major tools in increasing market share. Third, mergers and acquisitions are successful strategies to buy more market share especially if competitive market is highly fragmented.

Haider (2009) stated that there are essential guidelines for any business to win market share such as differentiation, focused advertising, customer relationship management, promotional schemes, and services after sale. Fillis *et al.* (2004) suggested that e-business offers the opportunity to increase market share and long term profitability.

Study Aim and Objectives

The main focal point of this study is to provide a deeper understanding of the current status of electronic networks (the use of internet: email and websites) in the Jordanian handicrafts sector More specifically, the research objectives of the study are to:

- Explore and understand the concept of electronic networks from the managers' perspectives in handicraft small businesses.
- Explore how small businesses utilise and employ the e-environment to develop their business activities.
- Identify the contribution of electronic networks in gaining market share in the

Jordanian handicrafts sector, and identify the challenges of using e-networks in gaining market share.

Methodological Considerations

To achieve the study aim and objectives, the study methodology has been employed based on the qualitative approach. More specifically, multi-cases study design has been adopted. The study adopts the qualitative case study approach (Bryman, 2008) to provide a deeper understanding of the current status of electronic networks in Jordanian small businesses which operate in the high quality handicraft sector.

In-depth interviews are used as data generation tool in this study. The purposive choice basis is employed to select the target interviewees. The qualitative data of each case have been analysed independently using the textual analysis of interviews transcripts. In the light of a holistic view of the study, cross cases analysis has been carried out to achieve the study aim and objectives.

This kind of study design provides in-depth analysis and highly takes into its consideration the reality of the research data and issues. Therefore, the data from the in-depth interviews were analysed for emergent themes, used together and integrated with the findings of case study and the literature to design the overall findings.

ANALYSIS OF CASE 1 (THE CANDLES PROJECT)

Interviewee Profile

The interviewee gender is female; her position is manager of the selected project. In term of experience, she has about 19 years of experience in handicraft sector. Moreover, she has BSc in Business Management.

The Current Status of Electronic Networks in the Project

The manager defined the use of E-networks in the project as "the use different websites and email to communicate with customers and marketing dealers, and the use of computerised systems to manage the internal work in the project"

She emphasised that the business use the email to communicate with the project marketers and showrooms of different products of the project. The project uses the electronic networks (email) to receive orders, submit reports, and discuss new designs. The business got an internet access. However, they still depend on manual work. The business case does not have an official website on the internet. The project depends on marketing agencies and dealers in products marketing and new market outlets.

The manager said:

I never tried to access any competitors' websites but we do not face any problem in contacting with our customers or dealers. We totally depend on market agencies to marketing our products. So, the dealers try to find us new outlets and we do not worry about marketing.

The Project Market Share and Use of Electronic Networks

The manger is not satisfied about the business market share. Comparing with the past years the business does not make any sales figures that cover its cost. Moreover, products design needs local women experts on handicrafts because it represents the traditional line of crafts. The project does not have the financial ability to recruit more employees or to increase the wages. Additionally, the business cannot make large orders or accepts order that comes on urgent basis. Accordingly, the project cannot increase the market share due to the previous issues. Furthermore, the use of

E-networks applications may not help on increase the market share as the project manager stated. The project manager said:

I am not happy with the current situation of our outlets, and our centers in Lebanon and Saudi Arabia have been closed because of the un-certainty in the political situation, today we manage our orders according to the number of women we have. We cannot accept more orders or big orders. Also, the seasons play a major role; on summer the women are much able to work on handicrafts orders.

ANALYSIS OF CASE 2 (DESIGN CENTRE PROJECT)

Interviewee Profile

The interviewee gender is female; her position is owner and manger the Project. In term of experience, she has about 15 years of experience in handicraft sector. She used to work as quality manager in a different business.

The Current Status of Electronic Networks in the Project

The project manager defined the use of electronic networks as communication tools that can be used to facilitate the daily work of the project such as marketing dealers and shows rooms communications. She emphasised that the business use the electronic networks to document the work, receive orders and to communicate with the project stakeholders. However, the project is not using the internet access efficiently because of the challenge of using the English language. The project manager said:

"We use the computerised systems to document our orders, stock items, raw materials, and our financial records. Additionally, we use the email to

communicate with our outlets, but we don't use the internet for any other purposes because it is hard to understand the English language probably".

The Project Market Share and Use of Electronic Networks

The manager is satisfied about the market share that the business has achieved. However, she believes on the ability of the business to improve its market share through the evaluation of the products designs and quality. The project adopts customers' feedback policy to improve its products. The project manager said:

Our products have been evaluated several times in terms of the quality and the design; many improvement touches have been added and tested in order to satisfy our customers. Today we have a good number of orders and a good sales figure. Our products are produced with high care and on a quality level. Moreover, we believe in continuous improvements of our products by taking the customers opinions.

Improving the project market share through contacting different marketing agencies is a key issue. According to the business manger's experience in marketing, the project identified that the main obstacles of sales drop is the lack of marketing distribution channels and the use of E-networks may help the project on create more marketing channels. The project manager stated that:

There is a large market for our products in the Middle East and in international markets. Moreover, it has been very hard to market our products in Jordan; the Jordanian market cannot be the only targeted market. However, the main problem on the business outreach is the far distance from the Capital Amman. I know the website will help and we going to develop website for our project.

ANALYSIS OF CASE 3 (NORTH JORDAN PROJECT)

Interviewee Profile

The interviewee is male; he is the manager of the project. In term of experience, he has 14 years of experience in handicraft sector. He has BSc degree in marketing.

The Current Status of Electronic Networks in the Project

The manger defined the electronic networks as all the internet activities and applications available to facilitate the daily work and communicate efficiently with other parties such as customers, suppliers and marketing outlets in a quicker and cheaper way. The project manager said:

Electronic networks allow us use of internet activities and computerised applications to convey and communicate efficiently with our customers, suppliers, markets in quick and cheap media.

Mainly, the project is using the electronic networks applications for the purpose of building relationships, and communication with customers, suppliers, marketers, and showrooms. Moreover, they use e-networks for managerial communications, sending and receiving reports, and raw material orders. However, the project manger is not completely satisfied about the level of using the E-networks and he believes that E-networks activities can make the work quicker and easier. The project manager said:

Actually, we use the internet to build relationships and communication with customers, supplier, and for marketing purposes in very limited way. We send and receive some reports by the internet. I am not satisfied about our situation for using the

internet I think we can get more benefits such as easy and quick work.

The Project Market Share and Use of Electronic Networks

The project manager is not satisfied about market share situation. The project is planning to develop their internet website and developing its own marketing outlets and channels in order to increase the market share locally, regionally, and internationally. Therefore, they will save the marketing cost for different products. Moreover, they adopt customers' feedbacks to develop their products. The project manager said:

We are planning to develop our electronic websites. We are also thinking to open our marketing channels to reach more customers in Jordan and outside Jordan; the next step is to develop new marketing ideas to reach project customer not from the marketing agencies and different showrooms. So we can save marketing cost. Also, e-mail helps us to contact customer satisfaction about our products.

ANALYSIS OF CASE 4 (THE WEAVING PROJECT)

Interviewee Profile

The interviewee is female; she is the project owner and manager. She has 10 years of experience in the handicraft sector. She has BSc in Quality Engineering.

The Current Status of Electronic Networks in the Project

The project manager defined the use of electronic networks as a communications tool that is being used for the purpose of communicating with different marketing advisors searching new products design, learning and improving the products shape and quality. The project manager said:

Electronic network is the use of internet to communicate with different advisors, to search some new designs, to learn and improve our products shape and quality.

The Project Market Share and Use of Electronic Networks

The project manager is not satisfied about the size of current market share. However, the project has ability to achieve more market share and increase the market demand for its products. The project manager said:

I am not satisfied about the market share that our project gains from the Jordanian market. I believe we can do better. The project has a very good number of direct orders. It is important to increase our market share and our profit in order to be able to develop our own centre.

The project attempts to develop training programmes in order to develop the managerial skills of the workers to increase their market share. The project manager believes that the use of E-networks applications help them to maximise their sales and profits.

CROSS CASES ANALYSIS

In the light of holistic view of the four selected cases, the researcher can extract some common similarities, varieties, and themes in the selected cases of the small Jordanian handicraft projects.

The Current Status of Electronic Networks

All the owners/ managers of the four projects cases were asked to identify the concept of the electronic networks from their own perspectives. Their definitions are shown in Table 1.

As shown in (Table 1), the use of electronic networks has been identified in different ways. However, all cases have defined the electronic networks as a communication tool that can be used to facilitate and manage the work. Among these cases, Case 4 considered the role of electronic networks in enhancing the business owner's skills of searching new products designs and quality. On the other hand, Case 3 defined the electronic networks as all internet activities and applications that help the business to make the work process quicker and easier.

Some previous studies mentioned that SMEs adoption for e-networks is growing for different purposes. For example, Andam (2003) stated that ICT usage patterns among SMEs in developing countries show a progression from the use of the Internet for communication (primarily e-mail) to

Table 1. Concepts of e-networks in the selected projects

Case no.	Electronic networks concept
Case 1	The use different websites and email to communicate with customers and marketing dealers, and the use of computerised systems to manage the internal work.
Case 2	Communication tools that can be used to facilitate the daily work of the project such as marketing dealers and shows rooms communications.
Case 3	All the internet activities and applications available to facilitate the daily work and communicate efficiently with other parties such as customers, suppliers and marketing outlets in a quicker and cheaper way.
Case 4	Communications tool that used for the purpose of communicating with different marketing advisors searching new products design, learning and improving the products shape and quality.

use of the Internet for research and information search, to the development of Web sites with static information about a firm's goods or services, and finally to use the Internet for e-commerce.

Doncombe and Heeks (2005) also mentioned that the networked use of ICTs, frequent use of email and the Web, and use of computers in various applications are being applied and adapted in such systems on a largely ad hoc basis. However, in many cases, they lack the employee skills to effectively manage the systems that have been developed. In other cases, the development process may be deficient.

How Small Handicraft Businesses Utilise the E-Environment

Almost, all the selected cases have an internet access and they mainly use the email to communicate with different parties, send and receive documents related to the project reporting, orders, and follow-ups. Table 2 presents how small handicrafts utilise the E-environment.

As shown in Table 2, one project (Case 4) is using the E-networks applications on searching for the purpose of developing the handicraft design and products. One of the cases is not using the E-networks application for any purpose and it is not recognising the benefits of using the E-networks applications. In general, the business cases that are utilising the E-networks are not satisfied about the level of participation on the electronic networks activities.

Earlier studies also confirmed that ICTs can create new, strong linkages between internal activities, and even coordinate these actions more closely with their consumers and suppliers to facilitate integration within the company (Leenders & Wierenga, 2002; Sánchez *et al.*, 2007). Leeders and Wierenga (2002) suggested that ICTs not only help to transfer knowledge among team members, but also support the creation of new knowledge within a particular area. Sánchez *et al.* (2007) also stated that ICTs enhance the company's ability to coordinate activities regionally, nationally and globally, creating many new interrelationships among them.

The Use of E-Networks and Gain Market Share

As shown in Table 3, the business cases recognised direct and indirect links between the use of E-networks and increase the market share. However, case 1 has not identified any link. Two projects (Cases 2 and 3) believe in e-networks as driver for products development through taking customers' feedback. In short, (Figure 1) represents the relationship between the use of E-networks and increasing the market share.

In this aspect, similar studies stated that E-networks enable SMEs to access to new environments as well as the generation of new markets

Table 2. How small businesses utilise E -environment

Expected benefits of E-environment	Case 1	Case 2	Case 3	Case 4
Communicate with projects customers, suppliers and marketing dealers	✓	✓	✓	✓
Improve products design and quality				✓
Send and receive internal and external reports	✓	✓	✓	✓
Build customers relationships with continuous communications		✓	✓	
Make the work processes easier, quicker, and cheaper			✓	
Develop their own marketing outlet and channels		✓	✓	
Take customers feedback and satisfaction		✓	✓	

Table 3. The use of E-networks to increase the business market share

	Case 1	Case 2	Case 3	Case 4
The use of E-networks applications has no impact on increasing the business market share.	✓			
the use of E-networks may help the project on create more marketing channels		✓	✓	
The participation on the E-networks activities is the way to increase the direct sales.			✓	
The use of E-networks lead to increase the market share			✓	✓
The use of E-networks facilitates the development of the business that will lead directly to increase the market share				✓
The use of e-networks to take customers feedback as products development driver		✓	✓	

and business models (Sánchez *et al.,* 2007). Al-lahawiah et al. (2010) concluded that internet supports many SMEs to maintain contact with their customers. They can use the Internet for transnational marketing and transactions, thereby globalizing their sales and allow SMEs to improve relations with their suppliers and customers.

Challenges of Use E-Networks to Gain Market Share

As shown in Table 4, the four cases confirms that the major challenges for using e-networks to gain make share are external marketing agencies and lack of staff skills. However, three projects (Cases 1, 3, and 4) consider that difficulty in accessing regional markets is an additional major challenge.

Furthermore, Stansfield and Grant (2003) concluded that policy makers need to address the current attitudes and support mechanisms with regards to how to develop a positive approach to training staff with the skills needed to capitalise on Internet related technologies. Andam (2003) also concluded that there are many challenges faced by SMEs in their use of ICT in business or in engaging in e-commerce in developing countries such as lack of awareness for ICT value and lack of ICT knowledge and skills

Figure 1. Links identified between uses of E-networks and gaining of market share

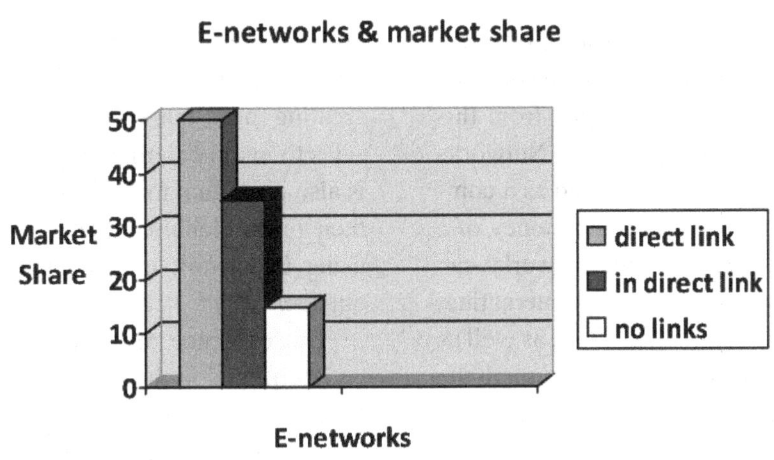

Table 4. Challenges of use E-networks to gain market share

	Case 1	Case 2	Case 3	Case 4
The project depends on external marketing agencies and dealers	✓	✓	✓	✓
Lack of staff skills such as English language difficulties	✓	✓	✓	✓
The project has difficulty accessing regional markets	✓		✓	✓
Long distance from the capital city (Amman)		✓		
Lack of expert workers in handicraft products	✓			
The project has seasonal demand	✓			

In addition to these, some previous studies confirmed that continuous training can play an important role in increasing the awareness of the huge potentialities of ICTs. Entrepreneurs can acquire a learning culture, integrating the training in their work activities and understanding in depth the potentialities of communication and information tools (Brady *et al.,* 2002; Sánchez *et al.,* 2007)

RESULTS AND CONCLUSIONS

The purpose of this study was to provide a deep understanding of the current status of electronic networks in the Jordanian handicrafts sector from managers' perspectives. More specifically, the study investigated the contribution of electronic networks as a key success factor to gain market share in some selected handicraft small businesses in Jordan.

In the light of the textual analysis of business case transcripts and the holistic analysis of cross cases, several findings have emerged from this study. First, a definition for Electronic Networks has been developed. It can be defined as a communication tool that saves time and money of a business. Furthermore, electronic networks can be used for the purpose of searching, interacting, learning, facilitating the internal work, as well as developing the production. Second, although the majority of projects do strongly believe in the importance of E-networks to gain market share

to develop the handicraft sector in Jordan, the selected cases are not satisfied with the level E-networks activities deployment in their projects, as email were indicated to be the main electronic networks utilised. Finally, the major barriers of E-networks use are depending on external marketing agencies, lack of staff skills especially English language, and difficulty in having access to regional markets.

In the light of the study findings and insights, the following recommendations are proposed for the Jordanian handicraft businesses. First, businesses should consider the decision of e-networks adoption in their future plans to take advantages of electronic networks applications in a manner that go beyond e-mails applications. Second, businesses should adopt the internal marketing concept through proper employees selection and proper training for their staff skills and capabilities to enhance their IT and English language skills. Third, businesses should take steps forward in utilising marketing through designing their own interactive internet website that is essential in creating new marketing channels with direct sales to avoid external marketing agencies. This is also important to aid businesses in developing their promotional campaigns for their products using E-network to build their projects image outside Jordan.

The evidence reported in this study should be interpreted in the light of several limitations. Notably, this study scope was limited to Jordanian handicraft businesses sector within a specific small country context, thus caution has to be exercised when generalising the present findings.

RECOMMENDATIONS FOR FURTHER RESEARCH

In the light of study limitations, the future studies can test the different stages of electronic networks adoption in handicraft sectors. Moreover, potential applications of electronic networks using various handicraft sectors can be investigated. Furthermore, learning processes from other sectors experience can be considered by handicrafts sector. Finally, e-networks can be disseminated as another evolutionary open innovation concept for business development among the small firms arena in the context of utilising knowledge from within the business and outside the business to promote value gain.

REFERENCES

Adekunle, P., & Tella, A. (2008). Nigeria SMEs participation in electronic economy: Problems and the way forward. *Journal of Internet Banking and Commerce, 12*(3).

Allahawiah, S., Altarawneh, H., & Alamro, S. (2010). *The Internet and small medium-sized enterprises (SMEs) in Jordan.* Retrieved from http://www.waset.org/journals/waset/v62/v62-54.pdf

Andam, Z. (2003). *E-commerce and e-business.* Retrieved from http://www.apdip.net/publications/iespprimers/eprimer-ecom.pdf

Brady, M., Saren, M., & Tzokas, N. (2002). Integrating information technology into marketing practice – the IT realize of contemporary marketing practice. *Journal of Marketing Management, 18*, 555–577. doi:10.1362/0267257022683703

Bryman, A. (2008). *Social research methods* (3rd ed.). New York, NY: Oxford University Press.

Chesbrough, H. W. (2003). *Open innovation: The new imperative for creating and profiting from technology.* Boston, MA: Harvard Business School Press.

Chitura, T., Mupemhi, S., Dube, T., & Bolongkikit, J. (2008). Barriers to electronic commerce adoption in small and medium enterprises: A critical literature review. *Journal of Internet Banking and Commerce, 13*(2).

Chussil, M. (1991). Does market share really matter. *Strategy and Leadership, 19*(5), 31–37. doi:10.1108/eb054336

Collins, C., Buhalis, D., & Peters, M. (2003). Enhancing SMEs' business performance through the internet and E-learning platforms. *Education + Training, 45*(8-9), 483-494.

Doncombe, R., & Heeks, R. (2005). *Information & communication technologies (ICTs), poverty reduction and micro, small &medium-scale enterprises (MSMEs): A framework for understanding ICT applications for MSMEs in developing countries.* Retrieved from http://www.unido.org/fileadmin/media/documents/pdf/Services_Modules/ict_brochure_report.pdf

Falkenberg, A. (1984). Modeling market share: A study of Japanese and U.S. performance in the U.S. Auto market. *Journal of the Academy of Marketing Science, 12*(4), 145–160. doi:10.1007/BF02721805

Fillis, I. (2002). Barriers to internationalisation: An investigation of the craft microenterprise. *European Journal of Marketing, 36*(7-8), 912–917. doi:10.1108/03090560210430872

Fillis, I., Johanson, U., & Wagner, B. (2004). Factors impacting on e-business adoption and development in the smaller firm. *International Journal of Entrepreneurial Behaviour & Research, 10*(3), 178–191. doi:10.1108/13552550410536762

Fink, D., & Disterer, G. (2006). International case studies: To what extent is ICT infused into the operations of SMEs. *Journal of Enterprise Information Management*, *19*(6), 608–624. doi:10.1108/17410390610708490

Haider, A. (2009). *How to gain market share?* Retrieved from http://article.abc-directory.com/article/5907

Hunaiti, Z., Masa'deh, R., Mansour, M., & Nawaf-leh, A. (2009). Electronic commerce adoption barriers in small and medium-sized enterprises (SMEs) in developing countries: The case of Libya. *IBIMA Business Review*, *2*, 37–45.

Kulmala, H., & Rauva, E. (2005). Network as a business environment: Experience from software industry. *Supply Chain Management: An International Journal*, *10*(3), 169–178. doi:10.1108/13598540510606223

Kuzma, A., & Shanklin, W. (1992). How medium-market-share companies achieve superior profitability. *Journal of Consumer Marketing*, *9*(1), 39–46. doi:10.1108/EUM0000000002595

Lal, K. (2005). Determinants of the adoption of e-business technologies. *Telematics and Informatics*, *22*(3), 181–199. doi:10.1016/j.tele.2004.07.001

Lawrence, J. (2008). The challenges and utilization of e-commerce: Use of Internet by small to medium–sized enterprises in the United Kingdom. *Information. Social Justice (San Francisco, Calif.)*, *1*(2), 99–113.

Leenders, M. A. A. M., & Wierenga, B. (2002). The effectiveness of different mechanisms for integrating marketing and R&D. *Journal of Product Innovation Management*, *19*(4), 305–317. doi:10.1016/S0737-6782(02)00147-9

Liu, C., & Arentt, K. (2000). Exploring the factors associated with website success in the context of electronic commerce. *Information & Management*, *38*(1), 23–33. doi:10.1016/S0378-7206(00)00049-5

McAuley, A., & Fillies, I. (2006). *A future in the making: A socio-economic study of makers in Northern Ireland 2006*. Belfast, Ireland: Craft Northern Ireland.

Mculey, A., & Fillis, I. (2004). *A socio-economic study of crafts businesses in England and Wales*. London, UK: Crafts Council, Arts Council England, and Arts Council Wales.

O'Toole, T. (2003). E-relationships: Emergence and the small firm. *Marketing Intelligence & Planning*, *21*(2), 115–122. doi:10.1108/02634500310465434

Poon, S., & Swatman, P. (1998). An exploratory study of small business Internet commerce issues. *Information & Management*, *35*(1), 9–18. doi:10.1016/S0378-7206(98)00079-2

Ramsey, E., Ibbotson, P., Bell, J., & Gray, B. (2003). E-opportunities of service sector SMEs: An Irish cross-border study. *Journal of Small Business and Enterprise Development*, *10*(3), 250–264. doi:10.1108/14626000310489709

Sánchez, V., Ruiz, M., & Zarco, A. (2007). Drivers, benefits and challenges of ICT adoption by small and medium sized enterprises (SMEs): A literature review. *Problems and Perspectives in Management*, *5*(1), 103–114.

Serbanica, D., & Militaru, G. (2008). Competitive advantage by integrated e-business in supply chains: A strategic approach. *Management and Marketing- Craiova*, *1*, 27-36.

Shanklin, W. (1992). Market share is not destiny. *Journal of Product and Brand Management*, *1*(3), 33–44. doi:10.1108/10610429210036843

Stanfield, M., & Grant, K. (2003). Barriers to the take-up of electronic commerce among small-medium sized enterprises. *Informing Science*, 737–745.

Stockdale, R., & Standing, C. (2004). Benefits and barriers of electronic marketplace participation: An SME perspective. *Journal of Enterprise Information Management*, *17*(4), 301–311. doi:10.1108/17410390410548715

Stockdale, R., & Standing, C. (2006). A classification model to support SME e-commerce adoption initiatives. *Journal of Small Business and Enterprise Development*, *13*(3), 381–394. doi:10.1108/14626000610680262

Tang, N., Burridge, M., & Ang, A. (2003). Development of an electronic-business planning model for small and medium-sized enterprises. *International Journal of Logistics Research and Applications*, *6*(4), 289–304. doi:10.1080/13675 560310001627043

Taylor, M., & Murphy, A. (2004). SMEs and e-business. *Journal of Small Business and Enterprise Development*, *11*(3), 280–289. doi:10.1108/14626000410551546

Thomas, B., & Sparkes, A. (2001). The use of Internet as a critical success factor for the marketing of Welsh agri-food SMEs in twenty first century. *British Food Journal*, *103*(5), 331–347. doi:10.1108/00070700110395368

This work was previously published in the International Journal of Information Communication Technologies and Human Development, Volume 3, Issue 3, edited by Susheel Chhabra and Hakikur Rahman, pp. 1-15, copyright 2011 by IGI Publishing (an imprint of IGI Global).

Chapter 9
From Rural Outsourcing to Rural Opportunities:
Developing an ICT Mediated Distributed Production Enterprise in Tamil Nadu, India

Aarti Kawlra
Indian Institute of Technology Madras, India

ABSTRACT

Inspired by the potential of Information and Communication Technologies, henceforth ICTs, for socio-economic development, and supported by a university based technology and business incubator, Rural Production Company, henceforth RPC, was set up in 2007 employing an ICT-mediated distributed production model. This paper reveals how RPC, initially an exploratory project whose key innovation was its Internet kiosk-facilitated model of crafts production and local empowerment, morphed into a social enterprise catering to global demands. The context of innovation provided by the Incubator led to a transformation of an ICT4D (ICT for Development) project into a business venture through the practice of formal and informal questioning at every stage of its implementation. This paper focuses on the iterative method adopted while highlighting the role of the incubator in the overall design and development process of the enterprise. This paper is a reflexive mapping of the organization's evolution from the original research agenda of outsourcing production cum rural employment, to one that privileges local networks both as a conscious business strategy and as an arena for collaborative change for human development.

INTRODUCTION

This paper follows the conception and growth of a social enterprise developed within the context of a university based incubator. It presents the unique incubation context of innovation and enterprise development of a production company involved in rural crafts by spotlighting the reflexive practices within its development process. The study is set against the backdrop of advancements in affordable technologies for rural connectivity (Jain & Raghuram, 2005; James, 2002; 2004; Jhunjhunwala, n. d.; Jhunjhunwala, Ramamurthi, & Gonsalves, 1998) on one hand, and research

DOI: 10.4018/978-1-4666-1957-9.ch009

in distributed production models (Holmstrom, 1993; Johansson, Kisch, & Mirata, 2005; Mathew, 1997; Oram & Doane, 2005) and crafts production (Brouwer, 1999; De Neve, 2005; Liebl & Roy, 2004; Mies, 1982; Kawlra, 1998; Venkatesan, 2009; Wood, 2000) on the other.

It's still wider relevance lies in going beyond narrow technological determinist views of ICT and development towards one that views technology as both facilitating and enhancing capabilities (Castells, 2000; Fukada-Parr, 2003; Grunfeld, 2009; Gurumurthy, 2008; Heeks, 2002, 2009; James, 2004; Sen, 1999). Presenting a detailed reflection of the stages in the growth of the organisation along with a conscious recognition of the role played by the incubator during its developmental course, it is hoped, would provide a closer look into the significance of academia-led innovation for a more dynamic and sustainable engagement with local actors in rural contexts. It will be appropriate, therefore, to commence the discussion with an understanding of incubators in general and the distinguishing features of the specific incubator in particular.

THE INNOVATION CONTEXT OF UNIVERSITY BASED INCUBATION

Incubators, in general, are seen as innovation spaces where entrepreneurs and business ventures receive various kinds of support for a sustained period of time to develop and commercialize new products, new technologies, or services. Typically this is accomplished through "job-creation" and "wealth generation" which are viewed as a means to focus on the wider community through the agency of the entrepreneur often, mediated through technology (Almirall, 2008; Carayannis et al., 2006; Castells, 2000; Chesbrough, 2003; Scaramuzzi, 2002; Sein & Harindranath, 2004; Schaffers et al., 2007; Schaffers & Kulkki, 2007; Steyaert, 2000).

The aims and approaches of incubators vary from country to country and cater to the unique entrepreneurial ecosystem of its country of location (Akcomak, 2009; Chandra, 2007; Lalkaka, 2001). In the developing world, incubators are viewed as important means of economic development through the promotion and growth of micro, small and medium enterprises and actively supported through programmatic funding and policies by governments through business incubation (Scaramuzzi, 2002). The various functions and services of incubators include – physical space and business centre facilities; technology and human resources; management and administrative (accounting and legal) support; information and data support; mentoring, diagnostic and crisis support; and access to finance and venture capitalists.

University-based incubators, in particular, are usually set up in or near the institution's campus, have the involvement of its students and faculty, and vary in model, size and goals. Typically they are committed to forge linkages between academia, the industry and the government towards the macro-goal of economic development. This approach has been termed the "triple helix model" of regional development where entrepreneurial universities transfer knowledge to the industry via the mechanism of incubators, for the benefit of society (Etzkowitz, 2002). While it is believed that knowledge-based growth would in turn foster more research funding and stimulate greater interaction (networks) between the three partners or stakeholders and in turn also sustain the incubators, the triple helix model has shown limited success (Cooke, 2005; Gunasekara, 2006). Other "innovation intermediaries" like the European Living Labs ('living laboratories') also support business innovation by providing a structured environment within which new technologies, products and services are designed and validated with the participation and feedback of actual users in real life settings (Almirall, 2008; Schaffers et al., 2007; Schaffers & Kulkki, 2007).

However, while they are committed to the multiple stakeholders concerned, they do not necessarily involve academia.

As a formal arrangement for the interaction between academia, governmental and nongovernmental organisations and the private industry, university-based incubators are innovation spaces where new ideas and structures of change are co-created and co-developed. As in recent advances in the development of IT, the incubation context presented in this paper points to iterative methodologies in design processes involving the wider society including users (Dittrich, Eriksen, & Wessels, 2009; Kling, 2000). Negotiations and constructive discourse between the various actors and agents are central to the flexibility of the innovation process while confronting limitations and challenges. Indeed, innovation requires the ability to bring about change not only through a break from convention, but also through a reconfiguration of priorities and agendas while continuing to honour the original mission. Indeed the stated goal of the incubator under study is to design, pilot and build businesses that harness the power of ICT's in the areas of affordable connectivity, livelihood, health, education, agriculture and financial inclusion for empowering rural India.

The innovative character of the university-based incubator studied in this paper, it will be seen, is its openness to exploration in areas sans experience or demonstrated potential and its strategy to view challenges as lessons that enrich its wider eco-system of incubation. Most significantly, this paper will show how the incubator's processes provide entrepreneurs with a learning space for a sustained dialogue and collaboration with rural entrepreneurs, producers, governmental and non-governmental intermediaries, during the course of the development and maturity of the enterprise. Indeed, a key component of the incubation practice is the building of networks of relationships between urban entrepreneurs and local actors and leveraging the increasingly robust mobile and Internet connectivity in rural India for the same.

Rural Incubator (henceforth RI) was conceived by its academic founders as an incubator with a difference. In 2006, the year of its inception, it mission was defined to serve India's rural underserved population, characterised by significantly lower levels of education and employment, through the creation of innovative business models and ICT applications. Its original research context was the technical innovations in providing affordable and low-cost connectivity to rural India at the university on the one hand and, on the other, to conduct field based experiments in building locally appropriate applications and services for further influencing telecom policies. It was in this context and spirit of social entrepreneurship that rural production company (henceforth RPC) was set up in late 2007 at the RI with an initial funding from a global project on Information for Development. It was registered as a company by an entrepreneur who had some experience with working in microfinance and self-help groups (SHG's) in Madurai, Tamil Nadu and who had been at the RI exploring possibilities in an existing research project in rural IT outsourcing. The genealogy of the company, however, dates still further back a couple of years when it was a pilot project developing and testing an ICT enabled crafts production project.

The crafts sector in India is characterised on one hand by a high degree of dynamism and, on the other, by a potential that remains largely untapped (Liebl & Roy, 2003). Apart from the few successful traditional artisan community based enterprises, private enterprises, a host of governmental and non governmental bodies engaged in crafts production and some studio or designer led niche ventures, the sector continues to struggle with problems pertaining to market responsiveness, global competition and availability of raw materials among others (Liebl & Roy, 2003). The promotion of micro and small enterprises with an ethically inspired developmental focus for the creation of rural livelihoods has been an important approach favouring crafts and their producers (Brouwer, 1999; De Neve, 2005; Holmstrom, 1993; Karnani, 2007; Mathew, 1997; Miller, Dawans, & Alter, 2009; Randall, 2005; Solanki, 2002; Strawn & Littrell, 2006). Creating innovative ICT's based solutions for enabling greater sustainability and scalability of rural craft-based production enterprises, therefore, was among the objectives in the ICT4D vision of the Incubator.

THE ICT4D PROJECT: EXPLORATORY PHASE

The inception of RPC has its roots in the academic context of technology innovations for providing low-cost connectivity to rural India as part of the twin global projects of bridging the "digital divide" through the spread and diffusion of ICT's (James, 2004; Kenniston, 2000; Norris, 2001) on the one hand, and finding "fortune at the bottom of the pyramid" on the other (Prahalad, 2002, 2004). It was also preceded by the several experiments in delivering affordable and low-cost Internet and telecom facilities to rural India since the late 1990's (Garai & Shadrach, 2006; James, 2004). Among these ICT for rural experiments was the *rural* Internet service provider company, henceforth ISP Company, which had been recently been incubated as the result of commercialisation of academic research with a business and delivery model believed to be appropriate for scaling throughout rural India (James, 2004; Jhunjhunwala, Ramachandran, & Bandhopadhyay, 2004; Paul, 2004).

The Internet Kiosk Model of ICT Access and Services Delivery

Its model inspired by the earlier success of expanding STD (subscriber trunk-dialling) access across India by sharing revenues with the local level operator, was designed as a three-tier franchise with entrepreneurs at every level. At the level of the city the ISP Company was responsible for the management and delivery of Internet services throughout its network. At the district level were the Local Service Providers (LSP) who invest in setting up the Access Centre and were responsible for managing and expanding the network to nearby villages. At the third tier were the many village-level entrepreneurs, or kiosk operators (KO) recruited by LSP's and who invest in and set up Internet kiosks with the infrastructural and technical training support of the ISP Company. These KO's in turn were positioned to provide a variety of Internet and computer based services for the rural market.

The ISP Company's rural networks across Tamil Nadu at the district and village levels formed the "rural access" nodes to RPC's first pilot forays in outsourcing production as the Project. Its rural outreach was mediated by the persona of the kiosk operator (KO), who performed the role of a local coordinator for organizing women's self-help groups (SHG's) and other rural producers to come under the fold of the Project. The many KO's were further coordinated under each district by Project field staff to provide technical and other support to the KO as well as seek out other producer groups in the vicinity of the kiosk.

Given that a three tier model for "penetration" into rural Tamil Nadu was already available – along the lines of the fibre optic cable – and offering existing relations with the different KO's and LSP's, the Project was initiated by taking forward a significant lesson learned from some existing projects on craft production at the university. The failure of two such experiments had been largely attributed to the problem of transportation of raw material from cities to the kiosk villages and back again to the urban client or company. This important lesson from the academic knowledge pool was responsible for re-orienting the production towards products for which raw materials were abundantly available in rural areas.

From Information Entrepreneurship to Craft Entrepreneurship

RPC in its original Project mode commenced its development by identifying and selecting KO's from banana plantation villages in the ISP Company's rural network for producing banana bark rope for a client in Bangalore. Given the fact that banana bark rope making is not a specialized skill and is not unknown to agricultural workers in the three districts chosen, the main endeavour was to enlist KO's who would be willing to expand their work description to include the organization of banana rope production. Raw material or bark collection and storage, training on banana bark splicing, rope twisting, rope grading, quality checking, packaging, delivery, invoicing and receipts were some of the main tasks involved, which were envisioned by the Project to be facilitated by a combination of technology mediated and face to face interactions.

Within a few months, five KO's from the three districts had been enlisted as local entrepreneurs ready to take on production for the Project and which was carried out in the households and streets of the producers' own villages. Exposure to the different products made from the rope at the client's facility in Bangalore, and subsequent interactions between KO's with trainers and quality managers immediately made it clear to all concerned that variations in rope quality was locality specific. Each KO/ Project Centre was thus given a specific product to develop based upon the quality of the rope they produced and the expertise available in and around the region. Thus, for instance, while some qualities were good for making table and floor mats, others were fine enough to crochet into fashion accessories, while a third could be used as weft in weaving table runners by coarse count handloom weavers in the vicinity. In this way, each KO was envisioned to expand his/her production capacity and product portfolio by training new producer groups while at the same time handling production orders for

the Project. In the meantime, the Project was to handle business development and find markets outside India among fair trade organizations and eco-friendly craft product retailers.

Within six months the Project had started registering revenues and was in a position to think of itself less as a research pilot and more as an enterprise in the making with an innovative business model in the field of craft production. In a poster submission at an international conference held at the university in August 2007, RPC presented its ICT enabled distributed production model publicly for the first time as below:

The Company mediates between the production Centre(s) and the Client(s) at a macro level while at the micro level of analysis, RPC is engaged in the distribution and aggregation of production orders to and from its many franchises or village-based ICT enabled Production Centres for the benefit of its many clients, each with their individual product specifications. Its particular Distributive Production Management System (C3) includes a Centre-wise product and skill database as well as a portfolio of craft workers differentiated on the basis of their skill levels and product specialties.

The role of RPC, apart from business development, is essentially to provide quality filters and production standards on the one hand and, on the other, mentorship to village based ICT entrepreneurs engaged in production coordination. This not only provides a unique model for community-based production organization outside the traditional artisan community fold but also offers transparencies, efficiencies and risk distribution in craft production hitherto unimaginable"(Kawlra & Sreejith, 2007, p. 4).

As a paradigm for ICT applications for livelihoods creation, this was an ideal typical model and the feedback for it was positive as well. However, the reality on the ground presented a very different picture.

The incubator's project reviews were based on two key milestones – successful completion of client orders and sustained revenue at the local Internet kiosk. This, according to its "incubation pathway", would take the Project to its next level – to that of being a pilot – or a "venture in the making" where the various technical, business and production processes are fine-tuned for different geographies and eventual scaling. The difficulty, however, was that while the Project's implementation plans appeared sound on paper, the said targets were far from achieved on account of irregularities in the supply and quality of products from the production units. The problems faced were related to the fact that the various local partners – the kiosk operators – were primarily "information entrepreneurs" providing ICT based services and only secondarily organizers of production. Moreover, the investments in the kiosk were fixed and required little working capital, something that they were unprepared for. Added to that, the exigencies of production required that the Project move to locations where raw material or skills were available which, unfortunately, did not necessarily coincide with kiosk presence.

Rethinking the approach of the ICT based kiosk facilitated model for craft production was clearly required. Some of the questions that came up during brainstorming sessions at the incubator were: Was it a top down imposition? But had not the Project looked at raw material resources and skills availability among other things before selecting its local partners for ensuring continuity? Is there a need to redefine the initial goals of service applications at Internet kiosks? It was clear that the Project's mission was not product-led but rather employment-led production. So why was the Project investing so much in product diversification and new skills development? Again, why was it focusing on the sustainability of individual kiosk operators who did not have production domain expertise?

The arguments were clearly guiding RPC to move away from the BoP (Bottom of the Pyramid)

model of viewing the rural as an emerging market for ICT products to a perspective that views rural citizens not merely as consumers but, significantly, as producers with capabilities and potential that could be developed (Karnani, 2007; Sen, 1999). The incubator suggested stepping out of the project mode of development intervention and moving on to that of a for-profit business without compromising on the original mission of wealth creation in rural India. An IT enabled venture catering to business process outsourcing to rural areas was part of the incubation eco-system and served to provide the Project with many a lesson from its own experience in business modelling. One of the aspects inadvertently adopted, was its model of outsourcing to rural areas for its comparative cost advantage vis-à-vis the urban.

This change, however, was made possible only after it had been decided subsequent to much deliberation that RPC was not a handicrafts company producing skill intensive, low volume-high margin products for the niche market, but rather one focused on high volume-low skill handmade products to generate large scale rural employment. Its aim, therefore, was not the production of custom made designer products but rather, the custom production of handmade products. This newly articulated vision and mission, however, demanded a full time executive at its helm. So the initial research project, of enabling crafts production through ICT kiosks, gradually gave way to an enterprise in the making through a formal incorporation of the project as a company with its principal project staff as the first board members.

THE EMERGENT RURAL (CRAFT) PRODUCTION COMPANY (RPC)

The move towards larger production scales was a confident one as it meant not only demonstrating the use of ICT's in creating greater efficiencies in production across geographies but also in piloting the distributed production model as a way to mitigate its unsustainable practices and consequences. Under this model, production is organised in small micro-units that are flexible and interrelated with each other in accordance with individual product or client production cycles (Christopher, 2000; Holmstrom, 1993; Johansson, Kisch, & Mirata, 2005).

RPC was now repositioned as a production organization employing ICT's for enhancing standardized, efficient and transparent production in rural areas. The problem addressed and value addition proposed by the emergent enterprise was defined in a report to an international funder in October 2007 as one addressing the pitfalls of the existing informal sector - delivery, quality, communication and credibility on the demand side and, on the supply side, it would provide employment opportunities to a workforce hitherto untrained or exposed to global demand.

RI's academic environment ensured that the company's operational model would shift from that of Internet kiosk facilitation, but also be wary of the pitfalls of the factory model with its attendant social and environmental implications. The local entrepreneurs this time were not to be ICT kiosk operators but those focused and experienced in craft production. So what was eventually envisioned was a rural production-outsourcing model or contractual production in micro-production units in villages in dispersed locations. Each of these production centres was to specialize in a core set of skills and production capabilities and capacities for individual clients and together be coordinated through the company's ICT platform for efficient production and delivery. The model was that of horizontally placed, autonomous modular units of production linked to a single buyer or organiser of production.

Moreover, this was also the rhetoric and production mantra of the 80's where "outsourcing" meant that firms decided to purchase fabricated or manufactured inputs into their own assembly line without actually setting up their own in-house facility to do the same (Friedman, 2005). So in

the leather footwear industry, for instance, the raw material is sourced from one country, the tanning done in yet another, the uppers in still another, while the design and the final shoe is made in the company's own country. "Could this be a model worth emulating?" RPC's CEO and others at the RI were not sure but for a while, continued with the flow led by the buoyancy of the incubation environment. However, it soon became evident that in the context of the use of ICT's, production process outsourcing was very different from business process outsourcing. RPC was transporting physical goods and not transmitting services over the Internet or other virtual communication channels (Bhagwati, 2004). The issues of quantity, quality and costs were highly vulnerable areas and could not be outsourced to still fledgling units and instead required greater vertical integration.

The company's next milestone, therefore, was to become more than just a coordinator of production entrepreneurs located in geographically dispersed centres. This would, it was believed, be addressed by the ICT interface that could be developed through the support of the incubator and presented a fairly surmountable challenge. What was more crucial was the fact that systems had to be developed and put in place in order to handle rural manufacturing at larger scales profitably. This meant a vertical integration of the production process and the creation of micro units based not on local entrepreneurs' production capacity but on specific skills, raw materials and stage in the production process. The aim was to have closer monitoring and standardization of processes for achieving higher production quality and quantity at lower costs.

It was decided, therefore, that mid-level organizers of production, would no longer provide the working capital or share revenues. This would mitigate a number of risks and challenges that had already been experienced with regard to quality, quantity and costs. At this stage RPC was more confident of its production and marketing capabilities and less so of handling local producers and the management took the decision to outsource labour mobilisation, recruitment and administration to local partners while keeping training and product development and production monitoring in house. By now RPC's revenues had started to mount as had the number of big clients together with their production compliance requirements. The company soon moved from coordinating dispersed production entrepreneurs to that of investing in its own production units in rural Tamil Nadu.

SEARCHING FOR (BRAND) IDENTITY: FROM OUTSOURCING TO OPPORTUNITIES

Economic self-sufficiency was a very important criterion for moving onto the next phase of incubation – that of an early stage Start-up. A round of funding was initiated by the RI to take the company forward in this direction of graduation from its fold. This in turn led to an expansion of the Board as well as the induction of industry and academic advisors to support this move. The regular budgetary reviews at the RI discontinued and instead the role of monitoring progress was taken up by the Board which included an RI representative. In the first year of its operation as a graduated company, the growth imperative guided much of RPC's business strategy. This objective of expansion is clearly stated and evident in RPC's second Annual Report of the assessment year 2008-09:

... to provide global customers with access to rural artisans who manufacture diverse products .... In the first year of its operation the company was engaged in the business of manufacture and sale of eco-friendly products made from natural fibres like banana and jute. The product segments ...during this period were corporate gift items like bags and folders and furnishings like mats, carpets and window blinds. (Sreejith, 2009, p. 1).

Consequently, its rural production partners as well as central organizational structure also underwent many expansive changes.

In that year (2008-09) RPC's production units grew from being located in two districts of Tamil Nadu – Madurai and Thanjavur – to seven other districts. The demand for corporate products led to further expansion so that the company was now locating its product finishing units outside Chennai city. In October 2008, the company had its own warehouse cum design studio in Chennai. By mid-2009 RPC was well underway in its large-scale production of handmade potpourri bags for a prestigious multinational company and was slowly dedicating staff and resources to build infrastructure and conduct training workshops to cater to the growing demand. It became imperative therefore that communication design inputs be provided for all the company's client presentations, promotional literature and website. This, it was believed, would evoke positive imagery of a professional enterprise engaged in rural production and employment generation while at the same time build a natural fibre focused brand identity.

After numerous brainstorming sessions, two important revelations were made, with obvious implications for RPC's future development and strategy. The first was the question of its name and the second was to do with its product range – both had to be altered to suit the changed market positioning of the company. Originally the term "outsourcing" had been central to the name of the company. Now the "o" of outsourcing became the "o" of opportunities in the name, which itself is an acronym. The website records this change by highlighting the active involvement of small rural producers with artisanal skills as "opportunities". According to the CEO, the term 'outsourced' confused some customers with regard to RPC's business model, as it appeared to be a trading organization offering no value additions of its own. The chosen term 'opportunity' on the other hand, did not imply this imagery and better captured the true essence of an ethical production organization. And while there was a clear economic rational to the said amendments, the conceptual basis for the same was no less significant. The repositioning of RPC's products as eco-friendly meant a fresh look at all parameters of production from the environmental perspective, in addition to that of equity, which had already been part of the original research design. The mission statement of the company now incorporated economy, equity and environment as the organization's triple bottom line.

The market repositioning also meant a clearer agenda and it was decided therefore to concentrate on key clients with larger and repeat orders. As it was unlikely to find such customers in the corporate products segment, RPC decided to withdraw from this segment and focus solely on handmade or handloom woven home accessories. In October 2009, the company's website formally announced that they had "discontinued small orders to focus exclusively on larger key accounts. This was done so that ... (RPC) could best fulfill our customers' needs while obtaining maximum social impact...,"thus reinforcing the company's new found production vision.

RPC had to move out of the corporate products segment for other reasons as well. Work pressure had continued to rise and the company was facing difficulties in meeting production schedules and quantities from multiple small clients. Various demands – pertaining to funds, new client orders, coordinating diverse production centres, marketing, sampling and the like – continued, until it was finally concluded that RPC was facing the conundrum of a very top heavy organization. It was at this time that the management, the board and academic advisors at RI together re-stated the company's commitment to the distributed production model and RPC was strategically transformed into a lean organizational structure at the head office in Chennai with its own production centres in dispersed locations in rural Tamil Nadu.

The priority areas for the company were now reformulated using a perspective that consciously views local resources as opportunities for mutual growth: limiting the diversity of raw materials to maintain quality standards; improving their sourcing and procurement procedures; using the volume and continuity of key account orders to negotiate better rates with local suppliers by building long term relations with them; directly working with the rural producers instead of mediating entrepreneurs; creating a productivity based incentive system to remunerate workers; using existing rural infrastructure like marriage halls and vacant buildings for production instead of building or purchasing specially for the purpose.

RPC had transformed from a company focusing on corporate and conference bespoke products for national and international customers to one focusing on large whole sale buyers of mass-produced natural fibre handmade products alone. Accordingly, its product portfolio and marketing message to customers changed in the company's website. The products featured on the website were intended to showcase the portfolio of skills and raw materials that the company could work with. RPC was now offering to its international customers, not certain products but capabilities in the form of flexible production units with the ability to quickly respond to market signals, to enable collaborative prototyping and product innovations. These capabilities could then be mutually utilized by the clients and the company designers to realistically assess future production capacities and client orders respectively.

Both the decision to focus on the large scale manufacture of natural fibres and products and the name change came from the realization that a sustainable and competitive business model must leverage existing rural opportunities and strengths, which is aptly reflected in the company's by-line "Rural skills meeting global demand". Most recently its CEO conceptualized RPC by contrasting it with other craft product companies along the following lines:

- RPC focuses on eco-friendly home accessories and packaging products with plans for product diversification into other products and innovative applications of natural fibres like natural fibre wall panels, seed beds, leaf plates and so on.

- Its business proposition is that of bringing mass production methods and systems like assembly line production into a rural distributed production context, enabling standardization, large volumes and consistent quality.

- It employs agricultural workers, who are trained in the skills required and work in a convivial atmosphere close to their homes.

- Production takes place in a number of geographically dispersed units. Each micro-production unit caters to client order specifications and capacities and functions under work compliance and certified conditions.

- It makes use of ICTs to coordinate production and supply chain management. Technology is used for daily updated MIS, design communication, streamlining procurement and material flow, production processes and quality control. Currently, the company is in the process of developing mobile phone-based reporting systems from all the centres and in customizing its resource management (ERP) system for enhancing production efficiencies and scale.

- Finally, it organizes production in a web or network of multiple hubs associated with still more numerous spokes. Each hub, usually located at the district or town level, is a nodal point of aggregation of materials and finished products, quality check point, packaging and delivery end, sampling site and coordinating and monitoring station for its respective spokes or production units. Each spoke at the village level is engaged in production, recruitment, training, and production reporting.

The continuous evaluation and reformulation of the model in conceptual and operational terms within a larger incubation eco-system had by now provided the company with a market positioning for itself. Not only was it self-consciously characterised as an innovative model, but was also overtly perceived as one sensitive to the wider human developmental goals of its incubator, now reconstituted as its own. RPC had grown from being a small ICT4D exploratory project to an enterprise in the making and finally into a start-up company with a sizeable turnover and prestigious international clients for natural fibre based handmade products. However, the road ahead for RPC, though much better defined, was still not free from challenges.

NEW CHALLENGES IN OPERATIONS

The difficulties in meeting international compliance norms from geographically distributed units in irregular settings, however, soon became so magnified that at one point the RPC management even considered the possibility of a dedicated production campus with a capacity of at least 250 workers managed entirely along the lines of an offshore factory. While this would have provided greater control over production, it was soon realised that the idea was in opposition to the original commitment of sustainable wealth creation using ICTs and could lead to fresh problems associated with centralised large scale manufacture.

RPC's current distributed production model had also evolved over a period of two years from a model of total outsourcing of production - where the company coordinated with multiple local entrepreneurs in different locations for its client order; to partial outsourcing using local partners primarily for its HR function of accessing rural producers, while handling production and marketing themselves. This model however, was also soon to change in the face of developments that took place *vis a vis* a local partner compelling the company to completely discontinue the modality of outsourcing from its operations portfolio.

A conflict situation arose between the company and its local HR partner in one of its biggest production centres handling nearly 300 craft producers. The issue involved a small local NGO who had been engaged by RPC for contract production on a revenue sharing basis. The problem had arisen when the NGO's role had recently been changed to that of an agent for the recruitment and HR compliance at a fixed monthly remuneration. Loss of a significant role and partnership, as an organiser of production and goods supplier, had prompted the aforesaid to harbour resentment against this decision taken by RPC.

The differences between RPC and the local agent reached a pinnacle point when false allegations were made by them and an official complaint registered against RPC as to who in fact had greater commitment from and rights over, the different producers under each of the production units. A confrontation before the local police inspector decided the case in favour of neither and producers were asked to choose between the two organisers of production – the local agent or RPC. In due course of settlement of the dispute, the complaint was withdrawn, a legal agreement drawn and RPC opened the doors of the production units once again to find a return of all but 25 of the full strength of its employees.

The lessons learnt from these developments were clearly articulated by RPC management – the strengthening of other centres in the distant vicinity and adding another centre in a different geographical location to handle production overflow in order to significantly reduce dependency on this particular site. It was also further decided to take cognisance of the fact that RPC had left the most crucial aspect of production – human resource relations – to an outside agency and thereby lost the opportunity of learning in-house the issues pertaining to rural producers in disbursed units. Most importantly, the lesson reiterated for RPC the efficacy and significance of the distributed production model involving smaller but numerous units over the factory based one involving large number of producers under a single roof.

RPC had come a long way in building its networks of interaction and collaboration with local actors. From working directly with ICT kiosk entrepreneurs, RPC had moved to working with the producer-suppliers and artisans in their neighbourhood and in the business relations developed initially by them. RPC had also developed links with small and big NGO's and semi-governmental bodies in different districts and variously partnered with them. Its hub and spoke production model too required licenses and approvals from local governmental authorities for smooth functioning and certification in each of the districts. The foundation of all these local networks of association has been built upon a matrix of good will created by RPC in the areas of its operation in rural Tamil Nadu. The company is now well poised in its unique model of ICT enabled distributed production, as a significant player in the field of handmade natural fibre based products, practising open innovation, by taking advantage of its wider ecology of networks for continued value addition and growth.

FUTURE ISSUES

The initial umbilical cord of the company with its incubator, though formally severed is far from detached. The road ahead to achieving sustainability and scalability are dependent on continuous rounds of funding and investments that would propel the company to its next phase of operation and scale. Whether it is for a state of the art design studio or a business development office and team located abroad to cater to its global clients, RPC must continue to leverage and sustain the linkages it had originally developed in the eco-system of RI.

Equally, apart from the official financial agreements between the two, RI continues to see to the growth of RPC towards its next phase of development as a member of its board, fund raiser and technology mentor. Moreover, RI's unique position as a university-based incubator allows it to be at the cutting edge of academic research and collaboration enabling access to both R&D funding, expertise and industry linkages world-wide. Indeed, RI continues to be engaged in national and international level research projects where RPC's own network of associations located in and around its dispersed production units, become "living labs" for RI's innovations in ICT applications for distributed production and work practices.

CONCLUSION

This paper has described the evolution of a university led rural-inclusive business venture that aims to strategically employ ICTs in the maintenance of an ever-expanding production network cutting across the traditional rural-urban divide in the context of enterprise building. It has shown the inception and transformation of the venture from an ICT for development project into a distributed production enterprise, ethically inspired and facilitated by global level processes and research in technology and production.

In addition, this case study has revealed the changing consciousness of the team that altered from the implementation of an ICT4D project for creating a profitable business to one that is also environmentally sensitive and socially conscious. At every stage of its growth, focusing on local actors, resources and linkages was a business strategy, be it the cooperative participation or lack thereof of partners in the different rural production sites or the availability or non-availability of natural or human resources. The emergent rural eco-system associated with RPC was in turn

directly responsible for the company's future trajectory. The study presented here is relevant not only for those interested in the promotion of social entrepreneurship through crafts but also for those keen on rural empowerment through technology based enterprise development. It is a study that views socio-economic development as the continuous and dynamic engagement with local actors through collaborative action and extending networks.

Finally, this case study is significant to innovation design on two accounts. In the first place it is an ethnographic reflection, the value of which lies in its "thick descriptions" (Geertz, 1975) offering a more nuanced narrative for deep insights. It is a record of the "conditions" of the creation of both the research project and enterprise building endeavour in a discursive manner. It points to the dynamic interplay between the incubators goals and the emergent company's goals and, in that sense, a self conscious exercise in constructive discourse and negotiation (Roth, 1989; Tedlock, 1991).

Indeed, the paper presents an example of the incubator as a space of high reflexivity with the demonstrated potential for tremendous autonomy of action. Secondly, it presents the specific RI's design process as more individualised and practice-based, enabling multiple iterations in support of the specific situation at hand (Suchman, 2001). It also points towards the possibility of an open space of incubation and innovation created for the fulfillment of mutual goals more sustainably. The case of RPC encourages the development of innovative solutions at every horizontal or vertical step of enterprise building, thereby creating a wider, more dynamic social ecology of collaboration for technology design and human development.

ACKNOWLEDGMENT

Material for this paper was collected by the author as a member of the staff and participant observer at the RI as well as a member of the board of RPC. Details of the organisation's later development process were generously provided by RPC's founder and CEO for which the author is very grateful. Thanks are due to C. Shambu Prasad of Xavier Institute of Management, Bhubaneswar, Vijay Baskar of Madras Institute of Development Studies and John B. Lourdusamy of IIT Madras for their comments on earlier drafts of this paper and to the Dept. of Humanities & Social Sciences, IIT Madras for providing the space to work.

REFERENCES

Akcomak, S. (2009). *Incubators as tools for entrepreneurship promotion in developing countries*. Tokyo, Japan: United Nations University.

Almirall, E. (2008). Living labs and open innovation: Roles and applicability. *Electronic Journal for Virtual Organizations and Networks, 10*, 21–26.

Brouwer, J. (1999). Modern and indigenous perceptions in small enterprises. *Economic and Political Weekly, 34*(48), 152–156.

Carayannis, E. G., Popescu, D., Sipp, C., & Stewart, M. (2006). Technological learning for entrepreneurial development (TL4ED) in the knowledge economy (KE): Case studies and lessons learned. *Technovation, 26*, 419–443. doi:10.1016/j.technovation.2005.04.003

Castells, M. (1996). *The rise of the network society, the information age: Economy, society and culture* (*Vol. 1*). Oxford, UK: Blackwell.

Chandra, A. (2007). *Approaches to business incubation: A comparative study of the United States, China and Brazil. Terre Haute*. IN: Indiana State University.

Chesbrough, H. W. (2003). *Open innovation: The new imperative for creating and profiting from technology*. Boston, MA: Harvard Business School Press.

Christopher, M. (2000). The agile supply chain: Competing in volatile markets. *Industrial Marketing Management, 29*(1), 37–44. doi:10.1016/S0019-8501(99)00110-8

Cooke, P. (2005). Regionally asymmetric knowledge capabilities and open innovation: Exploring 'Globalisation 2' a new model of industry organisation. *Research Policy, 34*(8), 1128–1149. doi:10.1016/j.respol.2004.12.005

De Neve, G. (2005). Weaving for IKEA in South India: Subcontracting, labour markets and gender relations in a global value chain. In Fuller, C. J., & Assayag, J. (Eds.), *Globalising India: Perpectives from below*. London, UK: Anthem Press.

Dittrich, Y., Eriksen, S., & Wessels, B. (2009). *From knowledge transfer to situated innovation: Cultivating spaces for cooperation in innovation and design between academics, user groups and ICT providers* (Tech. Rep. No. 2009:1). Ronneby, Sweden: Blekinge Institute of Technology.

Etzkowitz, H. (2002). Incubation of incubators: Innovation as a triple helix of university-industry-government networks. *Science & Public Policy, 29*, 115–128. doi:10.3152/147154302781781056

Friedman, T. L. (2005). *The world is flat: A brief history of the twenty-first century*. New York, NY: Farrar, Straus and Giroux.

Fukada-Parr, S. (2003). The human development paradigm: Operationalising Sen's ideas on capabilities. *Feminist Economics, 9*(2-3), 301–317.

Garai, A., & Shadrach, B. (2006). *Taking ICT to every Indian village: Opportunities and challenges*. New Delhi, India: One World South Asia.

Geertz, C. (1975). *The interpretation of cultures: Selected essays*. London, UK: Hutchinson.

Grunfeld, H. (2009). *Operationalising the capability approach for evaluating the contribution of ICT to development at ICT4D project in Bangladesh.* Victoria, Australia: Victoria University.

Gunasekara, C. (2006). Reframing the role of universities in the development of regional innovation systems. *The Journal of Technology Transfer, 31*(1), 101–113. doi:10.1007/s10961-005-5016-4

Gurumurthy, A. (2008). *Gender equality through ICT access and appropriation: Taking a rights-based approach.* Bangalore, India: IT for Change.

Heeks, R. (2002). Information systems and developing countries: Failure, success, and local improvisations. *The Information Society, 18,* 101–112. doi:10.1080/01972240290075039

Heeks, R. (2009). *The ICT4D 2.0 manifesto: Where next for ICT's and international development.* Manchester, UK: Development Informatics Group, Institute of Development Policy and Management.

Holmstrom, M. (1993). Flexible specialisation in India? *Economic and Political Weekly, 28*(35), 82–86.

Jagdish, B., Panagariya, A., & Srinivasan, T. N. (2004). The muddles over outsourcing. *Journal of Economic Perspectives. American Economic Association, 18*(4), 93–114.

Jain, R., & Raghuram, G. (2005). *Study on accelerated provisions of rural telecommunication services (ARTS).* Ahmedabad, India: Indian Institute of Management. Retrieved from http://www.iimahd.ernet.in/ctps/pdf/Final%20Report%20Edited.pdf

James, J. (2002). Low-cost information technology in developing countries: Current opportunities and emerging possibilities. *Habitat International, 26,* 21–31. doi:10.1016/S0197-3975(01)00030-3

James, J. (2004). *Information technologies and development: A new paradigm for delivering the Internet to rural areas in developing countries.* London, UK: Routledge.

Jhunjhunwala, A. (n. d). *Unleashing telecom and Internet in India.* Retrieved from http://www.tenet.res.in

Jhunjhunwala, A., Ramachandran, A., & Bandyopadhyay, A. (2004). n-Logue: The story of a rural service provider in India. *Journal of Community Informatics, 1*(1), 30–38.

Jhunjhunwala, A., Ramamurthi, B., & Gonsalves, T. A. (1998). The role of technology in telecom expansion in India. *IEEE Communications Magazine,* 88–94. doi:10.1109/35.733480

Johansson, A., Kisch, P., & Mirata, M. (2005). Distributed economies – a new engine for innovation. *Journal of Cleaner Production, 13,* 971–979. doi:10.1016/j.jclepro.2004.12.015

Karnani, A. (2007). The mirage of marketing to the bottom of the pyramid: How the private sector can help alleviate poverty. *California Management Review, 49*(4), 90–111.

Kawlra, A. (1998). *Weaving as praxis: The case of the Padma Saliyars.* Unpublished doctoral dissertation, Indian Institute of Technology, Delhi, India.

Kawlra, A., & Sreejith, N. N. (2007, August 22-25). *An ICT-based model for Craft (distributive) production in India.* Paper presented at the International Conference on Home/Community Oriented IT for the Next Billion, Madras, India.

Kenniston, K., & Kumar, D. (Eds.). (2000). *Bridging the digital divide: Lessons from India.* Bangalore, India: National Institute of Advanced Study.

Kenniston, K., & Kumar, D. (Eds.). (2003). *The four digital divides.* New Delhi, India: Sage.

Kling, R. (2000). Learning about information technologies and social change: The contribution of social informatics. *The Information Society, 16*(3), 217–223. doi:10.1080/01972240050133661

Lalkala, R. (2001, November). Best practices in business incubation: Lessons yet to be learned. In *Proceedings of the International Conference on Business Centres: Actors for Economic and Social Development*, Brussels, Belgium (pp. 14-15).

Liebl, M., & Roy, T. (2003). Handmade in India: Preliminary analysis of Crafts producers and Crafts production. *Economic and Political Weekly, 38*(51-52), 5366–5376.

Mathew, P. M. (1997). From beautiful 'small' to flexible specialisation: Asian experience of small enterprise development. *Economic and Political Weekly, 32*(3), 84–86.

Mies, M. (1982). *The lace makers of Narsapur: Indian housewives produce for the world market*. London, UK: Zed Press.

Miller, L., Dawans, V., & Alter, K. (2009). *Industree Craft: A case study in social enterprise development using the four lenses approach*. Seattle, WA: Virtue Ventures, LLC.

Norris, P. (2001). *Digital divide: Civic engagement, information poverty, and the Internet worldwide*. Cambridge, UK: Cambridge University Press.

Oram, J., & Doane, D. (2005). Size matters: The need for human-scale economic institutions for development. *Development in Practice, 15*(3-4), 439–450. doi:10.1080/09614520500076233

Paul, J. (2004). *What works: n-Logue's rural connectivity model: Deploying wirelessly-connected Internet kiosks in villages throughout India*. Washington, DC: World Resources Institute.

Prahalad, C. K. (2006). *The fortune at the bottom of the pyramid: Eradicating poverty through profits*. Upper Saddle River, NJ: Wharton School Publishing.

Prahalad, C. K., & Hammond, A. (2002). Serving the world's poor, profitably. *Harvard Business Review, 80*(9), 48–57.

Randall, D. C. (2005). An exploration of opportunities for the growth of the fair trade market: Three cases of Craft organisations. *Journal of Business Ethics, 56*(1), 55–67. doi:10.1007/s10551-004-1756-6

Roth, P. A. (1989). Ethnography without tears. *Current Anthropology, 30*(5), 555–569. doi:10.1086/203784

Scaramuzzi, E. (2002). *Incubators in developing countries: Status and development perspectives*. Washington, DC: World Bank.

Schaffers, H., Cordoba, M., Hongisto, P., Kallai, T., Merz, C., & Van Renzburg, J. (2007, June 4-6). *Exploring business models for open innovation in rural living labs*. Paper presented at 13th International Conference on Concurrent Enterprising, Sophia-Antipolis, France.

Schaffers, H., & Kulkki, S. (2007). Living labs, an open innovation concept fostering rural development. *Tech Monitor*, 30-38.

Sein, M. K., & Harindranath, G. (2004). Conceptualising the ICT artifact: Toward understanding the role of ICT in national development. *The Information Society, 20*, 15–24. doi:10.1080/01972240490269942

Sen, A. (1999). *Development as freedom*. New York, NY: Knopf.

Solanki, S. S. (2002). Migration of rural artisans: Evidence from Haryana and Rajasthan. *Economic and Political Weekly, 37*(35), 3579–3580.

Sreejith, N. N., & Kawlra, A. (2009). *Director's report for the year ended 31st March 2009*. Chennai, India.

Steyaert, C. (2000, June 18-20). *Creating worlds: Political agendas of entrepreneurship*. Paper presented at the 11th Nordic Conference on Small Business Research, Aarhus, Denmark.

Strawn, S., & Littrell, M. A. (2006). Beyond capabilities: A case study of three artisan enterprises in India. *Clothing & Textiles Research Journal*, *24*(3), 207–213. doi:10.1177/0887302X06294686

Suchman, L. (2001). Building bridges: Practice-based ethnographies. In Schiffer, M. B. (Ed.), *Anthropological perspectives in technology*. Albuquerque, NM: University of New Mexico Press.

Tedlock, B. (1991). From participant observation to the observation of participation: The emergence of narrative ethnography. *Journal of Anthropological Research*, *47*(1), 69–94.

Venkatesan, S. (2009). *Craft matters: Artisans, development and the Indian nation*. New Delhi, India: Orient Blackswan.

Wood, W. W. (2000). Flexible production, households, and fieldwork: Multisited Zapotec weavers in the era of late capitalism. *Ethnology*, *39*(2), 133–148. doi:10.2307/3773840

This work was previously published in the International Journal of Information Communication Technologies and Human Development, Volume 3, Issue 3, edited by Susheel Chhabra and Hakikur Rahman, pp. 16-30, copyright 2011 by IGI Publishing (an imprint of IGI Global).

Chapter 10
Factors Affecting E–Commerce Adoption by Small Businesses in a Developing Country:
A Case Study of a Small Hotel

Ali Acılar
Bilecik University, Turkey

Çağlar Karamaşa
Bilecik University, Turkey

ABSTRACT

Internet use has grown and spread rapidly around the world during the last decade. Today, computers and the Internet have become an integral part of modern societies. The Internet has created a new medium for communication and commerce for businesses. It is hard to imagine a business working without using a computer. These technological advances have also largely affected small and medium-sized enterprises (SMEs). While large companies have been quick to adopt the information and communication technologies (ICTs), SMEs have been slow to adopt these technologies in general for various reasons, especially in developing countries. This study explores the factors affecting the adoption of e-commerce by small businesses in a developing country. To attain this purpose a case study was conducted in a small hotel, which is using its website to keep up with customer expectations and competition in a small Turkish city. Conclusions and suggestions derived from this study provide a meaningful contribution to the understanding of e-commerce adoption among small businesses in developing countries.

DOI: 10.4018/978-1-4666-1957-9.ch010

INTRODUCTION

The ICTs are developing at a fast pace, affecting almost all aspects of our daily lives. Today, computers and the Internet have become an indispensable part of modern societies. According to Internet World Stats (2010) it is estimated that there are approximately 2 billion (28.7% of the world's population) Internet users in the world. From 2000 to 2010, the number of Internet users around the world increased by 444.8% (Internet World Stats, 2010) and Internet use in all areas of life has become more common over the time. The use of Internet for commercial purposes has also greatly increased. According to the United States Census Bureau, the total volume of e-commerce transactions in the United States was about 3,704 billion dollars in 2008, and among them 92.2% were B2B (United States Census Bureau, 2010).

Computers and the Internet have changed the way we live, the way we communicate, the way we get education, and the way we make business (Lee & Chan, 2008). Today, many businesses depend on computers and the Internet for their daily operations.

In terms of entrepreneurships, apart from assisting large corporate enterprises, the Internet has also providing many benefits and advantages to small businesses. It serves the small businesses in many ways. As a means of transaction, the Internet serves as a marketplace to bring sellers and buyers together for conducting sales; as a communication medium, the World Wide Web provides an inexpensive, easy and fast way for interacting with customers, suppliers and other businesses, and a company's Web presence helps enhance credibility, gather feedback, improve customer service, and facilitate business process (Chen et al., 2003).

However, SMEs face various difficulties when adopting the Internet and e-commerce. These difficulties are mainly related with SME's structure and their surrounding environment (Al-Qirim, 2007). Small businesses usually lack the technical knowledge, the financial power, the know-how, and the experience (Al-Hawari, Al-Yamani, & Izzawa, 2008). Overall, the literature suggests that Internet use is not prevalent among small enterprises (Karanasios, 2007), especially in developing countries.

Since the tourism and hospitality industry is very important for developing countries to prevent unemployment and to achieve economic development, tourism is the top national priority for economic development in many developing countries, and because of its relatively low start-up costs and its high potential to attract foreign capital, e-tourism is being promoted (Bui, Le, & Jones, 2006). The vast majority of hospitality businesses around the world are small and medium sized, belong to local entrepreneurs, are run by family, generally employ members of the local society (Main, 2002). Because small and medium sized hospitality organizations provide stable employment opportunities and support the integration of local economies in peripheral areas, even during recession periods, despite their size, these organizations are very important (Buhalis & Main, 1998).

The tourism and hospitality industry has relied mainly on information, while tourism services are produced and consumed in a physical world in a regional or local context, purchase decision of a tourism product is generally based on information received through direct or intermediary market channels; prior knowledge; word of mouth; and perceptions of trust and service quality (Braun, 2006). In this case, the ICTs, especially the World Wide Web, can provide the information to customers looking for data as part of their purchase process.

The tourism and hospitality enterprises can obtain a wide range of benefits from using the ICTs. These technologies help the tourism and hospitality enterprises to reduce costs, enhance operational efficiency, and improve service quality and customer experience (Law, Leung, & Buhalis, 2009). The Internet can create a direct link between the members of the hospitality industry and consumers, and also websites can provide information about the services and create an instant confirmation response to an inquiry such as room availability (Braun, 2006). Despite these apparent benefits and advantages, the small hospitality business owners do not use the Internet to its full advantage (Lituchy & Rail, 2000; Hudson & Gilbert, 2006).

Given these issues, the main objective of this paper is to examine the factors affecting e-commerce adoption by small businesses in a developing country by using a case study approach. For this reason, this paper investigates the case of a family owned small hotel, which is using its website to keep up with customer expectations and competition in a small Turkish city.

LITERATURE REVIEW

There is a digital divide between developed and developing countries in terms of accessing and using the ICTs. There is even a digital divide within developed countries. ICT adoption rates among enterprises differ between and within industries. Since today tourism and hospitality industry is highly dependent on information and the ICTs, the digital divide phenomenon also exists in this industry. There are a variety of technological divides (motivational, physical, informational, etc.) between tourists and destinations within developed countries and between developed and developing countries (Minghetti & Buhalis, 2009). While high-tech tourists and regions or enterprises meet in an electronic marketplace and communicate directly through electronic channels, medium- and low-digital-access tourists and destinations still depend on analog transactions and physical intermediaries for their vacation planning process and transactions (Minghetti & Buhalis, 2009). Factors affecting e-commerce adoption in small businesses are discussed in the following paragraphs.

Factors Affecting E-Commerce Adoption in Small Businesses

Several factors were identified from the literature reviewed as having considerable influence on the adoption of e-commerce among small businesses. These factors can be listed as: organizational factors, technological factors, individual factors, and environmental factors (Al-Qirim, 2007; Upadhyaya & Mohanan, 2009; Rogers, 2003; Cloete, Courtney, & Fintz, 2002). These affecting factors could be briefly summarized as follows: *Organizational factors*: user involvement, external/internal communications, quality of internal IT systems and capability, top management support, size, information intensity of products, specialization; *Technological factors*: observability, trialability, relative advantage, cost, complexity, compatibility, image; *Individual factors*: CEO's innovativeness, CEO's prior information systems/e-commerce knowledge, characteristics of owner/entrepreneur, educational qualification, etc., and *Environmental factors*: vertical linkages, government, competition, external pressure from suppliers/buyers, external support from technology vendors (Al-Qirim, 2007; Upadhyaya & Mohanan, 2009; Rogers, 2003; Cloete, Courtney, & Fintz, 2002).

Auger and Gallaugher (1997) studied factors affecting the adoption of an Internet-based sales presence for small businesses. They identified six factors that impacted the decision to go online: low development and maintenance costs, an interest in experimenting with a new marketing tool, the desire to promote products and build the company's image, financial considerations, benefits in obtaining and disseminating information, and competitive considerations. According to their study results, among these factors, low development and maintenance cost was revealed as the most significant. Auger and Gallaugher (1997) also found that small businesses that have made the decision to go on-line perceive that deploying a Web-based sales presence is a relatively low-risk, and high reward strategy.

Poon and Swatman (1999) found that the perception of long-term benefits and potential business opportunities drive small business to adopt Internet commerce. Premkumar and Roberts (1999) studied factors that influence the adoption of various communications technologies in small businesses located in rural communities in the United States and they found that relative advantage, top management support, organizational size, external pressure and competitive pressure are important determinants of adoption.

Riemenschneider and McKinney (2002) analyzed the differences in the belief of small business executives regarding the adoption of Web-based e-commerce. They found that security and cost were barriers to adoption of Web-based e-commerce. Daniel and Grimshaw (2002) found that the use of e-commerce for responding to competitors, providing enhanced customer services and improving relations with suppliers was driving the uptake by smaller businesses to a greater extent than by their larger counterparts.

Cloete, Courtney, and Fintz (2002) identified factors affecting e-commerce adoption in small businesses as: the owner's perception and acceptance of e-commerce, characteristics of the organization, and the context in which the business find itself. According to Cloete, Courtney, and Fintz (2002), adoption of e-commerce is mainly based on perceived benefit. Chen et al. (2003) studied the e-commerce case of a small traditional retailer and identified six critical success factors for the firm, as follows: incremental e-commerce involvement, allocating resources widely, outsourcing the development, changing business process, studying the customer, and revising and evaluating results.

Jennex, Amoroso, and Adelakun (2004) investigated the key infrastructure factors affecting the success of small companies in developing economies that are establishing B2B e-commerce ventures. They found that workers' skills, client interface, and technical infrastructure are the most important factors to the success of a B2B e-commerce relationship. Jeon, Han, and Lee (2006) investigated determining factors for the successful adoption of e-business by SMEs in Korea and they determined several factors for e-business adoption, i.e., CEO's knowledge of IT/e-business, the relative advantages and benefits from adopting e-business, governmental support for e-business, and using e-business as a globalization strategy for market expansion. They also found that business size, the cost of e-business adoption and competitive pressures from the industry do not seem to be an important factor in adopting e-business by SMEs in Korea.

Pearson and Grandon (2005) surveyed managers/owners of SMEs in the Midwest region of the United States to identify variables that differentiate between adopters and non-adopters of e-commerce. They found that organizational readiness, perceived usefulness, compatibility, and external pressure differentiated between adopters and non-adopters of e-commerce.

Al-Qirim (2007) investigated the impact of technological, organizational, individual and environmental factors on e-commerce adoption in New Zealand SMEs. He found that technological factors such as complexity, the compatibility, and the cost are affecting significantly, but observability and trialability are not. Image was found to play a supplementary role in his study. At organizational level, factors such as user involvement, external/internal communications, quality of IT systems and capabilities, and specialization were found as insignificant. At the individual level, the study found CEO's innovativeness played an important role in e-commerce adoption in SMEs. At the environmental level, pressure from supplier/buyer on their adoption decision of e-commerce was identified as important in his study.

Bharadwaj and Soni (2007) found that a major reason for businesses not engaging in e-commerce is their perception that it is not strategically important for their businesses.

Upadhyaya and Mohanan (2009) researched the factors affecting electronic marketplace adoption among manufacturing SMEs in India. They found that the owner's knowledge of computers and the Internet, organization's familiarity with Internet-based applications and size of the firm are the factors that contribute to the e-marketplace adoption. According to their study, the government support and the extent to which the firm is globalized does not have any influence on manufacturing SMEs to adopt e-marketplace.

Factors Affecting E-Commerce Adoption in Small Businesses in the Tourism and Hospitality Industry

Buhalis and Main (1998) studied the process of information technology adoption in small and medium-sized hospitality organizations (SMHOs) and identified several reasons for the lack of use of information technology in these organizations as follows: a) the lack of training, b) the age, educational level, and family arrangements of the SMHOs' proprietors, c) the deficiency of rational management and marketing functions, and d) the short-term, operational focus of managers.

Raymond (2001) administered a survey to travel agencies to study determinants of website implementation in small businesses. He identified various factors determining the assimilation of e-commerce by small enterprises in the form of informational, transactional, and strategic implementation of a website. Raymond (2001) found that the informational implementation and transactional implementation are determined by environmental context (business partners' influence and environmental uncertainty), whereas strategic implementation is determined by travel agencies' marketing strategy (in terms of distribution and communication), the organizational context (type of ownership, nature of business), and the characteristics of e-commerce (perceived advantages and technology attributes).

Morrison and King (2002) explored the perceptions and attitudes of small tourism business owner-operators in regional areas towards investigating e-commerce as an element of destination marketing. They identified two major challenges for small tourism enterprises: First, the impact of online technologies supporting e-commerce in tourism is likely to increase rather than diminish, because they enable and support new organizational configurations and have the capacity to re-engineer market places and supply chains. Secondly, the success of many destination marketing businesses is dependent upon the effective engagement of a significant proportion of small tourism businesses. Morrison and King (2002) suggested that public sector destination marketing organizations need to: accept and work with the innate characteristics of the population; ensure the utility and functionality of the proposed technology; enhance owner-operator understanding of the benefits and costs of Internet-based trade; and utilize a combination of coercive push and voluntary pull factors to engage them in both individual and destination-based e-commerce strategies.

Warden and Tunzelana (2004) found that organizational barriers exist in e-commerce adoption initiatives of SMMEs (Small Medium Micro Enterprises) in the South African Tourism industry.

Hudson and Gilbert (2006) studied small hospitality businesses to identify the underlying success factors in utilizing the Internet as a marketing tool in the tourism and hospitality sector. Their study results suggest that bed & breakfast hotel owners are using the Internet as a low-cost method of increasing their customer base, especially from overseas markets. Hudson and Gilbert (2006) found that success in adoption of the Internet is closely related to online experience, the measurement of website efficiency, prompt responses to inquiries, making it easy for customers to make a reservation, the development of relationships with customers, customer adoption of technology, and the existence of online partners.

Karanasios (2007) identified four major Internet adoption obstacles in small tourism enterprises in Ecuador, as: the cost of adoption, inadequate and poor ICT infrastructure, a lack of government support, and a lack of the ICT skills.

Innovation Strategies in Tourism Industry

Innovation in the service industry has been a topic of growing interest among researchers and policy makers (Nybakk & Hansen, 2008). Innovations in tourism industry can be categorized as follows: product or service innovations, process innovations, managerial innovations, management innovations, and institutional innovations (Hjalager, 2010). Aldebert, Dang, and Longhi (in press) studied the evolution of innovative activities in the tourism industry through the empirical analysis of annual Tourism@ events which is an important trade fair in Europe that brings together major actors related to the tourism industry. They found that 70.7% of innovation in tourism is product or service innovation.

In order to be able to survive in today's competitive business world, SMEs must keep pace with the changes in their environment using limited resources. One of the ways to accomplish this goal for SMEs is applying open innovation in their business strategies. According to (Chesbrough, 2006, p. 43) "Open innovation means that valuable ideas can come from inside or outside the company and can go to market from inside or outside the company as well". Open innovation process includes purposive outflows of knowledge as well as purposive inflows of knowledge (Van de Vrande et al., 2009). Purposive outflows of knowledge mean innovation activities to leverage existing technological capabilities outside the boundaries of the organization and purposive inflows of knowledge imply innovation activities to capture and benefit from external sources of knowledge to enhance current technological developments in organization (Van de Vrande et al., 2009).

UNIZO, the Belgian federation of independent entrepreneurs, classified sources of open innovation for SMEs, such as: customers, suppliers, personnel, research organizations and universities, consultants and advisors, internal research and results from market research (Evens, 2009). Internet is an important medium of open innovation sources for small tourism and hospitality businesses. For example, INNOTOUR (www.innotour. com) is a center for innovation in tourism (Liburd & Hjalager, 2009). INNOTOUR defines itself as: "INNOTOUR is an open platform for tourism educators, researchers, students and businesses and dissemination of knowledge in the field of tourism innovation. The purpose is to build with colleagues a living website to maximize student relevance and learning, collaborative research and innovation in tourism businesses" (INNOTOUR). Open innovation initiatives in the tourism sector are usually a response to an external threat or crisis (Sandulli, 2009). Affecting factors of the success of these initiatives are the transfer of explicit knowledge and the presence of a strong player that takes the risk of innovating (Sandulli, 2009).

METHODOLOGY

The main aim of the present study is to explore the factors affecting e-commerce adoption by small businesses in a developing country. The study uses a single-case research methodology. According to Dul and Hak, (2008, p. 4) "A case study is in which (a) one case (single case study) or a small number of cases (comparative case study) in their real life context are selected, and (b) scores obtained from these cases are analysed in a qualitative manner." A family owned small hotel using its website since 2009 was selected for the study. The authors conducted interviews with the owner of the hotel to explore the factors affecting e-commerce adoption in a small business. The owner of the hotel was visited and interviewed three times by the authors. In interviews, the authors gathered information on the background of the hotel and its owner, Internet and Web use in the hotel, benefits of these technologies to the hotel and then the authors examined the factors affecting e-commerce adoption. In addition to the interview, the website of the hotel was also explored.

CASE STUDY

Otel Gören is a three-generation family owned and operated small hotel. It was established in 1952 and since then has served its customers. Otel Gören is located in one of the main streets of Bilecik, a small but a historical city in the northwest of Turkey. Bilecik's population is about 45,000.

Besides the owner, the hotel currently employs four people; one of them is his wife. The owner works on a full time basis in the hotel. The hotel is a bed and breakfast hotel. It serves approximately 3000 customers annually with 20 rooms and 40 beds.

Taner Gören is the owner of the hotel. He is forty years old, graduated from commercial high school, married and has one child. His computer skill is neither expert nor novice. The owner indicates his computer skill as moderate.

Information technology resources of the hotel are limited. There are two computers in the hotel; one is in the owner's office and the other one is on the reception desk. The hotel has an ADSL Internet connection. Customer records are kept on the computer at the reception desk. The Hotel has been using the Internet since 2000, but not mainly for business purposes until 2005. In Turkey, Hotels have to report the identification information of their guests to the appropriate Turkish authorities every day. Since 2005, keeping customer records on a computer and sending to the police department via the Internet have become mandatory for the hotels above a certain size. For this reason, Mr. Taner has started using ADSL broadband Internet connection since 2005. The

hotel also provides wireless Internet connection to its customers. Communication (E-mail), sending the identification information of the guests to the police, information search and gathering were the main uses of the Internet in the hotel.

At present, room reservations are usually made via telephone enquiries direct to the hotel. Some customers use e-mail to book a room. Approximately 10% of the bookings were made via e-mail in 2010. Since the customers cannot get instant response via e-mail they may prefer to book a room via phone.

Last year, Mr. Taner decided to renovate the hotel and then the hotel building was completely refurbished inside and out. With this renovation he wanted to have a website. The hotel's website was launched in 2009. The owner is aware of the importance of the Internet for businesses and he believes that today, it is necessary to have a website. The website of the hotel was designed by a local Web solutions firm and was registered with one of the main search engines. The content of the website is in Turkish. The hotel's website is relatively basic, simple and easy to use and navigate. It contains some sample pictures of the rooms, a list of the services provided by the hotel, contact information and daily weather of Bilecik. Audio, video and 360-degree photography were not used in the website. The hotel's website does not include Web-based booking system and does not offer online payment. Because of owner's concerns regarding the technology, he does not want to use Web-based booking system. He believes that it may cause some problems. For now, Web-based booking system is not seen as necessary by the owner. It seems that the main reasons for that the hotel is not using Web-based booking system are the lack of technical knowledge of the owner about the system and for now, it is not seen as necessary by the owner. The owner of the hotel has not registered the hotel's website to a booking portal yet. He stated that he did not know that there is such a service exists in the Internet. But when asked, he states that he might register to an online booking portal in the future.

The introduction of the website has provided the following benefits to the hotel:

- **Availability:** The information on the hotel's website is available to potential customers 24 hours a day, 7 days a week. This provides convenience to the customers and to the hotel. Today, the most popular and convenient way of looking for a hotel is the Web.
- **Credibility:** The website gives the hotel a mark of credibility and creates an image.
- **Keeping up with the Competition:** Having a website helps the hotel to keep up with the competition.
- **Cost Saving:** The website provides cost saving comparing to other media in terms of advertising.

In terms of e-commerce, it cannot be said that the hotel is successful. However, the hotel has not been benefitting fully from the Web's potential. The hotel has not completed the e-commerce adoption process yet.

Besides Hotel Gören, there are five more hotels in Bilecik. Two of them do not have a website yet. Among the hotels having a website, just one of them has been using an online reservation system on its website and this hotel was also registered to a well known international booking portal (www. booking.com). Most of the hotels in Bilecik are registered to national portals (e.g. www.otelrezervasyonu.gen.tr).

RECOMMENDATIONS AND CONCLUSIONS

Today, computers and the Internet have become an important part of the business life. The Internet has affected many industries, but the hospitality industry has been one of the most impacted. Nevertheless, the small hospitality business owners do not use the Internet to its full advantage and only a small number use a secure server for online bookings (Hudson & Gilbert, 2006). To be able to survive in the fast-changing environment, the small businesses in the hospitality industry have to adapt technological advances such as e-commerce to stay competitive. However, practicing e-commerce in developing countries is a major challenge (Bui, Le, & Jones, 2006) for especially small businesses with scarce resources.

The main aim of this study was to explore the factors affecting e-commerce adoption by small businesses in a developing country. For this reason, a family owned and operated small hotel in a small Turkish city was examined as a case study.

The owner of the hotel appreciates the value of the Internet. However, it cannot be said that the hotel makes full use of the Internet. E-mail, sending the identification information of the guests to the police, information search and gathering were the main uses of the Internet in the hotel. The hotel has a basic website that is not having Web-based booking system. Having a website has provided the opportunity for the hotel to reach more customers, to improve its service, to save costs, and to promote its image and credibility. Having a website can be accepted as the first step to e-commerce for most businesses in the Internet. But, it is not enough for a successful e-commerce application. In order to be successful in the Internet, the small hospitality businesses should also add value to their websites with, such as Web-based booking system, tourist information, and maps. Also, developing a website in only one language for a hotel may not be sufficient in the hospitality industry. The hotel website should provide information in common languages of the world, such as English and German in order to attract tourists.

The authors of the study suggest that the most important factor affecting the adoption of e-commerce in the case hotel is the perceived benefits by the owner. Other factors are identified as follows: customer expectations, competition and the increased use of the Internet by people. The main reasons for not using the Web-based booking in the website of the case hotel are found as following: the owner lacks the technical knowledge and, for now, Web-based booking is not seen as necessary by the owner.

In order to keep up with competition in the era of Internet, e-commerce awareness among small businesses should be increased especially in the developing countries. In addition to increasing awareness, it is required to support small businesses with knowledge and experience about e-commerce. Because most small businesses cannot afford the necessary training, consulting or outsourcing for e-commerce implementations, it is possible for chambers of commerce, or small-business associations to organize training sessions for small businesses to attend at an affordable price (Lituchy & Rail, 2000).

There are a number of limitations of this study. The first limitation is that the authors used a single case study methodology, and investigated only one small business. The second limitation is that investigated business is a hotel in the hospitality industry. The factors affecting adoption of e-commerce in small businesses may differ in different industries. Another limitation is that the study focused on a business that has not completed the e-commerce adoption process, yet. Finally, the study was conducted in Turkey. Therefore the generalization of the conclusions may not be applicable. Future studies in this topic area in other developing countries will help to learn more about the factors affecting the adoption of e-commerce by small businesses in developing countries.

ACKNOWLEDGMENT

An earlier version of this paper was presented at the International Conference on Entrepreneurship, Family Business and Innovation, 21-23 October 2010, Çankaya University, Ankara, Turkey.

REFERENCES

Al-Hawari, M., Al-Yamani, H., & Izwawa, B. (2008). Small businesses' decision to have a website Saudi Arabia case study. *World Academy of Science. Engineering and Technology*, *37*, 308–312.

Al-Qirim, N. A. (2007). E-commerce adoption in small businesses-cases from New Zealand. *Journal of Information Technology Case and Application Research*, *9*(2), 28–57.

Aldebert, B., Dang, R. J., & Longhi, C. (2011). Innovation in the tourism industry: The case of Tourism@. *Tourism Management*, *32*(5), 1204–1213. doi:.doi:10.1016/j.physletb.2003.10.071

Auger, P., & Gallaugher, J. M. (1997). Factors affecting the adoption of an Internet-based sales presence for small businesses. *The Information Society*, *13*, 55–74. doi:10.1080/019722497129287

Bharadwaj, P. N., & Soni, R. G. (2007). E-commerce usage and perception of e-commerce issues among small firms: Results and implications from an empirical study. *Journal of Small Business Management*, *45*(4), 501–521. doi:10.1111/j.1540-627X.2007.00225.x

Braun, P. (2006). E-commerce and small tourism firms. In Marshall, S., Taylor, W., & Yu, X. (Eds.), *Encyclopedia of developing regional communities with information and communication technology* (pp. 233–238). Hershey, PA: IGI Global. doi:10.4018/9781591405757.ch041

Buhalis, D., & Main, H. (1998). Information technology in peripheral small and medium hospitality enterprises: Strategic analysis and critical factors. *International Journal of Contemporary Hospitality Management*, *10*(5), 198–202. doi:10.1108/09596119810227811

Bui, T. X., Le, T., & Jones, W. D. (2006). An exploratory case study of hotel e-marketing in Ho Chi Minh City. *Thunderbird International Business Review, 48*(3), 369–388. doi:10.1002/tie.20100

Chen, L., Haney, S., Pandzik, A., Spigarelli, J., & Jesseman, C. (2003). Small business Internet commerce: A case study. *Information Resources Management Journal, 16*(3), 17–41. doi:10.4018/irmj.2003070102

Chesbrough, H. W. (2006). *Open innovation: The new imperative for creating and profiting from technology*. Boston, MA: Harvard Business School Press.

Cloete, E., Courtney, S., & Fintz, J. (2002). Small business' acceptance and adoption of e-commerce in the Western-Cape Province of South Africa. *Electronic Journal on Information Systems in Developing Countries, 10*(4), 1–13.

Daniel, E. M., & Grimshaw, D. J. (2002). An exploratory comparison of electronic commerce adoption in large and small enterprises. *Journal of Information Technology, 17*, 133–147. doi:10.1080/0268396022000018409

Dul, J., & Hak, T. (2008). *Case study methodology in business research*. Burlington, MA: Butterworth-Heinemann.

Evens, W. (2009). *How can SMEs benefit from open innovation?* Unpublished master's thesis, Hasselt University, Diepenbeek, Belgium.

Hjalager, A. M. (2010). A review of innovation research in tourism. *Tourism Management, 31*, 1–12. doi:10.1016/j.tourman.2009.08.012

Hudson, S., & Gilbert, D. (2006). The Internet and small hospitality businesses: B&B marketing in Canada. *Journal of Hospitality Marketing & Management, 14*(1), 99–116.

Internet World Stats. (2010). *Internet usage statistics*. Retrieved from http://www.internet-worldstats.com/stats.htm

Jennex, M. E., Amoroso, D., & Adelakun, O. (2004). E-commerce infrastructure success factors for small companies in developing economies. *Electronic Commerce Research, 4*, 263–286. doi:10.1023/B:ELEC.0000027983.36409.d4

Jeon, B. N., Han, K. S., & Lee, M. J. (2006). Determining factors for the adoption of e-business: The case of SMEs in Korea. *Applied Economics, 38*(16), 1905–1916. doi:10.1080/00036840500427262

Karanasios, S. (2007). Ecuador, the digital divide and small tourism enterprises. *Journal of Business Systems. Governance and Ethics, 2*(3), 21–34.

Law, R., Leung, R., & Buhalis, D. (2009). Information technology applications in hospitality and tourism: A review of publications from 2005 to 2007. *Journal of Travel & Tourism Marketing, 26*, 599–623. doi:10.1080/10548400903163160

Lee, W. W., & Chan, A. K. K. (2008, December). *Computer ethics: An argument for rethinking business ethics*. Paper presented at the 2nd World Business Ethics Forum: Rethinking the Value of Business Ethics, Hong Kong, China.

Liburd, J., & Hjalager, A. M. (2009). *Valuing open innovation environments in tourism education and research-the case of INNOTOUR*. Paper presented at the Think Tank 9 on The Importance of Values in Sustainable Tourism, Singapore.

Lituchy, T. R., & Rail, A. (2000). Bed and breakfasts, small inns, and the Internet: The impact of technology on the globalization of small businesses. *Journal of International Marketing, 8*(2), 86–97. doi:10.1509/jimk.8.2.86.19625

Main, H. C. (2002). The expansion of technology in small and medium hospitality enterprises with a focus on net technology. *Information Technology & Tourism, 4*, 167–174.

Minghetti, V., & Buhalis, D. (2010). Digital divide in tourism. *Journal of Travel Research, 49*(3), 267–281. doi:10.1177/0047287509346843

Morrison, A. J., & King, B. E. M. (2002). Small tourism businesses and e-commerce: Victorian tourism online. *Tourism and Hospitality Research, 4*(2), 104–115.

Nybakk, E., & Hansen, E. (2008). Entrepreneurial attitude, innovation and performance among Norwegian nature-based tourism enterprises. *Forest Policy and Economics, 10*, 473–479. doi:10.1016/j.forpol.2008.04.004

Pearson, J. M., & Grandon, E. E. (2005). An empirical study of factors that influence e-commerce adoption/non-adoption in small and medium sized businesses. *Journal of Internet Commerce, 4*(4), 1–21. doi:10.1300/J179v04n04_01

Poon, S., & Swatman, P. M. C. (1999). An exploratory study of small business Internet commerce issues. *Information & Management, 35*, 9–18. doi:10.1016/S0378-7206(98)00079-2

Premkumar, G., & Roberts, M. (1999). Adoption of new information technologies in rural small businesses. *Omega. International Journal of Management Science, 27*, 467–484.

Raymond, L. (2001). Determinants of web site implementation in small businesses. *Internet Research, 11*(5), 411–422. doi:10.1108/10662240110410363

Riemenschneider, C. K., & McKinney, V. R. (2001-2002). Assessing belief differences in small business adopters and non-adopters of web-based e-commerce. *Journal of Computer Information Systems, 42*(2), 101–107.

Rogers, E. (2003). *Diffusion of innovations*. New York, NY: Free Press.

Sandulli, F. D. (2009). *Challenges and opportunities of open innovation and open business models in tourism*. Paper presented at the First International Conference on the Measurement and Economic Analysis of Regional Tourism Donostia, San Sebastian, Spain.

United States Census Bureau. (2010). *E-Stats*. Retrieved from http://www.census.gov/econ/estats/2008/2008reportfinal.pdf

Upadhyaya, P., & Mohanan, P. (2009). Electronic marketplace adoption: A case study of manufacturing SMEs. *ICFAIAN Journal of Management Research, 8*(6), 30–40.

Van de Vrande, V., de Jong, J. P. J., Vanhaverbeke, W., & de Rochemont, M. (2009). Open innovation in SMEs: Trends, motives and management challenges. *Technovation, 29*, 423–437. doi:10.1016/j.technovation.2008.10.001

Warden, S. C., & Tunzelana, S. (2004). *E-commerce: A critical review of SME organisational barriers in tourism*. Paper presented at the 6th WWW Applications Conference, Johannesburg, South Africa.

This work was previously published in the International Journal of Information Communication Technologies and Human Development, Volume 3, Issue 3, edited by Susheel Chhabra and Hakikur Rahman, pp. 31-41, copyright 2011 by IGI Publishing (an imprint of IGI Global).

Chapter 11
Empowerment of SMEs Through Open Innovation Strategies:
Life Cycle of Technology Management

Hakikur Rahman
University of Minho, Portugal

Isabel Ramos
University of Minho, Portugal

ABSTRACT

Adoption of innovation strategies in entrepreneurship is an age old phenomenon, but inclusion of open innovation or collaborative innovation strategies in the business processes is a newly evolved concept. By far, most research reveals that the majority of successful global ventures are adopting open innovation strategies in their business proceedings. However, despite their contribution to entrepreneurship and national economy, the small and medium scale enterprises (SMEs) are well below the expectation level in terms of acquiring this newly emerged trend of doing business. Moreover, not much research is being conducted to investigate SMEs potencies, expectations, delivery channels and intricacies around the adoption, nourishment and dissemination of open innovation strategies. This research proposes a contextual framework leading to an operational framework to explore the lifecycle of open innovation strategy management activities focusing technology transfer (inbounds or outwards). It discusses a few issues on future research in empowering SMEs through utilization of open innovation strategies.

INTRODUCTION

While talking about successful entrepreneurship and value addition within an enterprise through open innovation (OI), one could realize that the innovation paradigm has been shifted from simple introduction of new ideas and products to accumulation of diversified actions, actors and agents along the process (Chesbrough, 2003a, 2006a). Furthermore, when the innovation process is not being restricted within the closed nature of it, the process takes many forms during its evolution (Rahman & Ramos, 2010). Definition of open innovation has also adopted many transformations along the path, incorporating innovations within

DOI: 10.4018/978-1-4666-1957-9.ch011

the products, process or service of an enterprise to organizational, marketing, or external entities and relations. Nature and scope of agents and actors even varies widely within the innovation dynamics, when the open innovation techniques are being applied to enterprises, designated as the small and medium enterprises (SMEs) (Schumpeter, 1934, 1982; Davenport, 1993; OECD, 1992, 1996, 2005; De Jong et al., 2007).

Due to the open and collaborative nature of this newly evolved perception, the primary focus of this paper has been kept within open nature of innovation (a more recently evolved terminology, which is better known as crowdsourcing[1] innovation), but not limited to other collaborative innovation, though it is not easy to put a restrictive boundary between them.

Being new in the research arena, on one hand the concept of open innovation has been flourished very progressively within a short span of time (Chesbrough, 2003b; Chesbrough, Vanhaverbeke, & West, 2006; Gassmann, 2006), but at the same time, it has evolved through various growth patterns in diversified directions involving different factors and parameters (Christensen, Olesen, & Kjaer, 2005; Chesbrough & Crowther, 2006; Dodgson, Gann, & Salter, 2006; Gassmann, 2006; Vanhaverbeke, 2006; West & Gallagher, 2006). Furthermore, as this research is related to SMEs[2], which are the steering factor of economic growth in the European countries, and especially in Europe where they comprise of over 98% (EC, 2008) of the entrepreneurships, the problem statements were constructed following multiple research studies along this aspect, though sufficient works towards the improvement of knowledge factors on SMEs development have not been found.

This research argues that to empower the SMEs through OI strategies, firstly the contextual framework need to be devised and then the operational framework has to be developed. The research also argues that the operational framework revolves around the life cycle of technology management activities that are either inbound to the enterprises or outbound from them. Depending on nature, scope, transparency and efficiency of the life cycle, the open innovation will grow among and within the entrepreneurships. The more efficient and focused the life cycle will be the growth factor of OI strategies will reach towards fulfilling the operational framework. In this discourse, this paper has tried to discuss the contextual framework in relevance to the OI strategies as the background concept, and to support the main thrust of the paper, which is the life-cycle of technology management, it has tried to develop an operational framework as the entry point.

CONTEXTUAL FRAMEWORK

Innovation is a way of performing something new. It may refer to incremental and emergent or radical and revolutionary changes in thinking, products, process development, or organizational development. Innovation, as seen by Schumpeter (1934) incorporates way of producing new products, new methods of production, new sources of supply, opening of new markets, and new ways of organizing businesses. Oslo manual (1992, 1996, 2005), after several adjustments has come into this argument, that innovation is the implementation of a new or significantly improved product (good or service), or process, a new marketing method, or a new organizational method in business practices, workplace organization or external relations.

However, other scholars and researchers in the field of innovation, has put forward definition of innovation in various formats and perspectives. Some definitions or arguments are being included below:

The creation of new ideas/processes which will lead to change in an enterprise's economic and social potential. (Drucker, 1998, p. 149)

This research will look into the economic and social aspect of open innovation process, but at the same time look into any technology parameters that are involved within the processes.

Tidd, Bessant, and Pavitt (2005) and Bessant and Tidd (2007) argued that there are four types of innovation, i.e., the innovator has four routes of innovation paths, such as product innovation (changes in the products or services [things] which an organization offers), process innovation (changes in the ways in which products or services are created and delivered), positioning innovation (changes in the context in which the products or services are introduced) and paradigm innovation (changes in the underlying mental models which outline what the organization does)[3].

This research would argue that these are the areas through which open innovation takes place in an enterprise.

However, in terms of the types of open innovation, Darsø (2001) argued that innovation can be incremental (improvements of processes, products and methods, often found by technicians or employees during their daily work), radical (novel, surprising and different approach or composition), social (spring from social needs, rather than from technology, and are related to new ways of interaction) and quantum (refers to the emergence of qualitatively new system states brought by small incremental changes).

Furthermore, talking about types of innovation, Henderson and Clark (1990) identified four; incremental innovation- improves component knowledge and leaves architectural knowledge unchanged; modular innovation- architectural knowledge unchanged, component knowledge of one or more components reduced in value; architectural innovation- component knowledge unchanged, architectural knowledge reduced in value; and radical innovation[4]- both component knowledge and architectural knowledge reduced in value.

Thus, innovation can be termed as introduction of new idea into the marketplace in the form of a new product or service, or an improvement in organization or process (http://www.mjward.

co.uk/Businesses-phrases-terms-jargon/Business-Phrases-Terms-1.html).

This definition enables one to concentrate on demand driven innovation, or innovation may be re-termed as a:

Process by which an idea or invention is translated into good or service for which people will pay" (Businessdictionary.com).

The final definition that this research has selected leads to the very basic parameters of innovation, where there are goods or services between buyer and the seller.

Hence, a functional equation (Figure 1) (by taking innovation as the most probable or prominent function in above definitions and arguments) can be deducted, as:

A context diagram (Figure 2) from the equation sets the primary problem statements of this research. If one argues that innovation generates new or improved products, process or services, then the following diagram can be derived:

However, one could observe that this context diagram does not necessarily lead to the open nature of innovation that can be built upon. Therefore, this research would like to modify the context diagram by connecting to an open platform utilizing various open innovation strategies (Figure 3).

Initially, this research would like to carry out investigation into the three aspects of open innovation (product, process and service). However, it will set its boundary within the various business processes through organizational transformations and capacity development initiatives incorporating open innovation strategies to empower SMEs. Furthermore, it will emphasize on technology diffusion and issues of technical nature to enable the SMEs community to innovate further in reaching out to their grass roots stakeholders. As the research progresses, depending on the survey responses, which this research would like to carry out, other parameters of open innovation

Figure 1. A functional equation mapping various definitions and arguments

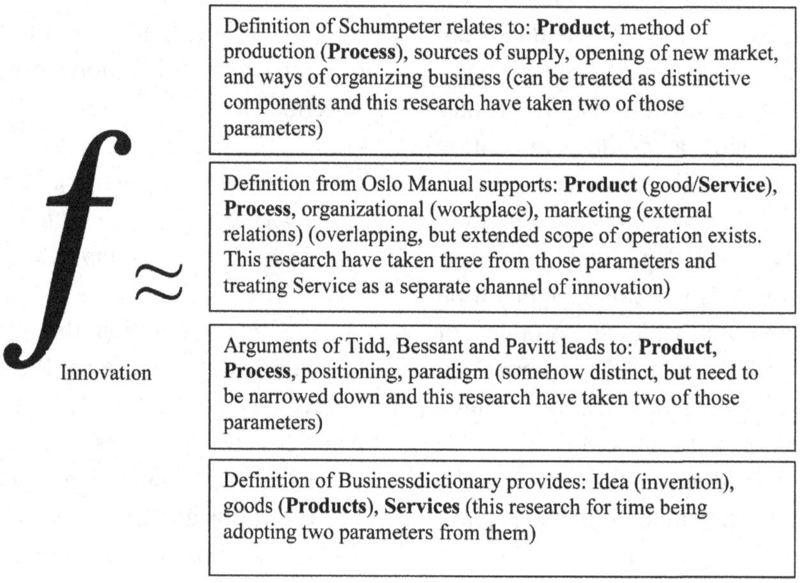

Definition of Schumpeter relates to: **Product**, method of production (**Process**), sources of supply, opening of new market, and ways of organizing business (can be treated as distinctive components and this research have taken two of those parameters)
Definition from Oslo Manual supports: **Product** (good/**Service**), **Process**, organizational (workplace), marketing (external relations) (overlapping, but extended scope of operation exists. This research have taken three from those parameters and treating Service as a separate channel of innovation)
Arguments of Tidd, Bessant and Pavitt leads to: **Product**, **Process**, positioning, paradigm (somehow distinct, but need to be narrowed down and this research have taken two of those parameters)
Definition of Businessdictionary provides: Idea (invention), goods (**Products**), **Services** (this research for time being adopting two parameters from them)
Innovation

strategies such as organizational and management aspects will be taken into account.

OPERATIONAL FRAMEWORK

In search of finding different patterns of open innovation and their relationships with SMEs, initial part of the research spent sufficient period of time (over a year or so) in literature review. Review was restricted to definite search strings, but was not confined to specific journals or search engines. However, to keep the credibility of the searched content most of the searches were limited to highly ranked journals and databases. Similarly, case studies were conducted and survey reports

Figure 2. A context diagram derived from the functional equation

Product
Process
Service
Result of an act or process
A course of action to achieve a result
Performance done by someone to benefit another

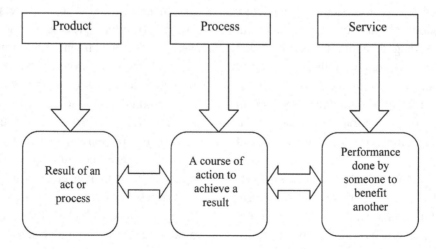

Figure 3. A context diagram with OI strategies

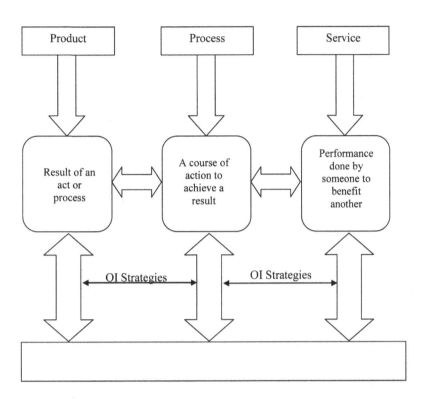

were being studied that were being operationalized or established or implemented by well reputed national and international agencies or institutes, such as European Commission, OECD, World Bank, UNDP, Vinnova, Innocentive and others. Moreover, literature review emphasized on empirical studies and cases illustrating activities on SMEs in reaching out to their broad based grass roots clientele.

Open Innovation, being latent within the product, process and service in an entrepreneurship grows naturally if these three could be intermingled further, such as incorporating new idea and changes through product development, process development and service development. In its simplest sense, open innovation will grow in an enterprise, if the bonding among them increases. As $f(P1,P2,S)$ moves inwards, bonding increases, and innovation grows (Figure 4), and

eventually an enterprise emerges as a cent percent innovative entity.

Given the potentiality of open innovation in an enterprise through improvement of the three parameters as shown in Figure 4, especially small and medium scale enterprises (SMEs), literature review gave primary focus to gather knowledge on opportunities and challenges that are being faced by SMEs when they are opening their windows of business processes through open innovation methods. Furthermore, to design an appropriate action plan for empowering them, a thorough literature review has been conducted on existing success cases utilizing open innovation strategies. These eventually assisted in developing the research design and survey methods. Readers may refer to Rahman and Ramos (2010) for an elaborate discussion on open innovation opportunities and challenges that are being faced by SMEs, and Rahman and Ramos (2010) illustrate an extended

Figure 4. Bonding of the three parameters of open innovation management

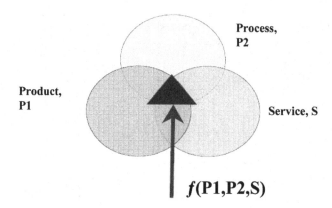

literature review on research and practices on open innovation strategies.

However, before progressing further, this study would like to give an insight into the product, process and service innovation, but not reinventing the wheel. Researchers mention that product innovation is linked to the analysis of changes and innovations within the product category. Product innovation allows one to map out changes in one's enterprise's product. It compels to determine how a product should evolve to meet needs of the client and be competitive in the future (Crawford, 1983; Hiebing & Cooper, 2003).

Process innovation combines the adoption of a new view of the business process with the application of innovation into key processes. The novel and distinctive feature of this combination is its enormous potential to assist an organization in achieving major reductions in process cost or process time, or major improvements in quality, flexibility, and service levels. In this perspective, the business must be viewed not in terms of functions, divisions, or products, but of key processes, they may include redesigning key processes from the beginning to the end, and employing whatever innovative technologies and organizational resources are available. However, a major challenge in process innovation is to make a successful transition to a continuous improve-

ment in environment. Referring to Davenport (1993), this research purview that, if a company that does not institute continuous improvement after implementing process innovation is likely to revert to old ways of doing business. Framework for process innovation may comprise of; identifying processes for innovation, identifying transformation enablers, developing a business vision and process objectives, understanding and measuring existing processes, and designing and creating a prototype of the new process (Zuboff, 1988; Walton, 1989).

Service innovation[5] systems are dynamic configurations of people, technologies, organizations and shared information that create and deliver value to customers, providers and partners through services. They are forming a growing proportion of the world economy and are becoming central activity for the businesses, governments, families and individuals. Nowadays, firms do not consider themselves to be 'services' or 'manufacturing' but providing solutions for customers that involve a combination of products and services. Preferably, service innovation can happen across all service sectors and one should look at all possible service activities rather than looking at specific service sectors (Van Ark, Broersma, & Den Hertog, 2003; Miles, 2005; IfM & IBM, 2008). Service innovation is more closely related to the depth than breadth (vertical than horizontal), and a deep relationship with external sources, such as customer needs of target markets are essential for service innovation (Lee et al., 2010).

To enhance the bonding state and increase the open innovation, one can think of an operational framework as shown in Table 1.

LIFE CYCLE OF TECHNOLOGY MANAGEMENT

As evolved from the very basic, but comprehensive definition of open innovation (Chesbrough, Vanhaverbeke, & West, 2006, p. 1), it is "the use of purposive inflows to accelerate internal innovation" and "the use of purposive outflows to expand the markets for external use of innovation", and thus, it comprises of outside-in and inside-out flow of ideas, knowledge and technologies. The outside-in movements may be termed as technology acquisition or technology exploration, while the inside-out movements may be termed as technology dissemination or technology exploration (Lichtenthaler, 2008; Van de Vrande, De Jong, Vanhaverbeke, & De Rochemont, 2009). Through technology exploration, SMEs can get acquainted with outside information, gain knowledge and utilize them for their empowerment by enhancing existing technology platform. On the other hand, through technology exploitation, SMEs can empower themselves by raising their knowledge platform (Chesbrough & Crowther, 2006; Lichtenthaler, 2008). Inter-firm collaborations (strategic alliances and joint ventures) are becoming essential instruments to improve competitiveness of enterprises in complex and critical environments (Hoffman & Schlosser, 2001).

Table 1. The operational framework

	Parameters of Innovation Management		
Operational activities	**Product innovation**	**Process innovation**	**Service innovation**
Relative interdependency	A product may come out with an entirely new idea	A process may respond to the need for better coordination and management of functional interdependencies	A service may establish a common language and shared platform or adopt interdisciplinary approach for research and education on service systems
Notable breakthrough	A product may offer improved performance against an existing function or desire or need or may provide a new approach for an existing product	A process intended to achieve radical business improvement	A service may provide solutions for challenges on service systems research
Integrated actions	The product may provide additional functions or features or may be an existing product, but targeting to a new segment of the market	The process may seem to be a discrete initiative but must be combined with other initiatives for ongoing transformations	The service may develop appropriate organizational arrangements to enhance industry-academic collaboration and promote learning programmes on service science, management and engineering
Intricately designed	A product may have a new price or value mix (promotion or other value addition) or may have improved packaging	A process can seldom be achieved in the absence of a carefully considered combination of both technological and human catalysts	A service may develop modular template-based platform of common interests
Localized ones	The product may have changes in appearance or forms as per the local demand	The process must suit the local business culture	The service need to work with partners within a sustainable framework

Along these two routes of open innovation, SMEs have the opportunities of increased customer involvement, external participation, networking among other partners, outsourcing of R&D and inward licensing of intellectual property (IP) through technology exploration, and they may have the opportunities of augmented venturing, inclusion of all-out staff involvement within the R&D processes and outward licensing of IP through technology exploitation (Van de Vrande, De Jong, Vanhaverbeke, & De Rochemont, 2009).

In the context of technology exploration and technology exploitation, parameters as mentioned above need further investigation. A few important activities under the category of technology exploration are being discussed next.

- **Increased Customer Involvement:** Researchers on open innovation recognize increased client involvement as an essential element to expedite internal innovation process (Gassmann, 2006). Apart from Von Hippel's (2005) initiating work, this has been supported by many other researchers (Olson & Bakke, 2001; Lilien et al., 2002; Bonner & Walker, 2004). Emphasis has been given to increased involvement of the customers at the beginning of the innovation process (Brockhoff, 2003; Von Hippel, 1998, 2005; Enkel et al., 2005). Firms may benefit from their customers' ideas, thoughts and innovations by developing better products that are currently offered or by producing products based on the designs of customers (Van de Vrande et al., 2009).

- **External Networking:** Another essential activity to innovate through open and collaborative innovation (Chesbrough et al., 2006), which includes acquiring and maintaining connections with external sources of social capital, organizations and individuals (Van de Vrande et al., 2009). External networking allows enterprises to

acquire specific knowledge without spending time, effort or money but to connect to external partners. Such collaborative network among non-competing entities can be utilized to create R&D alliances and acquire technological capabilities (Gomes-Casseres, 1997; Lee et al., 2010). Within the limited resources of SMEs, they must find ways to achieve production of economies of scale to market their products effectively, and at the same time provide satisfactory support services to their customers. On one hand, Lee et al. (2010) observed that SMEs are flexible and more innovative in new areas, but lack in resources and capabilities. On the other hand, larger firms may be less flexible, but have stronger trend to develop inventions into products or processes. These resources often attract SMEs to collaborate with large firms (Barney & Clark, 2007). But stronger ties with larger firms may limit opportunities and alternatives for SMEs, and they prefer to make external networks with other SMEs or institutions, such as universities, private research establishments or other forms of non-competitive intermediaries (Rothwell, 1991; Torkkeli et al., 2007; Herstad et al., 2008; Lee et al., 2010).

- **External Participation:** In fact this may refer to crowdsourcing in terms of open innovation strategies and it enables one to look into the minute details of innovation sequences in an enterprise which may seemingly unimportant or not promising before (Van de Vrande et al., 2009). A company's competitiveness is increasingly depending on its capabilities beyond the internal boundaries (Prügl & Schreier, 2006). During the start up stages, an enterprise can invest by keeping eyes on potential opportunities (Keil, 2002; Chesbrough, 2006b), and then explore further to increase the knowledge platform through external collaboration (Van de Vrande et al., 2009). Within the innovation process, companies are intensifying relationships and cooperation with resources located outside the firm, ranging from customers, research institutes, intermediaries and business partners to universities and intermediaries (Howells et al., 2003; Linder et al., 2003).

- **Outsourcing R&D:** Nowadays, enterprises are outsourcing R&D activities to acquire external knowledge and technical service providers, such as engineering firms or high-tech organizations are taking lead in the open innovation arena (Van de Vrande et al., 2009). The basic assumption is that enterprises may not be able to conduct all R&D activities by themselves, but capitalize on external knowledge through outsourcing, either by collaboration, or taking or purchasing license (Gassmann, 2006). In this context, collaborative R&D is a useful means by which strategic flexibility can be increased and access to new knowledge can be realized (Pisano, 1990; Quinn, 2000; Fritsch & Lukas, 2001). While R&D outsourcing has been targeted to cost savings in most companies, more and more managers are discovering the value of cooperative R&D to achieve higher innovation rates. Collaborative R&D are being utilized to make systematic use of the competences of suppliers, customers, universities and competitors in order to share risks and costs, enlarge the knowledge base, access the complementary tangible and intangible assets, keep up with market developments and meet customer demands (Nalebuff & Brandeburger, 1996; Boiugrain & Haudeville, 2002; Van Gils & Zwart, 2004; Christensen et al., 2005; De Jong et al., 2007). Furthermore, the not-invented-here syndrome, a severe barrier to innovation, can also be mitigated if external partners are increasingly involved in

the R&D processes (Katz & Allen, 1982) and the most important factor is that, in the open innovation paradigm, it is considered totally acceptable to acquire key development outside the organizational boundary (Prencipe, 2000).

- **Inward Licensing of Intellectual Property:** Intellectual Property (IP) can be termed as creative ideas and expressions of the human mind that have commercial value (http://www.c7.ca/glossary) or it can be seen as an idea, invention, formula, literary work, presentation, or other knowledge asset owned by an organization or individual (Utah Education Network, n. d.). The major legal mechanisms for protecting intellectual property rights are copyrights, patents, and trademarks. IP rights enable owners to select who may access and use their property and to protect it from unauthorized use. As Chesbrough (2006a) has mentioned IP as a catalyst of open business model, an enterprise can acquire intellectual property including the licensing of patents, copyrights or trademarks. This has been supported by Van de Vrande et al. (2009), as this process may strengthen one's business model and gear up the internal research engines. Inward licensing tend to be less costly than conducting in-house R&D, and the licensing payment can be used to control risks by prudent payment scheme, which reduces time to bring new products into market and lowers risk when an invention of similar nature has already been commercialized (Box, 2009; Darcy et al., 2009).

- Other issues like user innovation, non-supplier integration or external commercialization of technology fall under this category, but hardly have they formed any definitive trend channeling separate research aspects other than the activities mentioned above. However, as this research progress, efforts will be given to extract contents of similar interest and highlight them.

Before proceeding next, a few activities on technology exploitation are being discussed below:

- **Venturing:** A venture can be seen as an agreement among people to do things in service of a purpose and according to a set of values, and in this context, an entrepreneur is a venturer that carries primary responsibility for operating a venture (http://igniter.com/post56). Hence, venturing is the process of establishing and developing a venture, and can be defined as starting up new entrepreneurships drawing on internal knowledge, which implies spin-off and spin-out processes. In most cases, support from the parent organization includes finance, human capital, legal advice, or administrative services (Van de Vrande et al., 2009). Keil (2002) suggests that external corporate venturing unites both physical and intellectual assets of an enterprise by extending and exploiting the internal capabilities for continual regeneration and growth. Though earlier studies on open innovation have primarily focused on venturing activities in large enterprises (Chesbrough, 2003a; Lord et al., 2002), but the potential of venturing activities is regarded to be as enormous. Chesbrough (2003a) illustrated that the total market value of 11 projects which turned into new ventures exceeding that of their parent company, Xerox, by a factor of two.

- **Outward Licensing of Intellectual Property:** As mentioned earlier, IP plays a crucial role in open innovation as a result of the in-and-out flows of knowledge (Arora, 2002; Chesbrough, 2003a, 2006a; Lichtenthaler, 2007). Enterprises have opportunities to out-license their IP through

commercialization to obtain more value from it (Gassmann, 2006; Darcy et al., 2009). Darcy et al. (2009) mention that out-licensing of IPs bring opportunity of high profitability, allow multiple licensees to work together at the same time, seem less riskier than Foreign Direct Investment (FDI), simple to operate when less technology components exist, and especially suited for SMEs as this process lowers risk by eliminating need for downstream production facilities. Out-licensing of IPs allow them to profit from their IPs when other firms with different business models find them as profitable, and in this way IPs route to the market through external paths (Van de Vrande et al., 2009). By means of out-licensing, many firms have begun to actively commercialize technology. This increase in inward and outward technology transactions reflects the new paradigm of open innovation (Vujovic & Ulhøi, 2008; Lichtenthaler & Ernst, 2009). However, the decision of firms to license out depends on anticipated revenues and profit-dissipation effects (Arora et al., 2001), as whether the outward licensing generates revenues in the form of licensing payments, but current profits might decrease when licensees use their technology to compete in the same market (Van de Vrande et al., 2009). Moreover, these new forms of knowledge exploitation and creation of technology markets require the design of appropriate financial instruments to support the circulation and commercialization of knowledge (Darcy et al., 2009).

- **Involvement of Non-R&D Employees:** By capitalizing on the initiatives and knowledge of internal employees, active or non-active with the R&D exercises, an enterprise can be benefited (Van de Vrande et al., 2009). Chesbrough et al. (2006) has conducted case studies which illustrate the significance of informal ties of employees of one enterprise with employees of other enterprises, which are crucial in understanding of arrival of new products in the market and also the commercialization processes. Earlier researches (Van de Ven, 1986), also support this view that innovation by individual employees within an enterprise who are not involved in R&D, but involved in new idea generation could be effective in fostering the success of an enterprise. Moreover, along the context of currently evolved knowledge society, employees need to be involved in innovation processes in diversified ways, such as by encouraging them to generate new ideas and suggestions, exempting them to take initiatives beyond organizational boundaries, or introducing suggestion schemes such as idea boxes and internal competitions (Van Dijk & Van den Ende, 2002);

- There are other activities like spin-off (Ndonzuau et al., 2002), selling of results (OECD, 2008), transfer of technology (OECD, 2008), and transfer of know-how (OECD, 2008) that may fall under the activities of technology exploitation, which deserve further research and investigation.

In the perpetual scenario, one can portrait a picture as shown in Figure 5, as SMEs are acting as catalysts in the process of technology exploration and technology exploitation performing the necessary actions. But, in reality, they need to be under a strategically guided and managed environment to achieve their innovativeness and competitiveness to attain a sustainable economic platform (Sautter & Clar, 2008). This research would argue that a third party in between them is essential to take necessary initiatives, strategies and action plans for providing appropriate guidance, support and directives at the field level in tackling issue, difficulties and challenges on behalf of them. Furthermore, this form of support

should be carried out from a platform that would be institutional, so that in time of need, SMEs may rely on and feel dependable. In addition to these, if this institutional support comes from a locally generated perspective, they would feel confident and comfortable to be working with. This research argues that to expedite and make efficient use of the life cycle management, engagement of partners is essential. The partners could be a consortium of SMEs and external entities, like research houses, universities, association of entrepreneurs, intermediaries specialized in carrying out open innovation strategies in SMEs, not acting in isolation, but acting in close interactions.

Moreover, the life-cycle of technology exploration and technology exploitation (Figure 5) is not a perpetual one and demands a catalytic agent to make it roll or put in action. This research would like to put forward action plans in accomplishing the life-cycle management of the mentioned open innovation phenomena. It also affirms that a third party or agent of innovation can play the most important role in ascertaining pre-requisites at each entrepreneurship level, their networked level, or even at the level of their human skills. Among various action plans, establishment of a networked environment is pertinent. Utilizing ICT, an extended platform of communication and knowledge sharing can be established (D´Adderio, 2001; Antonelli, 2006), which can be physical or virtual.

However, apart from the mentioned benefits or opportunities mentioned above, as Professor Henry Chesbrough (2003a, 2003b, 2006a, 2006b, 2007) claims a fundamental shift in innovation paradigm from closed to open innovation and advocates collaborative and open innovation strategies and open business models to take the full benefit from collaborating with external partners, this research would continue building on the paradigm shift. It would explore to develop a sustainable business model adopting open innovation strategies to be applicable for SMEs operating at the grass roots (Rahman & Ramos,

Figure 5. Life-cycle of technology exploration and technology exploitation in SMEs

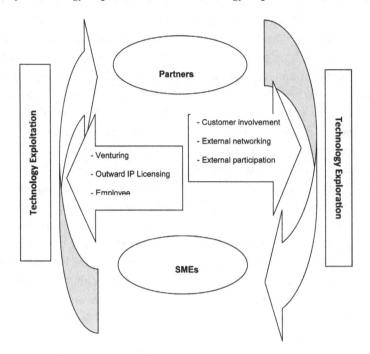

2010). Furthermore, as mentioned by Sautter and Clar (2008), this research would support that, it is beneficial to avail the competences of external partners meeting the challenges of increased complexity of research, technological development and innovation (RTDI), and growing global competition.

FUTURE RESEARCH SCOPES

In strategically guided and well managed groups, the enhanced innovativeness and competitiveness at the firm level would result in sustainable economic development (Sautter & Clar, 2008). However, in order to survive, for SMEs- especially those operating in an increasing dynamic and digitalized environment and at the grass roots level, but with potentiality and knowledge being the most indispensable and important resource for innovation- need to establish trusted relations to

aligned communities, networks and stakeholders (Hafkesbrink & Scholl, 2010).

Future of this research would like to examine the conditions for proactivity the effect that proactive agents have through the life cycle management and on the reminder of the population, as a joint platform of interactive partners. This would constitute a significant research effort, and while future research would aim to uncover unattended clues in this area, the focus will be on disseminating and improving innovation tool for SMEs at the grass roots (MacGregor et al., 2007) and dedicated to tools to empower them. With the research agenda and the survey result this study would like to support its hypotheses articulated so far.

CONCLUSION

It is clear that there are a variety of potential contribution that SMEs can make to economic development at the local, national and regional levels, that include employment and revenue generation, acting as supplier to larger companies and contributing to a more diversified economic strength through the development of new activities, particularly through new firm formation in service activities (Smallbone et al., 2003). An improved and efficient life cycle management would ensure engagement of applicable open innovation strategies to be adopted in SMEs to empower them for elevated socio-economic development. The survey, which will be conducted by the end of 2010 would enable to conclude further on adoption of open innovation strategies relating the nature, size, challenges, barriers, finance, competition and other form of collaborative innovation strategies.

REFERENCES

Antonelli, C. (2006). Localized technological change and factor markets: Constraints and inducements to innovation. *Structural Change and Economic Dynamics*, *17*, 224–247. doi:10.1016/j.strueco.2004.05.002

Arora, A. (2002). Licensing tacit knowledge: Intellectual property rights and the market for know-how. *Economics of Innovation and New Technology*, *4*(1), 41–59. doi:10.1080/10438599500000013

Barney, J., & Clark, D. (2007). *Resource-based theory: Creating and sustaining competitive advantage*. New York, NY: Oxford University Press.

Bessant, J., & Tidd, J. (2007). *Innovation and entrepreneurship*. New York, NY: John Wiley & Sons.

Boiugrain, F., & Haudeville, B. (2002). Innovation, collaboration and SMEs internal research capacities. *Research Policy*, *31*, 735–747. doi:10.1016/S0048-7333(01)00144-5

Bonner, J., & Walker, O. (2004). Selecting influential business-to-business customers in new product development: Relational embeddedness and knowledge heterogeneity considerations. *Journal of Product Innovation Management*, *21*, 155–169. doi:10.1111/j.0737-6782.2004.00067.x

Box, S. (2009). *OECD work on innovation- a stocktaking of existing work*. Paris, France: OECD Publishing.

Brockhoff, K. (2003). Customers' perspectives of involvement in new product development. *International Journal of Technology Management*, *26*(5-6), 464–481. doi:10.1504/IJTM.2003.003418

Chesbrough, H. (2003a). *Open innovation: The new imperative for creating and profiting from technology*. Boston, MA: Harvard Business School Press.

Chesbrough, H. (2003b). The era of open innovation. *MIT Sloan Management Review*, *44*(3), 35–41.

Chesbrough, H. (2006a). Open innovation: A new paradigm for understanding industrial innovation. In H. Chesbrough, W. Vanhaverbeke, & J. West (Eds.), *Open innovation: Researching a new paradigm* (pp. 1-27). Oxford, UK: Oxford University Press.

Chesbrough, H. (2006b). *Open business models: How to thrive in the new innovation landscape*. Boston, MA: Harvard Business School Press.

Chesbrough, H. (2007). The market for innovation: Implications for corporate strategy. *California Management Review*, *49*(3), 45–66.

Chesbrough, H., & Crowther, A. K. (2006). Beyond high tech: Early adopters of open innovation in other industries. *R & D Management*, *36*(3), 229–236. doi:10.1111/j.1467-9310.2006.00428.x

Chesbrough, H., Vanhaverbeke, W., & West, J. (Eds.). (2006). *Open innovation: Researching a new paradigm*. Oxford, UK: Oxford University Press.

Christensen, J. F., Olesen, M. H., & Kjær, J. S. (2005). The industrial dynamics of open innovation: Evidence from the transformation of consumer electronics. *Research Policy, 34*(10), 1533–1549. doi:10.1016/j.respol.2005.07.002

Crawford, C. M. (1983). *New products management*. Homewood, IL: Richard D. Irwin, Inc.

D'Adderio, L. (2001). Crafting the virtual prototype: How firms integrate knowledge and capabilities across organizational boundaries. *Research Policy, 30*, 1409–1424. doi:10.1016/S0048-7333(01)00159-7

Darcy, J., Kraemer-Eis, H., Guellec, D., & Debande, O. (2009). *Financing technology transfer*. Adenauer, Luxembourg: European Investment Fund.

Darsø, L. (2001). *Innovation in the making*. Frederiksberg, Denmark: Samfundslitteratur.

Davenport, T. H. (1993). *Process innovation: Reengineering work through information technology*. New York, NY: Ernst & Young.

De Jong, J. P. J., Vanhaverbeke, W., Van de Vrande, V., & De Rochemont, M. (2007). Open innovation in SMEs: Trends, motives and management challenges. In *Proceedings of the EURAM Conference*, Paris, France.

Dodgson, M., Gann, D., & Salter, A. (2006). The role of technology in the shift towards open innovation: The case of Procter & Gamble. *R & D Management, 36*(3), 333–346. doi:10.1111/j.1467-9310.2006.00429.x

Drucker, P. (1998). The discipline of innovation. *Harvard Business Review*, 149.

EC. (2008). *SBA fact sheet Portugal*. Brussels, Belgium: European Commission.

Enkel, E., Kausch, C., & Gassmann, O. (2005). Managing the risk of customer integration. *European Management Journal, 23*(2), 203–213. doi:10.1016/j.emj.2005.02.005

Fritsch, M., & Lukas, R. (2001). Who cooperates on R&D? *Research Policy, 30*(2), 297–312. doi:10.1016/S0048-7333(99)00115-8

Gassmann, O. (2006). Opening up the innovation process: Towards an agenda. *R & D Management, 36*(3), 223–228. doi:10.1111/j.1467-9310.2006.00437.x

Gomes-Casseres, B. (1997). Alliance strategies of small firms. *Small Business Economics, 9*, 33–44. doi:10.1023/A:1007947629435

Hafkesbrink, J., & Scholl, H. (2010). Web 2.0 learning- a case study on organizational competences in open content innovation. In Hafkesbrink, J., Hoppe, H. U., & Schlichter, J. (Eds.), *Competence management for open innovation- tools and IT-support to unlock the potential of open innovation*. Berlin, Germany: Eul Verlag.

Henderson, R. M., & Clark, K. B. (1990). Architectural innovation: The reconfiguration of existing product technologies and the failure of established firms. *Administrative Science Quarterly, 35*, 9–30. doi:10.2307/2393549

Herstad, S. J., Bloch, C., Ebersberger, B., & van de Velde, E. (2008). *Open innovation and globalisation: Theory, evidence and implications*. Retrieved from http://www.tem.fi/files/25709/Open_innovation_and_globalisation.pdf

Hiebing, R. G. Jr, & Cooper, S. W. (2003). *The successful marketing plan: A disciplined and comprehensive approach*. New York, NY: McGraw-Hill.

Hoffman, W. H., & Schlosser, R. (2001). Success factors of strategic alliances in small and medium-sized enterprises: An empirical study. *Long Range Planning, 34,* 357–381. doi:10.1016/S0024-6301(01)00041-3

Howells, J., James, A., & Malek, K. (2003). The sourcing of technological knowledge: Distributed innovation processes and dynamic change. *R & D Management, 33*(4), 395–409. doi:10.1111/1467-9310.00306

IfM and IBM. (2008). *Succeeding through service innovation: A service perspective for education, research, business and government*. Cambridge, UK: University of Cambridge Institute for Manufacturing.

Katz, R., & Allen, T. J. (1982). Investigating the not-invented-here (NIH)- syndrome: A look at performance, tenure and communication patterns of 50 R&D project groups. *R & D Management, 12,* 7–19. doi:10.1111/j.1467-9310.1982.tb00478.x

Keil, T. (2002). *External corporate venturing: Strategic renewal in rapidly changing industries.* Westport, CT: Quorum.

Lee, S., Park, G., Yoon, B., & Park, J. (2010). Open innovation in SMEs- an intermediated network model. *Research Policy, 39*(2), 290–300. doi:10.1016/j.respol.2009.12.009

Lichtenthaler, U. (2007). The drivers of technology licensing: An industry comparison. *California Management Review, 49*(4), 67–89.

Lichtenthaler, U. (2008). Open innovation in practice: An analysis of strategic approaches to technology transactions. *IEEE Transactions on Engineering Management, 55*(1), 148–157. doi:10.1109/TEM.2007.912932

Lichtenthaler, U., & Ernst, H. (2009). Opening up the innovation process: The role of technology aggressiveness. *R & D Management, 39*(1), 38–54. doi:10.1111/j.1467-9310.2008.00522.x

Lilien, G. L., Morrison, P. D., Searls, K., Sonnack, M., & von Hippel, E. (2002). Performance assessment of the lead user idea-generation process for new product development. *Management Science, 48*(8), 1042–1059. doi:10.1287/mnsc.48.8.1042.171

Linder, J. C., Jarvenpaa, S., & Davenport, T. H. (2003). Toward an innovation sourcing strategy. *MIT Sloan Management Review, 4447,* 43–49.

Lord, M. D., Mandel, S. W., & Wager, J. D. (2002). Spinning out a star. *Harvard Business Review, 80,* 115–121.

MacGregor, S., Bianchi, M., Hernandez, J. L., & Mendibil, K. (2007, October 29-30). Towards the tipping point for social innovation. In *Proceedings of the 12th International Conference on Towards Sustainable Product Design,* Surrey, UK (pp. 145-152).

Miles, I. (2005). Innovation in services. In Fagerberg, J., Mowery, D. C., & Nelson, R. R. (Eds.), *The Oxford handbook of innovation* (pp. 433–458). Oxford, UK: Oxford University Press.

Nalebuff, B. J., & Brandeburger, A. M. (1996). *Co-opetition*. London, UK: Harper Collins.

Ndonzuau, F. N., Pirnay, F., & Surlemont, B. (2002). A stage model of academic spin-off creation. *Technovation, 22,* 281–289. doi:10.1016/S0166-4972(01)00019-0

OECD. (1992). *Oslo manual* (1st ed.). Paris, France: OECD.

OECD. (1996). *Oslo manual* (2nd ed.). Paris, France: OECD.

OECD. (2005). *Oslo manual* (3rd ed.). Paris, France: OECD.

OECD. (2008). *Open innovation in global networks, policy brief.* Paris, France: OECD.

Olson, E., & Bakke, G. (2001). Implementing the lead user method in a high technology firm: A longitudinal study of intentions versus actions. *Journal of Product Innovation Management, 18*(2), 388–395. doi:10.1016/S0737-6782(01)00111-4

Pisano, G. P. (1990). The R&D boundaries of the firm: An empirical analysis. *Administrative Science Quarterly, 35*(1), 153–176. doi:10.2307/2393554

Prencipe, A. (2000). Breadth and depth of technological capabilities in CoPS: The case of the aircraft engine control system. *Research Policy, 29*(7-8), 895–911. doi:10.1016/S0048-7333(00)00111-6

Prügl, R., & Schreier, M. (2006). Learning from leading-edge customers at The Sims: Opening up the innovation process using toolkits. *R & D Management, 36*(3), 237–250. doi:10.1111/j.1467-9310.2006.00433.x

Quinn, J. B. (2000). Outsourcing innovation: The new engine of growth. *Sloan Management Review, 41*(4), 13–28.

Rahman, H., & Ramos, I. (2010). Open innovation in SMEs: From closed boundaries to networked paradigm. *Issues in Informing Science and Information Technology, 7,* 471–487.

Rothwell, R. (1991). External networking and innovation in small and medium-sized manufacturing firms in Europe. *Technovation, 11*(2), 93–112. doi:10.1016/0166-4972(91)90040-B

Sautter, B., & Clar, G. (2008). *Strategic capacity building in clusters to enhance future-oriented open innovation processes.* Brussels, Belgium: The European Foresight Monitoring Network.

Schumpeter, J. A. (1934). *The theory of economic development.* Cambridge, MA: Harvard University Press.

Schumpeter, J. A. (1982). *The theory of economic development: An inquiry into profits, capital, credit, interest, and the business cycle (1912/1934).* New Brunswick, NJ: Transaction Publishers.

Smallbone, D., North, D., & Vickers, I. (2003). The role and characteristics of SMEs. In Asheim, B., Nauwelers, C., & Todtling, F. (Eds.), *Regional innovation policy for small-medium enterprises* (pp. 3–20). Northampton, MA: Edward Elgar.

Tidd, J., Bessant, J., & Pavitt, K. (2005). *Managing innovation: Integrating technological, market and organizational change* (3rd ed.). Chichester, UK: John Wiley & Sons.

Torkkeli, M., Tiina Kotonen, T., & Pasi Ahonen, P. (2007). Regional open innovation system as a platform for SMEs: A survey. *International Journal of Foresight and Innovation Policy, 3*(4). doi:10.1504/IJFIP.2007.016456

Utah Education Network. (n. d.). *Ed technology glossary of terms.* Retrieved from http://www.uen.org/core/edtech/glossary.shtml

Van Ark, B., Broersma, L., & Den Hertog, P. (2003). *Service innovation, performance and policy: A review.* London, UK: The Ministry of Economic Affairs of the Netherlands.

Van de Ven, A. H., Schroeder, R., Scudder, G., & Polley, D. (1986). Managing innovation and change processes: Findings from the Minnesota innovation research program. *Agribusiness Management Journal, 2*(4), 501–523.

Van de Vrande, V., De Jong, J. P. J., Vanhaverbeke, W., & De Rochemont, M. (2009). Open innovation in SMEs: Trends, motives and management challenges. *Technovation, 29,* 423–437. doi:10.1016/j.technovation.2008.10.001

Van Dijk, C., & Van den Ende, J. (2002). Suggestion systems: Transferring employee creativity into practicable ideas. *R & D Management, 32*, 387–395. doi:10.1111/1467-9310.00270

Van Gils, A., & Zwart, P. (2004). Knowledge acquisition and learning in Dutch and Belgian SMEs: The role of strategic alliances. *European Management Journal, 22*(6), 685–692. doi:10.1016/j.emj.2004.09.031

Vanhaverbeke, W. (2006). The inter-organizational context of open innovation. In H. Chesbrough, W. Vanhaverbeke, & J. West (Eds.), *Open innovation: Researching a new paradigm* (pp. 205-219). Oxford, UK: Oxford University Press.

Von Hippel, E. (1998). Economics of product development by users: The impact of 'sticky' local information. *Management Science, 44*(5), 629–644. doi:10.1287/mnsc.44.5.629

Von Hippel, E. (2005). *Democratizing innovation*. Boston, MA: MIT Press.

Vujovic, S., & Ulhøi, J. P. (2008). Opening up the innovation process: Different organizational strategies. In Obel, B., & Burton, R. M. (Eds.), *Information and organization design series* (*Vol. 7*). New York, NY: Springer.

Walton, R. E. (1989). *Up and running: Integrating information technology and the organization*. Boston, MA: Harvard Business School Press.

West, J., & Gallagher, S. (2006). Challenges of open innovation: The paradox of firm investment in open-source software. *R & D Management, 36*(3), 319–331. doi:10.1111/j.1467-9310.2006.00436.x

Zuboff, S. (1988). *In the age of the smart machine: The future of work and power*. New York, NY: Basic Books.

ENDNOTES

[1] Crowdsourcing is a form of open innovation (and in some cases, user innovation) that attempts to involve a large pool of outsiders to solve a problem. Product recommendations at Amazon etc. are probably the most often seen example (Chesbrough, Vanhaverbeke, & West, 2006).

[2] Small and medium enterprises (also SMEs, small and medium businesses, SMBs, and variations thereof) are companies whose headcount or turnover falls below certain limits (http://en.wikipedia.org/wiki/SMEs).

[3] About Types of Innovation: Tidd et al. (2005) argue that there are four types of innovation; consequently the innovator has four pathways to investigate when searching for good ideas, such as: a) Product Innovation - new products or improvements on products (example- the new Mini or the updated VX Beetle, new models of mobile phones and so on.); b) Process Innovation - where some part of the process is improved to bring benefit (example- Just in Time); c) Positioning Innovation – for example- Lucozade used to be a medicinal drink but the was repositioned as a sports drink; and d) Paradigm Innovation - where major shifts in thinking cause change (example- during the time of the expensive mainframe, Bill Gates and others aimed to provide a home computer for everyone) (http://ezinearticles.com/?Types-of-Innovation&id=38384).

[4] Radical innovation concerns technology breakthrough, user embracement as well as new business models (Artemis, 2009).

[5] Examples of service innovation may include: On-line tax returns, e-commerce, helpdesk outsourcing, music download, loyalty

programs, home medical test kits, mobile phones, money market funds, ATMs and ticket kiosks, bar code, credit cards, binding arbitration, franchise chains, installment payment plans, leasing, patent system, public education and compound interest saving accounts (IfM & IBM, 2008, p. 17).

This work was previously published in the International Journal of Information Communication Technologies and Human Development, Volume 3, Issue 3, edited by Susheel Chhabra and Hakikur Rahman, pp. 42-57, copyright 2011 by IGI Publishing (an imprint of IGI Global).

Chapter 12
Web–Based Intellectual Property Marketplace:
A Survey of Current Practices

Isabel Ramos
Centre Algoritmi, University of Minho, Portugal

José Fernandes
Centre Algoritmi, University of Minho, Portugal

ABSTRACT

In the past year, knowledge and innovation management have acquired increasing relevance in organizations. In the last decade, open innovation strategy, and in particular, crowdsourcing innovation model has also gained increasing importance. This model is seen as a new innovation model, capable of accelerating the innovation process. Therefore, it is important to understand how organizations can best take advantage of this innovation model. This paper approaches in two ways for commercializing intellectual property: crowdsourcing innovation, and intellectual property marketplaces. Thus, with the intention of understanding the concepts and practices, the study started by collecting scientific articles through bibliographic data bases. The paper provides knowledge about concepts and practices underlying the ways for commercializing intellectual property. It also contributes with a proposal of architecture for an intellectual property marketplace, based on the analysis of practices about crowdsourcing innovation and intellectual property marketplaces. This architecture is still in a draft stage, but already includes helpful insights for organizations interested in applying the open innovation strategy.

INTRODUCTION

The Knowledge Management (KM) presents as goal the increase of efficiency and efficacy to the level of individual and collaborative work (Ramos & Carvalho, 2008). Thus, to better manage the organizational knowledge, it pretends to increase the innovation capacity as well as improve the decision processes. In the last years the KM has acquired increasingly preponderance in the international sphere.

This paper approaches two ways for commercializing Intellectual Property (IP): Crowdsourcing Innovation (CI) and IP marketplaces.

DOI: 10.4018/978-1-4666-1957-9.ch012

The CI is presented as a new way to innovate, capable of accelerating the innovation process (Adams & Ramos, 2009). This innovation model is supported by web platforms, for example, the platform of InnoCentive, and NineSigma, used to launch challenges for a community registered in the platform. The IP marketplaces are also supported by web platforms where registered members can promote their IP, namely patents. In this way, and considering the analysis made of some these marketplaces, the purpose of them is promoting the IP commercialization, providing the following services: selling, buying, and licensing of IP. It is important to refer that the two ways mentioned above are also important in the Small and Medium Enterprises (SMEs) scope, because these ways help them to promote their inventions with potential of commercialization as well as to enable them accessing to the innovation networks.

The study is mainly motivated by the growing interest that CI and IP marketplaces have raised. The main objective of this paper is to present the concepts and practices in CI and IP marketplaces, ending with a draft of a proposal of architecture for an IP Marketplace that systemize the practices of two ways for IP commercialization. As there is no available systemization that promotes a view about the IP commercialization market, the proposal of architecture presented here intends helping SMEs.

Thereafter the paper talks about IP commercialization, presents a review of current practices on CI and IP marketplaces, develops the architecture for an IP marketplace and put forward a few issues on future research before the conclusion.

INTELLECTUAL PROPERTY COMMERCIALIZATION

In recent years two ways for commercializing IP, CI and IP marketplaces, supported by web platforms have acquired increasing relevancy. The CI practice aims to promote the creativity with intention for creating new ideas and concepts; and the IP marketplaces aim to provide support for commercializing IP already patented, i.e., they are focused in the transferring of IP among IP owners and buyers.

To understand better the contents of the survey that are being discussed in the next section, some concepts related to crowdsourcing and IP marketplaces are being discussed next.

Created by How (2006), the crowdsourcing term is presented as a web-based business model, composed of a distributed network of individuals. The idea is to launch challenges, with the intention of creating innovative solutions. In other words, a company puts in a crowdsourcing platform a challenge, for what the associative creative network (designated by crowd) develop solutions (Brabham, 2008).

This study finds that there are two main definitions about crowdsourcing. The first one is given by Howe (2006): "Technological advances in everything from product design software to digital video cameras are breaking down the cost barriers that once separated amateurs from professionals. Hobbyists, part-timers, and dabblers suddenly have a market for their efforts, as smart companies in industries as disparate as pharmaceuticals and television discover ways to tap the latent talent of the crowd. The labor is not always free, but it costs a lot less than paying traditional employees. It's not outsourcing; it's crowdsourcing"(p. 3).

And the second definition was given by Brabham (2008): "Crowdsourcing is not just another buzzword, not another meme. It is not just a re-packaging of open philosophy for capitalist ends either. It is a model capable of aggregating talent, leveraging ingenuity while reducing the costs and time formerly needed to solve problems. Finally, Crowdsourcing is enabled only through the technology of the web, which is a creative mode of user interactivity, not merely a medium between messages and people" (p. 87).

However, to understand the activity in IP marketplaces and CI, it is necessary to consider important concepts related with IP which are IP rights, and patents. Therefore, these two concepts are being presented in the form of definitions.

The first, IP rights, "incorporate a variety of regulatory policies designed to improve the functioning of markets for technologies and information goods and services. These policies include patents, copyrights, trademarks, trade secrets (rules against unfair competition in acquiring private business information), and numerous related devices" (Maskus, 2008, p. 249); the second concept, about patents, is described by the same author as "temporary exclusive rights to use or license process technologies and to make and distribute the embodiments of ideas into new products" (p. 261).

The definition of an electronic marketplace is also relevant in this context. So, according to Bakos (1991) "an electronic marketplace (or electronic market system) is an inter-organizational information system that allows the participating buyers and sellers to exchange information about prices and *product offerings*" (p. 299); and in the context of this paper, the "product offerings" are seen as IP assets. In summary one can say that an IP Marketplace aims at promoting the IP commercialization, providing support for the interaction of IP owners and potential buyers.

The next section approaches the practices, complemented with some examples on the two ways of IP commercialization that are being discussed earlier.

A SURVEY OF CURRENT PRACTICES

Crowdsourcing Innovation

Practices

Over the years the organizations have demonstrated a great enthusiasm with the CI: "Enterprises are increasingly employing crowdsourcing to access scalable workforce on-line" (Vukovic, 2009, p. 686).

Considering that crowdsourcing converges for an opening in the investigation and development process, it is important to highlight the importance of web 2.0 (Trompette et al., 2008). This infrastructure facilitates the on-line resolution of innovation problems, in a distributed and more efficient way, ensuring scalability benefits and skilled manpower in a global scale (Vukovic, 2009). According to the same author, the CI process integrates three main actors: requestor; crowdsourcing platform; and provider. The requestor is responsible for submitting a task request on the crowdsourcing platforms, for initiating the process; the requestor pays or assigns awards for the successful execution of the task by one or more providers; and the crowdsourcing platform aims to ensure the successful execution of the task by providers, as well as, ensure that requestors pay the promised rewards (Vukovic, 2009).

Relatively to the rewards offered by participating in the CI platforms, according to Antikainen and Vaataja (2010), can be divided in two forms: monetary rewards and non-monetary rewards. The monetary rewards include money and products; while the non-monetary rewards consist in publishing different kinds of rankings about winners of challenges. Regarding the motivation to participate in CI platforms, according to Leimeister et al. (2009), is principally intrinsic or activated by external incentives. Rosenstiel (2007) described the activation of human behavior in a model designated by Motive-Incentive-Activation-Behavior (MIAB). In this, the activation is stimulated by incentives that later influence the behavior of people.

Another thing that should be highlighted is the benefits for organizations. Reichwald and Piller (2006) suggested three: reduction of the time in development of new products; reduction of the costs with innovation; and better consumer acceptance of the new products. So, it is important to refer four guidelines for successful crowdsourcing suggested by Hempel (2006). These guidelines are:

- The defined challenge should be clear in relation to its objective and expected results
- It is essential to define adequate filters to select the best idea for a challenge, because generally several solutions are received through crowdsourcing
- It is important to have a rigorous process for attracting new elements, being essential to have in consideration the diversity and quality of skills
- It is important to create a sense of belonging to a friendly community. The offered rewards are important to recruit people from the crowd, but it is also important to create conditions that allow the building of friendship relations within the crowd. These are two ways to maintain people in the community for a long time.

The intermediation platforms, designated by some authors as innovation intermediaries, aim to provide support for CI practice. According to Trompette et al. (2008) the intermediary can play the following main roles:

- **Broker:** These intermediaries connect companies seeking innovative ideas with those individuals and small teams that have the knowledge and skills to provide those ideas.
- **Agent:** These intermediaries know individuals and small teams that have innovative ideas and technologies and pro-actively find the companies that can benefit from them.
- **Scout:** These intermediaries work for companies that have innovation needs and search for the technologies being developed in Universities and other R&D entities that can fulfill those needs.

Furthermore, according to Trompette et al. (2008), the intermediation platforms are trying to conjugate a private investment model (profits aiming) and a collective action model. In the private investment model the innovation is financed by private investment, i.e., use private resources for creating and developing the new ideas/concepts; while the collective action model aims at getting the results of the collaborative work of innovators (e.g. an innovation, a service, etc) and make them available for public use. The idea in the Trompette et al.'s (2008) paper is to create a private-collective model, identical to suggested by Hippel and Krogh (2003) for applying in open source software projects. Model of this study conjugates the best things of the two models mentioned above, aiming the maximum benefits.

Examples

Regarding to the examples of CI platforms, the Open Innovators is a website that provides many examples of platforms that give support to CI practice. Through this website it has been possible to identify four examples of CI platforms. The examples are: InnoCentive, IdeaConnection, NineSigma, categorized as research and development platforms; and Cambrian House – Chaordix categorized as intermediary of Open Innovation (OI) service.

Relatively to the platform characteristics, after analyse them, it can be noticed that they all focus on the creation and sustaining a crowd, trying to continuously add new members with diversified knowledge and skills (Diener & Piller, 2010). The crowd provides solutions for challenges that companies make available to the platform, or for challenges that an owner company of a CI platform decide to launch by its own initiative. Among the four platforms that are being analyzed here, only one – InnoCentive – presents a public challenge center where the crowd members can submit their solutions for posted challenges. This can be understood as a way to maintain confidentially about the challenges submitted by companies.

There are other elements that characterize this type of platforms, as it is the example of a blog. This aims to promote the debate of ideas as well as sharing of diverse elements about CI. Some platforms make available consulting services in OI.

Table 1 intends to give a perspective about a set of characteristics that were found in the analysis of four selected CI platforms. To obtain these characteristics this research has used as main reference the study realized by Diener and Piller (2010), which considered several characteristics about intermediation platforms that give support to the OI practice.

Intellectual Property Marketplaces

Practices

Regarding the practical issues about IP marketplaces, it is important to mention the evolution of IP legislation that, according to Webber and Cave (2007), has had a significant progress along the past thirty years. This is based in the fact that nowadays a growing number of specialists are focused on solving and debating issues related with the IP legislation.

According to Blackman (2007), the IP management has acquired increasingly importance for companies having in consideration that this is a strategic element for them. To reinforce this idea, and according to Kamiyama et al. (2006), companies have obtained competitive advantages through their own IP, such as the improvement of their competitive position; generation of a higher volume of incomes; and improvement of the access to financing.

However, one of the most important challenges for IP marketplaces is the IP valuation (Kamiyama et al., 2006). The same authors showed that several specialists have proposed methods for facilitating the IP valuation that can be categorized in two groups: qualitative methods and quantitative methods. According to the same authors, the qualitative methods aim at evaluating patents based in some factors, namely: strength and breadth of the patents rights; and evaluating the legal security of these same rights. Regarding the quantitative methods, these aim at determining the monetary value of a patent. According to Smith and Parr (2000), this value can be obtained by one of three approaches: cost approach, income approach, and market approach.

Another aspect that assumes relevancy for organizations is the patent licensing (Kamiyama et al., 2006). It is suggested, three types of licensing: cross-licensing, patent pools, and unilateral licensing. However, it is relevant to say that in some situations, to develop an innovation, the patent license may not be enough and it may be necessary to get additional know-how or technologies.

Table 1. A set of standard characteristics related to CI platforms (adapted from Diener & Piller, 2010)

Characteristics	Covered Topics
CI platforms industry focus	Automotive, Engineering, Telecom, Computer / IT, Design, Consumer electronics, Medicine / Health, and Pharmaceutical / Chemical
Focus of CI platforms on stages of the innovation process	Ideation, New product development, and commercialization
Types of open innovation approaches	Managing community, Providing software, and Open innovation consultant
Methodological approaches of CI platforms to accomplish open innovation	Workshops, Challenges, and Toolkit
Type of community support by CI platforms	Collaborative space, Discussion forum, and Panel of specialists
Type of community access	Restricted and Non-restricted

According to Blackman (2007), IP marketplaces can also instigate the technology diffusion, the appearing of new companies, as well as an increase in competition. As Chesbrough (2006) says, "A small number of intermediary firms have arisen in recent years to assist in the process of identification, negotiation, and transfer of patents from one firm to another" (p. 3).

Examples

IP marketplaces also appear in result of the necessity for finding or monitor the external knowledge, taking for marketplaces the effort of developing required skills and resources (Lee & Lee, 2010). There are many IP marketplaces on the web promoting the IP commercialization. For this paper four examples have been selected. These examples are: Yet2.com, IPMarket, IdeaBuyer, and Tynax. In general, this type of Marketplaces provides services that aim to promote the transactions between the IP owners (vendors) and the potential buyers. Usually, IP marketplaces arrange patents into categories to make searches of IP easier. The IP available is mainly patents; in some cases are inventions. Therefore, IP marketplaces also provide a patents license service.

In respect to the commercialization, the IP prices are not usually listed on-line. In the analyzed IP marketplaces there were only small description of IP, and the details are only provided by contacting the Marketplace staff.

Table 2 aims to provide a synthesis about a set of standard services related with IP marketplaces. The presented services in this table were identified in the analyzed IP marketplaces.

DRAFT PROPOSAL OF A STANDARD ARCHITECTURE FOR AN INTELLECTUAL PROPERTY MARKETPLACE

Architecture Outlook

The proposal of architecture presented in the next subsection has resulted from the analyses of concepts and practices in CI and IP marketplaces. It intends to be a design of the main components that an IP Marketplace can integrate. Those components were the ones that these researchers found in the several studied marketplaces. Authors are not suggesting that all components should be implemented in all situations. They are

Table 2. A set of standard services related to IP marketplaces

Services	Description
Selling IP	It aims at helping the IP owners to realize gains with their IP, providing a way to promote IP for potential buyers.
Buying IP	It provides a web place in which the IP owners (vendors) can expose their IP for potential buyers, being created the ideal conditions for realizing IP transactions among vendors and buyers.
Licensing IP	It intends to provide support in licensing agreements of IP assets, namely patents.
Patents wanted	It provides a place in which the Marketplace members, namely companies, make available requests for patents needed for solving innovation problems.
Strategic alliance	It aims at encouraging the creation of agreements among companies for achieving a strategic goal. These agreements include international licensing, contract management and joint entrepreneurship.
Training	It provides a set of educational materials to help the IP owners better understanding the dynamic of the IP market which is in continuous change.
Strategic advising	It provides services to help Marketplace members to define the best strategies for maximizing the value of their IP assets, mainly their patents portfolio.

only proposing a systemized understanding of the components that can be part of marketplaces, so that managers can find the knowledge they need to implement a specific Marketplace initiative.

Proposal of Architecture

The draft proposal is presented in Figure 1, which is composed by three layers: Infrastructure, Applications, and Services.

Figure 1. Draft proposal of a standard architecture for an IP marketplace

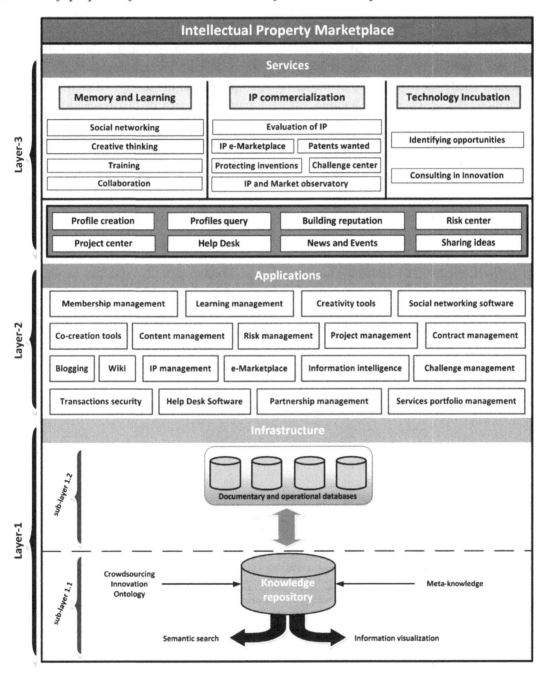

- **Layer 1 – Infrastructure:** Integrated in two sub-layers: on the sub-layer 1.1 is represented the knowledge repository where all information is stored. This repository is kept autonomous in relation to the documentary and operational databases (sub-layer 1.2). It is necessary to define a crowd-sourcing innovation ontology and also indexing techniques to enable analysis to the stored data in the Knowledge Repository as well as other pertinent queries; the sub-layer 1.2 presents a set of operational databases holding the actual information. These databases holding all generated information by the several operations performed in each service available in the Marketplace. Beyond this, they intend to take the interlocutor function among the applications that support the several services and the Knowledge Repository.

- **Layer 2 – Applications:** Presents the set of applications that are responsible for giving support to the several services available in the Marketplace. In this scope searches were conducted to identify applications that could be adopted here. This study has found that it may be needed to develop new applications related with Information Intelligence and e-Marketplace, because this study did not find any available in the market. Tables 3, 4, 5, and 6 presents the support applications for each service.

- **Layer 3 – Services:** Depicts the services available in the Marketplace, focused on three value creation processes: Memory and Learning, IP Commercialization, and Technology Incubation. The layer-3 also presents a set of shared services.

Description about the three value creation processes are given below, which are being incorporated in the layer-3 of architecture (as the main focus area of this research), as well as a corresponding table that synthesizes the features of services.

- **Memory and Learning:** Includes a set of services that aims to encourage the members' creativity with the intention of creating new inventions/concepts. Table 3 aims at providing a perspective about the features of the services available in this process.

  IP Commercialization: Includes a set of services focused in the transferring of IP assets, promoting the interaction among IP owners and potential buyers. Table 4 intends to give a perspective about the features of the services defined for this process.

Table 3. Memory and learning services

Services	Description	Support application(s)
Social networking	It aims at providing a sense of belonging to a community in which the members have the possibility for sharing contents.	Social networking software
Creative thinking	It intends providing a set of tools to integrate the creativity.	Creativity tools
Training	It aims providing training about several topics in the open innovation area.	Learning management
Collaboration	It intends giving support for helping evaluate available technologies, for solving problems of technologic innovation, and for discussing technology and market trends.	Co-creation tools and Information intelligence

Table 4. IP commercialization services

Services	Description	Support application(s)
Evaluation of IP	It intends to provide support to evaluate IP assets.	IP management and risk management
IP e-Marketplace	It aims at providing the services of buying and selling IP (e.g. patents, technology, software, code for software, literature review, thesis, market studies), and licensing patents. This research proposes that buying IP and licensing patents should be supported by a mechanism allowing on-line transactions.	IP management, e-Marketplace, and Transactions security
Patents wanted	It intends to provide companies with the possibility of making available a description of their innovation needs, expecting the submission of patents as solutions to those needs.	IP management
Protecting inventions	It intends to provide support for protecting inventions through patents.	IP management
Challenge center	It aims at providing an opportunity to make challenges available, distributed by several categories. The members can submit their solutions to these challenges.	Challenge management
IP and Market observatory	It intends to provide access to several worldwide IP databases. This service also should provide a surveillance component focused in the technologic and market trends.	Content management and Informational intelligence

Table 5. Technology incubation services

Services	Description	Support application(s)
Identifying opportunities	It aims at identifying investment/financing opportunities. It also intends to help companies in developing the acquired technology into an innovation with high commercial potential.	Partnership management and Informational intelligence
Consulting in innovation	It intends to help companies to develop mature innovation processes.	Services portfolio management

• **Technology Incubation:** The services supporting this process aim at enabling the development of the acquired IP in commercially successful innovations. Table 5 describes the features of defined services.

Beyond of three value creation processes described above, the layer-3 of architecture includes a set of services that are shared by these three processes. Table 6 synthesizes the features of the shared services.

This section presents and discusses a draft proposal of a standard architecture for an IP marketplace that provides useful services for helping companies to adopt an open innovation strategy. This was done by describing the layers and com-

ponents of architecture. In the next section future developments are explored.

FUTURE ISSUES

Given the results of the work developed so far, this study suggests four scenarios for future investigation:

• Ideating a mechanism for online intellectual property transactions based in an electronic contract.
• Improving the proposal of architecture presented in the subsection by integrating the architecture principles of SOA (Service-

Table 6. Shared services

Services	Description	Support application(s)
Profile creation	It enables individual and companies to describe themselves and to create a unique identification within the community.	Membership management
Profiles query	It aims at providing access to the members' profile.	Membership management
Building reputation	This service aims at creating a reputation index about each community member.	Membership management
Risk center	It intends to help in risk management associated with innovation strategy adoption, project execution, innovation process management, protecting inventions, and IP commercialization.	Risk management
Project center	It aims at helping to develop new projects as well as giving support on project contracts management.	Project management and Contract management
Help Desk	It intends to provide support to the several services available in the Marketplace, namely to clarify issues, and solve specific problems.	Help Desk software
New and Events	It aims at providing resources about topics related with the three value creation processes.	Content management
Sharing ideas	It intends to provide opportunities to share ideas, for example opinion articles. The aim is to promote the discussion among members.	Blogging and Wiki

Oriented Architecture) and SaaS (Software as a Service).

- Detailing specification of all services as well as the applications that support those services.
- Exploring issues that Small and Medium Enterprises can face to access some services available in the proposal of architecture presented above and identify ways that help them to attenuate these difficulties.

CONCLUSION

This paper addresses concepts and practices related to Crowdsourcing Innovation (CI) and Intellectual Property (IP) marketplaces. It presents some examples to complement the theoretical explanation. Based on this information, it was possible to design a draft proposal of architecture for an IP marketplace.

In sum, this paper aimed at presenting a proposal of architecture for an IP marketplace that includes a set of services that can be useful for

organizations interested in implementing an open innovation strategy.

REFERENCES

Adams, C., & Ramos, I. (2009). Crowdsourcing: A social networking approach to outsourcing. *Cutter IT Journal, 22*(10).

Antikainen, M. J., & Vaataja, H. K. (2010). Rewarding in open innovation communities – how to motivate members. *International Journal of Entrepreneurship and Innovation Management, 11*(4), 440–456. doi:10.1504/IJEIM.2010.032267

Bakos, J. Y. (1991). A strategic analysis of electronic marketplaces. *Management Information Systems Quarterly, 15*(3), 295–310. doi:10.2307/249641

Blackman, M. (2007). Patents: Realising and securing value. *World Patent Information, 29*(2), 186–187. doi:10.1016/j.wpi.2006.11.002

Brabham, D. C. (2008). Crowdsourcing as a model for problem solving: An introduction and cases. *International Journal of Research into New Media Technologies*, *14*(1), 75–90. doi:10.1177/1354856507084420

Chesbrough, H. (2006). *Emerging secondary markets for intellectual property: US and Japan comparisons*. Retrieved from http://www.ryutu. inpit.go.jp/en/pdf/ESMIP.pdf

Diener, K., & Piller, F. (2010). *The market for open innovation: Increasing the efficiency and effectiveness of the innovation process*. Aachen, The Netherlands: RWTH-TIM Group.

Hempel, J. (2006). *Crowdsourcing: Milk the masses for inspiration*. Retrieved from http://www.businessweek.com/magazine/content/06_39/b4002422.htm

Hippel, E. V., & Krogh, G. V. (2003). Open source software and the private-collective model: Issues for organization science. *Organization Science*, *14*(2), 209–223. doi:10.1287/orsc.14.2.209.14992

Howe, J. (2006). The rise of crowdsourcing. *Wired Magazine*, *14*(6), 1–4.

Kamiyama, S., Sheehan, J., & Martinez, C. (2006). *Valuation and exploitation of intellectual property*. Paris, France: OECD Publishing.

Lee, Y. G., & Lee, J. H. (2010). Different characteristics between auctioned and non-auctioned patents. *Scientometrics*, *82*(1), 135–148. doi:10.1007/s11192-009-0029-7

Leimeister, J. M., Huber, M., Bretschneider, U., & Krcmar, H. (2009). Leveraging crowdsourcing: Activation-supporting components for IT-based idea competitions. *Journal of Management Information Systems*, *26*(1), 197–224. doi:10.2753/MIS0742-1222260108

Maskus, K. E. (2008). The globalization of intellectual property rights and innovation in services. *Journal of Industry, Competition and Trade*, *8*(3), 247–267. doi:10.1007/s10842-008-0040-3

Ramos, I., & Carvalho, J. A. (2008). Organizational mind: A new perspective on knowledge management. In Koohang, A., & Harman, K. (Eds.), *Knowledge management: Theoretical foundations*. Hershey, PA: IGI Global.

Reichwald, R., & Piller, F. (2006). *Interaktive wertschöpfung: Open innovation, individualiserung und neue formen der arbeitsteilung*. Berlin, Germany: Gabler Verlag.

Rosenstiel, L. V. (2007). *Grundlagen der organisations-psychologie: Basiswissen und Anwendungshinweise*. Stuttgart, Germany: Schäffer-Poeschel.

Smith, G. V., & Parr, R. L. (2000). *Valuation of intellectual property and intangible assets* (3rd ed.). New York, NY: John Wiley & Sons.

Trompette, P., Chanal, V., & Pelissier, C. (2008, July 10-12). Crowdsourcing as a way to access external knowledge for innovation: Control, incentive and coordination in hybrid forms of innovation. In *Proceedings of the 24th EGOS Colloquium*, Amsterdam, Netherlands.

Vukovic, M. (2009). Crowdsourcing for enterprises. In *Proceedings of the World Congress on Services-I* (pp. 686-692).

Webber, D., & Cave, D. C. (2007). Intellectual property – challenges for the future. In *Proceedings of the IEEE Region 10 TENCON Conference* (pp. 1-5).

This work was previously published in the International Journal of Information Communication Technologies and Human Development, Volume 3, Issue 3, edited by Susheel Chhabra and Hakikur Rahman, pp. 58-68, copyright 2011 by IGI Publishing (an imprint of IGI Global).

Chapter 13
An Application of the UTAUT Model for Understanding Acceptance and Use of ICT by Nigerian University Academicians

N. D. Oye
Universiti Teknologi Malaysia, Malaysia

N. A. Iahad
Universiti Teknologi Malaysia, Malaysia

Nor Zairah Ab Rahim
Universiti Teknologi Malaysia, Malaysia

ABSTRACT

This study examines the acceptance and use of ICT by Nigerian university academicians. The model validated is the Unified Theory of Acceptance and Use of Technology (UTAUT). Using a pilot study, one hundred questionnaires were administered and collected at the University of Jos Plateau State, Nigeria. The construct was significantly correlated with behavioral intention (BI). This implies that the university ICT system makes tasks easier to accomplish, thereby making academicians more productive. The survey shows that 86.5% agree. Effort expectancy (EE) was significantly correlated with BI. The result shows that 84.3% agreed that they could use ICT. Among the four UTAUT constructs, performance expectancy exerted the strongest effect. The UTAUT model shows age effects for older workers and a stronger willingness for the younger workers to adopt new IT products. According to this study age and gender do not have significant effect on acceptance and use of ICT. Performance expectancy (PE) and Effort expectancy (EE) are found to be the most significant predictors of academic staffs' acceptance of ICT and use.

DOI: 10.4018/978-1-4666-1957-9.ch013

INTRODUCTION

Information and communications Technology (ICT) has the potential to improve all aspects of our social, economic and cultural life. The introduction of ICT into universities clearly changes the way education is conducted. ICT also paves way for a new pedagogical approach, where students are expected to play more active than before (Alabi, 2004). ICT focuses on the crucial issues of how people communicate and learn in electronic environment. ICT in learning depends on effective communication of human knowledge, which may either occur in synchronous or asynchronous and blended learning situation as the case may. The role of Information and Communications Technology (ICT) in human development has received growing attention among development practitioners, policy makers, government and civil society in recent years due to the growing proliferation of the Internet, convergence in IT and telecommunications technologies and increasing globalization.

According to Bandele (2006), ICT is a revolution that involves the use of computers, internet and other telecommunication technology in every aspect of human endeavour. Ozoji in Jimoh (2007) defined ICT as the handling and processing of information (texts, images, graphs, instruction etc) for use, by means of electronic and communication devices such as computers, cameras, telephone. Ofodu (2007) also refers to ICT as electronic or computerized devices, assisted by human and interactive materials that can be used for a wide range of teaching and learning as well as for personal use. From these definitions, ICT could therefore be defined as processing and sharing of information using all kinds of electronic device, an umbrella that includes all technologies for the manipulation and communication of information. This new development is a strong indication that the era of teachers without ICT skills are gone. Any classroom teacher with adequate and professional skills in ICT utilization will definitely have his students perform better in classroom

learning. Teaching and learning has gone beyond the teacher standing in front of a group of pupils and disseminating information to them without the students' adequate participation (Ajayi, 2008).

The ICT facilities used in the teaching learning process in schools according to Bandele (2006), Bolaji (2003), Bryers (2004), and Ofodu (2007) include; radio, television, computers, overhead projectors, optical fibers, fax machines, CD-Rom, Internet, electronic notice board, slides, digital multimedia, video/VCD machine and so on. In fact some of the facilities are not sufficiently provided for teaching – learning process in the institutions of learning. Undoubtedly, this might account for why teachers are not making use of them in their teaching.

In Nigeria the available infrastructure for ICT in most of these universities are grossly inadequate. It was observed that most university students still visit internet off campus because of too much demand on the internet on-campus. The bandwidths shared on most of these systems at cyber Cafés are still low, hence much time is still wasted on internet browsing. Olaniyi (2006) was of the view that most of the institutions of higher learning in Nigeria have started building their ICT centres but they focus mainly on internet facilities without considering other components that make up ICT Centre. However ICT infrastructure has not been the priority of government. Government policy has been the deregulation of telecommunication industry. ICT infrastructures are therefore mostly provided by private entrepreneur for business purpose (Akinsola, Marlien, & Jacobs, 2005).

Adoption of ICT in Higher Education Institutions

In developing countries Nigeria precisely, preliminary investigations show that only a few organizations in the economy have adopted the IT, but there has not been formal study to determine the level of diffusion and the factors affecting its efficiency on organizations. Achimugu, Oluwagbemi, Oluwaranti, and Afolabi (2009) opined that the adoption of Information Technology (IT) in Developing Countries is one of the most pressing current developmental issues. Since IT became commercial in the early 1990s, it has diffused rapidly in developed countries but generally slowly in developing ones. Nigerian universities are focusing on curricula that might contribute more directly to economic growth and network. In the case of Nigeria today, individuals may not use ICT service for different reasons ranging from lack of interest, illiteracy, lack of awareness, exorbitant rate of services, poor quality of service and low per capita income.

The United Nations have identified four major sets of indicators for complete information technology diffusion in a country (Chiemeke & Longe, 2007): (a) ICT infrastructure and access. (b) Access to and use of ICT by households and individuals. (c) Use of ICT by businesses and (d) ICT sector and trade in ICT goods.

Oyelaran-Oyeyinka and Adeya (2004) investigated the level and depth of use of computers by university staff. From our survey, in Nigeria, 58.5% use computers for word processing, 32.2% use it for spreadsheet and data processing and 20.5% use it for programming. 66.9% use it for e-mail/Internet while 9.4% use the computer for other purposes apart from the aforementioned. Respondents suggest that resources be directed at training lecturers/ and researchers to incorporate the use of computer applications in academic functions. There is a higher degree of e-mail and Internet use within the private universities compared to the public universities. The main reason could be a result of better facilities at some of the private universities coupled with lower densities of users per access point. This implies faster connections, shorter waiting times, less congestion and lower cost as the private institutions often provide free access for the staff.

Somekh (2008) opined that pedagogical adoption of ICT is complex and requires an integration of vision, system-wide experimentation and new roles and relationships for teachers and students. ICTs, when used in ways that make use of their affordances, are a powerful driver for change. Let us not forget that classrooms have never been ideal learning environments and teachers in public education systems have always been somewhat burdened by working with students who are there under compulsion. ICTs can help to make schools less-stressful workplaces for both teachers and students.

Technology Acceptance Model

The Technology Acceptance Model or TAM (Davis, Bagozzi, & Warshaw, 1989) is one of the most profound frameworks frequently used in studies to predict and explain the use of computer based applications and solutions. The model asserts that the adoption of a technology is determined by the user's intention to use, which in turn is influenced by his or her attitudes towards the technology. It is very likely that the variability in these attitudinal and behavioral constructs depends on the user's perceptions — perceived usefulness (PU) and perceived ease of use (PEOU). While PU indicates the extent to which the use of the technology is promising to advance one's work, PEOU represents the degree to which the technology seems to be free of effort (Davis et al., 1989). This model posits that attitudes and behavioral intention mediate the effects of PU and PEOU, the two constructs of extrinsic motivation. With the ongoing development of ICT and the diversification of the fields it affects, various theoretical studies have been carried out in order to ensure better understanding concerning its diffusion, adoption, acceptance, and usage (Davis et al., 1989; Rogers, 2003; Taylor & Todd, 1995; Venkatesh & Davis, 2000; Venkatesh,, Morris, Davis, & Davis, 2003; Yi 2006). See Figure 1, Figure 2, and Figure 3.

TAM2 is the extension of TAM which includes social influence process such as subjective norms and cognitive instrumental process. See Figure 4.

Figure 1. TRA theory proposed by Fishbein and Ajzen (1975) that an individuals' attitudes towards behavior and the surrounding subjective norms influence their behavioral intention

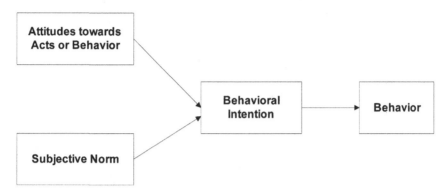

Figure 2. Theory of planned behavior (Ajzen, 1991). According to Ajzen, intention is an immediate predictor of behavior

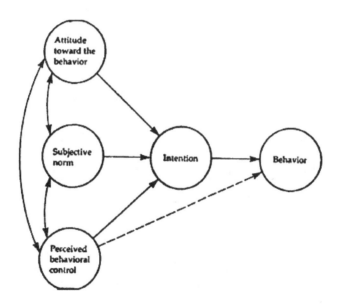

Figure 3. The TAM to explain the computer usage and acceptance of IT (Davis et al., 1989; Davis, 1985), developed TAM to explain computer usage and acceptance of IT

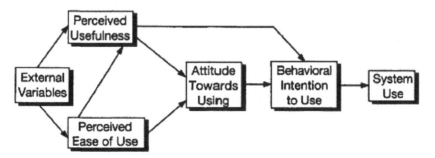

Figure 4. TAM2 (Venkatesh & Davis, 2000) added to original TAM Model, subjective norm, etc

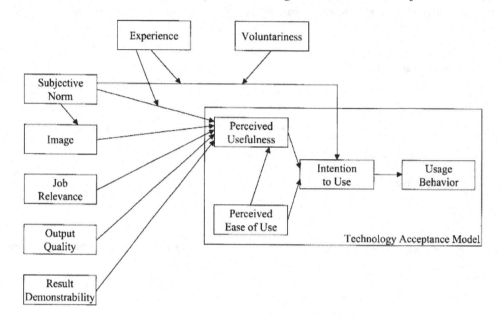

Limitations of TAM

- TAM is only capable of predicting technology adoption success of 30%.
- TAM2 (TAM Extension) can predict 40%.
- The call for a modified model gave birth to UTAUT model by Venkatesh et al. (2003).

UTAUT Model

UTAUT has condensed the 32 variables found in the existing eight models into four main effect and four moderating factors. The combinations of the constructs and moderating factors have increased the predictive efficiency to 70%, a major improvement over previous TAM model rates. See Figure 5 and Figure 6.

- **UTAUT:** Unified Theory of Acceptance and Use of Technology
- **TRA:** Theory of Reason Action
- **TPB:** Theory of Planned Behavior
- **TAM:** Technology Acceptance Model
- **MM:** Motivational Model

- **C-TPB-TAM:** Combine Theory of Planned Behavior and Technology Acceptance Model
- **MPCU:** Model of PC utilization
- **IDT:** Innovation Diffusion Theory
- **SCT:** Social Cognitive Theory
- **PE:** The extent an individual believes the system will help them do their jobs better (PU).
- **EE:** Relates to how ease an individual believes the system is to use (PEOU).
- **SI:** Relates to whether or not important others' influence an individuals' intention to use the system.
- **FC:** Whether individuals have the personal knowledge and institutional resources available to use the system.

In the UTAUT model, PE and EE were used to incorporate the constructs of perceived usefulness and ease of use in the original TAM. PEOU can be expected to be more noticeable only in the early stages of using a new technology. UTAUT also addresses how individual differences determine

Figure 5. UTAUT model structure

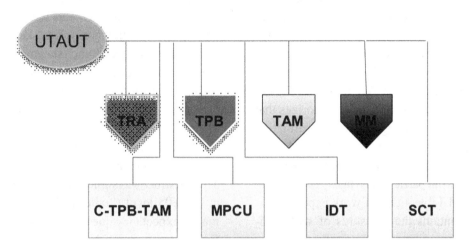

the acceptance and use of technology. Precisely speaking, the connection between PU, PEOU, and intention to use can be moderated by age, gender, and experience For instance, the strength between PU and intention to use varies with age and gender such that it is more significant for male and young workers. Again the effect of PEOU on intention is also moderated by gender and age such that it is more significant for female and older workers, and the effect decrease with experiences. The UTAUT

model accounted for 70% of the variance in usage intention, better than any of TAM studies alone.

METHODOLOGY

This study was conducted at the university of Jos Plateau state, Nigeria, as a pilot study. One hundred questionnaires were administered and collected, containing 23 UTAUT survey questions and 9 demographic statements totaling 32

Figure 6. UTAUT model

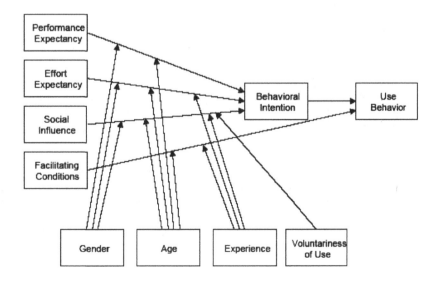

questions. In addition, 75% were male and 43% were female. The respondents are the university academicians. The survey tool presented modified questions based on UTAUT model. The expectations are that the survey will provide evidence of the acceptance and use of ICT by the university academicians. The UTAUT model theorizes that four constructs have a significant determination on user acceptance of IT innovations (Venkatesh et al., 2003) as seen in Table 1. Table 2 provides a summary of the participants' ages, Table 3 that of gender and Table 4 that of work experience.

Table 5 contains the measures of scale reliabilities for the constructs. Generally reliability numbers greater than 0.6 are considered acceptable in technology acceptance literature (Zhang, Li, & Sun, 2006). As summarized in the Table 6, a reliability analysis was conducted, for the 23 items using Cronbach's Alpha. The UTAUT constructs appears to have a good degree of reliability of above .70.

RESULTS

Descriptive Analysis

A descriptive statistical analysis is described in this section in order to provide a broad understanding of the academician's view of ICT acceptance and use for teaching and learning. Table 7 summarizes the frequencies and the corresponding percentages. Participants were asked to rate their level of agreement with each statement or question with appropriate responses on a five item Likert scale. Where (1) is "Strongly Disagree", (2) is "Disagree" (3) is "Neither Agree nor Disagree", (4) is 'Agree", and (5) is "Strongly Agree."

Performance expectancy had a mean response of 4.32 and standard deviation of .665 for (PE1). The construct was significantly correlated with BI at the 0.05 level (2tailed). Responses to performance expectancy questions (Q1-Q4) are related to the extent an individual believes ICT helps them to do their job better. The overall results for these series of questions associated to the perceived usefulness of ICT to the University academic staff were positive. This implies that the university ICT system make task more easily accomplished, thereby making them more productive. The result from the survey shows that 86.5% agree. When one looked at questions Q1,Q2,and Q3 the notable thing with these question group is that nobody disagree with the usefulness of ICT, thus the disagree rate is 0%. Again responses to Q4 have 78% agreeing rate believing that using ICT in the job would increase their chance of getting a raise (promotion). The 78% agreement is suggesting that there is perceived monetary reward incentive

Table 1. Definitions and root constructs for the four constructs (Venkatesh et al., 2003)

Construct	Definition	Root Constructs
Performance expectancy	The degree to which an individual believes that using the system will help him or her to attain gains in performance. (p. 447)	'Perceived Usefulness 'from TAM and C-TAM-TPB, 'extrinsic motivation' from MM, 'Job-fit' from MPCU, 'relative advantage' from IDT, and 'Outcome expectations' from SCT.
Effort expectancy	The degree of ease associated with the use of the system (p. 450)	'Perceived ease of use' from TAM, 'Complexity' from MPCU, and 'ease of use' from IDT
Social influence	The degree to which an individual perceived that important others believe he or she should use the new system (p. 451)	'Subjective norm' in TRA, TAM2, TPB and C-TAM-TPB, 'social factors' in MPCU, and 'Image' in IDT.
Facilitating conditions	The degree to which an individual believes that an organizational and technical infrastructure exists to support use of the system.	'Perceived behavioral control' from TPB, C-TAM-TPB, 'facilitating conditions' from MPCU, and 'Compatibility' from IDT.

Table 2. Participant age (n= 100)

AGE					
		Frequency	Percent	Valid Percent	Cumulative Percent
Valid	UNDER 30YEARS	12	12.0	12.0	12.0
	30-44 YEARS	75	75.0	75.0	87.0
	45 YEARS AND ABOVE	13	13.0	13.0	100.0
	Total	100	100.0	100.0	

Table 3. Participant gender (n =100)

GENDER					
		Frequency	Percent	Valid Percent	Cumulative Percent
Valid	MALE	57	57.0	57.0	57.0
	FEMALE	43	43.0	43.0	100.0
	Total	100	100.0	100.0	

Table 4. Participant work experience (n = 100)

WORK EXPERIENCE					
		Frequency	Percent	Valid Percent	Cumulative Percent
Valid	1-5YEARS	8	8.0	8.0	8.0
	6-10YEARS	72	72.0	72.0	80.0
	MORE THAN ABOVE	20	20.0	20.0	100.0
	Total	100	100.0	100.0	

Table 5. Reliability

Case Processing Summary			
		N	%
Cases	Valid	100	100.0
	Excluded[a]	0	.0
	Total	100	100.0

a. Listwise deletion based on all variables in the procedure.

Table 6. Reliability statistics

Cronbach's Alpha	N of Items
.786	23

linked with ICT usage and a future prospect of getting a better job with higher pay.

Effort expectancy (See Table 8) construct had a mean response of 3.87 and standard deviation of .562. EE was significantly correlated with BI at the 0.01 level (2-tailed). Responses to effort expectancy questions (Q5-Q8) are related to how easy an individual believes the ICT system is to use. Overall results for this series of questions were perceived as being positive with individual ability to easily use and understand the current ICT, which are always user friendly. The result shows that, 84.3% agreed that they could use ICT. EE has the highest correlation with BI, all the constructs were significantly correlated with BI but the strongest correlation was Q6(EE2),

Table 7. Summary of survey responses (n= 100)

	Strongly Disagree	Disagree	Neither Agree or Disagree	Agree	Strongly Agree
Performance Expectancy	1	2	3	4	5
Q1(PE1) I find the ICT systems offered at my institution useful in my job	0.0% (0)	0.0% (0)	10% (10)	49% (49)	42% (42)
Q2(PE2) Using the ICT systems available enable me to accomplish task more easily	0.0% (0)	0.0% (0)	3% (3)	73% (73)	24% (24)
Q3(PE3) Using the ICT systems available increases my productivity	0.0% (0)	0.0% (0)	21% (21)	50% (50)	30% (30)
Q4(PE4) If I use the current ICT systems, it will increase my chance of getting a rise	0.0% (0)	4% (3)	18% (18)	48% (48)	30% (30)

which states that: 'It is simple for me to the use existing ICT technology.'

Social influence (See Table 9) had a mean of 3.03 and a standard deviation of .300. This construct was significantly correlated with BI with a correlation coefficient of .096. Responses to social influence questions (Q9-Q12) are related to whether or not important others' influence an individual's intention to use the ICT system. Overall results for this series of questions were perceived as being slightly positive with regard to personal and institutional support, and other's influence on their ICT system use. Correspondingly, 57% agreed with these sentiments and 3% disagreeing with 40% neither agreeing nor disagreeing. In general, senior officials would support the use of technology for teaching and learning. Q11 (SI3) had an overwhelming positive response with 86% of the respondents "agree" or "strongly agree".

Facilitating condition (Table 10) had a mean of 3.75 and standard deviation of .592. FC was significantly correlated with BI at the 0.05 level (2-tailed). Responses to facilitating condition questions (Q13-Q20) asks if individual's have the personal knowledge and institutional resources available to use the ICT: Overall results for this series of questions were perceived as being slightly positive with respondents stating that they possess the knowledge to use the ICT systems and that their institution's have a support structure

available to users, should they need assistance. There was one notable exception in this group regarding the negative wording of Q15 that will necessitate reverse scoring for this item to get a true indication of the responses. As a result 58.9% agree with these sentiments and 13.5% disagrees while 27.5% neither agreeing nor disagreeing. Q17(FC5) had a negative result, probably the question need to be reframe to be clearly understood.

Behavioral intention (Table 11) had a mean of 3.31 and standard deviation of .465. Responses for behavioral intention questions (Q21-Q23), is grounded in the theoretical relationship between several technology acceptance and use models incorporating intention to use a given technology with the actual usage of that technology. Thus, if a person's intention is to use ICT, it is theorized that they will likely do so as intention is a good predictor of usage. The overall results for this series of questions were perceived as being negatively responded to, as 38.7% agreed that they intend to use ICT within the next 3months and only 1% stated that they did not intend to use ICT with 60.3% neither agreeing nor disagreeing that they intended to use ICT. The notable fact in this group is that the disagreeing rate is extremely very low that is 1% and that of "neither agree nor disagree is very high which is 60.3%.

When we consider the responses on Behavioral Intention for all the three items, less than

Table 8. Effort expectancy (n=100)

Effort Expectancy	1	2	3	4	5
Q5(EE1) My interaction with the ICT systems available is clear and understandable	0.0% (0)	0.0% (0)	20% (20)	70% (70)	10% (10)
Q6(EE2) It is simple for me to use the existing ICT technology	0.0% (0)	0.0% (0)	4% (4)	86% (86)	10% (10)
Q7(EE3) Whatever ICT I come across, it will be simple to operate	0.0% (0)	0.0% (0)	28% (28)	66% (66)	6% (6)
Q8(EE4) The knowledge of using ICT is simple for me.	0.0% (0)	0.0% (0)	11% (11)	84% (84)	5% (5)

Table 9. Social influence (n= 100)

Social Influence	1	2	3	4	5
Q9(SI1) People who influence my action suppose that I apply ICT technology.	0.0% (0)	3% (3)	83% (83)	6% (6)	8% (8)
Q10(SI2) People who are important to me think I should use the ICT systems	0.0% (0)	3% (3)	55% (55)	41% (41)	1% (1)
Q11(SI3) The senior management of this institution has been helpful in the use of the ICT system	0.0% (0)	4% (4)	10% (10)	65% (65)	21% (21)
Q12(SI4) In general, the organization has supported the use of ICT systems	0.0% (0)	2% (2)	12% (12)	64% (64)	22% (22)

Table 10. Facilitating conditions

Facilitating Condition	1	2	3	4	5
Q13 (FC1) I have the resources necessary to use the current ICT	0.0% (0)	8% (8)	12% (12)	80% (80)	0.0% (0)
Q14(FC2) I have adequate ability to operate ICT technology.	0.0% (0)	0.0% (0)	8% (8)	90% (90)	2% (2)
Q15(FC3) The technology did not match the ICT I operate	0.0% (0)	80% (80)	16% (16)	4% (4)	0.0% (0)
Q16(FC4) Some people are present to help me with ICT system problems.	8% (8)	5% (5)	35% (35)	52% (52)	0.0% (0)
Q17 (FC5) I could finish the work of ICT system.. when nobody is available to assist.	0.0% (0)	8% (8)	92% (92)	0.0% (0)	0.0% (0)
Q18(FC6) I could complete the job or task using the ICT system…if I could call someone for help if I got stuck	0.0% (0)	0.0% (0)	14% (14)	58% (58)	28% (28)
Q19 (FC7) I can finish the work with ICT system if I have enough time.	0.0% (0)	0.0% (0)	9% (9)	56% (56)	35% (35)
Q20 (FC8) I could complete the job or task using the ICT system..if I had just built-in help facility for assistance	0.0% (0)	0.0% (0)	34% (34)	60% (60)	6% (6)

Table 11. Behavioral intention

Behavioral Intention	1	2	3	4	5
Q21 (BI1) I guess I can operate ICT in three months.	0.0% (0)	0.0% (0)	67% (67)	33% (33)	0.0% (0)
Q22(BI2) I predict I will use the ICT system in the next three months	0.0% (0)	3% (3)	56% (56)	41% (41)	0.0% (0)
Q23(BI3) I plan to use the ICT system in the next three months	0.0% (0)	0.0% (0)	58% (58)	42% (42)	0.0% (0)

half of the participants responded "agree" or "strongly agree" to the statement, thus we have 33%, 41% and 42% respectively for Q21, Q22, and Q23. These results indicate that the majority of the participants are not quite confident of their intention to use ICT. No wonder we have 60.3% of participants responding to "neither agreeing nor disagreeing" that they intended to use ICT. See Table 12 and Table 13.

CONCLUSION

This study describes the acceptance and use of ICT by Nigerian university academicians. The results shows that the intention to accept and use ICT by the academic staff is a function of various concepts including the understanding that educational IT is useful, it is not difficult to use, important others believes that he/she should use ICT for teaching

Table 12. Correlations

		Facilitating Condition	Performance Expectancy	Effort Expectancy	Social Influence	Behavioral Intention
Facilitating Condition	Pearson Correlation	1	-.057	.045	-.053	.209*
	Sig. (2-tailed)		.570	.657	.604	.037
	N	100	100	100	100	100
Performance Expectancy	Pearson Correlation	-.057	1	.576**	.659**	.223*
	Sig. (2-tailed)	.570		.000	.000	.026
	N	100	100	100	100	100
Effort Expectancy	Pearson Correlation	.045	.576**	1	.674**	-.382**
	Sig. (2-tailed)	.657	.000		.000	.000
	N	100	100	100	100	100
Social Influence	Pearson Correlation	-.053	.659**	.674**	1	.096
	Sig. (2-tailed)	.604	.000	.000		.340
	N	100	100	100	100	100
Behavioral Intention	Pearson Correlation	.209*	.223*	-.382**	.096	1
	Sig. (2-tailed)	.037	.026	.000	.340	
	N	100	100	100	100	100

*. Correlation is significant at the 0.05 level (2-tailed).

**. Correlation is significant at the 0.01 level (2-tailed).

Table 13. Descriptive statistics

	N	Minimum	Maximum	Mean	Std. Deviation
PE1	100	3	5	4.32	.665
PE2	100	3	5	4.22	.484
PE3	100	3	5	4.08	.720
PE4	100	2	5	4.05	.783
EE1	100	3	5	3.87	.562
EE2	100	4	5	4.10	.302
EE3	100	3	4	3.60	.492
EE4	100	3	4	3.96	.197
SI1	100	2	4	3.03	.300
SI2	100	2	5	3.41	.570
SI3	100	2	5	4.09	.605
SI4	100	3	5	4.09	.570
FC1	100	2	4	3.75	.592
FC2	100	3	4	3.91	.288
FC3	100	2	4	2.29	.574
FC4	100	1	4	3.37	.884
FC5	100	2	4	2.91	.321
FC6	100	3	5	4.14	.652
FC7	100	3	5	4.28	.604
FC8	100	3	4	3.66	.476
BI1	100	3	4	3.31	.465
BI2	100	2	4	3.36	.542
BI3	100	3	4	3.39	.490
Valid N (listwise)	100				

and learning. Again the perception of free will to use ICT should also determine the intention to use.

The findings have important implications for teaching and learning. PE and EE are found to be the most significant predictors of academic staff acceptance of ICT and use. Therefore the university academicians need to be aware of the possibility of using ICT for teaching and learning without too much difficulty. They need to learn the basics of the technologies that will be most useful in their teaching and learning.

This study confirms the validity of the UTAUT model in the field context of a developing country's

educational system. Knowledge gained from the study is beneficial to both the university academic staff and the Nigerian ICT policy makers. Due to the limited sample size of the study, further research is needed, for testing the fitness of the UTAUT model based on these questions: ' Does the UTAUT model fit well with large organization?" Does the scales and measuring constructs in the UTAUT model need to be revised?'

RECOMMENDATIONS

The use of internet as a communication channel in Nigeria has led to increased productivity in sectors such as the educational, banking, communication and security, while Nigeria is gradually joining the league of globalizes nations. Modupe and Binuomote (2007) examined the awareness and adoption of Information Communication Technology (ICT) among secretarial staffs of Ladoke Akintola University of Technology, Ogbomoso. It was discovered that the level of adoption of Information Communication Technology (ICT) among the staffs in still low, information will have to be processed in a daily bases. However, recognizing the key roles that secretarial staffs play in University administration, it is recommended based on the findings of the study that more computer facilities are provided for these staffs, the coupled with a good access to internet facilities.

Recommendations made were that, all employed teachers in Federal, State and Private universities in Nigeria, should undertake mandatory training and retraining on ICT programmes. This is to provide them with practical and functional knowledge of computer, internet and associated areas of ICT for improved effectiveness and efficiency. The government should develop ICT policies and practices that would support lecturers in their academic work and students in their learning. ICT tools should be made more accessible to both academic staff and students.

ACKNOWLEDGMENT

The authors would like to thank Prof. V. Venkatesh for allowing the use of UTAUT for this research. In addition, the authors gratefully acknowledge UTM, Research University, Malaysia for their support and encouragement.

REFERENCES

Achimugu, P., Oluwagbemi, O., Oluwaranti, A., & Afolabi, B. (2009). Adoption of information and communication technologies in developing countries: An impact analysis. *Journal of Information Technology Impact, 9*, 37–46.

Ajayi, T. O., Salawu, I. O., & Adeoye, F. A. (2008). E-learning and distance education in Nigeria. *Turkish Online Journal of Educational Technology, 7*(4).

Ajzen, I. (1991). The theory of planned behavior. *Organizational Behavior and Human Decision Processes, 50*, 179–211. doi:10.1016/0749-5978(91)90020-T

Akinsola, O. S., Marlien, E. H., & Jacobs, S. J. (2005). ICT provision to disadvantage urban communities: A study in South Africa and Nigeria. *International Journal of Education and Development Using Information and Communication Technology.*

Alabi, A. (2004). Evolving role of ICT in teaching, research and publishing. *Nigeria Tribunal*, 30-31.

Bandele, S. O. (Ed.). (2006). *Development of modern ICT and internet system.* Abuja, Nigeria: Panof Press.

Bolaji, O. A., & Babajide, V. F. T. (2003). Perception of lecturers and service teachers towards the use of communication media in teching pure and applied science related disciplines. In *Proceedings of the 44th Annual STAN Conference* (pp. 33-36).

Bryers, J. D., & Ratner, B. D. (2004). Bioinspired implant materials befuddle bacteria. *ASM News, 70*, 232–237.

Chiemeke, O. B., & Longe, S. C. (2007). Information communication technology in Nigeria: Prospecta, challenges and metrics. *Asian Journal of Information Technology, 45*, 12–19.

Davis, F. D. (1985). *A technology acceptance model for empirical testing new end users information systems: Theory and results.* Cambridge, MA: MIT Sloan School of Management.

Davis, F. D., Bagozzi, R. P., & Warshaw, P. R. (1989). User acceptance of computer technology: A comparison of two theoretical models. *Management Science, 35*, 982–1003. doi:10.1287/mnsc.35.8.982

Fishbein, M., & Ajzen, I. (1975). Belief, attitude, intention, and behavior. In Wharton, A. S. (Ed.), *An introduction to theory and research reading.* Reading, MA: Addison-Wesley.

Jimoh, A. T. (2007). Students' attitude towards ICT in Nigeria tertiary institutions. *Education Focus, 1*(1), 73–79.

Modupe, M., & Binuomote, M. O. (2007). Awareness and adoption of information and communication technology among secretarial staff of Ladoke Akintola University of Technology, Ogbomaso, Nigeria. *Social Science, 2*, 57–59.

Ofodu, G. O. (2007). Nigeria literacy educators and their technological needs in a digital age. *Education Focus, 1*(1), 22–30.

Olaniyi, S. S. (2006). E-learning technology: The Nigeria experience [Electronic Version]. *Shape the Change*, 8-13, Oyelaran-Oyeyinka, B., & Adeya, C. N. (2004). Dynamics of adoption and usage of ICT in African universities: A study of Kenya and Nigeria. *Technovation, 24*(10), 841–851.

Rogers, M. E. (2003). *Diffusion of innovations* (5th ed.). New York, NY: Free Press.

Somekh, B. (2008). Factors affecting teachers' pedagogical adoption of ICT. *International Handbook of Information Technology in Primary and Secondary Education, 11*(3), 449-460.

Taylor, S., & Todd, P. (1995). Assessing IT usage: The role of prior experience. *Management Information Systems Quarterly, 19*(4), 561–570. doi:10.2307/249633

Venkatesh, V., & Davis, F. D. (2000). A theoretical extension of technology acceptance model: Four longitudinal field studies. *Management Science, 46*(2), 186–204. doi:10.1287/mnsc.46.2.186.11926

Venkatesh, V., Morris, M. G., Davis, G. B., & Davis, F. D. (2003). User acceptance of information technology: Towards a unified view. *Management Information Systems Quarterly, 27*(3), 425–478.

Yi, M. Y., Jackson, J. D., Park, J. S., & Probst, J. C. (2006). Understanding informatiom technology acceptance by individual professionals: Towards an intergrative view. *Information & Management, 43*, 350–363. doi:10.1016/j.im.2005.08.006

Zhang, P., Li, N., & Sun, H. (2006). Affective quality and cognitive absorption: Extending technology acceptance research. In *Proceedings of the Hawaii International Conference on System Sciences* (Vol. 8).

APPENDIX

Pilot Questionnaire

Directions: When completing the questionnaire, please keep in mind that we are using ICT in the context of teaching and learning, by the university academicians. ICT here refers to the application of digital equipments to all aspects of teaching and learning, which encompasses (PC, TV, Radio, Cellular phones, Laptops, overhead projectors, slide projectors, power-point projector, electronic boards, internet, hardware, software, and any technology specific to your teaching area).

Please rate each of the following on 1-5 scale, where (1) is "Strongly Disagree," (2) is "Disagree", (3) is" Neither Agree or Disagree", (4) is "Agree", and (5) is "Strongly Agree".

Performance expectancy (PE), Effort expectancy (EE), Social influence (SI), Facilitating condition (FC) and Behavioral intention (BI).

Section A: The UTAUT Survey

[1]PE1. I find the ICT systems offered at my institution useful in my job.[ ]
[2]PE2. Using the ICT systems available enables me to accomplish tasks more quickly [ ]
[3]PE3. Using the ICT systems available increases my productivity.[ ]
[4]PE4. If I use the current ICT system, I will increase my chances of getting a raise. [ ]
[5]EE1. My interaction with the ICT systems available is clear and understandable.[ ]
[6]EE2. It would be easy for me to become skillful at using the current ICT system.[ ]
[7]EE3. I would find whatever ICT system available easy to use.[ ]
[8]EE4. Learning to operate an ICT system is easy for me.[ ]
[9]SI1. People who influence my behavior think I should use the ICT system.[ ]
[10]SI2. People who are important to me think I should use the ICT system. [ ]
[11]SI3. The senior management of this institution has been helpful in the use of the ICT system.[ ]
[12]SI4. In general, the organization has supported the use of the ICT system.[ ]
[13]FC1. I have the resources necessary to use the current ICT system.[ ]
[14]FC2. I have the knowledge necessary to use the ICT system.[ ]
[15]FC3. The system is not compatible with other ICT systems I use.[ ]
[16]FC4. A specific person (or group) is available for assistance with ICT system difficulties.[ ]
[17]FC5. I could complete the job or task using the ICT system ... .if there was no one around to tell me what to do as I go.[ ]
[18]FC6. I could complete the job or task using the ICT system ... .if I could call someone for help if I got stuck. [ ]
[19]FC7. I could complete the job or task using the ICT system ... .if I had a lot of time to complete the job for which the software was provided.[ ]
[20]FC8. I could complete the job or task using the ICT system ... .if I had just built-in help facility for assistance.[ ]
[21]BI1. I intend to use the ICT system in the next 3 months.[ ]
[22]BI2. I predict I would use the ICT system in the next 3 months.[ ]
[23]BI3. I plan to use the ICT system in the next 3 months.[ ]

Section B: Demographic Information

[24] Gender: 1=Male 2=Female.

[25] Age: 1= Under 30years, 2= 30-44 years, 3= 45years and above

[26] What is your job status: 1= Part-time, 2= Full-time.

[27] Work Experience: 1= 1-5years, 2= 6-10years, 3= more than 10years.

[28] What is your career rank? 1= Lecturer, 2= Senior Lecturer, 3= Ass. Professor, 5= professor

[29] What is your workload? 1= 0-1 course, 2= 2-3 courses, 3= 4-5 courses, 4= more than 5 courses.

[30] Is ICT system use mandatory or voluntary at your institution?
    1= Mandatory 2=Voluntary

[31] Technology (ICT) usage: 1= once or more a day, 2= once a week,
    3= twice a month, 4= once a month, 5= Never

[32] If you had tom pick one issue that is the greatest barrier to using ICT, what would it be?
    1= Time, 2= Technical support, 3= Cost, 4= Training, 5= Compensation,
    6= Does not fit my program, 7= Others, please specify

COVER LETTER

Dear Educational Partner,

My name is Oye,N.D, a Phd student at Universiti Teknologi Malaysia. My research is on "Acceptance and Use of ICT by Nigerians University Academicians" (Using the Unified Theory of Acceptance and Use of Technology [UTAUT]). This questionnaire serves as a pilot test to evaluate the effectiveness of the questionnaire. The data collected will only be used for research purpose s. Names and identification of individuals are not needed. The submission will be treated confidentially.

The questionnaire is divided into two sections A& B. Section A is the UTAUT survey and section B is the demographic information.

I am inviting you to participate in filling the online pilot questionnaire, this will take you about 10 to 15 minutes to complete. There are no long answers required and nearly all questions are point and click type responses.

I thank you in advance for your time and consideration.

Sincerely,

Oye Nathaniel David (Phd student...)

Department of Information Systems

Universiti Teknologi Malaysia

This work was previously published in the International Journal of Information Communication Technologies and Human Development, Volume 3, Issue 4, edited by Susheel Chhabra and Hakikur Rahman, pp. 1-16, copyright 2011 by IGI Publishing (an imprint of IGI Global).

Chapter 14
Leapfrogging the Digital Divide:
Myth or Reality for Emerging Regions?

Kavitha Ranganathan
Indian Institute of Management, Ahmedabad, India

ABSTRACT

The leapfrogging theory claims that instead of following the conventional digital trajectory set by the west, emerging regions can straightaway use cutting-edge technology to "leapfrog" the digital-divide. To explore the possibility of digital leapfrogging by an emerging region, this study looks at the three domains of hardware, software and connectivity. In each domain the default technology and its potential is evaluated as a digital inclusion tool while being juxtaposed with the latest "cutting-edge" alternative that could be used instead for "leapfrogging". Three specific scenarios are developed in telephony, banking and the World Wide Web, which illustrate how a combination of these different technologies help emerging regions 'leapfrog the digital divide.' Finally, the paper suggests certain leapfrogging trajectories that ICT4D projects should explore.

INTRODUCTION

The past decade has seen a radical change in information and communication technology (ICT) and its effects on our daily lives. Yet, significant parts of the world are yet to benefit from these technologies, hence, the so-called "digital divide" between the developed world and emerging regions. By the late 90's ICT was seen as the potential tool to help the developing world scramble out of its current state of impoverishment as was chiefly

featured in the UN's Millennium Development Goals. Terms like "bridging the digital divide" and ICT4D (information and communication technologies for development) became popular topics of discourse, leading to a whole gamut of initiatives both by governments in developing nations, world-wide organizations like the World Bank, the UN and other non-government enterprises. However, successful ICT4D projects that have made significant differences to the under-privileged in a sustainable and scalable way are

DOI: 10.4018/978-1-4666-1957-9.ch014

few and far between, with the limited success of many projects being attributed to either unsustainable business models or a lack of understanding of local needs or unsuitable technology to begin with (Kenniston, 2001).

In this paper, we explore the possibility of "leapfrogging" the digital divide. In other words, instead of using traditional digital technology which may be unsuitable to bridge the divide, is it possible for emerging regions to by-pass this technology and use the very latest information and communication technologies to "leapfrog" the divide? The term "leapfrogging" has been used in varied contexts like technology usage in the industrial settings, minimizing our environmental impact by using modern technology and more recently in the context of digital inclusion (Steinmueller, 2001; Davison, 2000; Singh, 1999).

The leapfrogging theory goes thus -- the developing world can be perceived to be at a relative advantage since it does not need to adopt the digital trajectory followed by the West. Instead, it can reap the benefits of years of research and development invested into by the West to straightaway adopt the very cutting-edge technological offerings, thereby bypassing intermediary ICTs that are used widely in the West.

Consider a typical digital-enabled home or office scenario - a desktop (probably running a proprietary operating system) with a wired broadband Internet connection and loaded with common proprietary office applications. To achieve digital inclusion, does this scene need to be re-created in say a rural village in India? We argue that most of these components in this familiar scenario are unsuitable for bridging the digital divide - the desktop, the wired connection, the proprietary operating system and the quintessential applications. Instead we analyze the latest technologies that might be better suited to bridge the divide, hence enabling emerging regions to "leapfrog" across the more traditional digital setup.

This paper looks at the three major spokes that make the digital wheel spin - the hardware, software, and connectivity. In each spoke we evaluate the default technology and its potential as a digital inclusion tool while juxtaposing it with the latest "cutting-edge" alternative that could be used instead for "leapfrogging." We closely study numerous recent ICT projects and technology to identify trends that promise a "leapfrogging" potential. We finally describe three comprehensive scenarios where a combination of these technologies can be effectively used to leapfrog the digital divide, in three different contexts.

HARDWARE: THE FIRST SPOKE

Traditional hardware used for computing has been the ubiquitous desktop. Many 'ICT4D' projects revolve around creating a "tele-center" which typically houses one or more desktops connected to the Internet. An entire village or multiple villages might share one such center. The government of India has embarked on a mammoth digital-inclusion project where more than 100,000 Common Services Centers (CSCs) (a typical tele-center,) are being established across the country, especially targeting rural areas (http://www.csc-india.org).

However the telecenter model of shared PCs has met with limited success. The National CSC scheme for example, which is modeled as a public-private partnership, after an initial euphoric phase had many of its public players backing out. Out of the total rollout of 85,000 plus CSCs, around 4,600 are currently non-operational (http://www.csc-india.org). In the Akshaya telecenter project in Kerala, India (Gurumurthy, 2005) nearly half of the 634 tele-centers created in the pilot phase in 2004 had shut-down after just three years of operation. Why has the "tele-center" model of shared desktops met with limited success, even as it continues to be the default choice for many ICT4D projects the world over?

As stated by Byfield,

its (the tele-center's) current formulation is becoming more responsive to the needs of funders, development agencies, and, possibly, investors, and less responsive to the needs of local beneficiaries." (Byfield, 2004)

Exclusion of marginalized, inaccessibility by the community and insecure locations (Heeks, 2001) are purported as some of the limitations in the execution of the tele-center model. One of the obvious reasons for these limitations is the "shared" aspect of a PC. A user does not have direct and immediate access to the device and its applications and has to travel to the shared location and access it almost always through an intermediary. The telecenter operator or kiosk owner is often the only access point for the computer and the information it provides. Unless both the telecenter operator and the location of the center are chosen carefully, the usage of the center often remains restricted to the more powerful and richer/upper sections of the village. The operator (who needs to be literate) is often of a high caste or affluent local family as they might be the only literate people in the region, further marginalizing the very poor of the area (Harris, 2003).

What restricts the desktop to a shared model? A regular desktop is relatively expensive, bulky, has high maintenance costs and has high electricity consumption. The target population on the other hand has limited spending capacity, probably lives in remote areas with unreliable and limited electricity supply and has no easy access to maintenance support (Surana, 2008), thus necessitating the shared access model.

Moreover, today, a typical desktop's computing capacity may be overkill for the kind of applications that the target population is typically interested in. Rarely is such a machine used for number-crunching or other CPU intensive applications. In the Akshaya project for example, the killer applications for their telecenters are email and on-line chats while in the e-Gram Vishwa Gram centers in Gujarat, India (www.egram.co.in), utility bill payments are the most popular application.

With the desktop PC clearly unsuitable for many digital inclusion initiatives, what are the hardware alternatives available? There is a clear opportunity to leapfrog over desktops and directly use state-of-the-art net books, which are cheaper, portable and much more power efficient (see Box 1). However, the possibility of eliminating the PC all together is more of a reality today with the advent of the mobile phone. Smart mobiles – mobile phones with an operating system - have now revolutionized the information and communication space. They are lighter and more portable than netbooks, more efficient in terms of power consumption and their costs are reducing drastically. By the end of 2010 smart-phones costing way less than $100 were available in the Indian market.

Mobile penetration rates in emerging market countries are expected to rise to 95% by 2013 (Emerging Mobile Markets 2008 Report), making

Box 1. Net books

Small, portable, light and inexpensive laptops have surged in popularity over the last couple of years. The One Laptop Per Child (OLPC) project can be attributed to have spurred the whole net
Book movement. The OLPC project which incubated at MIT Media Labs in 2006, used an innovative design to manufacture a rugged, lightweight and power efficient laptop which would cost around $100, a fraction of the cost of a regular laptop in 2007. The OLPC laptops (also known as XOs) used flash memory instead of a hard
Drive and contained a host of other innovations that brought the cost down substantially without compromising on functionality. Though these machines were targeted at children in developing countries, there turned out to be a huge regular market for these so called "net books". Intel soon launched their classmate PC at $295 a piece with Dell, Acer and a host of others companies following suit with their own versions of net books soon after.

it the ideal platform for those on the other side of the digital divide. In India for example, 45% of the poor have access to a mobile phone within their own household. With the right set of value added services, mobile phones can be used to fulfill a whole range of ICT needs of the poorer sections of society.

Many inclusion projects are already leveraging mobile phones with complementary applications to reach out to their target population. Some popular mobile based ventures targeted at inclusive development are BabaJob, Cell Bazaar, M-Pesa, Eko, M-Dhil, One97's Dakia and Nokia Life Tools (See Box 2 for details on these projects).

Hence net books and mobile phones to a larger extent - by their very nature of being more affordable - can enable users to leapfrog over the shared access model of PCs to individual devices. End-users can directly own a mobile and not depend on a third party for access. Furthermore, the content and information can be user-specific. Personalized information in the domains of health, education, weather and agricultural produce can directly be pushed to the end users using mobile applications. Projects like MDhil (www.MDhil.com) and Nokia Life Tools are experimenting with both push based and pull based models, where users can request for information on health related issues and agricultural information like crop prices and weather. While many projects are mushrooming in the VAS (Value Added Service) space for mobile phones, the vast majority of users currently own basic, text based mobiles. Services that leverage SMS technology or voiced based solutions have the potential to reach the remotest of users and transform their lives and livelihoods.

Box 2. Mobile based development projects

BabaJob.com, a start up based in Bangalore, India aims to connect job seekers in the informal sector to potential employees, using digital solutions. While they initially started out as a website, Babajob has eventually gravitated to using a mobile interface to reach out to their target population of job seekers in the informal sector. In a pilot program where they partnered with Airtel, BabaJob send out SMS messages to 10,000 of Airtel's least paying customers, asking them if they were interested in jobs like a driver or a cook. Interested seekers could then reply to the SMS and register at BabaJob. BabaJob now processes 250 to 300 mobile applications per day. They also provide an IVR (Interactive Voice Response) system, where users are directed by voice prompts and can register with BabaJob's database, using their mobile phones.

Cell Bazaar (www.cellbazzar.com), which originated as an MIT Media Lab project aims to be a "Craigslist" for mobile phone users in Bangladesh. Using their phones, users list, sell and buy a range of products and services, from rice and bananas to used refrigerators and phones. Cell Bazaar offers four different interfaces which are interconnected: Web, SMS, WAP and Voice. Cell Bazaar has recently begun a category for jobs. Users can either send Cell Bazaar an SMS about a job posting or use the WAP (Wireless Application Protocol) interface provided by Cell Bazaar. Using their mobile phones and Cell Bazaar's multiple interfaces, small farmers and entrepreneurs eliminate middlemen and directly interact with buyers, thus increasing profits.

Mobile based money transfers and cashless transactions hold tremendous promise to populations who have traditionally been unbanked. **M Pesa** (Hughes, 2007), a mobile phone based money transfer service initially launched by Vodafone in Kenya in 2007, has proved the tremendous potential of this technology. M Pesa currently has over 6.5 million subscribers with 2 million daily transactions in Kenya alone. The service has been extended to Tanzania and Afghanistan, with India and Egypt next on the expansion list.

Eko Financial Services, again in the m-banking domain, extends bank accounts to anybody who owns a basic mobile phone, and specifically targets the unbanked Bottom of the Pyramid (BOP) market. Using standard technology like text messages and missed calls, users can open a no-frills bank account and deposit, withdraw and remit money; all with their basic mobile phone. Eko started its services in 2009 and since then has served more than 100,000 customers and transactions worth `400 crore.

MDhil uses the mobile platform to provide customer-centric health information. Customers can access health information via SMS or USSD. Since their launch in March 2009, they have reached over 150,000 customers and are targeted to reach 3 million by 2011. Nokia Life Tools is a similar mobile service customized for farmers and other rural personnel and provides them with information specific to their livelihood and lifestyle, while Daki from One97 is similar to a personalized voicemail service for the farmer, providing him with updates regarding crop prices at the wholesale 'mandi,' electricity availability schedules for tube wells and the like.

SOFTWARE: THE SECOND SPOKE

We now move to the next layer in a digital service - the software, in which we explore the operating system, applications and user interface spaces.

Operating Systems and Applications

While over 90% of the digital world uses expensive proprietary operating systems and office software (like Microsoft's Windows OS and Office Suite) alternatives in the form of open source software are far more affordable. The opens source movement that started in the eighties has produced a vast range of software from operating systems to web tools to office suits. Open source software (OSS) is created by a distributed community of programmers who believe that software should not be expensive and the source code should be available to anyone who wants to customize it. Much of this software is free (called FLOSS for Free/Libre Open Source Software) or moderately priced and all of it is customizable to one's own requirements. With OSS, the standard version can be adapted to local languages, cultures and preferences. Moreover the end-user interface can be tailored to locals and indigenous populations, making it more user friendly.

The take-up by the Extremadura Region in Spain of open source through its support for the LinEx project (a localized, Spanish-language version of the GNU/Linux operating environment) has not just allowed the implementation of activities for a lower price, but activities especially in education and training which were simply not possible with proprietary software. (Ghosh, 2003)

While the initial versions of a lot of the open source code might have been lower in quality than their proprietary counterparts, years of collaboration and hard work by dedicated open-source evangelists and programmers have produced products that are at par or even better in quality than proprietary software. Some popular open-source products include - Mozilla Firefox Browser, Apache Web Server, Linux Operating System, Open Office and Drupal content manager.

With easy availability of OSS for a host of applications and devices including mobile phones, emerging economies can avail of free or moderately priced software, directly leapfrogging over propriety software, which entail prohibitive licensing fees and expensive upgrades every few years.

Another recent technological advancement - Cloud Computing, holds immense promise for cash-strapped start-ups in emerging economies. Cloud computing comprises of two main components - Software as a Service (SaaS) and Infrastructure as a Service (IaaS). With both software and infrastructure offered as a service over the Internet, organizations and companies that are young and probably cash-strapped can "rent" computing infrastructure and/or software. The obvious advantage of no capital expenditures and the pay-as-you-go model ensures that users pay only for what they need. The catch of-course is that there needs to be a reliable Internet connection to avail of cloud services. Hence, connectivity issues need to be solved in conjunction with the decision of choosing the hardware and software solution for any ICT4D initiative.

Eko financial services (www.eko.co.in), a young start up in India that provides m-banking to the BOP market has benefited greatly by using both OSS as well as IaaS. Eko uses an open-source banking solution developed by Grameen Bank, which was then customized to Eko's requirements. Eko also uses Wipro's IaaS offering instead of investing in its own hardware. This means, as Eko scales (and Eko is scaling exponentially) and its hardware needs increase, Wipro's cloud services can instantly upgrade Eko's allotted infrastructure. The elasticity provided by Cloud Computing, have helped Eko keep its costs low and even turn a profit in the burgeoning branchless-banking market in India.

Thus the opportunity to leap-frog over proprietary software (by using OSS) and fixed upfront investments in infrastructure and software (by using Cloud Computing services) is a promising model already adopted by some of the nascent inclusive projects in India.

User Interfaces

Apart from economic and financial issues, one of the major factors for digital exclusion is non-literacy - the inability to read and type. Even for a literate user who can read and write in a local language, the language itself becomes a barrier because most software interfaces are designed for users adept in English. English as a mode of communication is restricted to about 5% of India's population. Yet, while there are more than 1.5 million Indian websites in English, there are only 20,000 or so websites in various Indian languages.

However, in the light of technological advances in the user-interface space, the conventional notion of using a key-board for input and a text-heavy display for output can be seriously challenged.

Innovations in voice recognition/speech software, touch-screens and text-free user-interfaces allow users on the disadvantaged side of the digital-divide to circumvent the language and illiteracy barrier altogether (Pitrelli, 2006; Plauch, 2006; Sherwani, 2005).

Research projects like IBM's Spoken Web (Kumar, 2007), Microsoft's Text-Free User Interface (UI) and Prodem's successful implementation of voice-driven ATMs in the Bolivian countryside (Hernandez, 2003) promise opportunities for a paradigm shift in how non-literate or semi-literate users can access digital services (see Box 3 for details on these projects).

The technologies discussed above (some are proof-of-concept projects and others have been deployed and used widely) show the concrete possibility for emerging regions to leapfrog over traditional keyboard inputs and text displays to state-of-the-art text-free, graphics and speech driven or touch-based user interfaces. These innovations allow marginalized users to cross language and illiteracy barriers to be part of the digital world.

Box 3. Innovations in user interfaces

IBM's Spoken Web: The spoken web, also known as the World Wide Telecom Web (T-Web) (Kumar, 2007), is IBM's vision for a web parallel in function and use to the regular World Wide Web. The T-Web however is targeted at marginalized groups who are unable to read/write and hence be a part of the normal WWW. The T-Web comprises of a network of voice sites that are voice applications created and hosted by the users themselves. Using an ordinary telephone call, users can create a voice-site for themselves, and also link it to other voice sites. A plumber for example can set-up his voice site to include information about himself like charges for his services, references etc. A potential client visiting the site could furthermore, book an appointment for the plumbers services. The T-Web has the potential to allow masses to exploit services and applications similar to those available on the regular web.

Text-Free User Interfaces by Microsoft (Ghosh, 2003; Medhi, 2010): Microsoft is investigating the use of text-free interfaces for applications ranging from a job portal for the informal sector (Babajob.com) to mobile banking. Typically a text-free interface uses only graphics and/or spoken dialog and is devoid of or contains minimal text. BabaJob provides this computer-based text-free UI to informal sector workers like maids and drivers. Using this interface, non-literate users are able to navigate online through various job postings and narrow down to suitable openings (Medhi, 2007).

The m-banking application being developed by the same team was used in field studies that showed that non-literate and semi-literate users preferred the spoken dialog and rich multimedia interfaces to the text-based interface (Medhi, 2010). The rich multimedia interface is however not supported by the basic variety of phones used by most of the poor in the developing world and hence the spoken dialog interface might be a more viable option for such populations.

Prodem's Multi-lingual ATMS: Multi-lingual Smart ATMs in Bolivia have helped Prodem FFP (Hernandez, 2003) efficiently serve its target population of rural and indigenous Bolivians. The stand-alone ATMS are voice-driven and can speak three different local languages and have color-coded touch-screens to help the non-literate user choose the appropriate banking service and navigate through the ATM functions. More recently, Citibank introduced similar smart ATMs in India as part of its financial inclusion drive.

CONNECTIVITY: THE THIRD SPOKE

Wired (fiber or copper) connections have been the traditional solution in the west, for both telephony as well as data connectivity. Many developing countries have a very low fiber penetration and this leads to a big hurdle for any kind of digital solution. India for example has a broadband penetration of 0.74% with fiber connections mostly limited to major metropolitan areas. While wired solutions can be cost effective for regions with high user-density (typically found in urban areas) when it comes to rural areas with far-flung scattered population clusters, wired solutions prove to be prohibitively expensive. Moreover, the socio-economic environment in many places may not be conducive to laying cables – there are multiple instances where the government or another organization in India started laying cables to connect remote areas, only to have them dug up at night and sold by the local population. The other option, satellite connectivity, does not requiring wire-lines but is more suitable for remote areas with high paying capacity, due to costs which could reach US$2,000 per month for 1Mbps bandwidth (Pentland, 2004).

That brings us to wireless technologies, which are now at a stage where they are sufficiently reliable, can provide predictable coverage and are affordable given enough demand. Developing nations thus have the opportunity to skip the spread of wired connectivity and straightaway adopt wireless technologies as cost-effective and speedy solutions for connecting a larger part of their population.

While Wi-Fi solutions in the west were traditionally used for indoor settings like an office or coffee-shop, their ease of deployment and economic viability make them very suitable for the developing world. Moreover, Wi-Fi (802.11) operates in the unlicensed spectrum (unlike WiMax and others), making it suitable for use by local entrepreneurs. This is particularly important as there is then no dependence on telecom operators, who are usually hesitant to enter the rural low-user density market. Empowering the local communities to build or at least maintain their own connectivity solution (the model successfully followed by some projects like the Aravind Eye Hospital network and Air-Jaldi, is a definite possibility with a Wi-Fi solution).

While Wi-Fi was traditional meant to cover a small indoor area - an office block for example- modifications in the MAC layer of the 802.11 protocol make Wi-Fi suitable for long-distances and outdoor use. This new application of the Wi-Fi spectrum, termed as WiLD (Wi-Fi for Long Distances) has successfully been deployed in some pilot connectivity projects (Patra, 2007). Point to point connections can span large distances (up to 20 KM), leading to lesser base-stations which drastically reduce costs. While the backbone consists of point to point links mounted on towers, the local connectivity is provided by the access network radiating around each tower as shown in Figure 1. These solutions are ideal for covering low-density clusters of users scattered across larger geographical regions.

Figure 2 plots different connectivity solutions for different user densities and paying capacities: fiber for users with high purchasing power located in high-density areas, satellite for similar users located in low density areas, traditional wireless solutions for high density and low purchasing power populations (as typically found in urban slums) and WiLD networks for low density and low purchasing power populations.

The Digital Gangetic Plain, AirJaldi, Akshaya E-Literacy Network and Aravind Eye Hospital Network are some projects that have already demonstrated the viability of using Wi-Fi and similar wireless technologies for long-distance point-to-point connectivity (WiLD Networks). (See Box 4 for details on these projects).

A more recent technological development in the wireless domain is ad-hoc peer-to-peer mesh networks also called MANETs (Mobile Ad-Hoc Networks) (Figure 3). In such networks, mobile

Figure 1. Illustration of backbone and access networks structure used in WiLD networks

	High Demand /High Purchasing Power	Low Demand / Low Purchasing Power
High Density	Fiber	Wireless
Low Density	Satellite	WiLD (Low Cost Per Unit of Demand)

P o p u l a t i o n

Figure 2. Connectivity solutions for different user-densities and paying capacities

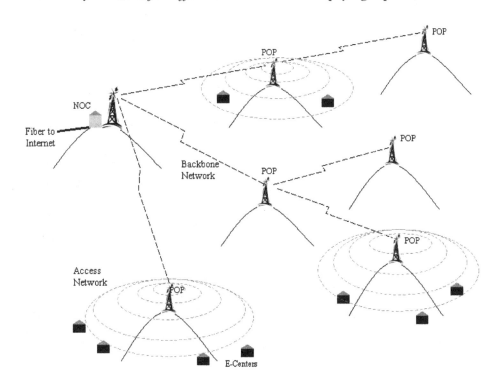

Box 4. Projects that use WiLD (Long Distance Wi-Fi) networks

The Digital Gangetic Plain (Raman, 2007), a rural wifi testbed in northern India, spans 80 KM in length and covers 100 sq Km. A joint collaboration of the Indian Institute of Technology – Kanpur and MIT Media Labs, it uses multihop directional wifi links. With around a million residents in the area, the cost of connectivity works out to less than $40 per subscriber. The Akshaya E literacy Network (www. akshaya.net) was started by the government of Kerala in 2003, to spread eliteracy in the state. The pilot project in Mallapuram district aimed to provide network connectivity to the entire population of around 3.6 million spread across an area of 35,000 Sq. Km. Due to the rugged mountainous terrain, wireless was considered the best solution. The connectivity solution consists of a high bandwidth wireless backbone and a wireless access network from the backbone to connect to individual centers (Figure 2). This network uses a mix of proprietary wireless technologies like VINE (Versatile Intelligent Network Environment) and WipLL (Wireless IP Local Loop), and is considered to be the biggest outdoor IP based wireless network in the world. Air Jaldi (www.drupal.airjaldi.com), an organization that specializes in providing wireless connectivity to rural regions operates three long distance wifi networks in the Himalayan Mountains in India, one each in Dharamshala, Tehri Garwal and Kumaon, providing much needed connectivity to these isolated Tibetan communities.

units (laptops or mobile phones) can directly communicate with one another within a certain range. More interestingly, each unit can act as a relay between two other units which are out of range from each other. Thus a bunch of such mobile units can form an ad-hoc network -- the more the number of units the larger the network can scale. Though MANETS are usually used for data communication, recent efforts (see Box 5)

Figure 3. Structure of a peer-to-peer mobile adhoc network

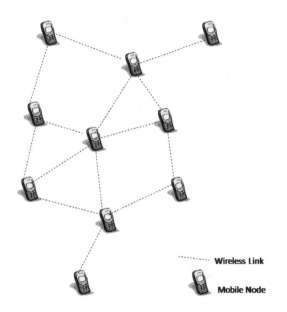

····· Wireless Link

Mobile Node

are experimenting with voice communication using specially designed mobile-phones. We call such networks MAPNETS (Mobile Ad-Hoc Phone Networks). There are no base-stations (cellular towers) or other costly infrastructure in this model, making such a system ideal for rural areas with low purchasing power. If one of these units is connected to the Internet, then the entire local network can communicate with the outside world through this gateway.

Four recent projects are experimenting with such networks for providing connectivity to rural regions, the One Laptop Per Child (OLPC) Program (also known as the XO laptops), the Village Telephony project that uses 'Mesh Potatoes", TerraNet, a Swedish mobile company and the Serval Research Project in Australia (See Box 5 for details). While Mesh Potatoes are not mobile and hence are configured as a static mesh network, the other three have mobile units that form an ad-hoc network among themselves.

MANET/MAPNET technology, though still in its infancy, holds tremendous promise for helping sparsely populated rural regions to leapfrog from zero connectivity, jump past traditional connectivity solutions which need cables or centralized base-stations to affordable, totally decentralized mesh networks providing voice and data connections.

Populations in far-flung rural areas need not wait for service providers to set-up costly infra-

Box 5. Mobile ad-hoc networks

The One Laptop Per Child program (laptop.org), aimed at underprivileged children in developing countries, has laptops with in-built wireless antennas which can automatically communicate with each other, up to a distance of 1 KM. Moreover each laptop can act as a relay between two other laptops, thus forming a multi-hop mesh network. If one laptop is connected to the Internet, then the entire network is indirectly connected to the Internet. Each laptop also has icons on its screen to denote other laptops that are within range and part of its mesh network.

TerraNet (www.terranet.se), a Swedish mobile company is experimenting with mobile phones that can form a similar ad-hoc mesh network. These phones contain special hardware that enables two phones to talk to each other directly if they are within a kilometer of each other. Phones also act as an intermediary, to route calls. Such a network can be connected to the outside world via a computer with an Internet connection. These networks however, cannot scale indefinitely. In TerraNet's proposal for example, there can be seven intermediaries who relay the voice data to the destination, before the latency gets too high for reasonable quality. Thus, an area of approximately 8 sq Km can be comfortably covered.

The Serval research project (www.servalproject.org) in Australia has developed a similar system where off-the-shelf mobiles phones have been programmed to form an ad-hoc network among themselves. This is an open-source project with all their software available in the public domain. Moreover, the Serval project claims that their software is hardware independent and can be used to mesh-enable any off the shelf mobile phone. Field tests show that the phones can be located a few hundred meters away from each other, and an end-to-end call can go through five intermediate hops. If one of these phones receives cellular or Internet coverage, then it can act as a gateway for the entire mesh network.

The Village Telephony project (www.villagetelco.org) uses 'mesh potatoes', which are specially designed telephones that can act as a router for phone calls. The first pilot called the Dili Village Telco, is a 100 node mesh telephony network in Dili, Timor Leste.

structure and related services before they have a functioning voice and/or data network. If there are enough mesh enabled phones or laptops in the region, a viable network will spring up quite automatically.

PUTTING IT TOGETHER

While we have discussed a range of technological advances in the hardware, software and connectivity spheres as possible leapfrogging devices, the set of technologies that will suit a possible situation can differ vastly. In large countries like India with over 600,000 villages and vastly different population profiles between the villages, the favorable technology for bridging the digital-divide could vary considerably from region to region and application to application. Factors like the population density and spread, literacy levels, adaptive capacity and purchasing power of the target population should play a critical role in the choice of the technology to be used.

Here we describe three possible digital-leapfrogging scenarios for three different target populations and applications:

Scenario 1: Village Telephony for Ultra-Rural Regions

Very remote and interior regions which do not currently have land-line telephony or mobile cellular coverage and are not expected to receive either of the two in the near future are good candidates for mobile adhoc phone networks (MAPNETs), which promise an alternate means of telephony. This telephone network can span an area of around 8 sq KM, beyond which the voice quality may suffer. Hence a single MAPNET can comfortably cover a single large village or a cluster of smaller villages. Since this is primarily a voice interface enabling users to talk to one another, the literacy levels of the population are irrelevant. Hence, the network could serve the entire population at these villages, as long as they can afford a mobile phone. These mesh enabled phones will automatically connect to one another forming an ad-hoc network.

The phones could be enabled for peer-to-peer routing of calls by using open-source protocols as promised by the Serval project (www.servalproject.org). Thus, mobile phones, mesh networks and open-source software could enable ultra-rural regions to leapfrogging across more traditional telephony like land-lines and cellular coverage. A MAPNET however limits the connectivity to the local region it is deployed in. If there is Internet or cellular connectivity available to one mesh-enabled phone that device can act as a gateway for the entire mesh. Thus investing in one satellite connection for VoIP calls could connect the entire set of remote villages to the outside world.

Scenario 2: Mobile Banking for Urban and Semi-Rural Regions

We envision a universal mobile banking eco-system for the bottom-of-the-pyramid population, on the lines of M-Pesa's (Hughes, 2007) and Eko's (www.eco.co.in) m-banking solutions. Since, this application depends on cellular coverage it will be limited to urban and semi-rural areas with reliable cellular network connectivity. The m-banking solution is targeted at those who typically find it difficult to visit a regular bank branch or ATM because it may entail a long trip to the nearest branch, eating hours or even days out of their regular work-day. This population may typically be semi-literate or just number literate but may own and know how to use the basic features of a mobile-phone. Eko estimates this population segment in India to be about half a billion.

Local shopkeepers act as 'Business Correspondents' (BCs) for a traditional brick and mortar bank, providing the last mile connectivity to users. Customers are allowed to withdraw, deposit and remit using their mobile phones, at these BC centers (again based on the M-Pesa model). We envision voice and icon based mobile user-interfaces (on the lines of Microsoft's text-free UIs) enabling these users to conduct their banking transactions, without the need to be literate. As seen in Eko's case, the back-end for these core-banking services can rely on open-source software and the infrastructure (including computing power and storage) can be leased from Cloud service providers, making it financially easier to boot-strap and scale such a service.

Scenario 3: WWW Applications for Large Rural Expanses using WiLD Networks

While P2P mesh networks can cover only a smaller region - say one village or a small group of villages within roughly 8 Sq KM, WiLD networks can cover a larger area spanning up to 100 Km in length, as in the case of the Digital Gangetic Plain discussed earlier. However, since the coverage is not blanket coverage, and only certain pockets are covered in the region, it is especially suited for rural expanses that have clusters of high density population. Each cluster of high-density users can be served by a separate access network, and all the access networks can be connected together by the back-bone network (as explained earlier on the section about WiLD Networks). WiLD networks also serve hilly terrain well, where the towers which form the backbone network can be placed on top of hills, and the valley population around a backbone tower can be served by the access network.

We envision a WiLD network providing Internet connectivity for such a rural expanse - one end of the network needs to be connected to a gateway to the Internet. Net Books could be used to connect to the Access network. The applications provided could be World Wide Web applications like email, VoIP and chat services, which are popular services for workers migrating to the city to communicate with the families they leave back in their villages. While chat services and VoIP do not need the user to be literate and their interface can be based solely on icons, email services imply that the users be able to read and type. Hence, this service can initially be targeted toward literates and semi-literate users in the region.

Thus, long distance point-to-point (WiLD) networks and net books provide a low-cost alternative to allow large expanses of rural regions to leapfrog over wired connectivity and desktops to the World Wide Web.

CONCLUSION

In this paper, we have looked at the possibility for emerging regions to adopt the latest in information and communication technologies, while bypassing intermediary technologies, as a means for digital inclusion. We discussed why the traditional digital trajectory followed by the West is unsuitable for many emerging regions and how the theory of "leapfrogging" can actually be implemented in the hardware, software and connectivity domains to achieve cost-effective digital inclusion.

By studying existing proof-of-concepts and pilots, we investigated the feasibility of a number of technologies for leapfrogging. We conclude that ICT4D initiatives should explore using the following leapfrogging trajectories:

- Mobiles instead of desktops for providing agriculture-based inputs, health and education based projects, banking services, job-portals etc.
- MAPNets (Mobile Ad-Hoc Phone Networks) instead of wired or cellular telephony for ultra-remote regions.
- WiLD (Wireless Long Distance) Networks instead of wired networks or satellites-dishes to provide connectivity to large rural regions.
- Voice and icon/graphic driven user-interfaces instead of text-based UIs.
- Open-source software instead of proprietary software for both back-end activity and user-facing applications.
- Availing cloud-based services instead of investing in software and hardware for back-end infrastructure.

We also developed three specific scenarios in telephony, banking and the World Wide Web, which illustrate how a combination of these different technologies can be used to 'leapfrog the digital divide'.

REFERENCES

Byfield, T. (2004). *Thoughts on the telecenter as a model for ICT in the rural "south"*. Unpublished manuscript, Social Sciences Research Council, Brooklyn, NY.

Davison, R., Vogel, D., Harris, R., & Jones, N. (2000). Technology leapfrogging in developing countries – An inevitable luxury? *Electronic Journal on Information Systems in Developing Countries, 1*(5), 1–10.

Ghosh, R. A. (2003). License fees and GDP per capita: The case for open source in developing countries. *First Monday, 8*(12).

Gurumurthy, A., Singh, P. J., & Kasinathan, G. (2005). Case study 5: The Akshaya experience: Community driven: Local entrepreneurs in ICT services. In S. Siochru & B. Girard (Eds.), *Poor access to ICTs: The case of Akshaya, India* (pp. 143-157). Retrieved from http://propoor- ict.comunica.org/content/pdfs/04_UNDP_Report_5-India.pdf

Harris, R. W., Kumar, A., & Balaji, V. (2003). Sustainable telecentres? Two cases from India. In Krishna, S., & Madon, S. (Eds.), *The digital challenge: Information technology in the development context* (pp. 124–135). Surrey, UK: Ashgate.

Heeks, R. (2001). *Understanding e-governance for development*. Manchester, UK: Institute for Development Policy and Management, University of Manchester.

Hernandez, R. (2003). *PRODEM FFP's multilingual smart ATMs for microfinance*. Washington, DC: World Research Institute.

Hughes, N., & Lonie, S. (2007). M-Pesa: Mobile money for the "unbanked": Turning cellphones into 24-hour tellers in Kenya. *Innovations: Technology, Governance, Globalization, 2*(1-2), 63–81. doi:10.1162/itgg.2007.2.1-2.63

Kenniston, K. (2001). *IT for the common man: Lessons from India*. Retrieved from http://web.mit.edu/~kken/Public/FILES/pubs.htm

Kumar, A., Rajput, N., Chakraborty, D., Agarwal, S. K., & Nanavati, A. A. (2007). WWTW: The world wide telecom web. In *Proceedings of the Workshop on Networked Systems for Developing Regions* (p. 7).

Medhi, I., Patnaik, S., Brunskill, E., Gautama, S. N. N., Thies, W., & Toyama, K. (2010). Designing mobile interfaces for novice and low-literacy users. *ACM Transactions on Computer-Human Interaction, 18*(1).

Medhi, I., Sagar, A., & Toyama, K. (2007). Text-free user interfaces for illiterate and semi-literate users. *Information Technologies and International Development, 4*(1), 37–50. doi:10.1162/itid.2007.4.1.37

Patra, R., Nedevschi, S., Surana, S., & Sheth, A. (2007). Wildnet: Design and implementation of high performance wifi based long distance networks. In *Proceedings of the 16th USENIX Security Symposium*.

Pentland, A., Fletcher, R., & Hasson, A. (2004). DakNet: Rethinking connectivity in developing nations. *Computer, 37*(1), 78–83. doi:10.1109/MC.2004.1260729

Pitrelli, J. F., Bakis, R., Eide, E. M., Fernandez, R., Hamza, W., & Picheny, M. A. (2006). The IBM expressive text-to-speech synthesis system for American English. *IEEE Transactions on Audio. Speech and Language Processing, 14*(4), 1099–1108. doi:10.1109/TASL.2006.876123

Plauch, M., & Prabaker, M. (2006). Tamil market: A spoken dialog system for rural India. In *Proceedings of the Extended Abstracts on Human Factors in Computing* (pp. 1619-1624).

Raman, B., & Chebrolu, K. (2007). Experiences in using WiFi for rural Internet in India. *IEEE Communications Magazine, 45*(1), 104–110. doi:10.1109/MCOM.2007.284545

Sherwani, J. (2005). *Are spoken dialog systems viable for under-served semi-literate populations?* Unpublished doctoral dissertation, Carnegie Mellon University, Pittsburgh, PA.

Singh, J. P. (1999). *Leapfrogging development? The political economy of telecommunications restructuring*. Albany, NY: State University of New York Press.

Steinmueller, E. (2001). ICTs and the possibilities for leapfrogging by developing countries. *International Labour Review, 140*(2), 194. doi:10.1111/j.1564-913X.2001.tb00220.x

Surana, S., Patra, R., Nedevschi, S., Ramos, M., Subramanian, L., Ben-David, Y., & Brewer, E. (2008). Beyond pilots: Keeping rural wireless networks alive. In *Proceedings of the 5th USENIX Symposium on Networked Systems Design and Implementation* (pp. 119-132).

Tarrif Consultancy. (2008). *Emerging mobile markets*. London, UK: Tarrif Consultancy.

This work was previously published in the International Journal of Information Communication Technologies and Human Development, Volume 3, Issue 4, edited by Susheel Chhabra and Hakikur Rahman, pp. 17-30, copyright 2011 by IGI Publishing (an imprint of IGI Global).

Chapter 15
Technology Related Trust Issues in SME B2B E–Commerce

Muneesh Kumar
University of Delhi, India and Groupe ESC-Pau, France

Mamta Sareen
University of Delhi, India

Susheel Chhabra
Lal Bahadur Shastri Institute of Management, India

ABSTRACT

There is increasing evidence that e-commerce adoption among SMEs is expanding rapidly. In spite of that, SMEs, particularly in developing countries, have not been able to adequately benefit from the new opportunities offered by e-commerce technologies. Previous studies have identified lack of trust as one of the major hurdles in achieving the potential benefits by the SMEs. This paper identifies technology-related trust issues that need to be addressed while building e-commerce infrastructure for SMEs. The evidence offered in the paper is based on a survey of the relevant practices regarding deployment and effective implementation of relevant technology tools to address these issues and enhance the levels of trust in e-commerce infrastructure. The paper also examines the relationship between the perceived level of trust and the level of assurance in respect of various technology-related trust issues. The paper suggests an approach of collaboration among the SMEs while building the e-commerce infrastructure and focusing their attention on the technology-related trust issues.

1. INTRODUCTION

Small and Medium Enterprises (SMEs) play a key role in the development of the economy of any country. SMEs are estimated to account for 80 percent of global economic growth (Jutla, Bodorik, & Dhaliwal, 2002). The relative importance of SMEs in many economies has been long recognized as different from large businesses (Gengatharen & Standing, 2005). It is stated that about 90% of all businesses in Australia (Mason, Castleman, & Parker, 2008), 96% in Malaysia (Alam et al.,

DOI: 10.4018/978-1-4666-1957-9.ch015

2008) and 85% in US (Levenburg & Klein, 2006) are characterized as SMEs. The contribution to generation of employment and distribution of economic power has always put SMEs in focus of national economic planning of most nations. In spite of this, SMEs continue to suffer from scarcity of resources and high degree of competition from their larger counterparts. However, with the advent of Internet, it was thought that SMEs would be greatly benefited by adoption of e-commerce technologies. Internet provided an opportunity to SMEs to enter the e-commerce environment at lower and affordable prices and thereby reduce transaction costs and expand the scope of marketing, by reaching new markets and partnering with suppliers and other collaborators (Payne et al., 2003). While anecdotal evidence and empirical results give the impression that e-commerce adoption among SMEs is expanding fast, the fact remains that many SMEs are still sitting on the sidelines (Daniel & McInerney, 2005; Teo, Wei, & Benbasat, 2003).

Most commonly, economists and information systems researchers view the spread of e-commerce as one of the main factors contributing to globalization by virtue of the speed with which it allows communication, information, and transactions to flow across large distances, thereby reducing coordination and search costs that formerly inhibited such trade (Bakos, 1997, 1998; Cairncross, 1997; Choi, Stahl, & Whinston, 1997). E-commerce has not only helped in reducing the cost of trading among SMEs but also has helped them to strengthen their relationships and collaboration among their trading partners for "just in time production" and "just in time delivery" (Ngai & Wat, 2002). Since SMEs do not have a well-established brand name, the participation of SMEs in e-commerce is more common than in B2C e-commerce (Deelmann, 2002). For SMEs, Internet and e-commerce are viewed as a means to overcome the barrier of distance and size in accessing global markets and building long-term relationships (Daniel & McInerney, 2005; Gen-

gatharen & Standing, 2005). Many SMEs are using e-commerce to restructure operations, streamline processes, reduce costs, improve sales and service, reach new markets, and distribute information. Most studies indicate that although there are growing levels of awareness and enthusiasm for e-commerce, only a small proportion of SMEs are realizing substantial benefits (Gengatharen & Standing, 2005). It has often been often cited that even though SMEs are adopting the e-commerce technologies, they are unable to fully exploit the potential, due to the high set up costs involved. Another barrier in the growth of e-commerce among SMEs is the lack of trust (Deelmann, 2002).

Though, a number of studies have been conducted relating trust to e-commerce, not much work seems to have been done on various issues regarding trust in e-commerce among SMEs (Ngai & Wat, 2002). Most of the studies have either focused on adoption of technology for e-commerce or on trust issues in e-commerce among SMEs. However, there is dearth of literature relating to use of technology for building trust in e-commerce among SMEs. The present paper focuses on the role of technology in enhancing levels of trust among SMEs.

2. LITERATURE REVIEW

A number of studies have been conducted that have focused on trust and e-commerce adoption. Some of these studies were relating to trust and e-commerce adoption, whereas others focused on technology related factors which have the potential to influence trust in e-commerce. A few studies specifically focused on SMEs and the issues relating to e-commerce adoption including trust related issues. Some of the significant studies in this regard are summarized.

Trust acts as a catalyst in many buyer–seller transactions that can provide consumers with high expectations of satisfying exchange relationships (Hawes, Kenneth, & Swan, 1989). Researchers have examined trust in various contexts: as related to bargaining (Schurr & Ozanne, 1985), buyer–seller relationships (Doney & Cannon, 1997), distribution channels (Dwyer, Schurr, & Oh, 1987), and the use of market research (Moorman, Deshpande, & Zaltman, 1993). Trust is considered to be more difficult to build and more critical in online as compared to offline trading environments (Hodges, 1997; Ratnasingham, 1998; Hoffman et al., 1999; Roy et al., 2001). Online transactions are more impersonal, anonymous and automated than offline transactions (Head et al., 2001) and hence, trust requirement becomes even more complex and challenging in the virtual environment of e-commerce (Moor, 1985; IDA, 2000). Dutton (2000) observed that users tend to be potential e-commerce customers if they find the e-vendor to be technically competent with their confidential transaction information and predictable in their behavior. Mcknight et al. (2002) empirically validated that impact of competence, benevolence, and integrity on trust in potential e-vendors. Lee and Turban (2001) presented a comprehensive model consisting of four antecedent dimensions of trust namely trustworthiness of Internet merchant, trustworthiness of Internet shopping medium, contextual factors and other factors. Trustworthiness of Internet shopping medium consisted of the technical competence, reliability, and familiarity with the medium. The contextual factors included effectiveness of security infrastructure and third party certifications. Milne and Boza (1999) found that consumer trust levels vary from industry to industry, depending on how much information is captured and whether it is shared. They emphasized that honest and full disclosure of information practices helps in enhancing the levels of online trust.

Since the underlying infrastructure of e-commerce is a set of technologies that facilitate the transactions, technology plays a vital role in trust building process. Certain issues pertaining to technology have been cited to impact trust. A number of challenges lurk in the path of the suc-cess of e-commerce. These include doubts about the reliability and security of the communication infrastructure and its vulnerability to hackers and system failures (Laudon et al., 2004), uncertainty about the credibility of trading partners (Head et al., 2002), concern that the confidentiality of transaction might be breached (Shim et al., 2000), lack of integration of trusted and secured financial services (Alexender et al., 2000) and confusion about the reality of price transparency (Zhu, 2002) on the Internet. Security, privacy and authentication have often been cited as the key factors influencing trust in e-commerce (Mahade-van & Venkatesh, 2000). Haiwook (2001) found that technological infrastructure in e-commerce systems provide a better means of coordination and help in enhancing the levels of trust. Hoffman, Novak, and Peralta (1999) argued that consumers' ability to control the actions of a web vendor directly affects their perception of security and privacy. Marco et al. (2002) addressed the trust and privacy problems concerning admittance to negotiation within e-marketplaces. Pavlou and Chellappa (2001) proposed a model to explain the relationship between perceived privacy and security with level of trust in e-commerce transactions. They observed strong relationship between the perceived security and level of trust in the transactions with online companies. A more comprehensive model relating trust with trust-related technology issues has been proposed by Kumar and Sareen (2009). They identified seven trust-related technology issues namely security, privacy and confidentiality, authentication and authorization, non-repudiation, web interface, and system performance and infrastructure.

Perhaps one of the most interesting studies that relate technology with trust is the one by Ratnasingam (2003). She introduced a new term "technology trust" which is supposed to be based on technical safeguards, protective measures and control mechanisms that aim to provide reliable transactions among the trading partners. Technology trust was found to be influenced by transaction integrity, authentication, confidentiality, non-repudiation and best business practices.

Mirchandani and Motwani (2001) identified factors that influence adoption of e-commerce in SMEs. They observed enthusiasm of top management, relative advantage of e-commerce, IT knowledge of employees as significant factors in taking decision to adopt e-commerce. Macgregor and Vrazlaic (2006) compared the purposes for which Swedish SMEs and Australian SMEs were using e-commerce. They found that Swedish SMEs (53%) were adopting e-commerce for more strategic purposes than their Australian counterparts (15.6%). Lack of technical know-how was posited as one of the major deterrent in e-commerce adoption in SMEs of both the countries. Security and privacy issues in e-transactions were identified as the primary determinants of e-commerce adoption among SMEs in Turkey (Abrizah, 2007). Gaynak et al. (2005) investigated the e-commerce adoption profile of SMEs in Turkey and also observed that the perceived benefits significantly influence e-commerce adoption in SMEs. Nabeel Al-Sirim (2007) investigated the impact of technology as one of the factors affecting the adoption of e-commerce among SMEs in New Zealand. Thatcher et al. (2006) identified organizational, industrial, governmental, and cultural factors having influence on e-commerce adoption in China. The United Nations Conference on Trade and Development (2002) primarily focused on the growth of SMEs in developing countries. Most of the report was on the issues relating to the regulatory interface and the telecom communications infrastructure. Mapping the UNCTAD's E-Commerce and Development Report 2002, Jennex examined the impact of five factors (namely People Factors, Technical Infrastructure, Client Interface, Business Infrastructure, and Regulatory Interface) on adoption and growth of e-commerce among SMEs. Extending this model, Behkamal et al. (2006) emphasized on the role of trust in SMEs e-commerce and observed that it could be developed through competence and predictability. Ruth

(2008) observed that insufficient knowledge of IT was one of the major obstacles in e-commerce adoption by SMEs. Grandon and Pearson (2004) investigated the adoption of e-commerce among SMEs and found that the operational support, managerial productivity, and strategic decision aids influenced the perceived strategic value of e-commerce.

Studies focusing on barriers to adoption of e-commerce among SMEs identified technological, organizational, environmental and individual aspects of the firm as the main factors (Rashid, 2001). The fear of losing trade secrets in e-business also creates reluctance for SMEs in the adoption of e-commerce (Killikanya, 2000). Factors such as managerial, market, and financial issues were also identified as reasons for success or failure of e-commerce among SMEs (Korgaonkar & O'Leary, 2006). Lack of technological expertise was also cited as one of the major challenges facing SMEs (Gengatharen & Standing, 2005). Lack of confidence and trust especially in security and legal issues concerning e-transactions were among the important inhibitor to growth of e-commerce among SMEs (PriceWaterHouseCooper, 1999). Many studies have identified information security problems as the main reason for the majority of SMEs for not making use of Internet technologies for their business transactions (Tagliavini et al., 2001). On the other hand, studies have found that SMEs engaging in e-commerce activities deploy security technologies such as firewalls and intrusion detection systems (IDS) to internally secure their information (Cavusoglu et al., 2002). Gallivan and Depledge (2003) pointed out that the use of various Internet technologies has the ability to enhance trust in e-commerce among SMEs. Bunduchi (2005) further stretched their findings and observed that level of IT functionalities used among SMEs influence the levels of trust. Soliman and Janz (2004) identified trust as a significant variable influencing the use of e-commerce among SMEs.

From the above summary of literature, it is evident that research related to trust issues in e-commerce among SMEs is still far from conclusive. Researchers have identified some of the technology related issues that need to be addressed in order to enhance levels of trust in e-commerce. However, no comprehensive study seems to have been conducted on technology issues in building trust in e-commerce among SMEs. The present paper makes a modest attempt in this direction. It empirically validates the relationship between various technology issues and the levels of trust in e-commerce among SMEs.

3. OBJECTIVE OF THE STUDY

The objective of the present paper is to investigate the relationship between the technology-related issues and levels of trust in e-commerce among SMEs. The technology issues in this regard include security, privacy and confidentiality, authentication and authorization, non-repudiation, and system performance and infrastructure (Kumar & Sareen, 2009). It is hypothesized that higher the level of assurance with regard to each of these issues, greater is the levels of trust in e-commerce. In view of this, the present paper aims at empirically testing the following hypotheses:

- **H1:** High level of Assurance regarding Security has the potential to influence trust in SMEs systems.
- **H2:** High level of Assurance regarding Privacy has the potential to influence trust in SMEs systems.
- **H3:** High level of Assurance regarding Authentication has the potential to influence trust in SMEs systems.
- **H4:** High level of Assurance regarding Non-Repudiation has the potential to influence trust in SMEs systems.
- **H5:** High level of Assurance regarding System Infrastructure and performance has the potential to influence trust in SMEs systems.

The technology issues and the related hypotheses to be investigated are represented in Figure 1.

The analysis presented in this paper is based on the practices followed by SMEs in order to address the trust-related technology issues.

4. SAMPLE SELECTION AND METHODOLOGY

The findings presented in this paper are primarily based on a part of the data collected through a survey of the companies that are using inter-

Figure 1. Trust and technology in e-commerce (adapted from Kumar & Sareen, 2009)

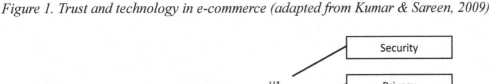
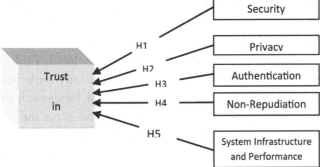

organizational systems for business relations. The survey was carried out in the year 2008. The data was collected with the help of a structured interview-guide administered during personal interviews. Out of one hundred six companies from cities like Delhi, Mumbai, Pune, Chennai, Hyderabad, Bangalore, Chandigarh, etc. that participated in the survey, thirty six (36) companies were SMEs. The present paper is based on the data collected from these 36 SMEs.

For the purpose of the present study, trust was taken as the dependent variable and independent variables related to the levels of assurance with respect to each of the technology issues. Each independent variable was measured on the basis of deployment of relevant technology tools and related practices that had the potential to address the concerned trust related technology issue. In order to determine the levels of assurance, sample companies were asked to indicate the deployed technology tools and their associated practices for their effective implementation. The technology tools and the associated practices used in this study are based on the set of technologies and benchmark practices identified by Kumar and Sareen (2009).

5. TECHNOLOGY TOOLS

Technology is the basic driver of e-commerce. As the cost of technology has fallen considerably due to both economies of scale and open-source initiatives, the cost of setting up and operating an infrastructure required for e-commerce is increasingly becoming affordable by SMEs. Although, a number of technology tools are available that influence the overall trustworthiness of the system, the present paper has taken the most relevant technologies among SMEs into consideration. These technology tools include Antivirus software solutions, Firewalls, IDS/IPS, VPN, SSL, PKI/ Digital Signatures, etc. Some of the other technologies

like IPSec, VLan, etc. are expensive technologies and may not be within the reach of SMEs.

The level of assurance of these technology tools is likely to be influenced by the extent to which the various technology practices are followed. A company was considered maintaining high level of assurance with respect to anti-virus solutions if it was following the practice of automatic scanning of data with latest and new versions of anti-virus solutions. A company was classified under high level of assurance in firewall technology, if it was found to have placed firewalls in all layers of the system architecture and created DMZ consisting of public servers only; it was documenting all the configurations and changes; and regularly monitoring the log files on daily basis. Similarly, a company maintaining high level of assurance with regard to IDS/IPS was the one that subscribed to latest IDS/IPS signatures placed them on all web repositories and regularly checked the IDS/IPS logs. With regard to VPN, the company was considered maintaining high level of assurance if it had installed an extranet based VPN with compulsory tunneling; the VPN installation was secure, scalable, flexible and able in preventing Denial of Service attacks. Table 1 presents the summary of the levels of assurance maintained by the sample SME companies with respect to each of the technology tools.

As can be observed from Table 1, only small proportion of sample companies was maintaining high levels of assurance in respect of these technology tools. One may explain this by arguing that SMEs are cost conscious and hesitate to install technology tools of higher costs. It is interesting to note that the significant proportion of the sample companies was maintaining medium level of assurance. These companies had deployed the technology tools but did not follow all the associated benchmark practices. This indicates that the cost is not the only reason for lower levels of assurance and perhaps lack of knowledge about the benchmark practices or their relevance

Table 1. Level of assurance with respect to deployed technology tools

Technology Tools	Deployed the Tool	Level of Assurance			
		High (3)	Medium(2)	Low (1)	Total
Anti-Virus	15(45%)	6 (17%)	9(25%)	21(58%)	36(100%)
Firewall	21(53%)	7(20%)	12(33%)	17(47%)	36(100%)
IDS/IPS	5(14%)	5(14%)	-	31(86%)	36(100%)
VPN	20(56%)	5(14%)	15(42%)	16(44%)	36(100%)
SSL	12 (33%)	12(33%)	24(67%)		36(100%)
PKI	18 (50%)	6(17%)	12(33%)	18(50%)	36(100%)

might be the other reasons for such low levels of assurance.

The respondents informally informed that 'Denial of Service' (DOS) attacks often give a 'lack of credibility' signal to their perspective trading partners that at times result in loss of revenue. However, most of the SMEs were aware of the vulnerability of their system environment but strongly believed that, in view of the smaller size of operation, no hacker would be interested in the information contained on their systems. Whereas some believed that the security attacks faced by them till now have not resulted in much loss of their confidential or important information. However, they seem to forget that even if any company does not lose information of value during a security attack, it loses time and money recovering the systems as well as potential cus-

tomers who were temporarily unable to access their systems. This might seriously impact their reputation, reliability and overall the trust of their trading partners on them.

As may be observed from Table 2, the aggregate level of assurance was higher in the case of firewall, VPN and PKI as compared to other technology tools. The need for enhancing the level of assurance in respect of each of these technologies is evident from this table. This may be achieved by deployment of new technology tools as well as adoption of suitable technology practices.

These technology tools play an important part in addressing the identified technology-related trust issues; hence an attempt has been made to relate the levels of assurance maintained by the sample companies regarding these tools with the technology-related trust issues.

Table 2. Level of assurance with respect to deployed technology tools: summary statistics

Technology Tools	Mean	Standard Deviation	T Value	Sig (2 tailed)
Anti Virus	1.58	0.770	12.338	0.000
Firewall	1.72	0.779	13.270	0.000
IDS/IPS	1.28	0.701	10.929	0.000
VPN	1.69	0.710	14.321	0.000
SSL	1.33	0.478	16.733	0.000
PKI	1.67	0.756	13.229	0.000

6. TECHNOLOGY ISSUES: LEVELS OF ASSURANCE

As pointed out earlier, the technology-related trust issues mainly relate to security, privacy, authentication non-repudiation, system infrastructure and performance and technology-related policies and procedures. Each of these issues can be addressed by adoption combination of the technology tools discussed above. Using the basis of categorization followed by Kumar and Sareen (2009), the sample companies were classified having high, medium and low levels of assurance with regard to trust-related technology issues.

As may be observed from Table 3, the mean level of assurance for each of the trust related technology issues was fairly low and did not exceed 1.7 in any of the issues. This highlights the need for paying attention to these issues. Table 4 presents the distribution of the respondents for different levels of assurance with regard to each of these issues.

7. RELATIONSHIP BETWEEN LEVELS OF TRUST AND TECHNOLOGY ISSUES

In order to understand the relationship between the levels of assurance of various technology issues and levels of trust, the respondents were asked to indicate the levels of trust of their e-commerce infrastructure as perceived by their trading partners on a 3 point Likert scale. This perceived level of trust was then related to levels of assurance with respect to each of the trust related technology issues. The findings relating to each of these issues are discussed in the following paragraphs.

7.1. Security

Security in e-commerce not only deals in accomplishing transaction security between the trading partners but also in making the environment less vulnerable to various security threats. Antivirus solutions, firewalls, IDS/IPS, VPN, SSL, and encryption mechanisms (using PKI) were identified

Table 3. Level of assurance in respect of technology- related trust issues: summary statistics

Technology Issues	Mean	Std. Deviation	t	Sig. (2 Tailed)
Security	1.69	0.710	14.321*	0.000
Privacy	1.58	0.732	12.979*	0.000
Authentication	1.61	0.688	14.055*	0.000
Non-Repudiation	1.14	0.351	19.483*	0.000
System Performance	1.67	0.676	14.790*	0.000

* df = 35

Table 4. Level of assurance in respect of trust-related technology issues

Technology Issues	High	Medium	Low	Total
Security	5(14%)	15(42%)	16(44%)	36(100%)
Privacy	5(14%)	11(31%)	20(55%)	36(100%)
Authentication	4(17%)	17(42.5%)	15(42.5%)	36(100%)
Non-Repudiation	-	5(14%)	31(86%)	36(100%)
System Infrastructure and Performance	4(12%)	16(44%)	16(44%)	36(100%)

for addressing the security related trust issue. For the purpose of determining the levels of assurance with respect to security, levels of assurance with respect to each technology tool was first converted into rating. The ratings of different technology tools deployed by the sample company were added to arrive at the overall ratings of the sample company. Based on these overall ratings, the sample companies were classified into three broad categories namely high, medium and low. The cutoff for this classification was based on careful observation and assessment of the data regarding practices.

As may be observed from Table 4, only 14% of the respondents were maintaining high level of assurance with respect to security. During the informal discussions, these companies informed that such levels helped in ensuring both their present and potential trading partners regarding the integrity of information. They also informed that often the trading partners enquired regarding the company's policies with respect to security of information and such high levels helped in enhancing the credibility and trust levels among them. This implies that SMEs need to follow appropriate practices for effective implementation of technologies to address the security related trust issue. Hence, the hypothesis H1 stating, "High level of Assurance regarding Security has the potential to influence trust in SMEs systems" could not be rejected.

7.2. Privacy

Privacy concerns usually follow security concerns. Most of the SMEs tend to be a part of supply chain and any leakage of confidential information regarding the business like, raw materials used etc. may be beneficial to the competitors. Hence, the information flow among the trading partners needs to be kept private and confidential. The trading parties require an assurance that their sensitive data will not be exposed to any unauthorized party, and that it will not be shared in any way without their express authorization. Lack of privacy can lead to breach of trust.

Based on the survey results, four technology tools were identified to address the privacy aspect of SMEs e-commerce environment. These technology tools include IDS/IPS, VPN, SSL, and PKI. Further, an overall level of assurance with regard to privacy issue of each of the sample company was also assessed. Since, most of the SMEs were a part of supply chain and thereby were aware of the importance of privacy. Hence, they had deployed most of the relevant policies and procedures to ensure the confidentiality of the transaction information. Hence, the hypothesis H2 stating, "High level of Assurance regarding Privacy has the potential to influence trust in SMEs systems" could not be rejected.

7.3. Authentication

Since the e-commerce transactions are conducted in a virtual environment without face-to-face interactions, one needs to be sure of the identity of the interacting party. Thus, the business interactions require authentication of the entities involved in the interactions. This issue attains greater importance in SMEs particularly due to fairly high value of transactions and major impact of loss on the revenue of the company. The SMEs need to ascertain that the party is correctly associated with who they are pretending to be and has the required authorization for the action. There is a need for a process that verifies whether an organization or an individual exists, has a name, and is entitled to use that name. Further, SMEs often become a part of supplier in the supply chain and the possibility of any long term association may be ruled out if proper authentication of the company is not assured with the trading partner. Technologies like VPN, SSL, PKI, Username and password id, etc. are widely used for authentication and authorization. Moreover, the use of digital certificates and USB smart card tokens are also becoming an important tool for authentication. For an effective authentication system, a number of practices need to be followed. There should be an active, strong authorization system, which should prompt the users to forcibly change the password on a regular basis. There should be variable level of authorization depending upon the sensitivity of information shared and it should be fully integrated into the enterprise-wide security policy. All authentication sessions should be monitored and tracked through the Log. Firm background checks done on employees with access to sensitive information and all inactive accounts should automatically be disabled.

As may be observed from Table 4, almost half of the respondents were maintaining medium to high level of assurance with regard to authentication. Since, many of the responding SMEs formed a part of supply chain and therefore it was found that they had laid relevant policies and procedures for active and strong authentication and authorization system using various technologies like VPN and USB smart card with digital certificates. However, many of the SMEs were conducting their e-commerce transactions in open virtual environment of e-Marketplaces and hence did not deploy relevant technologies for authentications. Since, high levels of assurance is related to higher trust levels in e-commerce, hence there is a need for the SMEs to incorporate the requisite practices to effectively address the authentication related trust issue. Hence, the hypothesis H3 stating "High level of Assurance regarding Authentication has the potential to influence trust in SMEs systems" could not be rejected.

7.4. Non-Repudiation

For online transactions of e-commerce, non-repudiation procedures ensure that transacting parties cannot disown the transaction or cannot subsequently repudiate (reject) a transaction by exploiting virtual nature of electronic transactions. To protect and ensure digital trust, various technologies exist like PKI using Digital Sig-

natures, which not only validate the sender, but also 'time stamp' the transaction, so it cannot be claimed subsequently that the transaction was not authorized or not carried out. The companies need to maintain audit logs for all the transactions conducted and the logs need to be archived to a secure log server. They must regularly perform audit checks on a daily, weekly or a predefined interval. The system should also provide the information about the type of event, date and time of event and the transaction information.

As may be observed from the Table 4, SMEs had not laid down relevant policies and procedures to address non-repudiation. The main reason behind this is that financial transactions were hardly carried through online medium by SMEs. Many of the SMEs stated that the financial transaction of their e-commerce activity was often conducted through bank drafts or cheques. Hence, the non-repudiation issue relating to financial transactions was not relevant. Yet, there had been various disputes regarding non-repudiation, particularly relating to other transaction information. Hence, now they have realized the need for their systems to provide convincing evidence of the other party's participation in a protocol session. Maintaining audit logs for all the transactions conducted, time stamping the transactions, regularly performing audit checks on a daily, weekly or a predefined interval are some of the practices that can help SME address the issue of non-repudiation. Hence, the hypothesis H4 stating "High level of Assurance regarding Non-Repudiation has the potential to influence trust in SMEs systems" could not be rejected.

7.5. System Infrastructure and Performance

The infrastructure is the foundation on which the building of e-commerce applications is built. If the infrastructure (both hardware and software) is unable to meet the demands of the environment, then the e-commerce applications are likely to suffer. To be effective in e-commerce, an enterprise must make a significant investment in hardware and application solution for the critical e-business areas. Various application solutions involve a different set of requirements, technologies and complexities, and there is a need for high degree of maintenance in order to ensure a high optimal performance and information availability. These types of enterprise applications depend on a complex mix of distributed, heterogeneous technologies running across multiple technology layers including both hardware and software. Failure to do so will create hurdles in the smooth functioning of the systems and may on accessions result in non-availability of the e-commerce system to the trading partners. This may adversely affect the trust levels in e-commerce and create doubts regarding the credibility and technical competence of the organization/trading partner.

The hardware requirements include having an application/web server, a database server, enterprise servers, application servers, networking and security equipments like routers, load balancers firewalls, etc. The software requirements include operating system with networking features, web authoring tools, database management system, programming platforms like Java or Active X, etc. or any other software required for the application. These hardware and software elements need to be properly integrated in a unified manner so as to meet the e-commerce demands and thereby build trust among the trading partners. The companies should use different servers like data server, file server web server etc with specific functions so as to avoid cluttering. The servers should be adequately bench marked for improved efficiency and proper and effective clustering of servers should be done The companies must develop the policy of installing various updation patches to keep pace with the latest in technology and also to gear the system against any latest security threat in the market. These patches are available freely to licensed software purchaser (subscribed).

As may be observed from Table 4, almost half of the SMEs had not deployed relevant infrastructure for their business activities. These respondents were conducting their e-commerce activities either through any e-Marketplace or through open virtual environment of Internet. Although these respondents realized the need that proper infrastructure for such activities may give a boost to their revenue but high IT costs prevented them for such an investment. The SMEs maintaining medium to high level of assurance asserted that such an environment had resulted in enhancing their credibility among their trading partners and have perceived revenue benefits also. This implies that maintaining high level of assurance with regard to system performance helps in enhancing levels of trust and SMEs need to take requisite steps in that direction. Hence, the hypothesis H5 stating "High level of Assurance regarding System Infrastructure and performance has the potential to influence trust in SMEs systems" could not be rejected.

8. RELATIONSHIP BETWEEN LEVELS OF TRUST AND TECHNOLOGY-RELATED TRUST ISSUES

The data presented in Table 4 and Table 5 and the subsequent analysis presented in the earlier sections help to accept all the proposed hypotheses. However, in order to examine the relationship between the level of trust in the e-commerce infrastructure and the level of assurance for the technology related trust issues, regression analysis was carried out. The respondents were asked to ascertain the level of trust as perceived by their trading partner on a 3-point Likert Scale. This level of trust was regressed with the levels of assurance in respect of the technology-related trust issues (as ascertained on the basis of practices relating to effective deployment and implementation of

Table 5. Level of trust and levels of assurance in respect of technology-related issues

Technology Issues / Trust	High	Medium	Low	Total
Security				
High levels of trust	4	-	-	4
Medium levels of trust	1	9	-	10
Low levels of trust	-	6	16	22
Total	**5**	**15**	**16**	**36**
Privacy				
High levels of trust	4	1	-	4
Medium levels of trust	-	8	3	10
Low levels of trust	-	1	19	22
Total				**36**
Authentication				
High levels of trust	4	-	-	4
Medium levels of trust	-	10	6	10
Low levels of trust	-	0	16	22
Total	**4**	**10**	**22**	**36**
Non-Repudiation				
High levels of trust				4
Medium levels of trust				10
Low levels of trust				22
Total				36
System Infrastructure and Performance				
High levels of trust	4	-	-	4
Medium levels of trust	-	10	6	10
Low levels of trust	-	6	10	22
Total	**4**	**16**	**16**	**36**

Note: **Security:** χ^2 =43.069 (78% < 5) at 0.00 (2 sided); Phi = 1.094 at 0.00; Cramer's V = 0.773 at 0.00; Kendall tau = 0.782 at 0.00 and Kappa = 0.674 at 0.00;

Privacy: χ^2 =45.521 (68% < 5) at 0.00 (2 sided); Phi = 1.124 at 0.00; Cramer's V = 0.795 at 0.00; Kendall tau = 0.817 at 0.00 and Kappa = 0.752 at 0.00;

Authentication: χ^2 =57.039 (68% < 5) at 0.00 (2 sided); Phi = 1.259 at 0.00; Cramer's V = 0.890 at 0.00; Kendall tau = 0.847 at 0.00 and Gamma = 0.806 at 0.00;

Non-Repudiation: χ^2 =28.475 (67% < 5) at 0.00 (2 sided); Phi = 0.889 at 0.00; Cramer's V = 0.889 at 0.00; Kendall tau = 0.629 at 0.00;

System Performance: χ^2 =52.364 (78% < 5) at 0.00 (2 sided); Phi = 1.206 at 0.00; Cramer's V = 0.853 at 0.00; Kendall tau = 0.788 at 0.00 and Kappa = 0.719 at 0.00;

technology tools in addressing). The adjusted R^2 obtained was 78%, indicating fairly high degree of relationship between the level of trust and the levels of assurance in respect of different technology related trust issues.

The results depicted in Table 6 provide evidence in support of four of the five hypotheses postulated earlier, indicating that these technology-related trust issues have significant influence on level of trust. The regression results eliminated the significant role of non-repudiation in influenc-

Table 6. Impact of technology-related trust issues on levels of trust: correlation results

Technology Related Issues	Security	Privacy	Authentication	Non-Repudiation	System Performance	Trust
Security	1.0					
Privacy	0.793*	1.0				
Authentication	0.916*	0.834*	1.0			
Non-Repudiation	0.655*	0.671*	0.608*	1.0		
System Performance	0.985*	0.768*	0.925*	0.596*	1.0	
Trust	0.801*	0.834*	0.853*	0.652*	0.797*	1.0

*Correlation is significant at the 0.01 level (2 tailed)

ing the levels of trust. The results indicated the relatively greater significance of Security, Privacy and Authentication related trust issue in determining the levels of trust in that order. Thus, the SMEs need to follow relevant practices in order to maintain high level of assurance regarding these technology-related trust issues.

9. FINDINGS AND LIMITATIONS

An important contribution of this paper is in terms of validating the 'Trust and Technology' model proposed by Kumar and Sareen (2009) in context of SMEs. The findings indicate that more than forty percent of the SMEs were maintaining low level of assurance with regards to the Security, privacy, authentication and system infrastructure and performance related trust issues. However, this percentage was fairly high (83%) in the case non-repudiation related trust issue. The low level of assurance was also observed in deployment and implementation of relevant technologies by fairly large proportion of the sample SMEs. Interestingly, many of the SMEs that made investment in the deployment of various technologies but had failed to put in place appropriate policies and procedures for effective implementation of them. This led to falling level of assurance with regards to the technology tools and thereby failing to effectively address the emerging technology-related trust is-

sue. The relationship between the levels of trust and technology-related trust issues like security, privacy, authentication and system infrastructure and performance was found to be highly significant. This highlights the need for attaining high level of assurance with regard to these issues by deploying and effectively implementing the relevant technologies in building the e-commerce infrastructure by SMEs. The evidence offered in this paper points to the deficiency in the effective implementation of various technologies by SMEs that have the potential to enhance levels of trust in B2B e-commerce.

It is, therefore, suggested that SMEs should make deliberate attempts to address the technology-related trust issues in order to ensure that the adoption of e-commerce helps in the realization of potential benefits. At times, in view of the resource constraints, some of the technologies are either not deployed or not effectively implemented by SMEs. Collaboration and sharing of resources is perhaps the answer to such a problem. SMEs need to collaborate among themselves and share infrastructure and expertise (IT skills) in order to ensure that higher levels of trust are maintained. Chambers of commerce and other trade associations have a role to play in bringing about such collaborations.

Like any other study of this kind, this study also suffers a number of limitations. The main limitation of this paper can be imputed to the research's coverage. The survey should have been distributed to a larger population, giving a more accurate representation of the participant's perceptions of trust in SMEs systems. This limits the generaliability of our results. Secondly, a potential limitation also comes from the some answers sought from the data. The empirical study was based on the perceived level of trust as indicated by the respondents as perceived by their trading partners. This may bias the results if the respondents have not given a true reflection of their trading partner's perceptions. Ideally, the trading partners of the SMEs should have been sought to answer their satisfaction levels. However, in spite of the limitation the study raises some of the important technology-related trust issues that deserve attention of SMEs.

REFERENCES

Alam, S. S., Ishak, N. A., & Khatibi, A. (2008). The effects of perceived characteristics on ICT adoption in SMEs in Malaysia. In *Proceedings of the 5th Global Conference on SMEs and Industrial Development in Asian Countries*.

Alexander, N., & Colgate, M. (2000). Retail financial services: Transaction to relationship marketing. *European Journal of Marketing, 34*(8), 938–953. doi:10.1108/03090560010331432

Bakos, J. Y. (1991). Information links and electronic marketplaces: The role of inter-organizational information systems in vertical markets. *Journal of Management Information Systems, 8*(2), 31–52.

Bunduchi, R. (2005). Business relationships in Internet-based electronic markets: The role of goodwill trust and transaction costs. *Information Systems Journal, 15*, 321–341. doi:10.1111/j.1365-2575.2005.00199.x

Cairncross, F. (1997). *The death of distance*. Boston, MA: Harvard Business School Press.

Carson, D. (1990). Some exploratory models for assessing small firms marketing performance (a qualitative approach). *European Journal of Marketing, 24*(11), 8–51. doi:10.1108/03090569010006056

Cavsoglu, H. (2009). Configuration of and interaction between information security technologies: The case of firewalls and intrusion detection systems. *Information Systems Research, 20*(2), 198–217. doi:10.1287/isre.1080.0180

Cheskin and Studio Archetype. (1999). *The Cheskin research and studio archetype/Sapient e-commerce trust study*. Retrieved from http://www.studioarchetype.com/ cheskin/html/phase1.html

Choi, S., Stahl, D. O., & Whinston, A. (1997). *The economics of electronic commerce: The essential economics of doing business in the electronic marketplace*. Indianapolis, IN: Macmillan.

Cox, J. (1999). *Trust, reciprocity, and other-regarding preferences of individuals and groups*. Tucson, AZ: University of Arizona.

Daniel, T. A., & McInerney, M. L. (2005). E-commerce and the "reluctant" small business owner: SME e-commerce and customer loyalty revisited how technology is changing the business model for small and medium-sized enterprises (SMEs). *International Journal of Applied Management and Technology, 3*, 183–206.

Deelmann, T., & Loos, P. (2002). Trust economy: Aspects of reputation and trust building for SMEs in e-business. In *Proceedings of the Eighth American Conference on Information Systems* (pp. 2213-2221).

Doney, M., & Cannon, P. (1997). An examination of the nature of trust in buyer-seller relationship. *Journal of Marketing, 61*(2), 35–51. doi:10.2307/1251829

Elia, E., Lefebvre, L., & Lefebvre, E. (2007). Focus of electronic commerce initiatives and related benefits in manufacturing SMEs. *Journal of Information Systems and E-Business Management, 5*, 1–23. doi:10.1007/s10257-006-0035-8

Gallivan, M. J., & Depledge, G. (2003). Trust, control and the role of interorganizational systems in electronic partnerships. *Information Systems Journal*, *13*, 159–190. doi:10.1046/j.1365-2575.2003.00146.x

Gengatharen, D., & Standing, C. (2005). A framework to assess the factors affecting success or failure of the implementation of government supported regional e-marketplaces for SMEs. *European Journal of Information Systems*, *14*, 417–433. doi:10.1057/palgrave.ejis.3000551

Grandon, E., & Pearson, J. M. (2004). E-commerce adoption: Perceptions of managers/owners of small and medium sized firms in Chile. *Communications of the Association for Information Systems*, *13*, 81–102.

Haiwook, C. (2001). The effects of inter-organisational information systems infrastructure on electronic cooperation: An investigation of the "move to the middle" (Doctoral dissertation, Morehead State University). *Proquest Digital Dissertations.* Retrieved from http://www.lib.umi.com/ dissertations

Hawes, J., Kenneth, E., & Swan, J. (1989). Trust earning perceptions of sellers and buyers. *Journal of Personal Selling & Sales Management*, *9*(1), 1–8.

Head, M. M., Yuan, Y., & Archer, N. (2001, January). Building trust in e-commerce: A theoretical framework. In *Proceedings of the Second World Congress on the Management of Electronic Commerce.*

Henderson, J. C. (1990). Plugging into strategic partnerships: The critical IS connection. *Sloan Management Review*, 7–18.

Hodges, M. (1997). Building a bond of trust. *Technology Review*, *100*(6), 26–27.

Hoffman, D. L., Novak, T. P., & Peralta, M. (1999). Building consumer trust on-line. *Communications of the ACM*, *42*(4), 80–84. doi:10.1145/299157.299175

IDA. (2000). *A proposed framework on building trust and confidence in electronic commerce.* Retrieved from http://unpan1.un.org/intradoc/ groups/public/ documents/apcity/unpan004855. pdf

Jennex, M. E. (2003). UNCTAD and e-commerce success. *Electronic Journal on Information Systems in Developing Countries*, *11*(11), 1–7.

Jutla, D., Bodorik, P., & Dhaliwal, J. (2002). Supporting the e-business readiness of small and medium-sized enterprises: Approaches and metrics. *Internet Research: Electronic Networking Applications and Policy*, *12*(2), 139–164. doi:10.1108/10662240210422512

Kaynak, E., Tatoglu, E., & Kula, V. (2005). An analysis of the factors affecting the adoption of electronic commerce by SMEs: Evidence from an emerging market. *International Marketing Review*, *22*(6), 623–640. doi:10.1108/02651330510630258

Killikanya, C. (2000). E-Commerce: Internet slow to make inroads. *Bangkok Post: Mid-year. Economic Review (Federal Reserve Bank of Atlanta)*, 32–35.

Korgaonkar, P., & O'Leary, B. (2006). Management, market, and financial factors separating winners and losers in e-business. *Journal of Computer-Mediated Communication*, *11*(4). doi:10.1111/j.1083-6101.2006.00311.x

Kumar, M., & Sareen, M. (2009). Trust and technology in inter-organizational business relations. *International Journal of Telecommunications and Human Development*, *1*(4), 40–57. doi:10.4018/ jicthd.2009091504

Laudon, K., & Traver, C. (2002). *E-Commerce: Business, technology, society*. Reading, MA: Addison-Wesley.

Levenburg, N., & Klein, H. (2006). Delivering customer services online: Identifying best practices of medium-sized enterprises. *Information Systems Journal, 16*, 135–147. doi:10.1111/j.1365-2575.2006.00212.x

Levin, C. (2000). *Web dropouts: Concerns about online privacy send some consumers off-line*. Retrieved from http://www.zdnet.com/

Macgregor, R., & Vrazlaic, L. (2006). Electronic business in small businesses: A global perspective. In Al-Qirim, N. (Ed.), *Global electronic business research: Opportunities and directions*. Hershey, PA: IGI Global.

Mahadevan, B., & Venkatesh, N. S. (2000). A framework for building on-line trust for business to business e-commerce. In *Proceedings of the IT Asia Millennium Conference*, Bombay, India.

Marchany, R. C., & Tront, J. G. (2002). E-commerce security issues. In *Proceedings of the 35th Hawaii International Conference on System Sciences*.

Mason, C., Castleman, T., & Parker, C. (2008). Systems factors influencing SME knowledge sharing online. In *Proceedings of the 19th Australasian Conference on Information Systems* (pp. 617-628).

Mayer, R. C., Davis, J. H., & Schoorman, F. D. (1995). An integrative model of organizational trust. *Academy of Management Review, 20*(3), 709–734.

Milne, G. R., & Boza, M. (1999). Trust and concern in consumers' perceptions of marketing information management practices. *Journal of Interactive Marketing, 13*(1), 5–24. doi:10.1002/(SICI)1520-6653(199924)13:1<5::AID-DIR2>3.0.CO;2-9

Mirchandani, A. A., & Motwani, J. (2001). Understanding small business electronic commerce adoption: An empirical analysis. *Journal of Computer Information Systems*, 70–73.

Moor, J. (1985). What is computer ethics? *Metaphilosophy, 16*(4). doi:10.1111/j.1467-9973.1985.tb00173.x

Moorman, C., Deshpande, R., & Zaltman, G. (1993). Factors affecting trust in market research relationships. *Journal of Marketing, 57*, 81–101. doi:10.2307/1252059

Ngai, E., & Wat, F. (2002). A literature review and classification of electronic commerce research. *Information & Management, 39*(5), 415–429. doi:10.1016/S0378-7206(01)00107-0

NOIE. (2002). *E-Commerce for small business*. Parkes, Australia: National Office for the Information Economy.

Patton, M. A., & Jøsang, A. (2004). Technologies for trust in electronic commerce. *Electronic Commerce Research, 4*(1), 9–21. doi:10.1023/B:ELEC.0000009279.89570.27

Payne, J. (2003). *E-Commerce readiness for SMEs in developing countries: A guide for development professionals*. Washington, DC: Learn Link.

Rashid, M. A., & Al-Qirim, N. A. (2001). E-Commerce technology adoption framework by New Zealand small to medium enterprises. *Research Letters Information Mathematical Science, 2*(1), 63–70.

Ratnasingham, P., & Klein, S. (2001). Perceived benefits of inter-organizational trust in ecommerce participation: A case study in the telecommunication industry. In *Proceedings of the Seventh Americas Conference on Information Systems*, Boston, MA (pp. 769-780).

Roy, M. C., Dewit, O., & Aubert, B. A. (2001). The impact of interface usability on trust in web retailers. *Internet Research: Electronic Networking Applications and Policy, 11*(5), 388–398. doi:10.1108/10662240110410165

Ruth, Z. (2008). *E-commerce and e-business.* Retrieved from http://www.bentley.edu/newsevents/ books.cfm

Sanayei, A., Rashidkabol, M., & Salehniai, M. (2008). A model of adoption of electronic commerce by small and medium-sized enterprises. In *Proceedings of the 3rd International Conference on E-Commerce with Focus on Developing Countries.*

Schurr, P. H., & Ozanne, J. L. (1985, March). Influences on exchange processes: buyers' preconceptions of a seller's trustworthiness and bargaining toughness. *The Journal of Consumer Research, 11*, 939–953. doi:10.1086/209028

Stockdale, R., & Standing, C. (2006). A classification model to support SME economic adoption initiatives. *Journal of Small Business and Enterprise Development, 13*(2), 381–394. doi:10.1108/14626000610680262

Teo, H. H., Wei, K. K., & Benbasat, I. (2003). Predicting intention to adopt interorganizational linkages: An institutional perspective. *Management Information Systems Quarterly, 27*, 19–49.

Thatcher, S. M. B., Foster, W., & Zhu, L. (2006). E-commerce adoption decisions in Taiwan: The interaction of culture and other institutional factors. *Electronic Commerce Research and Applications, 5*, 92–104. doi:10.1016/j.elerap.2005.10.005

UNCTAD. (2002). *e-Commerce and development report.* New York, NY: United Nations Conference on Trade and Development.

Westin, A., & Maurici, D. (1998). *E-commerce and privacy: What net users want.* Harrisburg, PA: Price Waterhouse Coopers.

Whiteley, D. (2000). *E-Commerce: Strategy, technologies and applications.* New York, NY: McGraw-Hill.

Ziad, H., Mansoor, M., & Nawafleh, A. (2009). Electronic commerce adoption barriers in small and medium sized enterprises (SMEs) in developing countries: The case of Libya. *IBIMA Business Review, 2*.

This work was previously published in the International Journal of Information Communication Technologies and Human Development, Volume 3, Issue 4, edited by Susheel Chhabra and Hakikur Rahman, pp. 31-46, copyright 2011 by IGI Publishing (an imprint of IGI Global).

Chapter 16
A Quasi-Experiment on Computer Multimedia Integration into AIDS Education:
A Study of Four Senior High Schools in Chennai, India

Chia-Wen Tsai
Ming Chuan University, Taiwan

Pei-Di Shen
Ming Chuan University, Taiwan

Yen-Ting Lin
Ming Chuan University, Taiwan

ABSTRACT

India is the third most HIV (Human Immunodeficiency Virus) /AIDS (Acquired Immune Deficiency Syndrome) -infected country in the world. The behavior of adolescents puts them at an increased risk for HIV and other STIs (Sexually Transmitted Infections). Additionally, their knowledge about HIV/AIDS is often inadequate. A quasi experiment was designed to be conducted at four high schools with a random sampling of 451 students. Two high schools used computers and other multimedia methods to promote AIDS education while two other schools used traditional lectures. Each school had two class-hours of AIDS education. Findings determined a gap in knowledge, attitude and behavior about HIV/AIDS issues within these different groups. The implications for current teaching approaches are discussed in this study.

DOI: 10.4018/978-1-4666-1957-9.ch016

INTRODUCTION

Globally, HIV (Human Immunodeficiency Virus) continues to exact a substantial toll on the health and well-being of millions, causing considerable suffering, morbidity, and death (DiClemente & Crosby, 2009). Asia, consisting of 60% of people in the world, is second only to sub-Saharan Africa in terms of the number of people living with HIV. India accounts for roughly half of Asia's HIV prevalence. India is one of the largest and most populated countries in the world, with over one billion inhabitants. Of this number, it's estimated that around 2.4 million people are currently living with HIV (UNAIDS, 2009). It is now recognized that, in India, AIDS (Acquired Immune Deficiency Syndrome) constitutes a humanitarian crisis of immense proportions.

Per a United Nations Development Programme (UNDP) 2010 report, India had 2.39 million people living with HIV at the end of 2009, up from 2.27 million in 2008. Adult prevalence also rose from 0.29% in 2008 to 0.31% in 2009 (Sharma, 2010). While this percentage may seem low, because India's population is so large, it places India third in the world of the terms of the number of people who are HIV infected.

Throughout 1990s, it was clear that even individual states and cities had some epidemics, but in the same decade HIV had spread to the general population. Increasingly, cases of HIV infection were observed among people that had earlier been seen as 'low-risk', such as housewives and high-ranking members of society (Baria, Menon, Nagchoudhury, David, & Menon, 1997). Furthermore, Nath (1998) indicates "HIV infection is now common in India; exactly what the prevalence is, is not really known, but it can be stated without any fear of being wrong that infection is widespread…It is spreading rapidly into those segments that society in India does not recognize as being at risk. AIDS is coming out of the closet."

The India Government subsequently set up an AIDS society, which aimed to focus on HIV prevention initiatives. A safe-sex campaign was launched, encouraging condom use and attacking the stigma and ignorance associated with HIV. In 2007, HIV prevalence among antenatal clinic attendees was 0.25%. HIV prevalence among injecting drug users was 16.8%, third highest out of all reporting states. HIV prevalence among men who have sex with men and female sex workers was 6.6% and 4.68% respectively.

For understanding the vast array of factors associated with Indian adolescents' HIV risk behavior and subsequent intervention, carefully calibrated programs of research that also engender community support are needed (DiClemente, Crosby, & Salazar, 2007). In this regard, it is necessary to educate people and students in India about HIV prevalence and to raise their awareness through HIV/AIDS education.

The International Problems of HIV/AIDS

HIV infections are not limited to India by any means, and a significant percentage of youth are affected worldwide. Chifunyise, Benoyb, and Mukiibi (2002) pointed out that twenty-five percent of all global HIV infections occur among people between the ages of 15 and 24 years, with new infections among some subgroups reaching record proportions. Africa has been disproportionately impacted by HIV; almost three quarters of all youth living with HIV/AIDS reside there, with HIV the leading cause of death among adolescents/young adults 15 to 29 years old.

Moreover, Zimbabwe is facing a serious AIDS epidemic. In the year 2000, 25% of adults were estimated to be HIV infected (UNAIDS, 2000). Young people are at a high risk of HIV infection because of their frequency of changing sexual partners.

In addition, Malawi has a serious rate of HIV infection. According to the Malawi National AIDS

Commission, there were 700,000 HIV/AIDS cases in Malawi in 2003. The HIV prevalence rate of adult Malawians was about 15%. Sub-Saharan Africa has just over 10% of the world's population, but is home to more than 60% of all people living with HIV, about 25.8 million (Kuo, 2006).

EDUCATION AS A SOLUTION

The prospect of HIV infection remains one of the most significant public health risks facing adolescents. Most of those infected might pass away between 25 and 35 years of age, which means they might have been infected during their high school years (Lee, 2003). Although India is the third most HIV-infected country, each state promotes health care regulations through their individual ministries. This might make the situation worse as there is no nation-wide education effort.

From a nationwide investigation between 1988 and 1995 in the United States, there was found to be a peak of 33% of male students who engaged in pre-marital sexual behavior, but through AIDS education and sex education, the rate decreased to 27%, which shows the impact of the education campaign (Haffner, 1996). This research shows that under the instruction of teaching students not to have sex before marriage, a positive attitude toward sex could make them reduce the number of sex partners, and use condoms, which indicates that HIV/AIDS education and sex education make a positive impact and it's worthwhile to integrate this content into high school instruction (Haffner, 1996). Another study showed that AIDS and sex education implemented during students' teenage years could lead them to have correct sexual knowledge and make the right decisions about sexual behavior (Denny, Young, Rausch, & Spear, 2002; Blinn-Pike, 1996). In the former study, after 18 months, the research results indicated that AIDS and sex education teach students sex can wait and help them toward positive knowledge, attitude, and behavior.

Aside from traditional education, how can the word be spread efficiently? Integrating information technology into instruction is one of the most popular strategies of smart teaching. Applying computer and Internet to a suitable topic, with the right timing and combination of subjects, can make teaching more interactive, more fun and more informative (Hsu, 2002). Through that type of stimulation, students may more easily change their behavior (Flora, 1988). Integrating information technology into instruction is commonly applied to many kinds of health and hygiene education such as diabetes, smoking, and sexual education (Lieberman, 1997). Moreover, Thomas, Cahill, and Santilli (1997) designed and developed an interactive CD-ROM game as learning material, which is shown to be beneficial and have positive impact on AIDS education. In this regard, we integrated computers and multimedia into PowerPoint slides and digital videos to help students learn about AIDS and HIV prevention in this study.

COMPUTER MULTIMEDIA INTEGRATION

There has been a lot of research exploring how to use technology to teach within the context of specific content areas. Mayer (2001) introduced his theory on designing effective multimedia learning environments which is based on Dual Coding, Active Processing and Limited Capacity theories, wherein learners perceive external information, select relevant data and organize them into meaningful information, and integrate this information with their prior knowledge.

Computer and multimedia need the same degree of interactivity that a school exercise book or a laboratory experiment has in order to remain a creditable learning medium. Educationists have shown that certain forms of learning become easier, and are retained more permanently if the learner participates in some way with the learning material.

In India, the use of computers in schools for educational purposes began very late (Aavishkar, 2002). Nowadays, we find every good school is equipped with computers for educating children. Teachers and students can use computers in many ways, for teaching the use of computers, assessing various data banks, viewing films, listening to music and browsing the Internet. But in the information literacy varies greatly from state to state in India, so in this study the researchers use basic computer multimedia integration in AIDS education.

RESEARCH GOALS

Researchers in this study conducted a quasi-experiment in four high schools with a random sampling of 451 students. In this study, we address two research questions. In this context, students are provided with an informative traditional lecture or an interactive computer multimedia lesson based on the same AIDS education material. By answering questions in three dimensions on an HIV/AIDS questionnaire as pretest and posttest survey, the researchers investigated the following:

1. Will computer multimedia involvement in AIDS education be associated with better, more reproducible AIDS knowledge, attitude, and behavior than that resulting from tradition lectures?
2. If there is a difference, will it vary by students' gender?

EMPIRICAL STUDY

Research Design

In the study, researchers were trained for 20 hours by the HIV/AIDS Foundation before the study

commenced. During the research stage, researchers were randomly sampling potential research subjects from four different secondary high schools in Chennai, India. After that, researchers divided subjects into four specific groups, which were (1) integrated computer multimedia in an all female school (PG), (2) integrated computer multimedia in a mixed gender school (PM), (3) traditional lecture in an all female school (TG), and (4) traditional lecture in a mixed gender school (TM). Before the experimental classes, students completed a questionnaire as a pretest. Researchers gave a two-hour-long class using the designed instruction as the experimental class. After six weeks, the research subjects were gathered together and the same questionnaire was administered as a posttest. The detailed research procedure is shown in Figure 1.

Subjects

Subjects were a random sample of students from each of four high schools with 132 (29.3%) male and 319 (70.7%) female students, a total of 451 subjects, in Chennai, India. Their ages are 17 (318 students, 70.5%) and 18 (133 students, 29.5%). There were 364 students (80.7%) who had heard of HIV/AIDS before the experiment, while others reported not knowing about HIV/AIDS beforehand. In order to test students' knowledge, attitude and behavior and students' gender effect from the computer multimedia integrated and traditional lecture setting, the researchers set up four different groups of subjects in the study.

Class Specifications

A two-hour-long class was delivered to both female and mixed gender high school students. Two types of experimental class were delivered, consisting of a teacher-centered, paper-based traditional lecture to the control groups and computer multimedia lesson with graphics, text, video, music, animation, sound, music and well-designed PowerPoint slides

Figure 1. The flow chart of the study

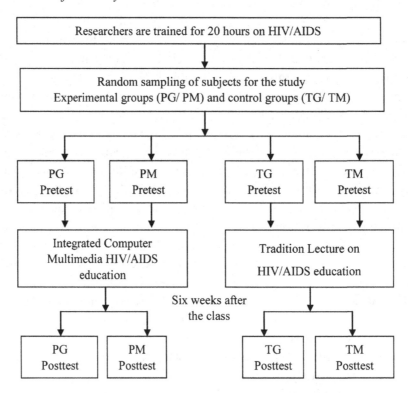

to the experimental groups. After training by the HIV/AIDS Foundation, the researchers created and designed the teaching material and content based on AIDS teaching instructions; the materials were approved by the Foundation instructor.

The experimental and control groups were taught based on the same content, including: introduction to the project, introduction to instructors, how HIV/AIDS affects the world, numbers and statistics in recent years, most infected countries, and how HIV is transmitted for the first hour; then the following hour comprised of interaction on taboos and the misery of HIV/AIDS. In this research, experimental lessons viewed integrated short video clips about how HIV infects the world, how HIV is transmitted, and caring for AIDS patients. Meanwhile, students from the control groups were taught the same content printed on papers, without video clips. Through the classes, the researchers excepted students could gain positive sexual behavior concepts, learn HIV/AIDS

knowledge, attitude and behavior leading toward awareness and positive attitudes, and this would lead to positive impact on society.

Experimental Design

Students were divided into four groups according to their gender and the class setting: (a) mixed gender with computer multimedia: 57 male students and 55 female students (112 students, 24.8%) (PM); (b) female students with computer multimedia: 109 female students (24.2%) (PG); (c) mixed gender with traditional lecture: 75 male students and 60 female students (135 students, 29.9%) (TM); (d) female students with traditional lecture: 95 female students (21.2%) (TG). In this study, PM and PG were experimental groups, while TM and TG were control groups. Students completed a questionnaire about HIV/AIDS knowledge, attitude, and behavior as a pretest, and then completed the same questionnaire six weeks after the experimental class as a posttest. The detailed subject and group numbers in the study are shown in Table 1.

Measurement

In this study, subjects were tested on their extended and long-lasting learning of HIV/AIDS knowledge, attitude, and behavior following the use of different teaching methods. Researchers adopted the questionnaire administered from Robertson (1999) to measure students' HIV/AIDS knowledge, attitude, and behavior. The questionnaire was designed with 37 questions using a Likert five-point scale and included items about students' gender, and age and sexual experiences. Any item which used professional or difficult words was replaced by simple words without changing its meaning (e.g., 'homosexuality' was changed to 'same sex behavior' or 'gay'). Also there was no time limit given, but the average time that students took to complete the instrument was 15~20 minutes. Participants anonymously completed the items on this instrument tailored to the outcome objectives of the project. The administration was pretest and posttest after six weeks; schools kept the students' name lists instead of the researchers. Students were tested with the same survey in the same conditions at both administrations. The questionnaire results are shown with figures and explanations in the following section.

RESULTS

In this study, students were asked about their knowledge, attitude, and behavior toward to HIV/AIDS at the beginning of the experiment and six weeks after. The pretest and posttest results are shown in Table 2. In this study, it is found that class setting and class setting with gender difference could result in significant improvement. In terms of class setting, the mean score at the pretest of computer multimedia integration into HIV/AIDS education at the all female school (PG group) is 101.98 and the posttest mean is 166.88, for a difference of 64.9 (Table 2). For students who joined the computer multimedia integrated instruction at the mixed gender school (PM group), the mean pretest score is 90.95, while the mean score at the posttest is 166.95, for a difference of 76.00. The all female class who joined the traditional lecture (TG group) scored a mean of 89.40 on the pretest, and 163.73 at the posttest, so the difference between pretest and posttest is 74.33. For the mixed gender group in traditional lecture (TM group), the mean score at the pretest is 97.11, with posttest at 159.48, and a difference of 62.37. From the class setting perspective, each setting shows significant difference between pretest and posttest.

Moreover, the results presented in Table 3 show significant difference in improved scores of students who received instruction integrating computers and multimedia (70.52) compared with those without computers and multimedia (67.31)

Table 1. Subject numbers in the study

Test Type		Pretest		Posttest	
Gender		**M**	**F**	**M**	**F**
Experimental Groups with Computer Multimedia	PG	0	109	0	109
	PM	57	55	57	55
Control Groups with Traditional Lecture	TG	0	95	0	95
	TM	75	60	75	60

F = female

M = male

Table 2. Difference between pretest and posttest among differing class settings in this study

Class Setting	Mean Pretest	Mean Posttest	Mean Difference	Sig.
PG	101.98	166.88	64.90	.000**
PM	90.95	166.95	76.00	.000**
TG	89.40	163.73	74.33	.000**
TM	97.11	159.48	62.37	.000**

*p<0.05, **p<0.01
PG=Computer Multimedia Integrated into Instruction at All Female School
PM=Computer Multimedia Integrated into Instruction at Mixed Gender School
TG=Traditional Lecture at All Female School
TM=Traditional Lecture at Mixed Gender School

($p = 0.018$). Therefore, it could be concluded that the effects of the instruction integrating computers and multimedia were positive, and higher than those without, in AIDS Education.

In this study, the mean score at the pretest for all female subjects is 96.74 (full score is 185), while that for male subjects is 91.25 (Table 4). At the posttest, the mean score of female participants is 164.55 and 162.72 for male subjects. In the Table 5, it is shown that male subjects had significantly better improvement (70.273) than female subjects (68.210) ($p = 0.014$).

From a gender perspective, mixed gender students have no significant difference of understanding HIV/AIDS knowledge, attitude, and behavior than male students. However, in Table 6 and Table 7, it is found that class setting and

class setting with gender difference could result in significant improvement. Moreover, in terms of class setting, the mean score at the pretest of computer multimedia integration into HIV/AIDS education at the all female school (PG group) is 101.98 and the posttest mean is 166.88, for a difference of 64.9 (Table 6). For students who joined the computer multimedia integrated instruction at the mixed gender school (PM group), the mean pretest score is 90.95, while the mean score at the posttest is 166.95, for a difference of 76.00. The all female class who joined the traditional lecture (TG group) scored a mean of 89.40 on the pretest, and 163.73 at the posttest, and the difference between pretest and posttest is 74.33. For the mixed gender group in traditional lecture (TM group), the mean score at the pretest is 97.11, with

Table 3. Comparison of scores: teaching with and without computers and multimedia

Group	n	Mean	Standard Error	t	d.f.	Sig.
With computers and multimedia	221	70.52	14.934	2.381	449	.018*
Without computers and multimedia	230	67.31	13.740			

*p<0.05, **p<0.01

Table 4. Difference between pretest and posttest among differing gender in this study

Gender	Mean Pretest	Mean Posttest	Mean Difference	S. D.	Sig.
M	91.25	162.72	71.47	1.256	.000**
F	96.74	164.55	67.81	.890	.000**

*p<0.05, **p<0.01

Table 5. Differences on subjects' improved mean score on gender

Gender	n	Mean Difference	S. D.	t	d. f.	Sig.
M	132	71.47	13.938	-2.464	449	.014*
F	319	67.81	14.490			

*p<0.05, **p<0.01
F = female
M = male

Table 6. Difference between pretest and posttest among differing class settings in this study

Class Setting	Mean Pretest	Mean Posttest	Mean Difference	Sig.
PG	101.98	166.88	64.90	.000**
PM	90.95	166.95	76.00	.000**
TG	89.40	163.73	74.33	.000**
TM	97.11	159.48	62.37	.000**

*p<0.05, **p<0.01
PG=Computer Multimedia Integrated into Instruction at All Female School
PM=Computer Multimedia Integrated into Instruction at Mixed Gender School
TG=Traditional Lecture at All Female School
TM=Traditional Lecture at Mixed Gender School

Table 7. Difference between pretest and posttest of HIV/AIDS knowledge, attitude, and behavior concepts

Class Setting	Gender	Test Type	Knowledge		Attitude		Behavior	
			Mean	Standard Deviation	Mean	Standard Deviation	Mean	Standard Deviation
PG	F	Pretest	2.87890	.578964	2.52706	.336962	3.23591	.777221
		Posttest	4.48073	.138428	4.53119	.109034	4.49279	.232055
TM	F	Pretest	2.70500	.519264	2.43417	.354331	2.77857	.816394
		Posttest	4.53000	.157631	4.54083	.130997	4.50000	.240345
	M	Pretest	2.60533	.568757	2.40600	.433711	2.68762	.952453
		Posttest	4.50000	.154220	4.55067	.136929	4.45905	.248873
TG	F	Pretest	2.52526	.377271	2.35158	.306182	2.44511	.748094
		Posttest	4.48105	.172155	4.36737	.159582	4.50977	.241802
PM	F	Pretest	2.83818	.590822	2.48818	.308065	3.15844	.740101
		Posttest	4.20727	.165389	4.49545	.114371	3.98182	.214822
	M	Pretest	2.72807	.556698	2.38596	.295918	2.72431	.499898
		Posttest	4.25263	.164865	4.45526	.122359	3.92732	.173127

F = female
M = male

posttest at 159.48, and a difference of 62.37. From the class setting perspective, each setting shows significant difference between pretest and posttest.

Table 7 and Table 8 show the means of HIV/AIDS knowledge, attitude, and behavior concepts in pretest and posttest, which indicates how subjects' improvement varied among the three concepts.

There were 20 questions about AIDS knowledge, with the most accurate answer equal to 5, the least 1 (same scale for each concept). The mean score of the PG group on the pretest is 2.87890 and at the posttest, 4.48073; for attitude concept there were 10 questions, with mean pretest score of 2.52706 and posttest, 4.53119; for behavior concept there were 7 questions, with mean pretest score of 3.23591 and posttest at 4.49279.

In the PM class setting, female students' mean score for knowledge at the pretest is 2.8381 and after six weeks the mean score at posttest is 4.49545; for male students at the pretest knowledge concept score is 2.72807, then at posttest the mean score is 4.25263. For the attitude concept, female students' mean score at the pretest is 2.48818 and mean score at the posttest is 4.49545; for males, the mean score at pretest is 2.38596 and at the

posttest the mean score is 4.45526. For behavior concept, female students' mean score at the pretest is 3.15844 and at the posttest is 3.98182, while for male students; the mean score at pretest is 2.72431, then 3.92732 at the posttest.

In the TG setting, for knowledge concept, the mean score at the pretest is 2.52526 and for the posttest the mean score is 4.48105; for attitude concept, the mean score at the pretest is 2.35158 and at the posttest is 4.36737; for behavior concept, the mean score at pretest is 2.44511, while at posttest it is 4.50977.

In TM group, female students' mean score for knowledge at the pretest is 2.70500 and at the posttest is 4.53000; for male students at the pretest of knowledge concept, the mean is 2.60533 and 4.50000 at the posttest. For attitude concept, female subjects' mean score at the pretest is 2.43417 and at the posttest, 4.54083; for male students the mean score at the pretest is 2.40600 and 4.55067 at the posttest. For behavior concept, female students' mean score at the pretest is 2.77857 and at the posttest, 4.50000; male students' mean score at the pretest is 2.68762, then for the posttest is 4.45905.

Table 8 shows that in different gender and class settings, students improve within three dif-

Table 8. Mean difference and significance in different class setting for three concepts between pretest and posttest

Class Setting	Gender	Concepts								
		Knowledge			Attitude			Behavior		
		Mean Difference	Std. Error	Sig.	Mean Difference	Std. Error	Sig.	Mean Difference	Std. Error	Sig.
PG	F	1.602	.057	.000**	2.004	.034	.000**	1.257	.078	.000**
TM	F	1.825	.070	.000**	2.107	.049	.000**	1.721	.110	.000**
	M	1.895	.068	.000**	2.145	.053	.000**	1.771	.114	.000**
TG	F	1.956	.043	.000**	2.016	.035	.000**	2.065	.081	.000**
PM	F	1.369	.083	.000**	2.007	.044	.000**	.823	.104	.000**
	M	1.525	.077	.000**	2.069	.042	.000**	1.203	.070	.000**

*$p<0.05$, **$p<0.01$

ferent concepts following HIV/AIDS education, and how significant the improvement is. In the class using computer multimedia integration for HIV/AIDS education at the all female school (PG group), students improved in knowledge with mean difference of 1.602, 2.004 in attitude, and 1.257 in behavior. Attitude is affected more than other concepts in the PG group. In PG group, the difference of the scores on the three concepts is statistically significant between pretest and posttest.

In the traditional lecture at the all female school (TG group), students improved in knowledge with a mean difference of 1.956, in attitude by 2.016, and in behavior by 2.065. In this setting, behavior improved the most. The difference of the scores on the three concepts is also statistically significant between pretest and posttest in the TG group.

Moreover, in the traditional lecture at the mixed gender school (TM group), female students improved on knowledge by a mean score of 1.825, while male students improved by 1.895. In words, male students improved more than female students. The mean difference in attitude improvement for female students is 2.107 and for male students is 2.145. For behavior concept, female students' mean improvement is 1.721, while for male students it is 1.771, putting male students' improvement higher in the study. All students in TM group show attitude concept improved more than the other two concepts, and improvements for all three concepts are significant.

For the computer and multimedia integration into instruction at the mixed gender school (PM group), female students improved in knowledge by a mean score of 1.369, while for male students, the improvement was somewhat greater, at 1.525. The mean improvement in attitude concept for females is 2.007, while for male students the improvement is 2.069, which is also slightly higher than that for females. In behavior concept, females' improvement mean is 0.823 and that for males is 1.203.

DISCUSSION AND CONCLUSION

In this study, the researchers designed different kinds of class settings and teaching methods to teach students about HIV/ AIDS, and also tested how their knowledge, attitude, and behavior concepts were improved following the teaching session. The researchers believe that the introduction of suitable methods for the validation of computer lesson presentation and the utilization of the multimedia power of computers to facilitate better understanding should be helpful in teaching about HIV/AIDS. Computer multimedia integrated into instruction seems to be a worldwide trend of teaching. It has been stated that the aims of the course and study should be clearly defined, and not merely a justification of the use of new media technology (Friedman, 1994).

Based on the findings in this study, the researchers identify several implications for teaching. In India, lessons on every subject usually follow a traditional, didactic approach to teaching, and don't usually involve interactions with students. In this study, the researchers tried to engage students in discussions and allowed them to ask questions, moreover, they integrated computers and multimedia into PowerPoint slides to present an informative HIV/AIDS education class. Through the process, students experienced cognitive dissonance related to their previous learning (Hewson, Beeth, & Thorley, 1998) and therefore, engaged in knowledge seeking (Edelson, 2001) in this HIV/AIDS education class. This enabled students to be more actively involved in the knowledge construction process, and have a chance to explore and reconsider their preconceptions. We believe it was through this means that the students were given the unusual opportunity to actively participate in classroom learning where their prior knowledge was elucidated (Driver, 1983; Clement, 1993).

As the data shows, each group, no matter using computer multimedia integration into HIV/AIDS education or traditional lecture, improved at least 62.37 points. Groups integrating computer and multimedia into HIV/AIDS education improved 64.90 at the all female school and up to 76.00 at mixed gender school. Meanwhile, the traditional lecture groups improved 62.37 at the mixed gender school and up to 74.33 at the all female school. The use of computer multimedia facilitates somewhat higher performance at the mixed gender school. However, for the all female school, there is no advantage from computer multimedia integration. The results of this study have similarities with Goodwin and Roscoe (1988), and Gaines, Iglar, Michal, and Patton (1988) regarding knowledge concept; likely arguments with Yan, Liu, and Lee (2001), and Chen (2003); and they illustrate the same points as Catania et al. (1992) for behavior concept in HIV/AIDS education research.

This research has its limitations with regard to subject sampling. In this study, the researchers chose the sample randomly from four different schools, and designed these into four different groups. This may affect students' diversity, thereby affecting the results. In this study, after students join the classes, they are not forced to practice and they do not have material to enhance their study of HIV/AIDS education, so at the posttest time, their situation could be assumed to be void of testing effect. Future studies may focus on testing students' extension of what was taught and effects on the duration of HIV/AIDS knowledge, attitude, and behavior by using different kind of teaching methods.

Although there has been much research on the implications of students' prior knowledge on learning, little research on engaging students' prior knowledge has been done in Indian classrooms. Any attempt to provide insight in this area is of benefit to the larger literature base and particularly relevant for Indian students. Moreover, this understanding informs the design of effective instructional strategies and curriculum materials. Findings from this study also help to sensitize teachers to the diverse understandings of HIV/AIDS that students bring, which also impact schools. The paper provides insights of the authors' achievements in use of computers for developing a different pedagogy for HIV/AIDS education, through computer and multimedia integration and traditional lecture. Although examples presented in this paper are based on students' responses to a questionnaire, the approach and methods highlighted can be equally beneficial to both future research and schools' further blueprint for HIV/AIDS education projects.

ACKNOWLEDGMENT

The author would like to express appreciation for the financial support of NSC99-2410-H-130-037- and NSC99-3113-S-214-001- from the National Science Council, Taiwan, R.O.C.

REFERENCES

Baria, F., Menon, S., Nagchoudhury, S., David, S., & Menon, V. (1997). Cover story: AIDS - striking home. India Today. Retrieved from http://www.sawnet.org/news/ aids.html

Blinn-Pike, L. (1996). Evaluation of a program to delay sexual activity among female adolescents in rural Appalachia. *Family Relations*, *45*(4), 380–386..doi:10.2307/585167

Catania, J. A., Coates, T. J., Kegeles, S., Fullilove, M. T., Peterson, J., & Marin, B. (1992). Condom use in multi-ethnic neighborhoods of San Francisco: The population-based AMEN (AIDS in multi-ethnic neighborhoods) study. *American Journal of Public Health*, *82*(2), 284–287..doi:10.2105/AJPH.82.2.284

Chen, P. R. (2003). The study of attitude toward AIDS and condom, the behavioral intension of using condom and relevant factors. Unpublished master's thesis, National Taiwan Normal University, Taipei, Taiwan.

Chifunyisea, T., Benoyb, H., & Mukiibi, B. (2002). An impact evaluation of student teacher training in HIV/AIDS education in Zimbabwe. *Evaluation and Program Planning, 25*(4), 377–385.. doi:10.1016/S0149-7189(02)00049-6

Clement, J. (1993). Using bridging analogies and anchoring intuitions to deal with students' preconceptions. *International Journal of Science Teaching, 30,* 1241–1257. doi:10.1002/tea.3660301007

Denny, D., Young, M., Rausch, S., & Spear, C. (2002). An evaluation of an abstinence education curriculum series: Sex can wait. *American Journal of Health Behavior, 26*(5), 366–377.

DiClemente, R. J., & Crosby, R. A. (2009). Preventing HIV among adolescents in Sub-Saharan Africa. *The Journal of Adolescent Health, 44*(2), 101–102..doi:10.1016/j.jadohealth.2008.12.001

DiClemente, R. J., Crosby, R. A., & Salazar, L. F. (2007). A review of STD/HIV preventive interventions for adolescents: Sustaining effects using an ecological approach. *Journal of Pediatric Psychology, 32*(8), 888–906..doi:10.1093/jpepsy/jsm056

Driver, R. (1983). *The pupil as a scientist.* Milton Keynes, UK: Open University Press.

Edelson, D. C. (2001). Learning for use: A framework for the design of technology-supported inquiry activities. *Journal of Research in Science Teaching, 38*(3), 335–385.. doi:10.1002/1098-2736(200103)38:3<355::AID-TEA1010>3.0.CO;2-M

Flora, J. A., & Thoresen, C. E. (1988). Reducing the risk of AIDS in adolescents. *Journal of African Psychology, 43*(11), 965–970.

Friedman, C. P. (1994). The research we should be doing. *Academic Medicine, 69*(6), 455–457.. doi:10.1097/00001888-199406000-00005

Gaines, J., Iglar, A. F., Michal, M. L., & Patton, R. D. (1998). Attitudes towards AIDS. *Health Values, 12*(4), 53–60.

Goodwin, M. P., & Roscoe, B. (1998). AIDS: Students' knowledge and attitudes at a Midwestern university. *Journal of American College Health, 36*(4), 214–222..doi:10.1080/07448481.1988.9939016

Haffner, D. W. (1996). Sexual health for American's adolescents. *The Journal of School Health, 66*(4), 151–152..doi:10.1111/j.1746-1561.1996.tb08237.x

Hewson, P. W., Beeth, M. E., & Thorley, R. N. (1998). Teaching for conceptual change. In Fraser, B. J., & Tobin, K. G. (Eds.), *International handbook of science education* (pp. 199–218). Boston, MA: Kluwer Academic.

Hsu, H. Y. (2002). The needs and meaning on teaching subjects integrating computers and technology. In Chang, H. T. (Ed.), *Teaching subjects integrating computers and technology* (pp. vii–x). Taipei, Taiwan: Pro-Ed.

Joint United Nations Programme on HIV/AIDS (UNAIDS) and World Health Organization. (WHO). (2000). AIDS epidemic. Geneva, Switzerland: UNAIDS.

Joint United Nations Programme on HIV/AIDS (UNAIDS) and World Health Organization. (WHO). (2009). AIDS epidemic. Geneva, Switzerland: UNAIDS.

Kuo, H. C. (2006). A survey on quality of life and needs among HIV/AIDS patients in the Northern Region of Malawi. Unpublished master's thesis, National Yang Ming University, Taipei, Taiwan.

Lee, M. P. (2003). *HIV/AIDS education instruction manual.* Taipei, Taiwan: Centers for Disease Control, Department of Health.

Lieberman, D. A. (1997). Interactive video games for health promotion effects on knowledge, self-efficacy, social support, and health. In Street, R. L. Jr., (Ed.), *Health promotion and interactive technology: Theoretical application and future directions* (pp. 103–120). Mahwah, NJ: Lawrence Erlbaum.

Mayer, R. E. (2001). *Multimedia learning*. Cambridge, UK: Cambridge University Press.

Nath, L. M. (1998). The epidemic in India: An overview. In Godwin, P. (Ed.), *The looming epidemic: The impact of HIV and AIDS in India* (p. 28). New Delhi, India: Mosaic Books.

Robertson, A., & Levin, M. L. (1999). AIDS knowledge, condom attitudes, and risk-taking sexual behavior of substance-abusing juvenile offenders on probation or parole. AIDS ducation and Prevention, 11(5), 450-461.

Sharma, S. (2010, December). Health care fails to reach migrants. Hindustan Times.

Srinivasan, T. M. (2002). *Use of computers and multimedia in education*. Rajasthan, India: Aavishkar Publisher Distributors.

Thomas, R., Cahill, J., & Santilli, I. (1997). Using an interactive computer game to increase skill and self-efficacy regarding safer sex negotiation: Field test results. *Health Education & Behavior, 24*(1), 71–86..doi:10.1177/109019819702400108

This work was previously published in the International Journal of Information Communication Technologies and Human Development, Volume 3, Issue 4, edited by Susheel Chhabra and Hakikur Rahman, pp. 47-58, copyright 2011 by IGI Publishing (an imprint of IGI Global).

Compilation of References

Aabo, S. (2005). The role and value of public libraries in the age of digital technologies. *Journal of Librarianship and Information Science*, *37*(4), 205–211. doi:10.1177/0961000605057855

Abbasi, S. (2007, August 30). *Role of Telecentres in Gender Empowerment: Do Telecentres Really Work for Women?* Paper presented at the Royal Holloway, University of London, London.

Abrahamson, J., & Fisher, K. E. (2007). What's past is prologue: Towards a general model of lay information mediary behaviour. *Information Research, 12*(4).

Abutaleb, A., & Li, V. (1997). Location Update Optimization in Personal Communication Systems. *International Journal of Wireless Networks*, *3*, 205–216. doi:10.1023/A:1019157217684

Acevedo, M. (2009). Network cooperation: Development cooperation in the network society. *International Journal of Information Communication Technologies and Human Development*, *1*(1). doi:10.4018/jicthd.2009010101

Achimugu, P., Oluwagbemi, O., Oluwaranti, A., & Afolabi, B. (2009). Adoption of information and communication technologies in developing countries: An impact analysis. *Journal of Information Technology Impact, 9*, 37–46.

Adams, C., & Ramos, I. (2009). Crowdsourcing: A social networking approach to outsourcing. *Cutter IT Journal*, *22*(10).

Adekunle, P., & Tella, A. (2008). Nigeria SMEs participation in electronic economy: Problems and the way forward. *Journal of Internet Banking and Commerce*, *12*(3).

Adkisson, H. (2002). *Identifying De-Facto Standards for E-Commerce Web Sites*. Retrieved from http://www.boxesandarrows.com/view

Agosto, D. E., Paone, K. L., & Ipock, G. S. (2007). The female-friendly public library: gender differences in adolescents' uses and perceptions of U.S. public libraries. *Library Trends*.

Ahmed, M., Hussein, R., Minakhatun, R., & Islam, R. (2007). Building consumers' confidence in adopting e-commerce: A Malaysian case. *International Journal of Business and Systems Research*, *1*(2), 236–255. doi:10.1504/IJBSR.2007.015378

Ajayi, T. O., Salawu, I. O., & Adeoye, F. A. (2008). E-learning and distance education in Nigeria. *Turkish Online Journal of Educational Technology, 7*(4).

Ajzen, I. (1991). The theory of planned behavior. *Organizational Behavior and Human Decision Processes*, *50*, 179–211. doi:10.1016/0749-5978(91)90020-T

Ajzen, I., & Fishbein, M. (1980). *Understanding Attitude and Predicting Social Behavior*. Upper Saddle River, NJ: Prentice-Hall, Inc.

Akcomak, S. (2009). *Incubators as tools for entrepreneurship promotion in developing countries*. Tokyo, Japan: United Nations University.

Akinsola, O. S., Marlien, E. H., & Jacobs, S. J. (2005). ICT provision to disadvantage urban communities: A study in South Africa and Nigeria. *International Journal of Education and Development Using Information and Communication Technology*.

Akyildiz, I., Ho, H., & Lin, Y. (1996). Movement-Based Location Update and Selective Paging for PCS Networks. *IEEWACM Transactions on Networking*, *4*(4), 629–638. doi:10.1109/90.532871

Akyildiz, I., McNair, J., Ho, J., Uzunalioglu, H., & Wang, W. (1999). Mobility Management in Next-Generation Wireless Systems. *Proceedings of the IEEE, 87*, 1347–1384. doi:10.1109/5.775420

Alabi, A. (2004). Evolving role of ICT in teaching, research and publishing. *Nigeria Tribunal*, 30-31.

Alam, S. S., Ishak, N. A., & Khatibi, A. (2008). The effects of perceived characteristics on ICT adoption in SMEs in Malaysia. In *Proceedings of the 5th Global Conference on SMEs and Industrial Development in Asian Countries*.

Albrecht, C. C., & Dean, D. L. (2005). Market Place and Technology Standards For B2B Ecommerce: Progress and Challenges. In *Proceedings of Standard Making: A Critical Research Frontier for Information Systems MISQ Special Issue Workshop* (p. 188).

Aldebert, B., Dang, R. J., & Longhi, C. (2011). Innovation in the tourism industry: The case of Tourism@. *Tourism Management, 32*(5), 1204–1213. doi:.doi:10.1016/j.physletb.2003.10.071

Alexander, N., & Colgate, M. (2000). Retail financial services: Transaction to relationship marketing. *European Journal of Marketing, 34*(8), 938–953. doi:10.1108/03090560010331432

Alfaro, F., Molina, J. P., & Camacho Jiménez, K. (2008). *Public access to information & ICTs final report: Dominican Republic*. Seattle, WA: University of Washington Center for Information & Society (CIS).

Al-Hawari, M., Al-Yamani, H., & Izwawa, B. (2008). Small businesses' decision to have a website Saudi Arabia case study. *World Academy of Science. Engineering and Technology, 37*, 308–312.

Aljadhai, A., & Znati, T. (2001). Predictive mobility support for QoS provisioning in mobile wireless environments. *IEEE Journal on Selected Areas in Communications, 19*(10), 1915–1930. doi:10.1109/49.957307

Allahawiah, S., Altarawneh, H., & Alamro, S. (2010). *The Internet and small medium-sized enterprises (SMEs) in Jordan*. Retrieved from http://www.waset.org/journals/waset/v62/v62-54.pdf

Almirall, E. (2008). Living labs and open innovation: Roles and applicability. *Electronic Journal for Virtual Organizations and Networks, 10*, 21–26.

Al-Qirim, N. A. (2007). E-commerce adoption in small businesses-cases from New Zealand. *Journal of Information Technology Case and Application Research, 9*(2), 28–57.

Ambrose, P. J., & Johnson, G. J. (1998). A Trust Model of Buying Behavior in Electronic Retailing. In *Proceedings of the Americas Conference on Information Systems (AMCIS)*, Baltimore, MD.

Andam, Z. (2003). *E-commerce and e-business*. Retrieved from http://www.apdip.net/publications/iespprimers/eprimer-ecom.pdf

Anderson, E., & Weitz, B. (1992). The Use of Pledges to Build and Sustain Commitment in Distribution Channels. *JMR, Journal of Marketing Research, 24*, 18–24. doi:10.2307/3172490

Anderson, J., & Weert, T. V. (Eds.). (2002). *Information and communication technology in education*. Paris, France: UNESCO.

Angenent, H. (1998). *Opvoeding en persoonlijkheidsontwikkeling*. Baarn, NL: Uitgeverij Intro.

Angenent, H. (2004). Psychological Antecedents of Institution-Based Consumer Trust in E-Retailing. *Information & Management, 42*(1), 159–177.

Antikainen, M. J., & Vaataja, H. K. (2010). Rewarding in open innovation communities – how to motivate members. *International Journal of Entrepreneurship and Innovation Management, 11*(4), 440–456. doi:10.1504/IJEIM.2010.032267

Antonelli, C. (2006). Localized technological change and factor markets: Constraints and inducements to innovation. *Structural Change and Economic Dynamics, 17*, 224–247. doi:10.1016/j.strueco.2004.05.002

Antonopoulou, E., Karetsos, S. T., Maliappis, M., & Sideridis, A. B. (2009). Web and mobile technologies in a prototype DSS for major field crops. *Computers and Electronics in Agriculture, 70*(2), 292–301. doi:10.1016/j.compag.2009.07.024

APC WNSP. (2005). *Gender Evaluation Methodology for Internet and ICTs: A Learning Tool for Change and Empowerment*. APC WNSP.

Applegate, R. (2008). Gender Differences in the Use of a Public Library. *Public Library Quarterly*, *27*(1), 19–31. doi:10.1080/01616840802122468

Arias, M., & Camacho Jiménez, K. (2008). *Public access to information & ICTs final report: Honduras*. Seattle, WA: University of Washington Center for Information & Society (CIS).

Ariunaa, L. (2008). *Public access to information & ICTs final report: Kyrgyzstan*. Seattle, WA: University of Washington Center for Information & Society (CIS).

Arora, A. (2002). Licensing tacit knowledge: Intellectual property rights and the market for know-how. *Economics of Innovation and New Technology*, *4*(1), 41–59. doi:10.1080/10438599500000013

Aubert, B. A., & Kelsey, B. L. (2000). *The Illusion of Trust and Performance*. CIRANO.

Auger, P., & Gallaugher, J. M. (1997). Factors affecting the adoption of an Internet-based sales presence for small businesses. *The Information Society*, *13*, 55–74. doi:10.1080/019722497129287

Bagozzi, R. P., & Fornell, C. (1982). Theoretical concepts, measurement, and meaning. In Fornell, C. (Ed.), *a Second Generation of Multivariate Analysis* (pp. 5–23). Praeger.

Baheshti, B. (2007). Review of Location Management in Cellular Networks. In *Proceedings of the IEEE Systems, Application and Technology Conference (LISAT 2007)* (pp. 1-6).

Bailey, A. (2009). Issues affecting the social sustainability of telecentres in developing contexts: A field study of sixteen telecentres in Jamaica. *The Electronic Journal on Information Systems in Developing Countries*, *36*(4), 1–18.

Bakos, J. Y. (1991). A strategic analysis of electronic marketplaces. *Management Information Systems Quarterly*, *15*(3), 295–310. doi:10.2307/249641

Bakos, J. Y. (1991). Information links and electronic marketplaces: The role of inter-organizational information systems in vertical markets. *Journal of Management Information Systems*, *8*(2), 31–52.

Bandele, S. O. (Ed.). (2006). *Development of modern ICT and internet system*. Abuja, Nigeria: Panof Press.

Bar, A., Feng, Y., & Golin, M. (2007). Paging mobile users efficiently and optimally. In *Proceedings of the IEEE Infocom 2007*.

Bar, A., Kessler, I., & Sidi, M. (1995). Mobile Users: To Update or Not to Update? *ACM/Baltzer. Wireless Networks*, *1*(2), 175–185. doi:10.1007/BF01202540

Baria, F., Menon, S., Nagchoudhury, S., David, S., & Menon, V. (1997). Cover story: AIDS - striking home. India Today. Retrieved from http://www.sawnet.org/news/ aids.html

Barney, J., & Clark, D. (2007). *Resource-based theory: Creating and sustaining competitive advantage*. New York, NY: Oxford University Press.

Barua, A., Konana, P., & Whinston, A. (2004). An empirical investigation of net-enabled business value. *Management Information Systems Quarterly*, *28*(4), 585–620.

Barzilai-Nahon, K., Gomez, R., & Ambikar, R. (2009). Conceptualizing a contextual measurement for digital divides: Using an integrated narrative. In Ferro, E., Dwivedi, Y. K., Gil-Garcia, J. R., & Williams, M. D. (Eds.), *Overcoming digital divides: Constructing an equitable and competitive information society* (pp. 630–644). Hershey, PA: IGI Global.

Basu, S. (2010). *Search engines to explore the invisible Web*. Retrieved from http://www.makeuseof.com/tag/10-search-engines-explore-deep-invisible-web/

Becker, S., Crandall, M. D., Fisher, K. E., Kinney, B., Landry, C., & Rocha, A. (2010). *Opportunity for All: How the American Public Benefits from Internet Access at U.S. Libraries*. Washington, DC: Institute of Museum and Library Services.

Bejerano, Y., Smith, M., Naor, J., & Immorlica, N. (2006). Efficient Location Area Planning for Personal Communication Systems. *IEEE/ACM Transactions on Networking*, *14*(2). doi:10.1109/TNET.2006.872555

Bergman, M. K. (2001). The deep web: Surfacing hidden value. *Journal of Electronic Publishing*, *7*(1). doi:10.3998/3336451.0007.104

Bertot, J. C., McClure, C. R., & Jaeger, P. T. (2008). The impacts of free public Internet access on public library patrons and communities. *The Library Quarterly*, *78*(3), 285–301. doi:10.1086/588445

Bertot, J. C., McClure, C. R., Thomas, S., Barton, K. M., & McGilvray, J. (2007). *Public Libraries and the Internet 2007: Report to the American Library Association*. Tallahassee, FL: College of Information, Florida State University.

Bessant, J., & Tidd, J. (2007). *Innovation and entrepreneurship*. New York, NY: John Wiley & Sons.

Best, M., & Kumar, R. (2008). Sustainability failures of rural telecentres: Challenges from the sustainable access in rural India (SARI) project. *Information Technologies & International Development, 4*(4), 14.

Bhadauria, V., & Sachan, R. (2009). The Cost effective Location Management Scheme using Mobility Information and Received Signal Strength of Mobile Users in Wireless Mobile Networks. *IEEE International Conference in Advance Computing (IACC)*, 878-882.

Bharadwaj, P. N., & Soni, R. G. (2007). E-commerce usage and perception of e-commerce issues among small firms: Results and implications from an empirical study. *Journal of Small Business Management, 45*(4), 501–521. doi:10.1111/j.1540-627X.2007.00225.x

Bhattacherjee, A. (2002). Individual Trust in Online Firms: Scale Development and Initial Test. *Journal of Management Information Systems, 19*, 211–241.

Biswash, S., & Kumar, C. (2009). Distance-Direction-Probability Based Location Management Scheme for Wireless Cellular Network. In *Proceedings of the National Seminar on Recent Advances on Information Technology (RAIT – 2009)* (pp. 30-38).

Biswash, S., & Kumar, C. (2009). Dynamic VLR Based Location Management Scheme for PCS Networks. In *Proceedings of the International IEEE Conference on Methods and Models in Computer Science (ICM2CS 09)* (pp. 276-280).

Blackman, M. (2007). Patents: Realising and securing value. *World Patent Information, 29*(2), 186–187. doi:10.1016/j.wpi.2006.11.002

Blinn-Pike, L. (1996). Evaluation of a program to delay sexual activity among female adolescents in rural Appalachia. *Family Relations, 45*(4), 380–386.. doi:10.2307/585167

Boiugrain, F., & Haudeville, B. (2002). Innovation, collaboration and SMEs internal research capacities. *Research Policy, 31*, 735–747. doi:10.1016/S0048-7333(01)00144-5

Bolaji, O. A., & Babajide, V. F. T. (2003). Perception of lecturers and service teachers towards the use of communication media in teching pure and applied science related disciplines. In *Proceedings of the 44th Annual STAN Conference* (pp. 33-36).

Boldi, P., Codenott, B., Santini, M., & Vigna, S. (2004). UbiCrawler: A scalable fully distributed web crawler. *Software, Practice & Experience, 34*(8), 721–726. doi:10.1002/spe.587

Bonner, J., & Walker, O. (2004). Selecting influential business-to-business customers in new product development: Relational embeddedness and knowledge heterogeneity considerations. *Journal of Product Innovation Management, 21*, 155–169. doi:10.1111/j.0737-6782.2004.00067.x

Bossio, J. F., & Sotomayor, K. (2008). *Public access to information & ICTs final report: Ecuador*. Seattle, WA: University of Washington Center for Information & Society (CIS).

Bossio, J. F. (2004). *Social Sustainability of Telecentres from the Viewpoint of Telecentre Operators: A Case Study from Sao Paulo, Brazil*. London: London School of Economics.

Box, S. (2009). *OECD work on innovation- a stocktaking of existing work*. Paris, France: OECD Publishing.

Brabham, D. C. (2008). Crowdsourcing as a model for problem solving: An introduction and cases. *International Journal of Research into New Media Technologies, 14*(1), 75–90. doi:10.1177/1354856507084420

Brabin, B., Wort, U. U., & Warsame, M. (2006). Birth outcomes in adolescent pregnancy in an area with intense malaria transmission in Tanzania. *Acta Obstetricia et Gynecologica Scandinavica, 85*(8), 949–954. doi:10.1080/00016340600756870

Brady, M., Saren, M., & Tzokas, N. (2002). Integrating information technology into marketing practice – the IT realize of contemporary marketing practice. *Journal of Marketing Management, 18*, 555–577. doi:10.1362/0267257022683703

Braga, C., & Primo, A. (2005). E-commerce Regulations: New game, new rules. *The Quarterly Review of Economics and Finance, 45*(2/3), 541–558.

Braun, P. (2006). E-commerce and small tourism firms. In Marshall, S., Taylor, W., & Yu, X. (Eds.), *Encyclopedia of developing regional communities with information and communication technology* (pp. 233–238). Hershey, PA: IGI Global. doi:10.4018/9781591405757.ch041

Brehm & Kassin. (1998). *Social Psychology*. Boston: Houghton.

Brin, S., & Page, L. (1998, April 14-18). The anatomy of a large-scale hyper textual web search engine. In *Proceedings of the Seventh International World-Wide Web Conference*, Brisbane, Australia.

Brockhoff, K. (2003). Customers' perspectives of involvement in new product development. *International Journal of Technology Management, 26*(5-6), 464–481. doi:10.1504/IJTM.2003.003418

Brouwer, J. (1999). Modern and indigenous perceptions in small enterprises. *Economic and Political Weekly, 34*(48), 152–156.

Brown, T. J., Dacin, P. A., Pratt, M. G., & Whetten, D. A. (2006). Identity, intended image, construed image, and reputation: An interdisciplinary framework and suggested terminology. *Journal of the Academy of Marketing Science, 34*(2), 99–106. doi:10.1177/0092070305284969

Brown, T., & Mohan, S. (1997). Mobility Management for Personal Communication Systems. *IEEE Transactions on Vehicular Technology, 46*(2), 269–278. doi:10.1109/25.580765

Bryceson, K. P. (2006). *E issues in agribusiness, the what, why, how*. Oxford, UK: Cabi Publishers. doi:10.1079/9781845930714.0000

Bryers, J. D., & Ratner, B. D. (2004). Bioinspired implant materials befuddle bacteria. *ASM News, 70*, 232–237.

Bryman, A. (2008). *Social research methods* (3rd ed.). New York, NY: Oxford University Press.

Buhalis, D., & Main, H. (1998). Information technology in peripheral small and medium hospitality enterprises: Strategic analysis and critical factors. *International Journal of Contemporary Hospitality Management, 10*(5), 198–202. doi:10.1108/09596119810227811

Bui, T. X., Le, T., & Jones, W. D. (2006). An exploratory case study of hotel e-marketing in Ho Chi Minh City. *Thunderbird International Business Review, 48*(3), 369–388. doi:10.1002/tie.20100

Bunduchi, R. (2005). Business relationships in Internet-based electronic markets: The role of goodwill trust and transaction costs. *Information Systems Journal, 15*, 321–341. doi:10.1111/j.1365-2575.2005.00199.x

Burke, K. (2009). Internet ICT use in agriculture: Micro-enterprises and SMEs. *Journal of Developmental Entrepreneurship, 14*, 233–254. doi:10.1142/S1084946709001260

Burt, R. S., & Knez, M. (1995). Trust and Third Party Gossip. In Kramer, R. M., & Tyler, T. R. (Eds.), *Trust in Organizations: Frontiers of Theory and Research* (pp. 68–89). Thousand Oaks, CA: Sage.

Butt, S., & Phillips, J. G. (2008). Personality and self reported mobile phone use. *Computers in Human Behavior, 24*(2), 346–360. doi:10.1016/j.chb.2007.01.019

Byfield, T. (2004). *Thoughts on the telecenter as a model for ICT in the rural "south"*. Unpublished manuscript, Social Sciences Research Council, Brooklyn, NY.

Cadiz, C. M. (2005). Communication for empowerment: The practice of participatory communication in development. In Hemer, O., & Tufte, T. (Eds.), *Media and glocal change: Rethinking communication for development* (pp. 145–158). Göteborg, Sweden: NORDICOM.

Cairncross, F. (1997). *The death of distance*. Boston, MA: Harvard Business School Press.

Cameron, H. (1996). Investing in Australian agribusiness companies: A challenge to the industry. *Australasian Agribusiness Review, 4*(1).

Canavari, M., Fritz, M., Hofstede, G., Matopoulos, A., & Vlachopoulou, M. (2010). The role of trust in the transition from traditional to electronic B2B relationships in agri-food chains. *Computers and Electronics in Agriculture*, *70*, 321–327. doi:10.1016/j.compag.2009.08.014

Carayannis, E. G., Popescu, D., Sipp, C., & Stewart, M. (2006). Technological learning for entrepreneurial development (TL4ED) in the knowledge economy (KE): Case studies and lessons learned. *Technovation*, *26*, 419–443. doi:10.1016/j.technovation.2005.04.003

Carson, D. (1990). Some exploratory models for assessing small firms marketing performance (a qualitative approach). *European Journal of Marketing*, *24*(11), 8–51. doi:10.1108/03090569010006056

Carver, C. S., & Scheier, M. F. (1992). *Perspective on Personality*. Boston: Allyn and Bacon.

Castells, M. (1996). *The rise of the network society, the information age: Economy, society and culture* (*Vol. 1*). Oxford, UK: Blackwell.

Castells, M. (2007). Communication, power, and couterpower in the network society. *International Journal of Communication*, *1*, 238–266.

Catania, J. A., Coates, T. J., Kegeles, S., Fullilove, M. T., Peterson, J., & Marin, B. (1992). Condom use in multiethnic neighborhoods of San Francisco: The population-based AMEN (AIDS in multi-ethnic neighborhoods) study. *American Journal of Public Health*, *82*(2), 284–287.. doi:10.2105/AJPH.82.2.284

Cavsoglu, H. (2009). Configuration of and interaction between information security technologies: The case of firewalls and intrusion detection systems. *Information Systems Research*, *20*(2), 198–217. doi:10.1287/isre.1080.0180

Central Intelligence Agency. (2007). *The world factbook*. Retrieved from https://www.cia.gov/library/publications/the-world-factbook/rankorder/2153rank.html

Chakrabarti, S., Berg, M., & Dom, B. (1999). Focused crawling: A new approach to topic-specific web resource discovery. In *Proceedings of the Eighth International Conference on World Wide Web* (pp. 1623-1640).

Chandra, A. (2007). *Approaches to business incubation: A comparative study of the United States, China and Brazil. Terre Haute*. IN: Indiana State University.

Chen, P. R. (2003). The study of attitude toward AIDS and condom, the behavioral intension of using condom and relevant factors. Unpublished master's thesis, National Taiwan Normal University, Taipei, Taiwan.

Chen, L., Haney, S., Pandzik, A., Spigarelli, J., & Jesseman, C. (2003). Small business Internet commerce: A case study. *Information Resources Management Journal*, *16*(3), 17–41. doi:10.4018/irmj.2003070102

Chesbrough, H. (2006). *Emerging secondary markets for intellectual property: US and Japan comparisons*. Retrieved from http://www.ryutu.inpit.go.jp/en/pdf/ESMIP.pdf

Chesbrough, H. (2006a). Open innovation: A new paradigm for understanding industrial innovation. In H. Chesbrough, W. Vanhaverbeke, & J. West (Eds.), *Open innovation: Researching a new paradigm* (pp. 1-27). Oxford, UK: Oxford University Press.

Chesbrough, H. (2003a). *Open innovation: The new imperative for creating and profiting from technology*. Boston, MA: Harvard Business School Press.

Chesbrough, H. (2003b). The era of open innovation. *MIT Sloan Management Review*, *44*(3), 35–41.

Chesbrough, H. (2006b). *Open business models: How to thrive in the new innovation landscape*. Boston, MA: Harvard Business School Press.

Chesbrough, H. (2007). The market for innovation: Implications for corporate strategy. *California Management Review*, *49*(3), 45–66.

Chesbrough, H., & Crowther, A. K. (2006). Beyond high tech: Early adopters of open innovation in other industries. *R & D Management*, *36*(3), 229–236. doi:10.1111/j.1467-9310.2006.00428.x

Chesbrough, H., Vanhaverbeke, W., & West, J. (Eds.). (2006). *Open innovation: Researching a new paradigm*. Oxford, UK: Oxford University Press.

Cheskin and Studio Archetype. (1999). *The Cheskin research and studio archetype/Sapient e-commerce trust study.* Retrieved from http://www.studioarchetype.com/cheskin/html/phase1.html

Cheskin. (2000). *Research, Trust in the Wired Americas.* Retrieved from http://www.cheskin.com/think/studies/trust2.html

Cheung, C., & Lee, M. K. O. (2000). Trust in Internet Shopping: A Proposed Model and Measurement Instrument. In *Proceedings of the Americas Conference on Information Systems (AMCIS)*, Long Beach, CA.

Chiemeke, O. B., & Longe, S. C. (2007). Information communication technology in Nigeria: Prospecta, challenges and metrics. *Asian Journal of Information Technology*, *45*, 12–19.

Chifunyisea, T., Benoyb, H., & Mukiibi, B. (2002). An impact evaluation of student teacher training in HIV/AIDS education in Zimbabwe. *Evaluation and Program Planning*, *25*(4), 377–385..doi:10.1016/S0149-7189(02)00049-6

Chircu, A. M., Kauffman, R. J., & Keskey, D. (2001). Maximizing the value of internet-based corporate travel reservation systems. *Communications of the ACM*, *44*(11), 57–63. doi:10.1145/384150.384162

Chitura, T., Mupemhi, S., Dube, T., & Bolongkikit, J. (2008). Barriers to electronic commerce adoption in small and medium enterprises: A critical literature review. *Journal of Internet Banking and Commerce*, *13*(2).

Choi, S., Stahl, D. O., & Whinston, A. (1997). *The economics of electronic commerce: The essential economics of doing business in the electronic marketplace.* Indianapolis, IN: Macmillan.

Choucri, N., Maugis, V., Madnick, S., & Siegel, M. (2003). *Global e-readiness- for what?* Retrieved from http://ebusiness.mit.edu

Christensen, J. F., Olesen, M. H., & Kjær, J. S. (2005). The industrial dynamics of open innovation: Evidence from the transformation of consumer electronics. *Research Policy*, *34*(10), 1533–1549. doi:10.1016/j.respol.2005.07.002

Christopher, M. (2000). The agile supply chain: Competing in volatile markets. *Industrial Marketing Management*, *29*(1), 37–44. doi:10.1016/S0019-8501(99)00110-8

Chussil, M. (1991). Does market share really matter. *Strategy and Leadership*, *19*(5), 31–37. doi:10.1108/eb054336

Clasen, M., & Muller, R. (2006). Success factors of agribusiness digital marketplaces. *Electronic Markets*, *16*(4), 349–360. doi:10.1080/10196780600999809

Clement, J. (1993). Using bridging analogies and anchoring intuitions to deal with students' preconceptions. *International Journal of Science Teaching*, *30*, 1241–1257. doi:10.1002/tea.3660301007

Cloete, E., Courtney, S., & Fintz, J. (2002). Small business' acceptance and adoption of e-commerce in the Western-Cape Province of South Africa. *Electronic Journal on Information Systems in Developing Countries*, *10*(4), 1–13.

Cloete, E., & Doens, M. (2008). B2B e marketplace adoption in South African agriculture. *Information Technology for Development*, *14*(3), 184–196. doi:10.1002/itdj.20105

Collins, C., Buhalis, D., & Peters, M. (2003). Enhancing SMEs' business performance through the internet and E-learning platforms. *Education + Training*, *45*(8-9), 483-494.

Connolly, R., & Bannister, B. (2007). E-commerce Trust beliefs: The influence of national culture. In *Proceedings of European and Mediterranean Conference on Information Systems (EMCIS2007)*, Polytechnic University of Valencia, Spain.

Cooke, P. (2005). Regionally asymmetric knowledge capabilities and open innovation: Exploring `Globalisation 2' a new model of industry organisation. *Research Policy*, *34*(8), 1128–1149. doi:10.1016/j.respol.2004.12.005

Corritore, C. L., Kracher, B., & Wiedenbeck, S. (2003). On-line Trust: Concepts, Evolving Themes, A Model. *International Journal of Human-Computer Studies*, *58*, 737–758. doi:10.1016/S1071-5819(03)00041-7

Cox, J. (1999). *Trust, reciprocity, and other-regarding preferences of individuals and groups.* Tucson, AZ: University of Arizona.

Craven, T. C. (2003). Html tags as extractor cues for web page. *Journal of Information Science*, *6*, 1–12.

Crawford, C. M. (1983). *New products management.* Homewood, IL: Richard D. Irwin, Inc.

D'Adderio, L. (2001). Crafting the virtual prototype: How firms integrate knowledge and capabilities across organizational boundaries. *Research Policy, 30*, 1409–1424. doi:10.1016/S0048-7333(01)00159-7

Daniel, E. M., & Grimshaw, D. J. (2002). An exploratory comparison of electronic commerce adoption in large and small enterprises. *Journal of Information Technology, 17*, 133–147. doi:10.1080/0268396022000018409

Daniel, T. A., & McInerney, M. L. (2005). E-commerce and the "reluctant" small business owner: SME e-commerce and customer loyalty revisited how technology is changing the business model for small and medium-sized enterprises (SMEs). *International Journal of Applied Management and Technology, 3*, 183–206.

Darcy, J., Kraemer-Eis, H., Guellec, D., & Debande, O. (2009). *Financing technology transfer*. Adenauer, Luxembourg: European Investment Fund.

Darsø, L. (2001). *Innovation in the making*. Frederiksberg, Denmark: Samfundslitteratur.

Das, T. K., & Teng, B. (1998). Between Trust and Control Developing Confidence in Partner Cooperation in Alliances. *Academy of Management Review, 23*(3), 491–512. doi:10.2307/259291

Davenport, T. H. (1993). *Process innovation: Reengineering work through information technology*. New York, NY: Ernst & Young.

Davis, F. D. (1985). *A technology acceptance model for empirical testing new end users information systems: Theory and results*. Cambridge, MA: MIT Sloan School of Management.

Davis, F. D. (1989). Perceived usefulness, perceived ease of use, and user acceptance of information technology. *Management Information Systems Quarterly, 13*(3), 319–340. doi:10.2307/249008

Davis, F. D., Bagozzi, R. P., & Warshaw, P. R. (1989). User acceptance of computer technology: A comparison of two theoretical models. *Management Science, 35*, 982–1003. doi:10.1287/mnsc.35.8.982

Davison, R., Vogel, D., Harris, R., & Jones, N. (2000). Technology leapfrogging in developing countries – An inevitable luxury? *Electronic Journal on Information Systems in Developing Countries, 1*(5), 1–10.

De Jong, J. P. J., Vanhaverbeke, W., Van de Vrande, V., & De Rochemont, M. (2007). Open innovation in SMEs: Trends, motives and management challenges. In *Proceedings of the EURAM Conference*, Paris, France.

De Neve, G. (2005). Weaving for IKEA in South India: Subcontracting, labour markets and gender relations in a global value chain. In Fuller, C. J., & Assayag, J. (Eds.), *Globalising India: Perpectives from below*. London, UK: Anthem Press.

Dean, D. L., Lee, J. D., Pendergast, M. O., Hickey, A. M., & Nunamaker, J. F. Jr. (1998). Enabling the Effective Involvement of Multiple Users: Methods and Tools for Collaborative Software Engineering. *Journal of Management Information Systems, 14*(3), 179–222.

Deelmann, T., & Loos, P. (2002). Trust economy: Aspects of reputation and trust building for SMEs in e-business. In *Proceedings of the Eighth American Conference on Information Systems* (pp. 2213-2221).

Demetre, L., Britta, O., & Debbie, M. (2008). *Information technology (IT) with a human face: A collaborative research project to improve higher nutrition training in Southern Africa*. Stellenbosch, South Africa: University of Stellenbosh.

Denny, D., Young, M., Rausch, S., & Spear, C. (2002). An evaluation of an abstinence education curriculum series: Sex can wait. *American Journal of Health Behavior, 26*(5), 366–377.

DiClemente, R. J., & Crosby, R. A. (2009). Preventing HIV among adolescents in Sub-Saharan Africa. *The Journal of Adolescent Health, 44*(2), 101–102..doi:10.1016/j.jadohealth.2008.12.001

DiClemente, R. J., Crosby, R. A., & Salazar, L. F. (2007). A review of STD/HIV preventive interventions for adolescents: Sustaining effects using an ecological approach. *Journal of Pediatric Psychology, 32*(8), 888–906..doi:10.1093/jpepsy/jsm056

Diener, K., & Piller, F. (2010). *The market for open innovation: Increasing the efficiency and effectiveness of the innovation process*. Aachen, The Netherlands: RWTH-TIM Group.

Dirks, K. T., & Ferrin, D. L. (2001). The role of trust in organizational settings. *Organization Science, 12*(4), 450–467. doi:10.1287/orsc.12.4.450.10640

Dittrich, Y., Eriksen, S., & Wessels, B. (2009). *From knowledge transfer to situated innovation: Cultivating spaces for cooperation in innovation and design between academics, user groups and ICT providers* (Tech. Rep. No. 2009:1). Ronneby, Sweden: Blekinge Institute of Technology.

Dodgson, M., Gann, D., & Salter, A. (2006). The role of technology in the shift towards open innovation: The case of Procter & Gamble. *R & D Management, 36*(3), 333–346. doi:10.1111/j.1467-9310.2006.00429.x

Doncombe, R., & Heeks, R. (2005). *Information & communication technologies (ICTs), poverty reduction and micro, small & medium-scale enterprises (MSMEs): A framework for understanding ICT applications for MSMEs in developing countries.* Retrieved from http://www.unido.org/fileadmin/media/documents/pdf/Services_Modules/ict_brochure_report.pdf

Doney, M., & Cannon, P. (1997). An examination of the nature of trust in buyer-seller relationship. *Journal of Marketing, 61*(2), 35–51. doi:10.2307/1251829

Doney, P. M., Cannon, J. P., & Mullen, M. R. (1998). Understanding the Influence of National Culture on the Development of Trust. *Academy of Management Review, 23*(3), 601–620. doi:10.2307/259297

Driver, R. (1983). *The pupil as a scientist.* Milton Keynes, UK: Open University Press.

Drucker, P. (1998). The discipline of innovation. *Harvard Business Review, 149.*

Dul, J., & Hak, T. (2008). *Case study methodology in business research.* Burlington, MA: Butterworth-Heinemann.

Dutta, S., & Mia, I. (2010). *The global information technology report 2009/2010.* Geneva, Switzerland: World Economic Forum.

ebXML. (2001). *ebXML Technical Architecture Specification.*

EC. (2008). *SBA fact sheet Portugal.* Brussels, Belgium: European Commission.

Edelson, D. C. (2001). Learning for use: A framework for the design of technology-supported inquiry activities. *Journal of Research in Science Teaching, 38*(3), 335–385.. doi:10.1002/1098-2736(200103)38:3<355::AID-TEA1010>3.0.CO;2-M

Ekman, B., Pathmanathan, I., & Liljestrand, J. (2008). Integrating health interventions for women, newborn babies, and children: A framework for action. *Lancet, 372*(9642), 990–1000. doi:10.1016/S0140-6736(08)61408-7

Elia, E., Lefebvre, L., & Lefebvre, E. (2007). Focus of electronic commerce initiatives and related benefits in manufacturing SMEs. *Journal of Information Systems and E-Business Management, 5,* 1–23. doi:10.1007/s10257-006-0035-8

Enkel, E., Kausch, C., & Gassmann, O. (2005). Managing the risk of customer integration. *European Management Journal, 23*(2), 203–213. doi:10.1016/j.emj.2005.02.005

Erdman, K. L., & Kain, K. C. (2007). Molecular diagnostic and surveillance tools for global malaria control. *Travel Medicine and Infectious Disease, 6*(1-2), 82–99. doi:10.1016/j.tmaid.2007.10.001

Etta, F., & Parvyn-Wamahiu, S. (2003). Information and communication technologies for development in Africa: *Vol. 2. The experience with community telecentres. Ottawa.* On, Canada: IDRC.

Etzkowitz, H. (2002). Incubation of incubators: Innovation as a triple helix of university-industry-government networks. *Science & Public Policy, 29,* 115–128. doi:10.3152/147154302781781056

European Commission (EC). (2008). *The European e-business report 2008: The impact of ICT and e-business on firms, sectors and the economy.* Retrieved from www.ebusiness-watch.org/key_reports/synthesis_reports.htm

Evens, W. (2009). *How can SMEs benefit from open innovation?* Unpublished master's thesis, Hasselt University, Diepenbeek, Belgium.

Fahamu. (2002). *Healthcare training and internet connectivity in Sub-Saharan Africa.* Retrieved from http://www.fahamu.org/downloads/Nuffieldwebreport.pdf

Falkenberg, A. (1984). Modeling market share: A study of Japanese and U.S. performance in the U.S. Auto market. *Journal of the Academy of Marketing Science, 12*(4), 145–160. doi:10.1007/BF02721805

Farrell, J., & Saloner, G. (1992). Converters, compatibility, and the control of interfaces. *The Journal of Industrial Economics, 40*(1), 9–35. doi:10.2307/2950625

Fillis, I. (2002). Barriers to internationalisation: An investigation of the craft microenterprise. *European Journal of Marketing, 36*(7-8), 912–917. doi:10.1108/03090560210430872

Fillis, I., Johanson, U., & Wagner, B. (2004). Factors impacting on e-business adoption and development in the smaller firm. *International Journal of Entrepreneurial Behaviour & Research, 10*(3), 178–191. doi:10.1108/13552550410536762

Fink, D., & Disterer, G. (2006). International case studies: To what extent is ICT infused into the operations of SMEs. *Journal of Enterprise Information Management, 19*(6), 608–624. doi:10.1108/17410390610708490

Finquelievich, S., & Prince, A. (2007). *El (involuntario) rol social de los cibercafés (Cibercafes' (involuntary) social role)*. Buenos Aires, Argentina: Editorial Dunken.

Finquelievich, S., & Prince, A. (2007). *El (involuntario) rol social de los cibercafés* [Cybercafes' (involuntary) social role]. Buenos Aires: Editorial Dunken.

Fishbein, M., & Ajzen, I. (1975). Belief, attitude, intention, and behavior. In Wharton, A. S. (Ed.), *An introduction to theory and research reading*. Reading, MA: Addison-Wesley.

Fishbein, M., & Ajzen, I. (1975). *Belief, Attitude, Intention, and Behavior: an Introduction to Theory and Research*. Reading, MA: Addison-Wesley.

Flora, J. A., & Thoresen, C. E. (1988). Reducing the risk of AIDS in adolescents. *Journal of African Psychology, 43*(11), 965–970.

Freedom House. (2007). *Map of press freedom*. Retrieved from http://www.freedomhouse.org/template.cfm?page=251&year=2007

Friedman, B., Kahn, P. H., & Howe, D. C. (2000). Trust Online. *Communications of the ACM, 43*(12), 34–40. doi:10.1145/355112.355120

Friedman, C. P. (1994). The research we should be doing. *Academic Medicine, 69*(6), 455–457.. doi:10.1097/00001888-199406000-00005

Friedman, T. L. (2005). *The world is flat: A brief history of the twenty-first century*. New York, NY: Farrar, Straus and Giroux.

Fritsch, M., & Lukas, R. (2001). Who cooperates on R&D? *Research Policy, 30*(2), 297–312. doi:10.1016/S0048-7333(99)00115-8

Fukada-Parr, S. (2003). The human development paradigm: Operationalising Sen's ideas on capabilities. *Feminist Economics, 9*(2-3), 301–317.

Gaines, J., Iglar, A. F., Michal, M. L., & Patton, R. D. (1998). Attitudes towards AIDS. *Health Values, 12*(4), 53–60.

Gallivan, M. J., & Depledge, G. (2003). Trust, control and the role of interorganizational systems in electronic partnerships. *Information Systems Journal, 13*, 159–190. doi:10.1046/j.1365-2575.2003.00146.x

Gambetta, D. G. (Ed.). (1988). *Trust: Making and Breaking Cooperative Relations*. New York: Basil Blackwell.

Ganesan, S. (1994). Determinants of long-term orientation in buyer-seller relationships. *Journal of Marketing, 58*, 1–19. doi:10.2307/1252265

Garai, A., & Shadrach, B. (2006). *Taking ICT to every Indian village: Opportunities and challenges*. New Delhi, India: One World South Asia.

Garbarino, E., & Johnson, S. (1999). The Different Roles of Satisfaction, Trust, and Commitment in Customer Relationships. *Journal of Marketing, 63*, 70–87. doi:10.2307/1251946

Garrido, M., Rothschild, C., & Oumar, T. (2009). *Technology for employability in Washington State: The role of ICT training on the employment, compensation and aspirations of low-skilled, older and unemployed workers*. Retrieved from https://digital.lib.washington.edu/dspace/handle/1773/16298

Gassmann, O. (2006). Opening up the innovation process: Towards an agenda. *R & D Management, 36*(3), 223–228. doi:10.1111/j.1467-9310.2006.00437.x

Geertz, C. (1975). *The interpretation of cultures: Selected essays*. London, UK: Hutchinson.

Gefen, D. (2000). E-Commerce: The Role of Familiarity and Trust. *Omega, 28*, 725–737. doi:10.1016/S0305-0483(00)00021-9

Gefen, D., & Heart, T. (2006). On the Need to Include National Culture as a Central Issue in E- Commerce Trust Beliefs. *Journal of Global Information Management, 14*(4), 1–30.

Gengatharen, D., & Standing, C. (2005). A framework to assess the factors affecting success or failure of the implementation of government supported regional e-marketplaces for SMEs. *European Journal of Information Systems, 14*, 417–433. doi:10.1057/palgrave.ejis.3000551

Ghosh, R. A. (2003). License fees and GDP per capita: The case for open source in developing countries. *First Monday, 8*(12).

Gichoya, D. (2005). Factors affecting the successful implementation of ICT projects in government. *The Electronic. Journal of E-Government, 3*(4), 175–184.

Giner, V., & Escalle, P. (2009). A Lookahead Strategy for Movement-Based Location Update in Wireless Cellular Networks. In *Proceedings of the Sixth International Conference on Information Technology* (pp. 1171-1177).

Gleitman, H. (1995). *Psychology*. New York: W. W. Norton & Company, Inc.

Goldfarb, A., & Prince, J. (2008). Internet adoption and usage patterns are different: Implications for the digital divide. *Information Economics and Policy, 20*, 2–15. doi:10.1016/j.infoecopol.2007.05.001

Goldring, J. P. D. (2009). *Malaria: Drugs, diagnostics and where is the vaccine? Royal society of South Africa lecture series*. Pietermaritzburg, South Africa: University of Kwazulu Natal.

Gomes-Casseres, B. (1997). Alliance strategies of small firms. *Small Business Economics, 9*, 33–44. doi:10.1023/A:1007947629435

Gomez, R. (2009). *Measuring Global Public Access to ICT: Landscape Summary Reports from 25 Countries Around the World (CIS Working Paper no. 7)*. Retrieved from http://www.cis.washington.edu/depository/landscape/documents/CIS-WorkingPaperNo7.pdf

Gomez, R. (2010). Structure and Flexibility in Global Research Design: Methodological Choices in Landscape Study of Public Access in 25 Countries. *Performance Measurement and Metrics, 11*.

Gomez, R. (Ed.). (2011). *Libraries, Telecentres, Cybercafes and Public Access to ICT: International Comparisons*. Hershey, PA: IGI Global.

Gomez, R., & Gould, E. (2010). The "cool factor" of public access to ICT: Users' perceptions of trust in libraries, telecentres and cybercafés in developing countries. *Information Technology & People, 23*(3), 247–264. doi:10.1108/09593841011069158

Gomez, R., & Hunt, P. (Eds.). (1999). *Telecentre evaluation: A global perspective*. Ottawa, ON, Canada: IDRC.

Gomez, R., & Ospina, A. (2001). The Lamp Without a Genie: using the Internet for development without expecting miracles. *The Journal of Development Communication, 12*(2).

Goodwin, M. P., & Roscoe, B. (1998). AIDS: Students' knowledge and attitudes at a Midwestern university. *Journal of American College Health, 36*(4), 214–222.. doi:10.1080/07448481.1988.9939016

Gould, E., Gomez, R., & Camacho, K. (2010). *Information needs in developing countries: How are they being served by public access venues?* Paper presented at the 16th Americas Conference on Information Systems AMCIS, Lima, Peru.

Grabner-Krauter, S., & Kaluscha, E. A. (2003). Empirical research in on-line trust: a review and critical assessment. *International Journal of Human-Computer Studies, 58*, 783–812. doi:10.1016/S1071-5819(03)00043-0

Grandon, E., & Pearson, J. M. (2004). E-commerce adoption: Perceptions of managers/owners of small and medium sized firms in Chile. *Communications of the Association for Information Systems, 13*, 81–102.

Griffith, D. A., Hu, M. Y., & Ryans, J. K. Jr. (2000). Process standardization across intra- and inter-cultural relationships. *Journal of International Business Studies, 31*(2), 303–323. doi:10.1057/palgrave.jibs.8490908

Grunfeld, H. (2009). *Operationalising the capability approach for evaluating the contribution of ICT to development at ICT4D project in Bangladesh*. Victoria, Australia: Victoria University.

Gunasekara, C. (2006). Reframing the role of universities in the development of regional innovation systems. *The Journal of Technology Transfer, 31*(1), 101–113. doi:10.1007/s10961-005-5016-4

Gurol, M., & Sevindik, T. (2007). Profile of Internet cafe users in Turkey. *Telematics and Informatics, 24*(1), 59–68. doi:10.1016/j.tele.2005.12.004

Gurstein, M. (2000). Community informatics: Enabling communities with information and communications technologies. In Gurstein, M. (Ed.), *Community informatics: Enabling communities with information and communications technologies* (pp. 1–30). Hershey, PA: IGI Global.

Gurstein, M. (2005). Editorial: Sustainability of community ICTs and its future. *The Journal of Community Informatics, 1*(2), 2–3.

Gurumurthy, A., Singh, P. J., & Kasinathan, G. (2005). Case study 5: The Akshaya experience: Community driven: Local entrepreneurs in ICT services. In S. Siochru & B. Girard (Eds.), *Poor access to ICTs: The case of Akshaya, India* (pp. 143-157). Retrieved from http://propoor-ict.comunica.org/content/pdfs/04_UNDP_Report_5-India.pdf

Gurumurthy, A. (2004). *Gender and ICTs*. Brighton, UK: Institute of Development Studies.

Gurumurthy, A. (2008). *Gender equality through ICT access and appropriation: Taking a rights-based approach*. Bangalore, India: IT for Change.

Haffner, D. W. (1996). Sexual health for American's adolescents. *The Journal of School Health, 66*(4), 151–152.. doi:10.1111/j.1746-1561.1996.tb08237.x

Hafkesbrink, J., & Scholl, H. (2010). Web 2.0 learning- a case study on organizational competences in open content innovation. In Hafkesbrink, J., Hoppe, H. U., & Schlichter, J. (Eds.), *Competence management for open innovation- tools and IT-support to unlock the potential of open innovation*. Berlin, Germany: Eul Verlag.

Haider, A. (2009). *How to gain market share?* Retrieved from http://article.abc-directory.com/article/5907

Hair, J. F., Black, W. C., & Babin, B. J. Anderson, R. E., & Tatham, R. L. (1995). *Multivariate data analysis* (6ᵗʰ ed.). Upper Saddle River, NJ: Prentice-Hall.

Haiwook, C. (2001). The effects of inter-organisational information systems infrastructure on electronic cooperation: An investigation of the "move to the middle" (Doctoral dissertation, Morehead State University). *Proquest Digital Dissertations*. Retrieved from http://www.lib.umi.com/ dissertations

Hamburger, A. Y., Wainpel, G., & Fox, S. (2002). On the Internet no one knows I'm an introvert: Extroversion, introversion, and Internet interaction. *Cyberpsychology & Behavior, 5*(2), 125–128. doi:10.1089/109493102753770507

Hani & Hsu. (2005). in Introducing Cultural Fit Factors to Investigate the Appropriateness of B2B Technology Adoption to Thailand by Savanid Vatanasakdakul. In *Proceedings of the 21st Bled eConference eCollaboration: Overcoming Boundaries through Multi-Channel Interaction*, Bled, Slovenia.

Harris, R. W., Kumar, A., & Balaji, V. (2003). Sustainable telecentres? Two cases from India. In Krishna, S., & Madon, S. (Eds.), *The digital challenge: Information technology in the development context* (pp. 124–135). Surrey, UK: Ashgate.

Haseloff, A. M. (2005). Cybercafes and their potential as community development tools in India. *The Journal of Community Informatics, 1*(3), 13.

Hawes, J., Kenneth, E., & Swan, J. (1989). Trust earning perceptions of sellers and buyers. *Journal of Personal Selling & Sales Management, 9*(1), 1–8.

Head, M. M., Yuan, Y., & Archer, N. (2001, January). Building trust in e-commerce: A theoretical framework. In *Proceedings of the Second World Congress on the Management of Electronic Commerce*.

Head, M. M., & Hassanein, K. (2002). Trust in e-Commerce: Evaluating the Impact of Third-Party Seals. *Quarterly Journal of Electronic Commerce, 3*(3), 307–325.

Heeks, R. (1999). *Information and communication technologies, poverty and development, development informatics.* Retrieved from http://www.man.ac.uk/

Heeks, R. (2001). *Understanding e-governance for development.* Manchester, UK: Institute for Development Policy and Management, University of Manchester.

Heeks, R. (2002). Information systems and developing countries: Failure, success, and local improvisations. *The Information Society, 18*(2), 101–112. doi:10.1080/01972240290075039

Heeks, R. (2009). *The ICT4D 2.0 manifesto: Where next for ICT's and international development.* Manchester, UK: Development Informatics Group, Institute of Development Policy and Management.

Hempel, J. (2006). *Crowdsourcing: Milk the masses for inspiration.* Retrieved from http://www.businessweek.com/magazine/content/06_39/b4002422.htm

Henderson, J. C. (1990). Plugging into strategic partnerships: The critical IS connection. *Sloan Management Review,* 7–18.

Henderson, R. M., & Clark, K. B. (1990). Architectural innovation: The reconfiguration of existing product technologies and the failure of established firms. *Administrative Science Quarterly, 35,* 9–30. doi:10.2307/2393549

Hernandez, R. (2003). *PRODEM FFP's multilingual smart ATMs for microfinance.* Washington, DC: World Research Institute.

Herstad, S. J., Bloch, C., Ebersberger, B., & van de Velde, E. (2008). *Open innovation and globalisation: Theory, evidence and implications.* Retrieved from http://www.tem.fi/files/25709/Open_innovation_and_globalisation.pdf

Hewett, E. W. (2006). Progressive challenges in horticultural supply chains: Some future challenges. *Acta Horticulturae, 712*(1), 39–50.

Hewson, P. W., Beeth, M. E., & Thorley, R. N. (1998). Teaching for conceptual change. In Fraser, B. J., & Tobin, K. G. (Eds.), *International handbook of science education* (pp. 199–218). Boston, MA: Kluwer Academic.

Hiebing, R. G. Jr, & Cooper, S. W. (2003). *The successful marketing plan: A disciplined and comprehensive approach.* New York, NY: McGraw-Hill.

Hillenbrand, C. (2005). Librarianship in the 21st century - crisis or transformation? *The Australian Library Journal, 54,* 164–181.

Hippel, E. V., & Krogh, G. V. (2003). Open source software and the private-collective model: Issues for organization science. *Organization Science, 14*(2), 209–223. doi:10.1287/orsc.14.2.209.14992

Hjalager, A. M. (2010). A review of innovation research in tourism. *Tourism Management, 31,* 1–12. doi:10.1016/j.tourman.2009.08.012

Hodges, M. (1997). Building a bond of trust. *Technology Review, 100*(6), 26–27.

Hoffman, D. L., Novak, T. P., & Peralta, M. (1999). Building consumer trust on-line. *Communications of the ACM, 42*(4), 80–84. doi:10.1145/299157.299175

Hoffman, W. H., & Schlosser, R. (2001). Success factors of strategic alliances in small and medium-sized enterprises: An empirical study. *Long Range Planning, 34,* 357–381. doi:10.1016/S0024-6301(01)00041-3

Hofstede, G. H. (1991). *Cultures and Organizations: Software of the Mind.* New York: McGraw-Hill.

Hofstede, G. H. (2001). *Culture's Consequences: Comparing Values, Behaviors, Institutions and Organizations across Nations.* Thousand Oaks, CA: Sage Publications.

Holmstrom, M. (1993). Flexible specialisation in India? *Economic and Political Weekly, 28*(35), 82–86.

Horticulture Associated Limited (HAL). (2009). *Value of horticulture.* Retrieved from http://www.horticulture.com.au/areas_of_Investment/Environment/Climate/value_horticulture.asp

Hossain, M., & Quaddus, M. (2010a, March 30-April 1). An adoption diffusion model of RFID-based livestock management system in Australia. In *Proceedings of the IFIP WG 8.2/8.6 International Working Conference* on *Human Benefit through the Diffusion of Information Systems Design Science Research,* Perth, Australia (pp. 179-191).

Hossain, M., & Quaddus, M. (2010b). Impact of external environmental factors on RFID adoption in Australian livestock industry: An exploratory study. In *Proceedings of the Asia-Pacific Conference on Information Systems* (p. 171).

Howe, J. (2006). The rise of crowdsourcing. *Wired Magazine, 14*(6), 1–4.

Howells, J., James, A., & Malek, K. (2003). The sourcing of technological knowledge: Distributed innovation processes and dynamic change. *R & D Management, 33*(4), 395–409. doi:10.1111/1467-9310.00306

Hsu, H. Y. (2002). The needs and meaning on teaching subjects integrating computers and technology. In Chang, H. T. (Ed.), *Teaching subjects integrating computers and technology* (pp. vii–x). Taipei, Taiwan: Pro-Ed.

Huang, H., Keser, C., Leland, J. W., & Shachat, J. (2003). Trust, the Internet and the Digital Divide. *IBM Systems Journal, 42*(3), 507–518. doi:10.1147/sj.423.0507

Huang, K., & Provan, G. K. (2007). Resource tangibility and patterns of interaction in a publicly funded health and human services networks. *Journal of Public Administration: Research and Theory, 17*(3), 435–454. doi:10.1093/jopart/mul011

Huang, Z., Brian, D., & Frolick, M. (2008). A comprehensive examination of Internet EDI adoption. *Information Systems Management, 25*(3), 273–286. doi:10.1080/10580530802151228

Hudson, S., & Gilbert, D. (2006). The Internet and small hospitality businesses: B&B marketing in Canada. *Journal of Hospitality Marketing & Management, 14*(1), 99–116.

Hughes, N., & Lonie, S. (2007). M-Pesa: Mobile money for the "unbanked": Turning cellphones into 24-hour tellers in Kenya. *Innovations: Technology, Governance, Globalization, 2*(1-2), 63–81. doi:10.1162/itgg.2007.2.1-2.63

Human Development Reports. (2001). *Human development report: Making new technologies work for human development*. Retrieved from http://hdr.undp.org/en/reports/global/hdr2001/

Human Development Reports. (2007). *Fighting climate change: Human solidarity in a divided world*. Retrieved from http://hdr.undp.org/en/reports/global/hdr2007-2008/

Human Development Reports. (2009). *M economy and inequality*. Retrieved from http://hdrstats.undp.org/en/indicators/161.html

Hunaiti, Z., Masa'deh, R., Mansour, M., & Nawafleh, A. (2009). Electronic commerce adoption barriers in small and medium-sized enterprises (SMEs) in developing countries: The case of Libya. *IBIMA Business Review, 2*, 37–45.

Hwang, H., Chang, M., & Tseng, C. (2000). A Direction-Based Location Update Scheme with a Line-Paging Strategy for PCS Networks. *IEEE Communications Letters, 4*(5), 149–151. doi:10.1109/4234.846494

Hyper History. (2010). *History education and information communication technologies (ICT)*. Retrieved from www.hyperhistory.org/images/assets/pdf/ict.pdf

ICT4D. (2008). *The sustainable use of ICTs to enable poor people and marginalised communities to use the potential of ICT to transform their lives*. Retrieved from http://www.gg.rhul.ac.uk/ict4d/Malaria.html

IDA. (2000). *A proposed framework on building trust and confidence in electronic commerce*. Retrieved from http://unpan1.un.org/intradoc/groups/public/documents/apcity/unpan004855.pdf

Ideacorp. (2008). *Public access to information & ICTs final report: Philippines*. Seattle, WA: University of Washington Center for Information & Society (CIS).

IFLA. (2007). *Access to libraries and information: Towards a fairer world* (*Vol. 7*). International Federation of Library Associations.

IfM and IBM. (2008). *Succeeding through service innovation: A service perspective for education, research, business and government*. Cambridge, UK: University of Cambridge Institute for Manufacturing.

Infoplease. (2009). *Tanzania*. Retrieved from http://www.infoplease.com/ipa/A0108028.html

International Telecommunications Union. (2007). *Measuring the information society: ICT opportunity index and world telecommunications/ICT indicators*. Retrieved from http://www.itu.int/ITU-D/ict/publications/ict-oi/2007/

International Telecommunications Union. (2010). *Measuring the information society.* Retrieved fromhttp://www.itu.int/ITU-D/ict/publications/idi/2010/Material/MIS_2010_without_annex_4-e.pdf

Internet World Stats. (2010). *Internet usage statistics.* Retrieved from http://www.internetworldstats.com/stats.htm

ITU. (2009). *Measuring the Information Society: The ICT Development Index.* Geneva, Switzerland: International Telecommunications Union.

Jagdish, B., Panagariya, A., & Srinivasan, T. N. (2004). The muddles over outsourcing. *Journal of Economic Perspectives. American Economic Association, 18*(4), 93–114.

Jain, R., & Raghuram, G. (2005). *Study on accelerated provisions of rural telecommunication services (ARTS).* Ahmedabad, India: Indian Institute of Management. Retrieved from http://www.iimahd.ernet.in/ctps/pdf/Final%20Report%20Edited.pdf

James, T., & Louw, M. (2008). *Public access to information & ICTs final report: Namibia.* Seattle, WA: University of Washington Center for Information & Society (CIS).

James, J. (2002). Low-cost information technology in developing countries: Current opportunities and emerging possibilities. *Habitat International, 26*, 21–31. doi:10.1016/S0197-3975(01)00030-3

James, J. (2004). *Information technologies and development: A new paradigm for delivering the Internet to rural areas in developing countries.* London, UK: Routledge.

Jarvenpaa, S. L., Tractinsky, N., & Vitale, M. (2000). Consumer Trust in an Internet Store. *Information Technology Management, 1*, 45–71. doi:10.1023/A:1019104520776

Jennex, M. E. (2003). UNCTAD and e-commerce success. *Electronic Journal on Information Systems in Developing Countries, 11*(11), 1–7.

Jennex, M. E., Amoroso, D., & Adelakun, O. (2004). E-commerce infrastructure success factors for small companies in developing economies. *Electronic Commerce Research, 4*, 263–286. doi:10.1023/B:ELEC.0000027983.36409.d4

Jensen, M., & Esterhuysen, A. (2001). *The telecentre cookbook for Africa: Recipes for self-sustainability.* Paris, France: UNESCO.

Jeon, B. N., Han, K. S., & Lee, M. J. (2006). Determining factors for the adoption of e-business: The case of SMEs in Korea. *Applied Economics, 38*(16), 1905–1916. doi:10.1080/00036840500427262

Jhunjhunwala, A. (n. d). *Unleashing telecom and Internet in India.* Retrieved from http://www.tenet.res.in

Jhunjhunwala, A., Ramachandran, A., & Bandyopadhyay, A. (2004). n-Logue: The story of a rural service provider in India. *Journal of Community Informatics, 1*(1), 30–38.

Jhunjhunwala, A., Ramamurthi, B., & Gonsalves, T. A. (1998). The role of technology in telecom expansion in India. *IEEE Communications Magazine*, 88–94. doi:10.1109/35.733480

Jimoh, A. T. (2007). Students' attitude towards ICT in Nigeria tertiary institutions. *Education Focus, 1*(1), 73–79.

Johansson, A., Kisch, P., & Mirata, M. (2005). Distributed economies – a new engine for innovation. *Journal of Cleaner Production, 13*, 971–979. doi:10.1016/j.jclepro.2004.12.015

Joint United Nations Programme on HIV/AIDS (UNAIDS) and World Health Organization. (WHO). (2000). AIDS epidemic. Geneva, Switzerland: UNAIDS.

Jutla, D., Bodorik, P., & Dhaliwal, J. (2002). Supporting the e-business readiness of small and medium-sized enterprises: Approaches and metrics. *Internet Research: Electronic Networking Applications and Policy, 12*(2), 139–164. doi:10.1108/10662240210422512

Kamiyama, S., Sheehan, J., & Martinez, C. (2006). *Valuation and exploitation of intellectual property.* Paris, France: OECD Publishing.

Kamssu, J. A., Siekpe, S. J., & Ellzy, A. J. (2004). Shortcomings to globalization: Using Internet technology and electronic commerce in developing countries. *Journal of Developing Areas, 38*(1), 151–169. doi:10.1353/jda.2005.0010

Kaplan, D., Iida, R., & Tokunaga, T. (2009). Automatic extraction of citation contexts for research paper summarization: a co reference-chain based approach. In *Proceedings of the Workshop on Text and Citation Analysis for Scholarly Digital Libraries* (pp. 88-95).

Karahanna, E., Evaristo, R., & Srite, M. (2002). Methodological issues in MIS cross-cultural research. *Journal of Global Information Management*, *10*(1), 48–56.

Karanasios, S. (2007). Ecuador, the digital divide and small tourism enterprises. *Journal of Business Systems. Governance and Ethics*, *2*(3), 21–34.

Karnani, A. (2007). The mirage of marketing to the bottom of the pyramid: How the private sector can help alleviate poverty. *California Management Review*, *49*(4), 90–111.

Katz, M. L., & Shapiro, C. (1994). Systems competition and network effects. *The Journal of Economic Perspectives*, *8*(2), 93–115.

Katz, R., & Allen, T. J. (1982). Investigating the not-invented-here (NIH)- syndrome: A look at performance, tenure and communication patterns of 50 R&D project groups. *R & D Management*, *12*, 7–19. doi:10.1111/j.1467-9310.1982.tb00478.x

Kawlra, A. (1998). *Weaving as praxis: The case of the Padma Saliyars.* Unpublished doctoral dissertation, Indian Institute of Technology, Delhi, India.

Kawlra, A., & Sreejith, N. N. (2007, August 22-25). *An ICT-based model for Craft (distributive) production in India.* Paper presented at the International Conference on Home/Community Oriented IT for the Next Billion, Madras, India.

Kaynak, E., Tatoglu, E., & Kula, V. (2005). An analysis of the factors affecting the adoption of electronic commerce by SMEs: Evidence from an emerging market. *International Marketing Review*, *22*(6), 623–640. doi:10.1108/02651330510630258

Keil, T. (2002). *External corporate venturing: Strategic renewal in rapidly changing industries*. Westport, CT: Quorum.

Kenniston, K. (2001). *IT for the common man: Lessons from India*. Retrieved from http://web.mit.edu/~kken/Public/FILES/pubs.htm

Kenniston, K., & Kumar, D. (Eds.). (2000). *Bridging the digital divide: Lessons from India*. Bangalore, India: National Institute of Advanced Study.

Kenniston, K., & Kumar, D. (Eds.). (2003). *The four digital divides*. New Delhi, India: Sage.

Killikanya, C. (2000). E-Commerce: Internet slow to make inroads. *Bangkok Post: Mid-year. Economic Review (Federal Reserve Bank of Atlanta)*, 32–35.

Kim, K., & Prbhakar, B. (2000). Initial Trust, Perceived Risk and Adoption of Internet Banking. In *Proceedings of the International Conference on Information Systems (ICIS)*, Brisbane, Australia.

Kim, K., & Choi, H. (2009). A Mobility Model and Performance Analysis in Wireless Cellular Network with General Distribution and Multi-Cell Model. *International Journal of Wireless Personal Communications*, *53*(2), 179–198. doi:10.1007/s11277-009-9678-3

Kim, S., Kim, I., Mani, V., Jun, H., & Agrawal, D. (2010). Partitioning of Mobile Network Into Location Areas Using Ant Colony Optimization. [ICIC]. *International Journal of Innovative Computing, Information, and Control*, *1*(1), 39–44.

Kling, R. (2000). Learning about information technologies and social change: The contribution of social informatics. *The Information Society*, *16*(3), 217–223. doi:10.1080/01972240050133661

Kondepu, K., & Kumar, C. (2009). An Effective Pointer-Based HLR Location Registration Scheme in Location Management for PCS Networks. In *Proceedings of the First IEEE International Conference on Communication Systems and Networks (COMSNETS-2009)* (pp. 570-571).

Kondepu, K., Kumar, C., & Tripathi, R. (2008). Partially Overlapping Super Location Area (POSLA): An Efficient Scheme for Location Management in PCS Networks. In *Proceedings of the IEEE 67th Vehicular Technology Conference (VTC-2008)* (pp. 2182-2187).

Konous, J., & Minoli, D. (2010). *Information Technology Risk Management in Enterprise Environments: A review of Industry practices and a pratical guide to risk management teams*. New York: John Wiley.

Korgaonkar, P., & O'Leary, B. (2006). Management, market, and financial factors separating winners and losers in e-business. *Journal of Computer-Mediated Communication*, *11*(4). doi:10.1111/j.1083-6101.2006.00311.x

Kulmala, H., & Rauva, E. (2005). Network as a business environment: Experience from software industry. *Supply Chain Management: An International Journal, 10*(3), 169–178. doi:10.1108/13598540510606223

Kumar, A., Rajput, N., Chakraborty, D., Agarwal, S. K., & Nanavati, A. A. (2007). WWTW: The world wide telecom web. In *Proceedings of the Workshop on Networked Systems for Developing Regions* (p. 7).

Kumar, C., & Tripathi, R. (2008). A Review of Mobility Management Schemes for the Wireless Networks. In *Proceedings of the National Seminar on Frontiers in Electronics, Communication, Instrumentation & Information Technology (FECIIT-2008)* (pp. 109-115).

Kumar, N., & Benbasat, I. (2001). Shopping as Experience and Website as a Social Actor: Web Interface Design and Para-Social Presence. In *Proceedings of the International Conference on Information Systems (ICIS)*, New Orleans, LA.

Kumar, M., & Sareen, M. (2009). Building trust in e-commerce through web interface. *International Journal of Information Communication Technologies and Human Development, 1*(1). doi:10.4018/jicthd.2009092205

Kumar, M., & Sareen, M. (2009). Trust and technology in inter-organizational business relations. *International Journal of Telecommunications and Human Development, 1*(4), 40–57. doi:10.4018/jicthd.2009091504

Kundu, A., & Sarangi, N. (2004). *ICT and human development: Towards building a composite index for Asia*. Amsterdam, The Netherlands: Elsevier.

Kuo, H. C. (2006). A survey on quality of life and needs among HIV/AIDS patients in the Northern Region of Malawi. Unpublished master's thesis, National Yang Ming University, Taipei, Taiwan.

Kuriyan, R., & Kitner, K. R. (2009). Constructing Class Boundaries: Gender, Aspirations and Shared Computing. *Information Technologies & International Development, 5*(1).

Kuriyan, R., & Toyama, K. (2007). *Review of Research on Rural PC Kiosks*. Retrieved from http://research.microsoft.com/research/tem/kiosks/

Kuzma, A., & Shanklin, W. (1992). How medium-market-share companies achieve superior profitability. *Journal of Consumer Marketing, 9*(1), 39–46. doi:10.1108/EUM0000000002595

Lai, F., Dahui, L., Wang, J., & Hutchinson, J. (2006). An empirical investigation of the effects of e-readiness factors on e-business adoption in China's international trading industry. *International Journal of Electronic Business, 4*(3-4), 320–339. doi:10.1504/IJEB.2006.010869

Lai, F., Wang, J., Hsieh, C., & Chen, J. (2007). On network externalities, e-business adoption and information asymmetry. *Industrial Management & Data Systems, 107*(5), 728–746. doi:10.1108/02635570710750453

Lal, K. (2005). Determinants of the adoption of e-business technologies. *Telematics and Informatics, 22*(3), 181–199. doi:10.1016/j.tele.2004.07.001

Lalkala, R. (2001, November). Best practices in business incubation: Lessons yet to be learned. In *Proceedings of the International Conference on Business Centres: Actors for Economic and Social Development*, Brussels, Belgium (pp. 14-15).

Laudon, K., & Traver, C. (2002). *E-Commerce: Business, technology, society*. Reading, MA: Addison-Wesley.

Law, R., Leung, R., & Buhalis, D. (2009). Information technology applications in hospitality and tourism: A review of publications from 2005 to 2007. *Journal of Travel & Tourism Marketing, 26*, 599–623. doi:10.1080/10548400903163160

Lawrence, J. (2008). The challenges and utilization of e-commerce: Use of Internet by small to medium –sized enterprises in the United Kingdom. *Information. Social Justice (San Francisco, Calif.), 1*(2), 99–113.

Lee, B., & Hwang, C. (1999). A Predictive paging scheme based on the movement direction of a mobile host. In *Proceeding of IEEE Vehicular Technology Conference (VTC)* (Vol. 4, pp. 2158-2162).

Lee, W. W., & Chan, A. K. K. (2008, December). *Computer ethics: An argument for rethinking business ethics*. Paper presented at the 2nd World Business Ethics Forum: Rethinking the Value of Business Ethics, Hong Kong, China.

Lee, M. P. (2003). *HIV/AIDS education instruction manual*. Taipei, Taiwan: Centers for Disease Control, Department of Health.

Leenders, M. A. A. M., & Wierenga, B. (2002). The effectiveness of different mechanisms for integrating marketing and R&D. *Journal of Product Innovation Management, 19*(4), 305–317. doi:10.1016/S0737-6782(02)00147-9

Lee, S., Park, G., Yoon, B., & Park, J. (2010). Open innovation in SMEs- an intermediated network model. *Research Policy, 39*(2), 290–300. doi:10.1016/j.respol.2009.12.009

Lee, Y. G., & Lee, J. H. (2010). Different characteristics between auctioned and non-auctioned patents. *Scientometrics, 82*(1), 135–148. doi:10.1007/s11192-009-0029-7

Leimeister, J. M., Huber, M., Bretschneider, U., & Krcmar, H. (2009). Leveraging crowdsourcing: Activation-supporting components for IT-based idea competitions. *Journal of Management Information Systems, 26*(1), 197–224. doi:10.2753/MIS0742-1222260108

Levenburg, N., & Klein, H. (2006). Delivering customer services online: Identifying best practices of medium-sized enterprises. *Information Systems Journal, 16*, 135–147. doi:10.1111/j.1365-2575.2006.00212.x

Levin, C. (2000). *Web dropouts: Concerns about online privacy send some consumers off-line.* Retrieved from http://www.zdnet.com/

Lewicki, R. J., & Bunker, B. B. (Eds.). (1995). *Trust in Relationships: A Model of Development and Decline.* San Francisco: Jossey-Bass.

Liburd, J., & Hjalager, A. M. (2009). *Valuing open innovation environments in tourism education and research-the case of INNOTOUR.* Paper presented at the Think Tank 9 on The Importance of Values in Sustainable Tourism, Singapore.

Lichtenthaler, U. (2007). The drivers of technology licensing: An industry comparison. *California Management Review, 49*(4), 67–89.

Lichtenthaler, U. (2008). Open innovation in practice: An analysis of strategic approaches to technology transactions. *IEEE Transactions on Engineering Management, 55*(1), 148–157. doi:10.1109/TEM.2007.912932

Lichtenthaler, U., & Ernst, H. (2009). Opening up the innovation process: The role of technology aggressiveness. *R & D Management, 39*(1), 38–54. doi:10.1111/j.1467-9310.2008.00522.x

Lieberman, D. A. (1997). Interactive video games for health promotion effects on knowledge, self-efficacy, social support, and health. In Street, R. L. Jr., (Ed.), *Health promotion and interactive technology: Theoretical application and future directions* (pp. 103–120). Mahwah, NJ: Lawrence Erlbaum.

Liebl, M., & Roy, T. (2003). Handmade in India: Preliminary analysis of Crafts producers and Crafts production. *Economic and Political Weekly, 38*(51-52), 5366–5376.

Lilien, G. L., Morrison, P. D., Searls, K., Sonnack, M., & von Hippel, E. (2002). Performance assessment of the lead user idea-generation process for new product development. *Management Science, 48*(8), 1042–1059. doi:10.1287/mnsc.48.8.1042.171

Linder, J. C., Jarvenpaa, S., & Davenport, T. H. (2003). Toward an innovation sourcing strategy. *MIT Sloan Management Review, 4447*, 43–49.

Lituchy, T. R., & Rail, A. (2000). Bed and breakfasts, small inns, and the Internet: The impact of technology on the globalization of small businesses. *Journal of International Marketing, 8*(2), 86–97. doi:10.1509/jimk.8.2.86.19625

Liu, C., & Arentt, K. (2000). Exploring the factors associated with website success in the context of electronic commerce. *Information & Management, 38*(1), 23–33. doi:10.1016/S0378-7206(00)00049-5

Lord, M. D., Mandel, S. W., & Wager, J. D. (2002). Spinning out a star. *Harvard Business Review, 80*, 115–121.

Lucas, H. (2008). Information and communications technology for future health systems in developing countries. *Social Science & Medicine, 66*(10), 2122–2132. doi:10.1016/j.socscimed.2008.01.033

Lumsden, J., & MacKay, L. (2006). How does personality affect trust in B2C e-commerce? In *Proceedings of the 8th international Conference on Electronic Commerce (ICEC '06)* (pp. 471-481).

MacGregor, S., Bianchi, M., Hernandez, J. L., & Mendibil, K. (2007, October 29-30). Towards the tipping point for social innovation. In *Proceedings of the 12ᵗʰ International Conference on Towards Sustainable Product Design*, Surrey, UK (pp. 145-152).

Macgregor, R., & Vrazlaic, L. (2006). Electronic business in small businesses: A global perspective. In Al-Qirim, N. (Ed.), *Global electronic business research: Opportunities and directions*. Hershey, PA: IGI Global.

Mahadevan, B., & Venkatesh, N. S. (2000). A framework for building on-line trust for business to business e-commerce. In *Proceedings of the IT Asia Millennium Conference*, Bombay, India.

Main, H. C. (2002). The expansion of technology in small and medium hospitality enterprises with a focus on net technology. *Information Technology & Tourism*, *4*, 167–174.

Malone, T. W., Yates, J., & Benjamin, R. I. (1987). Electronic markets and electronic hierarchies. *Communications of the ACM*, *30*(6), 484–497. doi:10.1145/214762.214766

Mäntymäki, M., & Salo, J. (2010). Trust, Social Presence and Customer Loyalty in Social Virtual Worlds. In *Proceedings of the 23rd Bled eConference eTrust: Implications for the Individual, Enterprises and Society*, Bled, Slovenia.

Marchant, T., Schellenberg, J. A., Edgar, T., Nathan, R., Abdulla, S., & Mukasa, O. (2002). Socially marketed insecticide-treated nets improve malaria and anemia in pregnancy in southern Tanzania. *Tropical Medicine & International Health*, *7*(2), 149–158. doi:10.1046/j.1365-3156.2002.00840.x

Marchany, R. C., & Tront, J. G. (2002). E-commerce security issues. In *Proceedings of the 35th Hawaii International Conference on System Sciences*.

Markande, S., & Bodhe, K. (2009). Cartesian Coordinate System based Dynamic Location Management Scheme. *International Journal of Electronics Engineering Research*, *1*(1), 63–69.

Marschollek, M., Mix, S., Wolf, K. H., Effertz, B., Haux, R., & Steinhagen-Thiessen, E. (2007). ICT-based health information services for elderly people: Past experiences, current trends, and future strategies. *Informatics for Health & Social Care*, *32*(4), 251–261. doi:10.1080/14639230701692736

Marshall, R. S., & Boush, D. M. (2001). Dynamic decision-making: a cross-cultural comparison of U.S. and Peruvian export managers. *Journal of International Business Studies*, *32*(4), 873–893. doi:10.1057/palgrave.jibs.8490998

Maskus, K. E. (2008). The globalization of intellectual property rights and innovation in services. *Journal of Industry, Competition and Trade*, *8*(3), 247–267. doi:10.1007/s10842-008-0040-3

Mason, C., Castleman, T., & Parker, C. (2008). Systems factors influencing SME knowledge sharing online. In *Proceedings of the 19ᵗʰ Australasian Conference on Information Systems* (pp. 617-628).

Mathew, P. M. (1997). From beautiful 'small' to flexible specialisation: Asian experience of small enterprise development. *Economic and Political Weekly*, *32*(3), 84–86.

Mayanja, M. (2006). Rethinking telecentre sustainability approaches: How to implement a social enterprise approach: Lessons from India and Africa. *The Journal of Community Informatics*, *2*(3).

Mayer, R. C., Davis, J. H., & Schoorman, F. D. (1995). An integrative model of organizational trust. *Academy of Management Review*, *20*(3), 709–734.

Mayer, R. E. (2001). *Multimedia learning*. Cambridge, UK: Cambridge University Press.

Mboera, L. E. G., Makundi, E. A., & Kitua, A. Y. (2007). *Uncertainty in malaria control in Tanzania: Crossroads and challenges for future interventions*. Dar es Salaam, Tanzania: National Institute for Medical Research.

McAuley, A., & Fillies, I. (2006). *A future in the making: A socio-economic study of makers in Northern Ireland 2006*. Belfast, Ireland: Craft Northern Ireland.

McCrae, R. R. (1992). The five-factor model: Issues and applications. *Journal of Personality*, *60*(2). doi:10.1111/j.1467-6494.1992.tb00970.x

McKnight, D. H., Choudhury, V., & Kacmar, C. (2002). Developing and Validating Trust Measures for ECommerce: An Integrative Typology. *Information Systems Research*, *13*(3), 334–359. doi:10.1287/isre.13.3.334.81

McKnight, D. H., Cummings, L. L., & Chervany, N. L. (1998). Initial Trust Formation in New Organizational Relationships. *Academy of Management Review*, *23*(3), 473–490. doi:10.2307/259290

Mculey, A., & Fillis, I. (2004). *A socio-economic study of crafts businesses in England and Wales*. London, UK: Crafts Council, Arts Council England, and Arts Council Wales.

Medhi, I., Patnaik, S., Brunskill, E., Gautama, S. N. N., Thies, W., & Toyama, K. (2010). Designing mobile interfaces for novice and low-literacy users. *ACM Transactions on Computer-Human Interaction*, *18*(1).

Medhi, I., Sagar, A., & Toyama, K. (2007). Text-free user interfaces for illiterate and semi-literate users. *Information Technologies and International Development*, *4*(1), 37–50. doi:10.1162/itid.2007.4.1.37

Melkote, S. R., & Steeves, H. L. (2001). *Communication for development in the third world. Theory and practice for empowerment* (2nd ed.). Thousand Oaks, CA: Sage.

Menda, A. (2010). *ICT education project amid rural connectivity challenges*. Retrieved from http://www.businesstimes.co.tz/index.php?option=com_content&view=article&id=200:ict-education-project-amid-rural-connectivity-challenges&catid=45:ict-news&Itemid=73

Mies, M. (1982). *The lace makers of Narsapur: Indian housewives produce for the world market*. London, UK: Zed Press.

Miles, I. (2005). Innovation in services. In Fagerberg, J., Mowery, D. C., & Nelson, R. R. (Eds.), *The Oxford handbook of innovation* (pp. 433–458). Oxford, UK: Oxford University Press.

Miller, L., Dawans, V., & Alter, K. (2009). *Industree Craft: A case study in social enterprise development using the four lenses approach*. Seattle, WA: Virtue Ventures, LLC.

Milne, G. R., & Boza, M. (1999). Trust and concern in consumers' perceptions of marketing information management practices. *Journal of Interactive Marketing*, *13*(1), 5–24. doi:10.1002/(SICI)1520-6653(199924)13:1<5::AID-DIR2>3.0.CO;2-9

Minghetti, V., & Buhalis, D. (2010). Digital divide in tourism. *Journal of Travel Research*, *49*(3), 267–281. doi:10.1177/0047287509346843

Mirchandani, A. A., & Motwani, J. (2001). Understanding small business electronic commerce adoption: An empirical analysis. *Journal of Computer Information Systems*, 70–73.

Modupe, M., & Binuomote, M. O. (2007). Awareness and adoption of information and communication technology among secretarial staff of Ladoke Akintola University of Technology, Ogbomaso, Nigeria. *Social Science*, *2*, 57–59.

Moghadam, A. H., & Assar, P. (2008). The Relationship Between National Culture and E-Adoption: A Case Study of Iran. *American Journal of Applied Sciences*, *5*(4), 369–377. doi:10.3844/ajassp.2008.369.377

Molla, A., & Licker, P. (2005a). eCommerce adoption in developing countries: A model and instrument. *Information & Management*, *42*, 877–899. doi:10.1016/j.im.2004.09.002

Molla, A., & Licker, P. (2005b). Perceived e-readiness factors in e-commerce adoption: An empirical investigation in a developing country. *International Journal of Electronic Commerce*, *10*(1), 83–110.

Molla, A., & Peszynski, K. (2009). E-Business diffusion among Australian horticulture firms. *Australian Agribusiness Review*, *17*, 78–93.

Molla, A., & Peszynski, K. (2010). The use of e-business in agribusiness: Investigating the influence of e-readiness and OTE factors. *Journal of Global Information Technology Management*, *13*(1), 1–30.

Money & Sharma. (2006). Referenced from Savanid Vatanasakdakul. 2008. Introducing Cultural Fit Factors to Investigate the Appropriateness of B2B Technology Adoption to Thailand. In *Proceedings of the 21st Bled eConference eCollaboration: Overcoming Boundaries through Multi-Channel Interaction*, Bled, Slovenia.

Montealegre, F., Thompson, S., & Eales, J. (2004, June 12-15). An empirical analysis of the determinants of success of food and agribusiness e-commerce firms. In *Proceedings of the IAMA Forum Symposium*, Montreux, Switzerland.

Moor, J. (1985). What is computer ethics? *Metaphilosophy*, *16*(4). doi:10.1111/j.1467-9973.1985.tb00173.x

Moorman, C., Deshpande, R., & Zaltman, G. (1993). Factors affecting trust in market research relationships. *Journal of Marketing*, *57*, 81–101. doi:10.2307/1252059

Moreno, C. (2001). Brief Overview of Selective Legal and Regulatory Issues in Electronic Commerce. In *Proceedings of the International Symposium on Government and Electronic Commerce Development*, Ningbo, China.

Morrison, A. J., & King, B. E. M. (2002). Small tourism businesses and e-commerce: Victorian tourism online. *Tourism and Hospitality Research*, *4*(2), 104–115.

Mueller, R. A. E. (2001). E-commerce and entrepreneurship in agricultural markets. *American Journal of Agricultural Economics*, *83*(5), 1243–1249. doi:10.1111/0002-9092.00274

Mutz, D. C. (2005). Social Trust and E-commerce experimental evidence for the effects of social trust on individuals' economic behavior. *Public Opinion Quarterly*, *69*(3), 393–416. doi:10.1093/poq/nfi029

Nalebuff, B. J., & Brandeburger, A. M. (1996). *Coopetition*. London, UK: Harper Collins.

Nath, L. M. (1998). The epidemic in India: An overview. In Godwin, P. (Ed.), *The looming epidemic: The impact of HIV and AIDS in India* (p. 28). New Delhi, India: Mosaic Books.

Ndonzuau, F. N., Pirnay, F., & Surlemont, B. (2002). A stage model of academic spin-off creation. *Technovation*, *22*, 281–289. doi:10.1016/S0166-4972(01)00019-0

Ngai, E., & Wat, F. (2002). A literature review and classification of electronic commerce research. *Information & Management*, *39*(5), 415–429. doi:10.1016/S0378-7206(01)00107-0

Ng, E. (2005). An empirical framework developed for selecting B2B e-business models: The case of Australian agribusiness firms. *Journal of Business and Industrial Marketing*, *20*(4-5), 218–225. doi:10.1108/08858620510603891

Ngwenyama, O., & Morawczynski, O. (2009). Factors affecting ICT expansion in emerging economies: An analysis of ICT infrastructure expansion in five Latin American countries. *Information Technology for Development*, *15*(4), 237–258. doi:10.1002/itdj.20128

Niwe Moses. (2006). Standards based B2B e-commerce Adoption. *Advances in Systems Modelling and ICT Applications*, 335-347.

NOIE. (2002). *E-Commerce for small business*. Parkes, Australia: National Office for the Information Economy.

Noor, A. M., Juliette, J., Mutheu, J. J., Andrew, J., Tatem, J. A., & Simon, I. (2009). Insecticide-treated net coverage in Africa: Mapping progress in 2000-07. *Lancet*, *373*, 58–67. doi:10.1016/S0140-6736(08)61596-2

Norris, P. (2001). *Digital divide: Civic engagement, information poverty, and the Internet worldwide*. Cambridge, UK: Cambridge University Press.

Nybakk, E., & Hansen, E. (2008). Entrepreneurial attitude, innovation and performance among Norwegian nature-based tourism enterprises. *Forest Policy and Economics*, *10*, 473–479. doi:10.1016/j.forpol.2008.04.004

O'Keeffe, M., & Mavondo, F. (2005). *Capabilities and competing: High performance in the food and beverage industry*. Retrieved from http://www.nfis.com.au/dmdocuments/final%20report.pdf

O'Toole, T. (2003). E-relationships: Emergence and the small firm. *Marketing Intelligence & Planning*, *21*(2), 115–122. doi:10.1108/02634500310465434

Obayelu, A. E., & Ogunlade, I. (2006). Analysis of the uses of information communication technology (ICT) for gender empowerment and sustainable poverty alleviation in Nigeria. *International Journal of Education and Development Using Information and Communication Technology*, *2*(3).

OECD. (1992). *Oslo manual* (1st ed.). Paris, France: OECD.

OECD. (1996). *Oslo manual* (2nd ed.). Paris, France: OECD.

OECD. (2005). *Oslo manual* (3rd ed.). Paris, France: OECD.

OECD. (2008). *Open innovation in global networks, policy brief.* Paris, France: OECD.

Ofodu, G. O. (2007). Nigeria literacy educators and their technological needs in a digital age. *Education Focus*, *1*(1), 22–30.

Olaniyi, S. S. (2006). E-learning technology: The Nigeria experience [Electronic Version]. *Shape the Change*, 8-13, Oyelaran-Oyeyinka, B., & Adeya, C. N. (2004). Dynamics of adoption and usage of ICT in African universities: A study of Kenya and Nigeria. *Technovation*, *24*(10), 841–851.

Olson, B. D., & Suls, J. (1998). Self-, Other-, and Ideal-Judgements of Risk and Caution as a Function of the Five-Factor Model of Personality. *Personality and Individual Differences*, *28*, 425–436. doi:10.1016/S0191-8869(99)00105-1

Olson, E., & Bakke, G. (2001). Implementing the lead user method in a high technology firm: A longitudinal study of intentions versus actions. *Journal of Product Innovation Management*, *18*(2), 388–395. doi:10.1016/S0737-6782(01)00111-4

Olson, J. S., & Olson, G. M. (2000). i2i Trust in E-Commerce. *Communications of the ACM*, *43*(12), 41–44. doi:10.1145/355112.355121

Oram, J., & Doane, D. (2005). Size matters: The need for human-scale economic institutions for development. *Development in Practice*, *15*(3-4), 439–450. doi:10.1080/09614520500076233

Pare, D. (2002). *B2B e-commerce services and developing countries: disentangling Myth from reality.* Retrieved from www.gapresearch.org/production/

Pare, D. (2003). Does this site deliver? B2B e-commerce services for developing countries. *The Information Society*, *19*, 123–134. doi:10.1080/01972240309457

Parkinson, S. (2005). *Telecentres, access and development: Experience and lessons from Uganda and South Africa* (p. 176). Ottawa, ON, Canada: IDRC.

Patra, R., Nedevschi, S., Surana, S., & Sheth, A. (2007). Wildnet: Design and implementation of high performance wifi based long distance networks. In *Proceedings of the 16th USENIX Security Symposium.*

Patton, M. A., & Jøsang, A. (2004). Technologies for trust in electronic commerce. *Electronic Commerce Research*, *4*(1), 9–21. doi:10.1023/B:ELEC.0000009279.89570.27

Paul, J. (2004). *What works: n-Logue's rural connectivity model: Deploying wirelessly-connected Internet kiosks in villages throughout India.* Washington, DC: World Resources Institute.

Pavlou, P. A., & Fygenson, M. (2006). Understanding and Predicting Electronic Commerce Adoption: An Extension of the Theory of Planned Behavior. *Management Information Systems Quarterly*, *30*(1), 115–143.

Payne, J. (2003). *E-Commerce readiness for SMEs in developing countries: A guide for development professionals.* Washington, DC: Learn Link.

Pearson, J. M., & Grandon, E. E. (2005). An empirical study of factors that influence e-commerce adoption/non-adoption in small and medium sized businesses. *Journal of Internet Commerce*, *4*(4), 1–21. doi:10.1300/J179v04n04_01

Pentland, A., Fletcher, R., & Hasson, A. (2004). DakNet: Rethinking connectivity in developing nations. *Computer*, *37*(1), 78–83. doi:10.1109/MC.2004.1260729

Pincus, A. (1999). *Hearing on the Role of Standards in the Growth of Global Electronic Commerce.* Senate Committee on Commerce, Science, and Transportation Subcommittee on Science, Technology, and Space.

Pisano, G. P. (1990). The R&D boundaries of the firm: An empirical analysis. *Administrative Science Quarterly*, *35*(1), 153–176. doi:10.2307/2393554

Pitrelli, J. F., Bakis, R., Eide, E. M., Fernandez, R., Hamza, W., & Picheny, M. A. (2006). The IBM expressive text-to-speech synthesis system for American English. *IEEE Transactions on Audio. Speech and Language Processing*, *14*(4), 1099–1108. doi:10.1109/TASL.2006.876123

Pitt, L., & Papania, L. (2007). In the words: Managerial approaches to exploring corporate intended image through content analysis. *Journal of General Management*, *32*(4), 1–16.

Plauch, M., & Prabaker, M. (2006). Tamil market: A spoken dialog system for rural India. In *Proceedings of the Extended Abstracts on Human Factors in Computing* (pp. 1619-1624).

Pollard, C. (2003). E-service adoption and use in small farms in Australia: Lessons learned from a government-sponsored programme. *Journal of Global Information Technology Management, 6*(2), 45–66.

Poon, S., & Swatman, P. (1998). An exploratory study of small business Internet commerce issues. *Information & Management, 35*(1), 9–18. doi:10.1016/S0378-7206(98)00079-2

Poon, S., & Swatman, P. M. C. (1999). An exploratory study of small business Internet commerce issues. *Information & Management, 35*, 9–18. doi:10.1016/S0378-7206(98)00079-2

Prahalad, C. K. (2006). *The fortune at the bottom of the pyramid*. Upper Saddle River, NJ: Wharton School Publishing.

Prahalad, C. K. (2006). *The fortune at the bottom of the pyramid: Eradicating poverty through profits*. Upper Saddle River, NJ: Wharton School Publishing.

Prahalad, C. K., & Hammond, A. (2002). Serving the world's poor, profitably. *Harvard Business Review, 80*(9), 48–57.

Prajapati, N., Agravat, R., & Hasan, M. (2010). Simulated Annealing for Location Area Planning in Cellular Networks. *International journal on applications of graph theory in wireless ad hoc networks and sensor networks (Graph-Hoc), 2*(1).

Pratim, B., Anilesh, D., & Saradindu, P. (2009). A New Fuzzy Logic Based Dynamic Location Update Scheme For Mobile Cellular Networks. *Advances in Wireless and Mobile Communications (AWMC) international journal, 2*(1).

Premkumar, G. (2000). Interorganization systems and supply chain management: An information processing perspective. *Information Systems Management.*

Premkumar, G., & Roberts, M. (1999). Adoption of new information technologies in rural small businesses. *Omega. International Journal of Management Science, 27*, 467–484.

Prencipe, A. (2000). Breadth and depth of technological capabilities in CoPS: The case of the aircraft engine control system. *Research Policy, 29*(7-8), 895–911. doi:10.1016/S0048-7333(00)00111-6

Price, G., & Sherman, C. (2001). *The invisible web: Uncovering information sources search engines can't see.* Medford, NJ: CyberAge Books.

Proenza, F., Bastidas-Buch, R., & Montero, G. (2002). *Telecenters for Socioeconomic and Rural Development in Latin America and the Caribbean. Inter-American Development Bank 17.* Retrieved from http://www.iadb.org/sds/itdev/telecenters/exsum.pdf

Proenza, F. (2001). Telecenter sustainability - myths and opportunities. *The Journal of Development Communication, 12*(2), 15.

Proenza, F. (2006). The Road to Broadband Development in Developing Countries Is through Competition Driven by Wireless and Internet Telephony. *Information Technologies & International Development, 3*(2), 21–39. doi:10.1162/itid.2007.3.2.21

Prügl, R., & Schreier, M. (2006). Learning from leading-edge customers at The Sims: Opening up the innovation process using toolkits. *R & D Management, 36*(3), 237–250. doi:10.1111/j.1467-9310.2006.00433.x

Quinn, J. B. (2000). Outsourcing innovation: The new engine of growth. *Sloan Management Review, 41*(4), 13–28.

Raban, Y., & Brynin, M. (2006). Older people and new technologies. In Kraut, M. B. R. E., & Kiesler, S. (Eds.), *Computers, phones, and the Internet: Domesticating information technology* (pp. 43–50). New York: Oxford University Press.

Rahman, H., & Ramos, I. (2010). Open innovation in SMEs: From closed boundaries to networked paradigm. *Issues in Informing Science and Information Technology, 7*, 471–487.

Raiti, G. C. (2007). The lost sheep of ICT4D research. *Information Technologies and International Development, 3*(4), 1–7. doi:10.1162/itid.2007.3.4.1

Rajagopal, S., Srinivasan, R., Narayan, R., & Petit, X. (2002). GPS-based Predictive Resource Allocation In Cellular Networks. In *Proceeding of the IEEE international conference on networks (IEEE ICON'02)* (pp. 229-234).

Raman, B., & Chebrolu, K. (2007). Experiences in using WiFi for rural Internet in India. *IEEE Communications Magazine*, *45*(1), 104–110. doi:10.1109/MCOM.2007.284545

Ramos, I., & Carvalho, J. A. (2008). Organizational mind: A new perspective on knowledge management. In Koohang, A., & Harman, K. (Eds.), *Knowledge management: Theoretical foundations*. Hershey, PA: IGI Global.

Ramsey, E., Ibbotson, P., Bell, J., & Gray, B. (2003). E-opportunities of service sector SMEs: An Irish cross-border study. *Journal of Small Business and Enterprise Development*, *10*(3), 250–264. doi:10.1108/14626000310489709

Randall, D. C. (2005). An exploration of opportunities for the growth of the fair trade market: Three cases of Craft organisations. *Journal of Business Ethics*, *56*(1), 55–67. doi:10.1007/s10551-004-1756-6

Rashid, M. A., & Al-Qirim, N. A. (2001). E-Commerce technology adoption framework by New Zealand small to medium enterprises. *Research Letters Information Mathematical Science*, *2*(1), 63–70.

Ratnasingam, P., & Pavlou, P. A. (2003). Technology trust in internet based inter-organizational electronic commerce. *Journal of Electronic Commerce in Organizations*, *1*, 17–41.

Ratnasingham, P., & Klein, S. (2001). Perceived benefits of inter-organizational trust in ecommerce participation: A case study in the telecommunication industry. In *Proceedings of the Seventh Americas Conference on Information Systems*, Boston, MA (pp. 769-780).

Ratnasingham, P. (1998). The importance of trust in electronic commerce. *Internet Research*, *8*(4), 3–321. doi:10.1108/10662249810231050

Rau, P.-L. P., & Liang, S.-F. M. (2003). A study of the cultural effects of designing a user interface for a web-based service. *International Journal of Services Technology and Management*, *4*(4-6), 480. doi:10.1504/IJSTM.2003.003627

Raymond, L. (2001). Determinants of web site implementation in small businesses. *Internet Research*, *11*(5), 411–422. doi:10.1108/10662240110410363

Raymond, L., Bergeron, F., & Blili, S. (2005). The assimilation of e-business in Manufacturing SMEs: Determinants and effects on growth and internationalisation. *Electronic Markets*, *15*(2), 106–118. doi:10.1080/10196780500083761

Reichwald, R., & Piller, F. (2006). *Interaktive wertschöpfung: Open innovation, individualisierung und neue formen der arbeitsteilung*. Berlin, Germany: Gabler Verlag.

Riemenschneider, C. K., & McKinney, V. R. (2001-2002). Assessing belief differences in small business adopters and non-adopters of web-based e-commerce. *Journal of Computer Information Systems*, *42*(2), 101–107.

Robertson, A., & Levin, M. L. (1999). AIDS knowledge, condom attitudes, and risk-taking sexual behavior of substance-abusing juvenile offenders on probation or parole. AIDS ducation and Prevention, 11(5), 450-461.

Robinson, S. (2004). Cybercafés and national elites: Constraints on community networking in Latin America. In Day, P., & Schuler, D. (Eds.), *Community practice in the network society* (p. 13). London, UK: Routledge.

Robinson, S. (2006). The potential role of information technology in international remittance transfers. In Deen, J., Anderson, J., & Lovink, G. (Eds.), *Reformatting Politics: Information Technology and Global Civil Society* (pp. 121–128). New York: Routledge.

Rogers, M. E. (2003). *Diffusion of innovations* (5th ed.). New York, NY: Free Press.

Roggio, A. (2010). *Ecommerce Know-how: Cloud Computing in the Ecommerce Forecast. Ecommerce Notes*. Retrieved from http://www.practicalecommerce.com/articles

Rose, C., & Yates, R. (1995). Minimizing the Average Cost of Paging under Delay Constraints. *International Journal of Wireless Networks*, *1*, 211–219. doi:10.1007/BF01202543

Rosenstiel, L. V. (2007). *Grundlagen der organisationspsychologie: Basiswissen und Anwendungs-hinweise*. Stuttgart, Germany: Schäffer-Poeschel.

RosettaNet. (2001). *RosettaNet Background Information*.

Roth, P. A. (1989). Ethnography without tears. *Current Anthropology*, *30*(5), 555–569. doi:10.1086/203784

Rothwell, R. (1991). External networking and innovation in small and medium-sized manufacturing firms in Europe. *Technovation*, *11*(2), 93–112. doi:10.1016/0166-4972(91)90040-B

Rotter, J. (1971). Generalised Expectancies for Interpersonal Trust. *The American Psychologist*, *26*, 443–452. doi:10.1037/h0031464

Rousseau, D. M., Sitkin, S. B., Burt, R. S., & Camerer, C. (1998). Not So Different After All: A Cross-Discipline View of Trust. *Academy of Management Review*, *23*(3), 393–404.

Rowland, M. (2007). Efficacy of pyrethroid-treated nets against malaria vectors and nuisance biting mosquitoes in Tanzania in areas with long-term insecticide-treated net use. *Tropical Medicine & International Health*, *12*(9), 1061–1073. doi:10.1111/j.1365-3156.2007.01883.x

Roy, M. C., Dewit, O., & Aubert, B. A. (2001). The impact of interface usability on trust in web retailers. *Internet Research: Electronic Networking Applications and Policy*, *11*(5), 388–398. doi:10.1108/10662240110410165

Rozengardt, A., & Finquelievich, S. (2008). *Public access to information & ICTs final report: Argentina*. Seattle, WA: University of Washington Center for Information & Society (CIS).

Ruth, Z. (2008). *E-commerce and e-business.* Retrieved from http://www.bentley.edu/newsevents/ books.cfm

Rutkauskiene, U. (2008). *Impact measures for public access computing in public libraries*. Lithuania: Vilnius University.

Salvador, T., Sherry, J. W., & Urrutia, A. E. (2005). Less cyber, more café: Enhancing existing small businesses across the digital divide with ICTs. *Information Technology for Development*, *11*(1), 77–95. doi:10.1002/itdj.20004

Sanayei, A., Rashidkabol, M., & Salehniai, M. (2008). A model of adoption of electronic commerce by small and medium-sized enterprises. In *Proceedings of the 3rd International Conference on E-Commerce with Focus on Developing Countries*.

Sanchez-Franco, M., & Bodaba, J. P. (2004). Personal Factors affecting users' web session lengths. *Internet Research: Electronic Networking Applications and Policy*, *14*(1), 62–80. doi:10.1108/10662240410516327

Sanchez-Franco, M., Francisco, J., Martínez-López, F., & Martín-Velicia, A. (2009). Exploring the impact of individualism and uncertainty avoidance in Web-based electronic learning: An empirical analysis in European higher education. *Computers & Education*, *53*(3), 588–598. doi:10.1016/j.compedu.2008.11.006

Sánchez, V., Ruiz, M., & Zarco, A. (2007). Drivers, benefits and challenges of ICT adoption by small and medium sized enterprises (SMEs): A literature review. *Problems and Perspectives in Management*, *5*(1), 103–114.

Sandulli, F. D. (2009). *Challenges and opportunities of open innovation and open business models in tourism.* Paper presented at the First International Conference on the Measurement and Economic Analysis of Regional Tourism Donostia, San Sebastian, Spain.

Sautter, B., & Clar, G. (2008). *Strategic capacity building in clusters to enhance future-oriented open innovation processes.* Brussels, Belgium: The European Foresight Monitoring Network.

Scaramuzzi, E. (2002). *Incubators in developing countries: Status and development perspectives.* Washington, DC: World Bank.

Schaffers, H., & Kulkki, S. (2007). Living labs, an open innovation concept fostering rural development. *Tech Monitor*, 30-38.

Schaffers, H., Cordoba, M., Hongisto, P., Kallai, T., Merz, C., & Van Renzburg, J. (2007, June 4-6). *Exploring business models for open innovation in rural living labs.* Paper presented at 13th International Conference on Concurrent Enterprising, Sophia-Antipolis, France.

Schellenberg, D., Menendez, C., Kahigwa, E., Aponte, J., Vidal, J., & Tanner, M. (2001). Intermittent treatment for malaria and anemia control at time of routine vaccinations in Tanzanian infants: A randomised, placebo-controlled trial. *Lancet*, *357*(9267), 1471–1477. doi:10.1016/S0140-6736(00)04643-2

Schilderman, T. (2002). *Strengthening the knowledge and information systems of the urban poor.* Rugby, UK: Department for International Development (DFID).

Schrammel, J., Köffel, C., & Tscheligi, M. (2009). Personality Traits, Usage Patterns and Information Disclosure in Online Communities. In *Proceedings of the HCI – People and Computers XXIII – Celebrating people and technology*.

Schumpeter, J. A. (1934). *The theory of economic development*. Cambridge, MA: Harvard University Press.

Schumpeter, J. A. (1982). *The theory of economic development: An inquiry into profits, capital, credit, interest, and the business cycle (1912/1934)*. New Brunswick, NJ: Transaction Publishers.

Schurr, P. H., & Ozanne, J. L. (1985, March). Influences on exchange processes: buyers' preconceptions of a seller's trustworthiness and bargaining toughness. *The Journal of Consumer Research*, *11*, 939–953. doi:10.1086/209028

Sein, M. K., & Harindranath, G. (2004). Conceptualising the ICT artifact: Toward understanding the role of ICT in national development. *The Information Society*, *20*, 15–24. doi:10.1080/01972240490269942

Selvan, C., Shanmugalakshmi, R., & Nirmala, V. (2010). Location Management Technique to Reduce Complexity in Cellular Networks. *IJCSI International Journal of Computer Science Issues, 7*(1).

Sen, A. (1999). *Development as freedom*. New York, NY: Knopf.

Serbanica, D., & Militaru, G. (2008). Competitive advantage by integrated e-business in supply chains: A strategic approach. *Management and Marketing- Craiova, 1*, 27-36.

Servaes, J. (Ed.). (2008). *Communication for development and social change*. Thousand Oaks, CA: Sage.

Servaes, J., & Malikhao, P. (2005). Participatory communication the new paradigm. In Hemer, O., & Tufte, T. (Eds.), *Media and glocal change: Rethinking communication for development* (pp. 91–103). Göteborg, Sweden: NORDICOM.

Sey, A., & Fellows, M. (2009). *Literature review on the impact of public access to information and communication technologies*. Seattle, WA: University of Washington.

Shanklin, W. (1992). Market share is not destiny. *Journal of Product and Brand Management, 1*(3), 33–44. doi:10.1108/10610429210036843

Sharma, S. (2010, December). Health care fails to reach migrants. Hindustan Times.

Sharma, D. K., & Sharma, A. K. (2010). Deep Web information retrieval process: A technical survey. *International Journal of Information Technology and Web Engineering*, *5*(1), 1–21. doi:10.4018/jitwe.2010010101

Sharma, D. K., & Sharma, A. K. (2011). A Novel Architecture for Deep Web Crawler. *International Journal of Information Technology and Web Engineering*, *6*(1), 25–48. doi:.doi:10.4018/jitwe.2011010103

Sharma, D. K., Varshneya, G., & Upadhyay, A. K. (2007). AJAX in development of web-based architecture for implementation of e-governance. *International Journal of Electronic Government Research*, *3*(3), 40–53. doi:10.4018/jegr.2007070103

Shavitt, S. (1989). Operationalizing functional theories of attitude. In Pratkanis, A., Breckler, S., & Greenwald, A. (Eds.), *Attitude Structure and Function* (pp. 311–337). Hillsdale, NJ: Lawrence Erlbaum.

Sherwani, J. (2005). *Are spoken dialog systems viable for under-served semi-literate populations?* Unpublished doctoral dissertation, Carnegie Mellon University, Pittsburgh, PA.

Shneiderman, B. (2002). *Leonardo's laptop: Human needs and the new computing technologies*. Cambridge, MA: MIT Press.

Singh, J., & Karnan, M. (2010). Intelligent Location Management Using Soft Computing Technique. In *Proceedings of the Second International Conference on Communication Software and Networks (ICCSN)* (pp. 343-346).

Singh, J., & Karnan, M. (2010). Using a Novel Intelligent Location Management Strategy in Cellular Networks. In *Proceedings of the International Conference on Signal Acquisition and Processing* (pp. 238-242).

Singh, J. P. (1999). *Leapfrogging development? The political economy of telecommunications restructuring*. Albany, NY: State University of New York Press.

Smallbone, D., North, D., & Vickers, I. (2003). The role and characteristics of SMEs. In Asheim, B., Nauwelers, C., & Todtling, F. (Eds.), *Regional innovation policy for small-medium enterprises* (pp. 3–20). Northampton, MA: Edward Elgar.

Smith, G. V., & Parr, R. L. (2000). *Valuation of intellectual property and intangible assets* (3rd ed.). New York, NY: John Wiley & Sons.

Solanki, S. S. (2002). Migration of rural artisans: Evidence from Haryana and Rajasthan. *Economic and Political Weekly, 37*(35), 3579–3580.

Somekh, B. (2008). Factors affecting teachers' pedagogical adoption of ICT. *International Handbook of Information Technology in Primary and Secondary Education, 11*(3), 449-460.

SOUL BEAT. Edutainment. (2007). *National malaria control programme (NMCP)*. Retrieved from http://www.comminit.com/en/node/135350/304

South Asia Partnership (SAP International). (2008). *Public access to information & ICTs final report: Nepal*. Seattle, WA: University of Washington Center for Information & Society (CIS).

Sreejith, N. N., & Kawlra, A. (2009). *Director's report for the year ended 31st March 2009*. Chennai, India.

Srinivasan, T. M. (2002). *Use of computers and multimedia in education*. Rajasthan, India: Aavishkar Publisher Distributors.

Stanfield, M., & Grant, K. (2003). Barriers to the take-up of electronic commerce among small-medium sized enterprises. *Informing Science*, 737–745.

Steinmueller, E. (2001). ICTs and the possibilities for leapfrogging by developing countries. *International Labour Review, 140*(2), 194. doi:10.1111/j.1564-913X.2001.tb00220.x

Steyaert, C. (2000, June 18-20). *Creating worlds: Political agendas of entrepreneurship*. Paper presented at the 11th Nordic Conference on Small Business Research, Aarhus, Denmark.

Stockdale, R., & Standing, C. (2004). Benefits and barriers of electronic marketplace participation: An SME perspective. *Journal of Enterprise Information Management, 17*(4), 301–311. doi:10.1108/17410390410548715

Stockdale, R., & Standing, C. (2006). A classification model to support SME e-commerce adoption initiatives. *Journal of Small Business and Enterprise Development, 13*(3), 381–394. doi:10.1108/14626000610680262

Strawn, S., & Littrell, M. A. (2006). Beyond capabilities: A case study of three artisan enterprises in India. *Clothing & Textiles Research Journal, 24*(3), 207–213. doi:10.1177/0887302X06294686

Stricker, S., Emmel, M., & Pape, J. (2003, July 5-9). Situation of agricultural ICT in Germany. In *Proceedings of the 4th Conference of the European Federation for Information Technology in Agriculture, Food and the Environment on Information Technology for a Better Agri-Food Sector, Environment and Rural Living,* Budapest, Hungary.

Suchman, L. (2001). Building bridges: Practice-based ethnographies. In Schiffer, M. B. (Ed.), *Anthropological perspectives in technology*. Albuquerque, NM: University of New Mexico Press.

Surana, S., Patra, R., Nedevschi, S., Ramos, M., Subramanian, L., Ben-David, Y., & Brewer, E. (2008). Beyond pilots: Keeping rural wireless networks alive. In *Proceedings of the 5th USENIX Symposium on Networked Systems Design and Implementation* (pp. 119-132).

Sutherland, P., & Tan, F. B. (2004). The Nature of Consumer Trust in B2C Electronic Commerce: A Multi-Dimensional Conceptualization. In *Proceedings of the International Conference of the Information Resources Management Association: Innovations Through Information Technology*, New Orleans, LA (pp. 611-614).

Swaminatha, J. M., & Tayur, S. R. (2003). Models for supply chains in e-business. *Management Science, 49*(10), 1387–1406. doi:10.1287/mnsc.49.10.1387.17309

Swedish International Development Cooperation Agency (SIDA). (2005). *ICTs for poverty alleviation: Basic tool and enabling sector*. Retrieved from http://www.eldis.org/fulltext/sidaictpoverty.pdf

Tang, N., Burridge, M., & Ang, A. (2003). Development of an electronic-business planning model for small and medium-sized enterprises. *International Journal of Logistics Research and Applications, 6*(4), 289–304. doi:10.1080/1367556031000162704

Tan, J., Tyler, K., & Manica, A. (2007). Business-to-business adoption of eCommerce in China. *Information & Management, 44*(3), 332–351. doi:10.1016/j.im.2007.04.001

Tarrif Consultancy. (2008). *Emerging mobile markets.* London, UK: Tarrif Consultancy.

Taylor, M., & Murphy, A. (2004). SMEs and e-business. *Journal of Small Business and Enterprise Development, 11*(3), 280–289. doi:10.1108/14626000410551546

Taylor, S., & Todd, P. (1995). Assessing IT usage: The role of prior experience. *Management Information Systems Quarterly, 19*(4), 561–570. doi:10.2307/249633

TechTargent. (2007). *ICT.* Retrieved from http://search-ciomidmarket.techtarget.com/

Tedlock, B. (1991). From participant observation to the observation of participation: The emergence of narrative ethnography. *Journal of Anthropological Research, 47*(1), 69–94.

Teo, H. H., Wei, K. K., & Benbasat, I. (2003). Predicting intention to adopt interorganizational linkages: An institutional perspective. *Management Information Systems Quarterly, 27*, 19–49.

Thatcher, S. M. B., Foster, W., & Zhu, L. (2006). E-commerce adoption decisions in Taiwan: The interaction of culture and other institutional factors. *Electronic Commerce Research and Applications, 5*, 92–104. doi:10.1016/j.elerap.2005.10.005

Thomas, B., & Sparkes, A. (2001). The use of Internet as a critical success factor for the marketing of Welsh agri-food SMEs in twenty first century. *British Food Journal, 103*(5), 331–347. doi:10.1108/00070700110395368

Thomas, R., Cahill, J., & Santilli, I. (1997). Using an interactive computer game to increase skill and self-efficacy regarding safer sex negotiation: Field test results. *Health Education & Behavior, 24*(1), 71–86.. doi:10.1177/109019819702400108

Tidd, J., Bessant, J., & Pavitt, K. (2005). *Managing innovation: Integrating technological, market and organizational change* (3rd ed.). Chichester, UK: John Wiley & Sons.

Tonsor, G. T., & Schroeder, T. C. (2006). Livestock identification: Lessons from the U.S. beef industry from the Australian system. *Journal of International Food & Agribusiness Marketing, 18*(4), 103–118. doi:10.1300/J047v18n03_07

Torkkeli, M., Tiina Kotonen, T., & Pasi Ahonen, P. (2007). Regional open innovation system as a platform for SMEs: A survey. *International Journal of Foresight and Innovation Policy, 3*(4). doi:10.1504/IJFIP.2007.016456

Toyama, K., Kiri, K., Menon, D., Pal, J., Sethi, S., & Srinivasan, J. (2005). *PC kiosk trends in rural India.* Paper presented at the Freedom, Sharing and Sustainability in the Global Network Society Conference, Tampere, Finland.

Transparency International. (2009). *Corruption perceptions index.* Retrieved from http://www.transparency.org/policy_research/surveys_indices/cpi/2009/cpi_2009_table

Trompette, P., Chanal, V., & Pelissier, C. (2008, July 10-12). Crowdsourcing as a way to access external knowledge for innovation: Control, incentive and coordination in hybrid forms of innovation. In *Proceedings of the 24th EGOS Colloquium*, Amsterdam, Netherlands.

Ubwani, Z. (2008). *Tanzania: Bush calls for use of nets in malaria war.* Retrieved from http://allafrica.com/stories/200802190005.html

UNCTAD. (2002). *e-Commerce and development report.* New York, NY: United Nations Conference on Trade and Development.

UNCTAD. (2010). *Information economy report 2010: ICTs, enterprises and poverty alleviation.* New York, NY: United Nations.

United States Census Bureau. (2010). *E-Stats.* Retrieved from http://www.census.gov/econ/estats/2008/2008reportfinal.pdf

UNSPSC. (2002). *United Nations Standard Products and Services Code.*

Unwin, T. (Ed.). (2009). *ICT4D: Information and communication technology for development.* Cambridge, UK: Cambridge University Press.

Upadhyaya, P., & Mohanan, P. (2009). Electronic marketplace adoption: A case study of manufacturing SMEs. *ICFAIAN Journal of Management Research, 8*(6), 30–40.

USAID. (2008). *President's malaria initiative: Malaria Operational Plan (MOP) Tanzania.* Retrieved from http://www.fightingmalaria.gov/countries/mops/fy09/tanzania_mop-fy09.pdf

Uslaner, E. M. (2000). Social capital and the net. *Communications of the ACM*, *43*(12), 60–64. doi:10.1145/355112.355125

Utah Education Network. (n. d.). *Ed technology glossary of terms*. Retrieved from http://www.uen.org/core/edtech/glossary.shtml

Uyaphi. (2008). *Tanzania malaria*. Retrieved from http://www.uyaphi.com/tanzania/malaria.htm

Van Ark, B., Broersma, L., & Den Hertog, P. (2003). *Service innovation, performance and policy: A review*. London, UK: The Ministry of Economic Affairs of the Netherlands.

Van de Ven, A. H., Schroeder, R., Scudder, G., & Polley, D. (1986). Managing innovation and change processes: Findings from the Minnesota innovation research program. *Agribusiness Management Journal*, *2*(4), 501–523.

Van de Vrande, V., de Jong, J. P. J., Vanhaverbeke, W., & de Rochemont, M. (2009). Open innovation in SMEs: Trends, motives and management challenges. *Technovation*, *29*, 423–437. doi:10.1016/j.technovation.2008.10.001

van Dijk, A. G. M. J. (2006). *The network society* (2nd ed.). Thousand Oaks, CA: Sage.

Van Dijk, C., & Van den Ende, J. (2002). Suggestion systems: Transferring employee creativity into practicable ideas. *R & D Management*, *32*, 387–395. doi:10.1111/1467-9310.00270

Van Gils, A., & Zwart, P. (2004). Knowledge acquisition and learning in Dutch and Belgian SMEs: The role of strategic alliances. *European Management Journal*, *22*(6), 685–692. doi:10.1016/j.emj.2004.09.031

Vanderheiden, G. (2000). Fundamental principles and priority setting for universal usability. In *Proceedings of the Conference on Universal Usability* (pp. 32-38).

Vanhaverbeke, W. (2006). The inter-organizational context of open innovation. In H. Chesbrough, W. Vanhaverbeke, & J. West (Eds.), *Open innovation: Researching a new paradigm* (pp. 205-219). Oxford, UK: Oxford University Press.

Vatanasakdakul, S., Tibben, W., & Cooper, J. (2004). What prevents B2B e-commerce adoption in developing countries? In *Proceedings of a socio-cultural perspective, in the 17th Bled eCommerce Conference on eGlobal*, Bled, Slovenia.

Veeraraghavan, R., Yasodhar, N., & Toyama, K. (2009). Warana unwired: Replacing PCs with mobile phones in a rural sugarcane cooperative. *Information Technologies & International Development*, *5*(1), 81–95.

Venkatesan, S. (2009). *Craft matters: Artisans, development and the Indian nation*. New Delhi, India: Orient Blackswan.

Venkatesh, V., & Davis, F. D. (2000). A theoretical extension of technology acceptance model: Four longitudinal field studies. *Management Science*, *46*(2), 186–204. doi:10.1287/mnsc.46.2.186.11926

Venkatesh, V., Morris, M. G., Davis, G. B., & Davis, F. D. (2003). User acceptance of information technology: Towards a unified view. *Management Information Systems Quarterly*, *27*(3), 425–478.

Vishwanath, A. (2003). Comparing online information effects: A cross-cultural comparison of online information and uncertainty avoidance. *Communication Research*, *30*(6), 579–598. doi:10.1177/0093650203257838

Voelcker, M. (2008). *Public access to information & ICTs final report: Brazil*. Seattle, WA: University of Washington Center for Information & Society (CIS).

Volpentesta, A. P., & Ammirato, S. (2007). Evaluating web interfaces of B2C e-commerce systems for typical agri-food products. *International Journal of Entrepreneurship and Innovation Management*, *7*(1), 74–91. doi:10.1504/IJEIM.2007.012174

Von Hippel, E. (1998). Economics of product development by users: The impact of 'sticky' local information. *Management Science*, *44*(5), 629–644. doi:10.1287/mnsc.44.5.629

Von Hippel, E. (2005). *Democratizing innovation*. Boston, MA: MIT Press.

Vujovic, S., & Ulhøi, J. P. (2008). Opening up the innovation process: Different organizational strategies. In Obel, B., & Burton, R. M. (Eds.), *Information and organization design series* (*Vol. 7*). New York, NY: Springer.

Vukovic, M. (2009). Crowdsourcing for enterprises. In *Proceedings of the World Congress on Services-I* (pp. 686-692).

W3C. (2002). *Web Services Architecture Working Group*.

Wachira, F. N. (2010). *Improving the management of human resources in the public service through application of information and communication technologies (ICTs)*. Paper presented at the APSHRMnet Workshop, Cotonou, Benin.

Walczuch, R., & Lundgren, H. (2004). Psychological Antecedents of Institution-Based Consumer Trust in E-Retailing. *Information & Management, 42*(1), 159–177.

Walkinshaw, B. P. (2007). *Why do Riecken libraries matter for rural development? A synthesis of findings from monitoring and evaluation*. Washington, DC: Riecken Foundation.

Walton, R. E. (1989). *Up and running: Integrating information technology and the organization*. Boston, MA: Harvard Business School Press.

Wanas, N. (2008). *Public access to information & ICTs final report: Egypt*. Seattle, WA: University of Washington Center for Information & Society (CIS).

Wanasundera, L. (2008). *Public access to information & ICTs final report: Sri Lanka*. Seattle, WA: University of Washington Center for Information & Society (CIS).

Wang, N., Zhang, N., & Wang, M. (2006). Wireless sensors in agriculture and food industry—recent development and future perspective. *Computers and Electronics in Agriculture, 50*(1), 1–14. doi:10.1016/j.compag.2005.09.003

Warden, S. C., & Tunzelana, S. (2004). *E-commerce: A critical review of SME organisational barriers in tourism*. Paper presented at the 6th WWW Applications Conference, Johannesburg, South Africa.

Warschauer, M. (2003). *Technology and social inclusion: Rethinking the digital divide*. Cambridge, MA: MIT Press.

Webber, D., & Cave, D. C. (2007). Intellectual property – challenges for the future. In *Proceedings of the IEEE Region 10 TENCON Conference* (pp. 1-5).

Westin, A., & Maurici, D. (1998). *E-commerce and privacy: What net users want*. Harrisburg, PA: Price Waterhouse Coopers.

West, J., & Gallagher, S. (2006). Challenges of open innovation: The paradox of firm investment in open-source software. *R & D Management, 36*(3), 319–331. doi:10.1111/j.1467-9310.2006.00436.x

Wheeler, D. (2007). Empowerment Zones? Women, Internet Cafes, and Life Transformations in Egypt. *Information Technologies & International Development, 4*(2), 16.

Whiteley, D. (2000). *E-Commerce: Strategy, technologies and applications*. New York, NY: McGraw-Hill.

Wolfradt, U., & Doll, J. (2001). Motives of adolescents to use the Internet as a function of personality traits, personal and social factors. *Journal of Educational Computing Research, 24*(1), 13–27. doi:10.2190/ANPM-LN97-AUT2-D2EJ

Wood, W. W. (2000). Flexible production, households, and fieldwork: Multisited Zapotec weavers in the era of late capitalism. *Ethnology, 39*(2), 133–148. doi:10.2307/3773840

Worcester, L., & Westbrook, L. (2004). Ways of knowing: Community information-needs analysis. *Texas Library Journal, 80*, 102–107.

Wordsmyth. (1999). *Experience*. Retrieved from http://www.wordsmyth.net/cgibin

World Bank. (2010). *Worldwide governance indicators*. Retrieved from http://info.worldbank.org/governance/wgi/sc_country.asp

World Economic Forum. (2010). *The global information technology report 2009-2010*. Retrieved from http://networkedreadiness.com/gitr/

World Health Organization. (2008). *World malaria report: The global fund: To fight AIDS, tuberculosis and malaria*. Retrieved from http://www.theglobalfund.org/en/malaria/background/

Xiaoping, Z., Wu, C., Tian, D., & Zhang, X. (2009). B2B e-marketplace adoption in agriculture. *Journal of Software, 4*(3), 232–239.

Xiao, Y. (2003). A Dynamic Anchor-Cell Assisted Paging with an Optimal Timer for PCS Networks. *IEEE Communications Letters*, *7*(8), 358–360. doi:10.1109/LCOMM.2003.813812

Xie, H., Tabbane, S., & Goodman, D. (1993). Dynamic Location Area Management and Performance Analysis. In *Proceedings of the 43rd IEEE Vehicular Technology Conference* (pp. 536-539).

Xu, S., Zhu, K., & Gibbs, J. (2004). Global technology, local adoption: A cross-country investigation of internet adoption by companies in the United States and China. *Electronic Markets*, *14*(1), 13–24. doi:10.1080/1019678042000175261

Xu, X., Duan, Y., Fu, Z., & Liu, X. (2009). Internet usage in the fresh produce supply chain in China. *Computer and Computing Technologies in Agriculture II*, *3*, 2151–2160.

Yadav, D., Sharma, A. K., & Gupta, J. P. (2008). Parallel crawler architecture and web page change detection techniques. *WSEAS Transactions on Computers*, *7*(7), 929–941.

Yi, M. Y., Jackson, J. D., Park, J. S., & Probst, J. C. (2006). Understanding informatiom technology acceptance by individual professionals: Towards an intergrative view. *Information & Management*, *43*, 350–363. doi:10.1016/j.im.2005.08.006

Zhang, P., Li, N., & Sun, H. (2006). Affective quality and cognitive absorption: Extending technology acceptance research. In *Proceedings of the Hawaii International Conference on System Sciences* (Vol. 8).

Zhang, Y., Laurence, T., Jianhua, Y., & Zheng, M. (2009). Quantitative Analysis of Location Management and QoS in Wireless Networks. *International Journal of Network and Computer Applications*, *32*(2), 483–489. doi:10.1016/j.jnca.2008.02.012

Zhao, C., Guo, W., & Liu, F. (2010). An adaptive distance-based location management of LEO system using coordinates approach. *The International Journal for Computation and Mathematics in Electrical and Electronic Engineering*, *29*(2), 468–476. doi:10.1108/03321641011014922

Ziad, H., Mansoor, M., & Nawafleh, A. (2009). Electronic commerce adoption barriers in small and medium sized enterprises (SMEs) in developing countries: The case of Libya. *IBIMA Business Review, 2*.

Zuboff, S. (1988). *In the age of the smart machine: The future of work and power*. New York, NY: Basic Books.

Zucker, L. G. (1986). Production of Trust: Institutional Sources of Economic Structure, 1840 – 1920. In Staw, B. M., & Cummings, L. L. (Eds.), *Research in Organizational Behavior* (*Vol. 8*, pp. 53–111). Greenwich, CT: JAI Press.

About the Contributors

Susheel Chhabra is Associate Professor of Information Technology at Lal Bahadur Shastri Institute of Management (Delhi, India) and is also acting as a Head-MCA. His areas of research and consultancy include e-government, e-business, computer networks, and software engineering. He has published several research papers on international and national level journals. He has co-authored a textbook on human resource information systems, edited a special issue of International Journal of E-Government Research on strategic e-business model for government, and also co-authored the edited book Integrating E-Business Models for Government Solutions: Citizen-Centric Service Oriented Methodologies and Processes (IGI Global, USA). He is currently engaged in several consultancy and training assignments on social change for human development, e-governance, e-business, and ERP for ISID, NTPC, LBSRC, etc.

* * *

Amjad A. Abu-ELSamen is an Assistant Professor of Marketing at the University of Jordan. He received his PhD from OklahomaState University, USA. His research interests include the applications of behavioral decision making theories, research methodology, services marketing, and B2B e-commerce. He has published several research papers in the field of marketing in international refereed business journals. Dr. Abu ELSamen has experience in teaching, lecturing, and supervising students in USA and Jordan. Dr. Abu ELSamen is among the few in Middle East to earn SAS predictive modeling certificate. He also received the SAS data mining certificate and won an international tournament in modeling and data mining.

Ali Acilar is an assistant professor in the Department of Business Administration, Bilecik University, Bilecik, Turkey. He graduated from the Department of Business Administration at Hacettepe University, Ankara, Turkey, received his MS in Operation Research and Statistics from Rensselaer Polytechnic Institute (RPI), Troy, NY, USA and obtained his Ph.D in Business Administration from Dumlupınar University, Kütahya, Turkey in 2007. His research interest includes information technology usage in SMEs, ethical use of information technology, gender issues in computer ethics, e-commerce and e-government.

Khalil Al-Hyari is an assistant professor at the faculty of planning and management, Al-Balqa Applied University, Al- Salt- Jordan. He has a PhD in SMEs Management from Glamorgan University, UK, 2009. His interests are in business research methods, SMEs management, manufacturing activities of SMEs in Jordan, internationalisation and export.

Marwan Al-Nsour is an associate professor at the faculty of planning and management, Al-Balqa Applied University, Al- Salt- Jordan. Dr. Al-Nsour has supervised and examined many PhD and master's theses in the Management area. His research interests are in operation management, quality management, and SMEs management. Currently, he is the dean of faculty of Management and Planning at Al-Balqa Applied University in Jordan.

Ghazi A. Al-Weshah is an Assistant Professor of Marketing at the Faculty of Planning and Management, Al-Balqa Applied University- Jordan. He has a PhD in Marketing from University of Wales, UK. His research interests are marketing information, competitive intelligences, and E-marketing. He had worked as an instructor in business and marketing for 4 year in Jordan and Saudi Arabia. Prior to academe he was working as a financial controller in the Jordanian banking industry.

Kemly Camacho is a Central American researcher based in Costa Rica. She is co-founder and president of the research cooperative Sulá Batsú, where she specializes on information and communication technologies for social transformation. She is a lecturer in Anthropology and in Program Evaluation at Universidad de Costa Rica.

Chia-Wen Tsai is an assistant professor in the Department of Information Management, Ming Chuan University. Dr. Tsai is one of the Editors-in-Chief of International Journal of Online Pedagogy and Course Design, and International Journal of Technology and Human Interaction. He is also the Associate Editor of Cyberpsychology, Behavior, and Social Networking. He is interested in online teaching methods and knowledge management.

Wanyenda Leonard Chilimo received her doctorate in information studies at the University of KwaZulu-Natal, South Africa in 2009. She has over 10 years of experience as an academic librarian, researcher, and lecturer in the information science field. She is currently working as a University Librarian at Pwani University College in Kenya.

José Joaquim Dias Fernandes has a master's degree in Information Systems Engineering and Management (2010). He was a researcher at Algoritmi Centre in the Information Systems Department of the Minho University. He also contributed in the PERCEPTUM Project – an open innovation brokering service.

Ricardo Gomez is Assistant Professor at University of Washington's Information School. He specializes in the social impacts of communication technologies, especially in community development settings. He is also interested in qualitative research methods, and in group facilitation and process design. He seeks creative ways to communicate complex ideas and research results in everyday language. He has worked with private, public and non-profit sectors around the world, with a particular focus on Latin America and the Caribbean. Before joining the University of Washington he worked with Microsoft Community Affairs, and with the International Development Research Center in Canada. He holds an MA from Université du Québec à Montréal (1992) and a Ph.D. from Cornell University (1997).

N.A. Iahad is faculty member at Department of Information System in at Universiti Technilogi Malaysia, Malaysia. She completed her PhD from School of Informatics, University of Manchester.

Çağlar Karamaşa graduated from the Department of Business Administration at Anadolu University, Eskişehir, Turkey in 2008. He is continuing his master's degree in Quantitative Methods at Anadolu University. He has been working as a research assistant in the Department of Business Administration at Bilecik University since 2010. His research interests include integer programming and applications, semi definite programming, dynamic programming, decision support systems, information technologies and e-commerce applications.

Aarti Kawlra is an associate faculty member of the Department of Humanities and Social Sciences, at the Indian Institute of Technology Madras. She has a PhD in Sociology/Social Anthropology from IIT Delhi on the community basis of production of silk handloom saris in Tamil Nadu. She is interested in decentralisation and networks with reference to both artisanal and information and communication technologies. Her wider academic focus is in material culture and, in particular, on notions of "work" and "community" in the context of technology design and use. Having been trained in ethnographic research methods her research emphasises reflexivity and the descriptive narrative. She has worked as a Consultant at the University based business Incubator under study and was engaged in a number of research projects entailing ICT4D applications for rural India, of which the present study is one. Currently, she is involved in a project on gender and citizenship through ICT's in Kerala.

Muneesh Kumar is a Professor at Department of Financial Studies, University of Delhi (India). His responsibilities include teaching banking and information systems related courses to students of Masters in Finance and Control (MFC) programme and supervising research. He has published several articles in international journals and presented papers in several international conferences. He has also authored three books and co-edited three books. He is associated with the several expert committees appointed by Government of India such as expert committee for IT projects of India Post and Market Participation Committee of Pension Fund Regulatory and Development Authority (PFRDA).

Alemayehu Molla is an Associate Professor, School of Business IT and Logistics, RMIT University. He holds a Bachelor degree in management, a Master degree in information science, and a PhD in information systems. He researches in the areas of Green IT, digital business, and development informatics with more than 80 publications including the European Journal of Information Systems, International Journal of E-commerce, Journal of E-commerce Research, Journal of E-commerce in Organizations, Information & Management, Internet Research and The Information Society Journal.

Restituta Thadeus Mushi, currently a PhD student, was born in Arusha and grew up in Kilimanjaro region in Tanzania. She btained early education in Tanzania and Masters in Information Studies at the University of KwaZulu-Natal South Africa. She received a B.A. in Information Science in 2008 from the University of Zulu-Land South. She is an employee of Sokoine University of Agriculture (SUA) Morogoro Tanzania. Mushi received different awards in leadership and academics such as: Overall Final Year Student in Information Science 2008, Higher Class Marks in Research Methodology, Field Work, and Knowledge Management, to mention a few.

N.D. Oye is PhD scholar at Department of Information system in Universiti Technologi Malaysia, Malaysia. Also, He is Lecturer in Federal University of Technology, School of Pure and Applied Science.

Pei-Di Shen now works as Director of the Teacher Education Center and professor of Graduate School of Education, Ming Chuan University, Taipei, Taiwan. Dr. Shen is one of the Editors-in-Chief of International Journal of Online Pedagogy and Course Design. Her primary interest areas are E-learning, Knowledge Management, Virtual Community, and Management Information Systems. Her research focus is the distance education in higher education.

Konrad Peszynski is a senior lecturer in the School of Business IT and Logistics, RMIT University. He holds Bachelor degrees in science (psychology) and commerce and administration (information systems with first class honours), a Master degree in education, and a PhD in information systems. His Phd explored the issue of power and politics in systems selection and implementation. His research interests include social media, supply chain management and associated green technologies, e-business, e-procurement and social issues in information systems.

Hakikur Rahman is an academic over 25 years has served leading education institutes and established various ICTD projects funded by ADB, UNDP and World Bank in Bangladesh. He is currently serving as a Post Doctoral Researcher at the University of Minho, Portugal. He has written and edited over 15 books on computer education, ICTs, knowledge management and research, and contributed over 50 book chapters, and journals and conference proceedings. Graduating from the Bangladesh University of Engineering and Technology in 1981, he has done his Master's of Engineering from the American University of Beirut in 1986 and completed his PhD in Computer Engineering from the Ansted University, BVI, UK in 2001.

Isabel Ramos has a doctorate degree in Information Technologies and Systems, specialization in Information Systems Engineering and Management (2001) and a master degree in Informatics for management. She is an Assistant Professor in the Information Systems Department of the Minho University, Portugal and Chair of the Information Systems Master Programs of the University. Dr. Ramos is Associate Editor of the International Journal of Technology and Human Interaction and member of the editorial board of Enterprise Information Systems. She is Secretary of the Technical Committee 8 (Information Systems) of IFIP – International Federation for Information Systems and awarded with the IFIP Outstanding Service Award in 2009. She is author and co-author of two books and more than 4 dozens of scientific and technical papers.

Kavitha Ranganathan received her PhD. in Computer Science from the University of Chicago. She then worked as a researcher at IBM's T.J Watson Research Center in New York. She is currently an assistant professor at the Indian Institute of Management, Ahmedabad, India. Her research interests broadly include distributed computer systems with a focus on resource scheduling and user behavior in large scale Grids and peer-to-peer systems. Her current research interests also include the use of information and communication technologies for development of emerging regions. She has published extensively in various international journals and conferences.

Ahmed I. Saleh received his B.Sc. in the department of Computer Engineering and Systems Department in the faculty of Engineering in Mansoura University, with general grade Excellent (1998). He got the master degree in the area of Mobile agents (2000). His Ph.D was in the area of web mining and search engines (2006). He has a good knowledge in networks Hardware and Software. Currently he is working as a Teacher at the faculty of Engineering, Mansoura University, Egypt. His interests are (Programming Languages, Networks and System Administration, and Database).

Mamta Sareen is an Associate Professor in Department of Computer Science, Kirori Mal College, University of Delhi, India. She has done her doctoral research in 'Trust and Technology in B2B e-commerce'. In addition, she is also pursuing research in areas like e-commerce, Internet banking, etc. She is teaching various courses on information technology like software engineering, management Information systems, Data Base Management Systems, etc. to various undergraduate and post graduate courses (B.Sc, MCA, MBA) of University of Delhi and I.P University, India.

A. K. Sharma received his M.Tech. (CST) with Honors from University of Roorkee (Presently I.I.T. Roorkee) and Ph.D (Fuzzy Expert Systems) from JMI, New Delhi and he obtained his second Ph.D. in Information Technology form IIITM, Gwalior in 2004. Presently he is working as the Dean, Faculty of Engineering and Technology & Chairman, Dept of Computer Engineering at YMCA University of Science and Technology, Faridabad. His research interest includes Fuzzy Systems, OOPS, Knowledge Representation and Internet Technologies. He has guided 9 Ph.D thesis and 8 more are in progress with about 175 research publications in International and National journals and conferences. The author of 7 books, is actively engaged in research related to Fuzzy logic, Knowledge based systems, MANETS, Design of crawlers. Besides being member of many BOS and Academic councils, he has been Visiting Professor at JMI, IIIT&M, and I.I.T. Roorkee.

Dilip Kumar Sharma is a B.Sc, B.E.(CSE), M.Tech.(IT), M.Tech. (CSE) and pursuing a Ph.D in Computer Engineering. He is life member of CSI, IETE, ISTE,, ISCA, SSI and member of CSTA, USA. He has attended 21 short term courses/workshops/seminars organized by various esteemed originations. He has published 25 research papers in International Journals /Conferences of repute and participated in 18 International/National conferences. Presently he is working as Reader in Department of Computer Science, IET at GLA University, Mathura, U.P. since March 2003 and he is also CSI Student branch Coordinator. His research interests are deep web information retrieval, Digital Watermarking and Software Engineering. He has guided various projects and seminars undertaken by the students of undergraduate/postgraduate.

Yen-Ting Lin is a graduate school student who majoring in Education and at the same time he also taking teacher education program in Ming Chuan University. Lin is a student and a part time teacher who like doing some experimental classes during his teaching which could solve problems while teachers may face at the real teaching environment. He also interested in international volunteer, which can combine his experiences between Taiwan and foreign countries.

Index